COMPLETE LIST OF MODEL DOCUMENTS

The Business Writer's Companion offers abundant examples of business writing, all of which are listed here for easy access. Additional figures throughout the book illustrate concepts, design elements, and types of visuals. For more model documents and resources for students and instructors, see the book's companion Web site at <bedfordstmartins.com/alred>.

9. PRESENTATIONS AND MEETINGS

THE
BUSINESS WRITER'S
COMPANION

ABOUT THE AUTHORS

Gerald J. Alred is Professor Emeritus of English at the University of Wisconsin–Milwaukee, where he teaches courses in the Professional Writing Program. He is the author of numerous scholarly articles and several standard bibliographies on business and technical communication, and he is a founding member of the editorial board of the *Journal of Business and Technical Communication*. He is a recipient of the prestigious Jay R. Gould Award for "profound scholarly and textbook contributions to the teaching of business and technical writing."

Charles T. Brusaw served as a faculty member at NCR Corporation's Management College, where he developed and taught courses in professional writing, editing, and presentation skills for the corporation worldwide. Previously, he worked in advertising, technical writing, public relations, and curriculum development. He has been a communications consultant, an invited speaker at academic conferences, and a teacher of business writing at Sinclair Community College.

Walter E. Oliu served as chief of the Publishing Services Branch at the U.S. Nuclear Regulatory Commission, where he managed the agency's printing, graphics, editing, and publishing programs. He also developed the public-access standards for and managed daily operations of the agency's public Web site. He has taught at Miami University of Ohio, Slippery Rock State University, and, as an adjunct faculty member, at Montgomery College and George Mason University.

SIXTH EDITION

THE
BUSINESS WRITER'S
COMPANION

Gerald J. Alred

Charles T. Brusaw

Walter E. Oliu

BEDFORD / ST. MARTIN'S   Boston ◆ New York

For Bedford/St. Martin's

Developmental Editor: Amy Gershman
Production Supervisor: Andrew Ensor
Senior Marketing Manager: Molly Parke
Text Design: Claire Seng-Niemoeller
Project Management: Books By Design, Inc.
Cover Design: Billy Boardman
Cover Photo: *Businesspeople in Meeting.* © John-Francis Bourke/Corbis.
Composition: MPS Limited, a Macmillan Company
Printing and Binding: RR Donnelley and Sons

President: Joan E. Feinberg
Editorial Director: Denise B. Wydra
Editor in Chief: Karen S. Henry
Director of Marketing: Karen R. Soeltz
Director of Production: Susan W. Brown
Associate Director, Editorial Production: Elise S. Kaiser
Manager, Publishing Services: Andrea Cava

Library of Congress Control Number: 2010906345

Manufactured in the United States of America.

5 4 3 2 1 0

f e d c b a

For information, write: Bedford/St. Martin's, 75 Arlington Street, Boston, MA 02116   (617-399-4000)

ISBN-13: 978-0-312-63132-1

Acknowledgments
Figure 3–3: "MLA Sample Page." Reprinted with the permission of Susan Litzinger, a student at Pennsylvania State University, Altoona.

Acknowledgments and copyrights are continued at the back of the book on page 407, which constitutes an extension of the copyright page.

Preface

The Business Writer's Companion is a concise yet comprehensive reference for writing in the classroom and on the job. A brief, topically arranged version of our popular *Business Writer's Handbook*, this easy-to-use guide addresses the most common types of business writing and communication. More than just a guide, however, the *Companion* places writing in a real-world context with quick access to more than seventy sample documents illustrating the most common types of business writing. With decades of combined academic and professional experience, we have developed the *Companion* as a reliable reference for the classroom and for the workplace.

Anticipating the needs of today's business writers, we have reorganized the sixth edition to include a new chapter called Workplace Technology that places all technology-related topics in one convenient place. New and updated digital tips address how to use workplace technology by addressing topics like covering hardware and software and working on collaborative documents. We also have been guided by the smart and generous reviews of colleagues and users around the country. In response to their suggestions, we've revised and updated entries throughout the book on topics such as blogs and forums, frequently asked questions, proposals, and more. A companion Web site works with the text to offer expanded online resources, including additional models and tips.

The *Companion*'s Organization and Cross-Referencing System

The *Companion*'s entries are thematically organized into twelve tabbed sections. At the beginning of each tabbed section, a brief preview lists and introduces the entries, which are alphabetically arranged within that section. Within each entry, underlined cross-references link readers to related entries both within that section and in other tabbed sections. When referencing an entry in a different tabbed section, the cross-reference includes a tab number in parentheses.

Features

Concise, comprehensive writing process coverage along with in-depth treatment of grammar and usage provides detailed help for every stage of writing—from preparation, audience analysis, and research, to drafting, revising, and proofreading.

Real-world sample documents offer students authentic and effective models of business correspondence for a variety of workplace situations. With additional annotated examples on the book's companion Web site, this edition offers reports, proposals, letters, memos, e-mail, résumés, and more.

A quick-reference design makes information easy to find. In addition to the cross-references throughout the book that help students find related entries, the Complete List of Model Documents provides easy access to sample documents. Tips and Checklists help students tackle complex tasks such as proofreading and revising, communicating with international audiences, and evaluating sources.

Up-to-date coverage of workplace technology gives students the latest advice on writing and designing for the Web, conducting Internet research, using software tools, and working with electronic documents.

New to This Edition

A new chapter on workplace technology gives an overview of the technologies that are integral to workplace writing—including e-mail, blogs, and text messaging—and offers guidelines for making effective use of these media. An entry on adapting to changing technology helps students evaluate and learn how to use new technology in a constantly evolving workplace context.

Updated Digital Tips focus on using technology to assist with a variety of writing and business tasks, such as using collaborative writing software, conducting meetings remotely, and working with Google documents.

New Professionalism Notes throughout the book highlight tips that advise students on how to act courteously and conscientiously in the workplace, from rehearsing presentations and proofreading work to meeting deadlines and being on time.

Revised coverage of research and documentation includes more models of electronic sources and reflects recent changes in both MLA and APA styles.

You Get More Digital Choices for *The Business Writer's Companion*

The Business Writer's Companion doesn't stop with a book. Online, you'll find both free and affordable premium resources to help students get even more out of the book and your course. You'll also find convenient instructor resources, such as sample syllabi, handouts, and in-class activities and suggested responses. To learn more about or to order any of the products below, contact your Bedford/St. Martin's sales representative, e-mail sales support (sales_support@bfwpub.com), or visit the Web site at bedfordstmartins.com/alredbwc/catalog.

Companion Web Site for *The Business Writer's Companion*

bedfordstmartins.com/alred
Send students to free and open resources, choose flexible premium resources to supplement your print text, or upgrade to an expanding collection of innovative digital content.

Free and open resources for *The Business Writer's Companion* provide students with easy-to-access reference materials, visual tutorials, and support for working with sources.

- 15 free Business Writing Lessons
- 30+ free Web and Research Projects
- Free Links Library for Business Writing
- Free expanded Digital Tips
- 30 free sample documents on *ModelDoc Central*
- 5 free videos of real writers from *VideoCentral*
- 3 free tutorials from *ix visual exercises* by Cheryl Ball and Kristin Arola
- *Research and Documentation Online* by Diana Hacker
- *Bedford Bibliographer*: a tool for collecting source information and making a bibliography in MLA, APA, and *Chicago* styles

VideoCentral is a growing collection of videos for the writing class that captures real-world, academic, and student writers talking about how and why they write. Writer and teacher Peter Berkow interviewed hundreds of people—from Michael Moore to Cynthia Selfe—to produce 50 brief videos about topics such as revising and getting feedback. *VideoCentral* can be packaged with *The Business Writer's Companion* at a significant discount. An activation code is required. To order *VideoCentral* packaged with the print book, use **ISBN-10: 0-312-57731-1** or **ISBN-13: 978-0-312-57731-5**.

Re:Writing Plus gathers all Bedford/St. Martin's premium digital content for writing into one online collection. It includes hundreds of model documents, exercises in visual rhetoric and documentation, and *VideoCentral*. *Re:Writing Plus* can be purchased separately or packaged with the print book at a significant discount. An activation code is required. To order *Re:Writing Plus* packaged with the print book, use **ISBN-10: 0-312-57730-3** or **ISBN-13: 978-0-312-57730-8**.

E-book Options

bedfordstmartins.com/alredbwc/catalog
Bedford/St. Martin's e-books let students do more and pay less. For about half the price of a print book, the e-book for *The Business Writer's Companion* offers the complete text of the print book combined with convenient digital tools such as highlighting, note-taking, and search. Both online and downloadable options are available.

Instructor Resources

bedfordstmartins.com/alredbwc/catalog
You have a lot to do in your course. Bedford/St. Martin's wants to make it easy for you to find the support you need—and to get it quickly.

Teaching Central offers the entire list of Bedford/St. Martin's print and online professional resources in one place. You'll find landmark reference works, sourcebooks on pedagogical issues, award-winning collections, and practical advice for the classroom—all free for instructors.

Bits collects creative ideas for teaching a range of composition topics in an easily searchable blog format. A community of teachers—leading scholars, authors, and editors—discuss revision, research, grammar and style, technology, peer review, and much more. Take, use, adapt, and pass the ideas around. Then, come back to the site to comment or share your own suggestion.

Content cartridges for the most common course management systems—Blackboard, WebCT, Angel, and Desire2Learn—allow you to easily download Bedford/St. Martin's digital materials for your course.

Acknowledgments

We are deeply grateful to the many instructors, students, professional writers, and others who have helped shape *The Business Writer's Companion*, Sixth Edition. For their sound advice on this revision, we wish to express our thanks to the following reviewers who completed questionnaires: John Adinolfi, Sacred Heart University; Diane Albertini, Dixie State College of Utah; Ian Barnard, California State University, Northridge; Barclay Barrios, Florida Atlantic University; Jim Black, Johnson State College; Stephen M. Byars, University of Southern California; Amber Dahlin, University of Colorado at Boulder; Scott Downing, DePaul University; Robert Goldberg, Prince George's Community College; Barbara Grunwaldt, Lakeland College; Tracey Hayes, Arizona State University; Terry Hinch, Carey Business School; Kathie Holland, University of Central Florida; Joanna Johnson, University of Miami; John Krajicek, Texas A&M University; Carolyn Leeb, DePaul University; Dorothy McCawley, University of Florida; James O'Rourke, University of Notre Dame; James Porter, Michigan State University; Jim Schwartz, Wright State University; Elayne Shapiro, University of Portland; Syd Slobodnik, University of Illinois at Urbana-Champaign; Christine Sneed, DePaul University; Jeffrey Walls, Indiana Institute of Technology; and Karen Weekes, Pennsylvania State University–Abington Campus.

For this edition, we especially thank Quinn Warnick, Iowa State University, for developing the new entry "adapting to new technologies" and Richard C. Hay of the RiCH Company for providing insightful developmental reviews of that entry as well as for help with the "blogs/forums" entry. We also thank Erik Thelen and Rachel Spilka for providing insights on the new chapter, Workplace Technology. For other special reviews and advice on the use and adaptation of workplace technology for business writing, we thank Michelle M. Schoenecker, Ulrike Mueller, Nick Carbone, and Paul Thomas. Finally, we thank Sally Stanton for expertly reviewing the "proposals" entry and developing the section on grant proposals.

For contributions to previous editions, we thank Rebekka Andersen for providing invaluable and fresh insights on many subjects, especially in the "proposals" entry. We thank Eileen Puechner, Senior Technical Editor at Johnson Controls, Inc., for her advice on workplace commu- nication. We are also grateful to Kim Isaacs, Advanced Career Systems, Inc.; Renee Tegge, Shorewood High School; Matthias Jonas, Niceware International, LLC; Lisa Rivero, Milwaukee School of Engineering; and Peter Sands, University of Wisconsin–Milwaukee.

We most gratefully acknowledge the leadership of Bedford/St. Martin's, beginning with Joan Feinberg, president; Denise Wydra, editorial director; Karen Henry, editor in chief; and Charles Christensen, retired president; for their support of this book. We would also like to acknowledge the contributions of others at Bedford/St. Martin's over the years — Nancy Lyman, who conceived the first edition of this book; Carla Samodulski, for her expert editorial guidance; Mimi Melek, for her editorial development of the second edition; Ellen Thibault, for editing the third edition; and Caroline Thompson, for editing the fourth edition; and Amy Gershman, for editing the fifth edition.

For this edition, we would like to thank Emily Berleth and Andrew Ensor of Bedford/St. Martin's for ensuring the high-quality production of the book, and Herb Nolan of Books By Design for his energy, care, and professionalism in turning manuscript into bound book. We are also pleased to acknowledge the unfailing support of Kate Mayhew, editorial assistant at Bedford/St. Martin's. Finally, we would like to thank Amy Gershman, associate editor at Bedford/St. Martin's, for her thoughtful and insightful editorial direction throughout the project.

We also gratefully acknowledge the ongoing contributions of many students and instructors at the University of Wisconsin–Milwaukee. Finally, special thanks go to Janice Alred for her many hours of substan- tive assistance and for continuing to hold everything together.

Gerald J. Alred
Charles T. Brusaw
Walter E. Oliu

Complete Contents

xviii   Complete Contents

11. Grammar   303

Five Steps to Successful Writing

Successful writing on the job is not the product of inspiration, nor is it merely the spoken word converted to print; it is the result of knowing how to structure information using both text and design to achieve an intended purpose for a clearly defined audience. The best way to ensure that your writing will succeed — whether it is in the form of a memo, a résumé, a proposal, or a Web page — is to approach writing using the following steps:

1. Preparation
2. Research
3. Organization
4. Writing
5. Revision

You will very likely need to follow those steps consciously — even self-consciously — at first. The same is true the first time you use new software, interview a candidate for a job, or chair a committee meeting. With practice, the steps become nearly automatic. That is not to suggest that writing becomes easy. It does not. However, the easiest and most efficient way to write effectively is to do it systematically.

As you master the five steps, keep in mind that they are interrelated and often overlap. For example, your readers' needs and your purpose, which you determine in step 1, will affect decisions you make in subsequent steps. You may also need to retrace steps. When you conduct research, for example, you may realize that you need to revise your initial impression of the document's purpose and audience. Similarly, when you begin to organize, you may discover the need to return to the research step to gather more information.

The time required for each step varies with different writing tasks. When writing an informal memo, for example, you might follow the first three steps (preparation, research, and organization) by simply listing the points in the order you want to cover them. In such situations, you gather and organize information mentally as you consider your purpose and audience. For a formal report, the first three steps require well-organized research, careful note-taking, and detailed outlining. For a routine e-mail message to a coworker, the first four steps merge as you type the information on the screen. In short, the five steps expand, contract, and at times must be repeated to fit the complexity or context of the writing task.

Dividing the writing process into steps is especially useful for collaborative writing, in which you typically divide the work among team members, keep track of a project, and save time by not duplicating effort. When you collaborate, you can use e-mail to share text and other files, suggest improvements to each other's work, and generally keep everyone informed of your progress as you follow the steps in the writing process. See also <u>collaborative writing</u> (Tab 1).*

Preparation

Writing, like most professional tasks, requires solid <u>preparation</u> (Tab 1). In fact, adequate preparation is as important as writing a draft. In preparation for writing, your goal is to accomplish the following four major tasks:

- Establish your primary purpose.
- Assess your audience (or readers) and the context.
- Determine the scope of your coverage.
- Select the appropriate medium.

Establishing Your Purpose. To establish your primary <u>purpose</u> (Tab 1), simply ask yourself what you want your readers to know, to believe, or to be able to do after they have finished reading what you have written. Be precise. Often a writer states a purpose so broadly that it is almost useless. A purpose such as "to report on possible locations for a new research facility" is too general. However, "to compare the relative advantages of Paris, Singapore, and San Francisco as possible locations for a new research facility so that top management can choose the best location" is a purpose statement that can guide you throughout the writing process. In addition to your primary purpose, consider possible secondary purposes for your document. For example, a secondary purpose of the research-facilities report might be to make corporate executive readers aware of the staffing needs of the new facility so that they can ensure its smooth operation in whichever location is selected.

Assessing Your Audience and Context. The next task is to assess your audience (Tab 1). Again, be precise and ask key questions. Who exactly is your reader? Do you have multiple readers? Who needs to see or use the document? What are your readers' needs in relation to your subject? What are your readers' attitudes about the subject? (Are they skeptical? supportive? anxious? bored?) What do your readers already know about the subject? Should you define basic terminology, or will such definitions merely bore, or even impede, your readers? Are you communicating with international readers and therefore dealing with issues inherent in <u>global communication</u> (Tab 1)?

---

*In this discussion, as elsewhere throughout this book, words and phrases shown as links—underlined and set in an alternate typeface—refer to specific alphabetical entries. The number in parentheses indicates the tabbed section in which the alphabetical entry can be found. If no tab number appears, the entry can be found in the same tabbed section as the entry you are reading.

For the research-facilities report, the readers are described as "top management." Who is included in that category? Will one of the people evaluating the report be the human resources manager? If so, that person likely would be interested in the availability of qualified professionals as well as in the presence of training, housing, and perhaps even recreational facilities available to potential employees in each city. The purchasing manager would be concerned about available sources for materials needed by the facility. The marketing manager would give priority to the facility's proximity to the primary markets for its products and services and to the transportation options that are available. The chief financial officer would want to know about land and building costs and about each country's tax structure. The chief executive officer would be interested in all this information and perhaps more. As with this example, many workplace documents have audiences composed of multiple readers. You can accommodate their needs through one of a number of approaches described in the entry audience (Tab 1).

In addition to knowing the needs and interests of your readers, learn as much as you can about the context (Tab 1). Simply put, context is the environment or circumstances in which writers produce documents and within which readers interpret their meanings. Everything is written in a context, as illustrated in many entries and examples throughout this book. To determine the effect of context on the research-facilities report, you might ask both specific and general questions about the situation and about your readers' backgrounds: Is this the company's first new facility, or has the company chosen locations for new facilities before? Have the readers visited all three cities? Have they already seen other reports on the three cities? What is the corporate culture in which your readers work, and what are its key values? What specific factors, such as competition, finance, and regulation, are recognized as important within the organization?

 TIP FOR CONSIDERING AUDIENCES

In the United States, conciseness (Tab 10), coherence (Tab 10), and clarity characterize good writing. Make sure readers can follow your writing, and say only what is necessary to communicate your message. Of course, no writing style is inherently better than another, but, to be a successful writer in any language, you must understand the cultural values that underlie the language in which you are writing. See also global communication (Tab 1), copyright (Tab 3), plagiarism (Tab 3), and awkwardness (Tab 10).

   Throughout this book, we have included ESL Tip boxes like this one with information that may be particularly helpful to nonnative speakers of English. The entry English as a second language (Tab 11) includes a list of entries that may be of particular help to ESL writers.

Determining the Scope.   Determining your purpose and assessing your readers and context will help you decide what to include and what not to include in your writing. Those decisions establish the <u>scope</u> (Tab 1) of your writing project. If you do not clearly define the scope, you will spend needless hours on research because you will not be sure what kind of information you need or even how much. Given the purpose and audience established for the report on facility locations, the scope would include such information as land and building costs, available labor force, cultural issues, transportation options, and proximity to suppliers. However, it probably would not include the early history of the cities being considered or their climate and geological features, unless those aspects were directly related to your particular business.

Selecting the Medium.   Finally, you need to determine the most appropriate medium for communicating your message. Professionals on the job face a wide array of options—from e-mail, fax, voice mail, videoconferencing, and Web sites to more traditional means, such as letters, memos, reports, telephone calls, and face-to-face meetings.

The most important considerations in selecting the appropriate medium are the audience and the purpose of the communication. For example, if you need to collaborate with someone to solve a problem or if you need to establish rapport with someone, written exchanges could be far less efficient than a phone call or a face-to-face meeting. However, if you need precise wording or you need to provide a record of a complex message, communicate in writing. If you need to make information that is frequently revised accessible to employees at a large company, the best choice might be to place the information on the company's intranet site. If reviewers need to make handwritten comments on a proposal, you may need to provide paper copies that can be faxed, or you may use word-processing software and insert comments electronically. The comparative advantages and primary characteristics of the most typical means of communication are discussed in <u>selecting the medium</u> (Tab 2). See also <u>Web design</u> (Tab 2), <u>writing for the Web</u> (Tab 2), and the entries in Tab 4, "Business Writing Documents and Elements."

Research

The only way to be sure that you can write about a complex subject is to thoroughly understand it. To do that, you must conduct adequate research, whether that means conducting an extensive investigation for a major proposal—through interviewing, library and Internet research, careful note-taking, and documenting sources—or simply checking a company Web site and jotting down points before you send an e-mail message to a colleague. The entries in Tab 3, "Research and Documentation," will help you with the research process.

Methods of Research.   Researchers frequently distinguish between primary and secondary <u>research</u> (Tab 3), depending on the types of sources consulted and the method of gathering information. *Primary research* refers to the gathering of raw data compiled from interviews, direct observation, surveys, experiments, questionnaires, and audio and video recordings, for example. In fact, direct observation and hands-on experience are the only ways to obtain certain kinds of information, such as the behavior of people and animals, certain natural phenomena, mechanical processes, and the operation of systems and equipment. *Secondary research* refers to gathering information that has been analyzed, assessed, evaluated, compiled, or otherwise organized into accessible form. Such forms or sources include books, articles, reports, Web documents, e-mail discussions, business letters, minutes of meetings, and brochures. Use the methods most appropriate to your needs, recognizing that some projects will require several types of research and that collaborative projects may require those research tasks to be distributed among team members.

Sources of Information.   As you conduct research, numerous sources of information are available to you.

- Your own knowledge and that of your colleagues
- The knowledge of people outside your workplace, gathered through <u>interviewing for information</u> (Tab 3)
- Internet sources, including Web sites, directories, archives, and discussion groups
- Library resources, including databases and indexes of articles as well as books and reference works
- Printed and electronic sources in the workplace, such as brochures, memos, e-mail, and Web documents

Consider all sources of information when you begin your research and use those that are appropriate and useful. The amount of research you will need to do depends on the scope of your project.

Organization

Without organization, the material gathered during your research will be incoherent to your readers. To organize information effectively, you need to determine the best way to structure your ideas; that is, you must choose a primary method of development. The entry <u>organization</u> (Tab 1) describes typical methods of development used in on-the-job writing.

Methods of Development.   An appropriate method of development is the writer's tool for keeping information under control and the readers' means of following the writer's presentation. As you analyze the information you have gathered, choose the method that best suits your subject, your readers' needs, and your purpose. For example, if you were writing instructions for assembling office equipment, you would naturally present the steps of the process in the order readers should perform them: the sequential method of development. If you were writing about the history of an organization, your account would most naturally go from the beginning to the present: the chronological method of development. If your subject naturally lends itself to a certain method of development, use it—do not attempt to impose another method on it.

Often you will need to combine methods of development. For example, a persuasive brochure for a charitable organization might combine a specific-to-general method of development with a cause-and-effect method of development. That is, you could begin with persuasive case histories of individual people in need and then move to general information about the positive effects of donations on recipients.

Outlining.   Once you have chosen a method of development, you are ready to prepare an outline. Outlining (Tab 1) breaks large or complex subjects into manageable parts. It also enables you to emphasize key points by placing them in the positions of greatest importance. By structuring your thinking at an early stage, a well-developed outline ensures that your document will be complete and logically organized, allowing you to focus exclusively on writing when you begin the rough draft. An outline can be especially helpful for maintaining a collaborative writing team's focus throughout a large project. However, even a short letter or memo needs the logic and structure that an outline provides, whether the outline exists in your mind or on-screen or on paper.

At this point, you must begin to consider layout and design elements that will be helpful to your readers and appropriate to your subject and purpose. For example, if visuals such as photographs or tables will be useful, this is a good time to think about where they may be deployed and what kinds of visual elements will be effective, especially if they need to be prepared by someone else while you are writing and revising the draft. The outline can also suggest where headings, lists, and other special design features may be useful. See Tab 6, "Design and Visuals."

Writing

When you have established your purpose, your readers' needs, and your scope, and you have completed your research and your outline, you will be well prepared to write a first draft. Expand your outline into paragraphs (Tab 1), without worrying about grammar, refinements of language usage, or punctuation. Writing and revising are different activities; refinements come with revision.

Write the rough draft, concentrating entirely on converting your outline into sentences and paragraphs. You might try writing as though you were explaining your subject to a reader sitting across from you. Do not worry about a good opening. Just start. Do not be concerned in the rough draft about exact word choice unless it comes quickly and easily—concentrate instead on ideas.

Even with good preparation, writing the draft remains a chore for many writers. The most effective way to get started and keep going is to use your outline as a map for your first draft. Do not wait for inspiration—you need to treat writing a draft as you would any on-the-job task. The entry <u>writing a draft</u> (Tab 1) describes tactics used by experienced writers—discover which ones are best suited to you and your task.

Consider writing the introduction last because then you will know more precisely what is in the body of the draft. Your opening should announce the subject and give readers essential background information, such as the document's primary purpose. For longer documents, an introduction should serve as a frame into which readers can fit the detailed information that follows. See <u>introductions</u> (Tab 1).

Finally, you will need to write a conclusion that ties the main ideas together and emphatically makes a final, significant point. The final point may be to recommend a course of action, make a prediction or judgment, or merely summarize your main points—the way you conclude depends on the purpose of your writing and your readers' needs. See <u>conclusions</u> (Tab 1).

Revision

The clearer a finished piece of writing seems to the reader, the more effort the writer has likely put into its <u>revision</u> (Tab 1). If you have followed the steps of the writing process to this point, you will have a rough draft that needs to be revised. Revising, however, requires a different frame of mind than does writing the draft. During revision, be eager to find and correct faults and be honest. Be hard on yourself for the benefit of your readers. Read and evaluate the draft as if you were a reader seeing it for the first time.

Check your draft for accuracy, completeness, and effectiveness in achieving your purpose and meeting your readers' needs and expectations. Trim extraneous information: Your writing should give readers exactly what they need, but it should not burden them with unnecessary information or sidetrack them into loosely related subjects.

Do not try to revise for everything at once. Read your rough draft several times, each time looking for and correcting a different set of problems or errors. Concentrate first on larger issues, such as <u>unity</u> (Tab 10) and <u>coherence</u> (Tab 10); save mechanical corrections, like spelling and punctuation, for later. See also <u>ethics in writing</u> (Tab 1).

Finally, for important documents, consider having others review your writing and make suggestions for improvement. For collaborative writing, of course, team members must review each other's work on segments of the document as well as the final master draft. For further advice and useful checklists, see <u>revision</u> (Tab 1) and <u>proofreading</u> (Tab 1).

1

The Writing Process

Preview

The "Five Steps to Successful Writing" essay (pages xxix–xxxvi) describes a systematic approach to writing and functions as a diagnostic tool for assessing problems. That is, when you find that a document is not achieving its primary purpose, the five steps can help you pinpoint where a problem occurred. Was the audience not fully assessed? Is additional research needed? Does the document need further revision? Many of the entries in this section expand on the topics introduced in the "Five Steps," such as **audience**, **collaborative writing**, **selecting the medium** (Tab 2), **writing a draft**, and others. Entries related to the research process, including such topics as finding, evaluating, and using sources, appear in Tab 3, "Research and Documentation."

audience

Considering the needs of your audience is crucial to achieving your purpose. When you are writing to a specific reader, for example, you may find it useful to visualize a reader sitting across from you as you write. (See correspondence, Tab 7.) Likewise, when writing to an audience composed of relatively homogeneous readers, you might create an image of a composite reader and write for *that* reader. In such cases, using the "you" viewpoint (Tab 10) and an appropriate tone (Tab 10) will help you meet the needs of your readers as well as achieve an effective business writing style (Tab 10). For meeting the needs of an audience composed of listeners, see presentations (Tab 9).

Analyzing Your Audience's Needs

The first step in analyzing your audience is to determine the readers' needs relative to your purpose and goals. Ask key questions during preparation.

- Who specifically is your reader? Do you have multiple readers? Who needs to see or use the document?
- What do your readers already know about your subject? What are your readers' attitudes about the subject? (Are they skeptical? supportive? anxious? bored?)
- What particular information about your readers (experience, training, and work habits, for example) might help you write at the appropriate level of detail?
- What does the context suggest about the readers' expectations for content or layout and design (Tab 6)?
- Do you need to adapt your message for international readers? If so, see global communication, global graphics (Tab 6), and international correspondence (Tab 7).

In the workplace, your readers are usually less familiar with the subject than you are. You have to be careful, therefore, when writing on a topic that is unique to your area of specialization. Be sensitive to the needs of those whose training or experience lies in other areas; provide definitions of nonstandard terms and explanations of principles that you, as a specialist, take for granted. See also defining terms.

Writing for Multiple Audiences

For documents aimed at multiple audiences with different needs, consider segmenting the document for different groups of readers: an executive summary for top managers, an appendix with detailed data for technical specialists, and the body for those readers who need to make decisions based on a detailed discussion. See also <u>proposals</u> (Tab 4) and <u>formal reports</u> (Tab 5).

When you have multiple audiences with various needs but cannot segment your document, first determine your primary or most important readers—such as those who will make decisions based on the document—and be sure to meet their needs. Then, meet the needs of secondary readers, such as those who need only some of the document's contents, as long as you do not sacrifice the needs of your primary readers. See also <u>persuasion</u> and "Five Steps to Successful Writing" (pages xxix–xxxvi).

collaborative writing

Collaborative writing occurs when two or more writers work together to produce a single document for which they share responsibility and decision-making authority. Collaborative writing teams are formed when (1) the size of a project or the time constraints imposed on it require collaboration, (2) the project involves multiple areas of expertise, or (3) the project requires the melding of divergent views into a single perspective that is acceptable to the whole team or to another group. Many types of collaborations are possible, from the collaboration of a primary writer with a variety of contributors and reviewers to a highly interactive collaboration in which everyone on a team plays a relatively equal role in shaping the document.

 DIGITAL TIP COLLABORATIVE WRITING SOFTWARE

Collaborative writing software helps teams of students, employees, researchers, and others work together on a common writing task whether they are in the same office or in different countries. Like word processing, collaborative writing software permits team members to draft, review, edit, and comment on their collective work. It also enables live text chat for brainstorming ideas, collaborative editing in real time, version tracking ("Is this the third or fourth draft?"), calendars to alert users of due dates, and spreadsheets to track work schedules. For more detailed information, go to *bedfordstmartins.com/alred*, and select *Digital Tips*, "Reviewing Collaborative Documents," "Using Collaborative Software," or "Using Wikis for Collaborative Work."

Tasks of the Collaborative Writing Team

The collaborating team strives to achieve a compatible working relationship by dividing the work in a way that uses each writer's expertise and experience to its advantage. The team should also designate a coordinator who will guide the team members' activities, organize the project, and ensure coherence and consistency within the document. The coordinator's duties can be determined by mutual agreement or, if the team often works together, assigned on a rotating basis.

Planning. The team conceptualizes the document to be produced as the members collectively identify the <u>audience</u>, <u>purpose</u>, <u>context</u>, and <u>scope</u> of the project. See also <u>meetings</u> (Tab 9) and "Five Steps to Successful Writing" (pages xxix–xxxvi).

At this stage, the team establishes a project plan that may include guidelines for communication among team members, version control (naming, dating, and managing document drafts), review procedures, and writing style standards that team members are expected to follow. The plan includes a schedule with due dates for completing initial research tasks, outlines, drafts, reviews, revisions, and the final document.

◼ PROFESSIONALISM NOTE Deadlines must be met, even if the drafts are not as polished as the individual writers would like. Team members rely on each other; one missed deadline can delay the entire project, which reflects poorly on the whole team. ✦

Researching and Writing. At this stage, the team completes initial research tasks, elicits comments from team members, creates a broad outline of the document (see <u>outlining</u>), and assigns writing tasks to individual team members, based on their expertise and the outline. Depending on the project, each team member further researches an assigned segment of the document, expands and develops the broad outline, and produces a draft from a detailed outline. See also <u>writing a draft</u> and <u>research</u> (Tab 3).

Reviewing. Keeping the audience's needs and the document's purpose in mind, each team member critically yet diplomatically reviews the other team members' drafts, from the overall organization to the clarity of each paragraph, and offers advice to help improve each writer's work. Team members can easily solicit feedback by sharing electronic files. Tracking and commenting features allow the reviewer to show the suggested changes without deleting the original text.

Revising. In this stage, individual writers evaluate their colleagues' reviews and accept, reject, or build on their suggestions. Then, the team coordinator can consolidate all drafts into a final master copy and maintain and evaluate it for consistency and coherence. See also <u>revision</u>.

◼ PROFESSIONALISM NOTE As you collaborate, be ready to tolerate some disharmony, but temper it with mutual respect. Team members may not agree on every subject, and differing perspectives can easily lead to conflict, ranging from mild differences over minor points to major showdowns. However, creative differences resolved respectfully can energize the team and, in fact, strengthen a finished document by compelling writers to reexamine assumptions and issues in unanticipated ways. See also <u>listening</u> (Tab 9). ✦

Writer's Checklist: Writing Collaboratively

- ☑ Designate one person as the team coordinator.
- ☑ Identify the audience, purpose, context, and scope of the project.
- ☑ Create a project plan, including a schedule and standards.
- ☑ Create a working outline of the document.
- ☑ Assign segments or tasks to each team member.
- ☑ Research and write drafts of document segments.
- ☑ Follow the schedule: due dates for drafts, revisions, and final versions.
- ☑ Use the agreed-upon standards for style and format.
- ☑ Exchange segments for team member reviews.
- ☑ Revise segments as needed.
- ☑ Meet the established deadlines.

conclusions

The conclusion of a document ties the main ideas together and can clinch a final significant point. This final point may, for example, make a prediction or a judgment, summarize the key findings of a study, or recommend a course of action. Figure 1–1 is a conclusion from a proposal to reduce health-care costs by increasing employee fitness through health-club subsidies. Notice that it makes a recommendation, summarizes key points, and points out several benefits of implementing the recommendation.

The way you conclude depends on your <u>purpose</u>, the needs of your <u>audience</u>, and the <u>context</u>. For example, a lengthy sales proposal might conclude persuasively with a summary of the proposal's salient points and the company's relevant strengths. The following examples are typical concluding strategies.

RECOMMENDATION

Our findings suggest that you need to alter your marketing to adjust to the changing demographics for your products.

SUMMARY

As this report describes, we would attract more recent graduates with the following strategies:

1. Establish a Web site where students can register and submit online résumés.
2. Increase our advertising in local student newspapers and our attendance at college career fairs.
3. Expand our local co-op program.

1
The Writing Process

> **Conclusion and Recommendation**
> I recommend that ABO, Inc., participate in the corporate membership
> program at AeroFitness Clubs, Inc., by subsidizing employee
> memberships. Offering this benefit to employees will demonstrate
> ABO's commitment to the importance of a healthy workforce. Club
> membership allows employees at all five ABO warehouses to participate
> in the program. The more employees who participate, the greater the
> long-term savings in ABO's health-care costs.
>
> Enrolling employees in the corporate program at AeroFitness would
> allow them to receive a one-month free trial membership. Those interested
> in continuing could then join the club and pay half of the one-time
> membership fee of $900 and receive a 30 percent discount on the
> $600 yearly fee. The other half of the membership fee ($450) would
> be paid for by ABO. If employees leave the company, they would have
> the option of purchasing ABO's share of the membership to continue at
> AeroFitness or selling their half of the membership to another ABO
> employee wishing to join AeroFitness.
>
> Implementing this program will help ABO, Inc., reduce its health-care costs
> while building stronger employee relations by offering employees a desirable
> benefit. If this proposal is adopted, I have some additional thoughts about
> publicizing the program to encourage employee participation that I would
> be pleased to share.

Makes a
recommen-
dation

Summarizes
key points

Points to
benefits

FIGURE 1–1. Conclusion

JUDGMENT

Based on the scope and degree of the tornado's damage, the current construction code for roofing on light industrial facilities is inadequate.

IMPLICATION

Although our estimate calls for a substantially higher budget than in the three previous years, we believe that it is reasonable given our planned expansion.

PREDICTION

Although I have exceeded my original estimate for equipment, I have reduced my labor costs; therefore, I will easily stay within the original bid.

The concluding statement may merely present ideas for consideration, may present a call for action, or may deliberately provoke thought.

IDEAS FOR CONSIDERATION

The new prices become effective the first of the year. Price adjustments are routine for the company, but some of your customers will not consider them acceptable. Please bear in mind the needs of both your customers and the company as you implement these price adjustments.

CALL FOR ACTION

Please send us a check for $250 now if you wish to keep your account active. If you have not responded to our previous letters because of some special circumstance, I will be glad to work out a solution with you.

THOUGHT-PROVOKING STATEMENT

Can we continue to accept the losses incurred by inefficiency? Or should we take the necessary steps to control it now?

Be especially careful not to introduce a new topic when you conclude. A conclusion should always relate to and reinforce the ideas presented earlier in your writing. Moreover, the conclusions must be consistent with what the <u>introduction</u> promised the report would examine (its purpose) and how it would do so (its method).

For guidance about the location of the conclusion section in a report, see <u>formal reports</u> (Tab 5). For other short closings, see <u>correspondence</u> (Tab 7) and entries on specific types of documents throughout this book.

context

Context is the environment or circumstances in which writers produce documents and within which readers interpret the meanings of those documents. Everything is written in a context, as illustrated in many entries and examples throughout this book. This entry considers the significance of context for workplace writing and suggests how you can be aware of it as you write. See also <u>audience</u>.

The context for any document, such as a proposal or report, is determined by interrelated events or circumstances both inside and outside an organization.* For example, when you write a proposal to fund a project within your company, the economic condition of that company is part of the context that will determine how your proposal is received. If the company has recently laid off a dozen employees, its management may not be inclined to approve a proposal to expand its operations—regardless of how well the proposal is written.

---

*For a detailed illustration of specific documents that have been affected by factors within particular contexts, see Linda Driskill, "Understanding the Writing Context in Organizations," in *Central Works in Technical Communication*, ed. Johndan Johnson-Eilola and Stuart Selber, 55–69 (New York: Oxford University Press, 2004).

When you correspond with someone, the events that prompted you to write shape the context of the message and will affect what you say and how you say it. If you write to a customer in response to a complaint, for example, the tone and approach of your message will be determined by the context—what you find when you investigate the issue. Is your company fully or partly at fault? Has the customer incorrectly used a product? contributed to a problem? (See also <u>adjustments</u>, Tab 7.) If you write instructions for office staff who must use high-volume document-processing equipment, other questions will reveal the context. What are the lighting and other physical conditions near the equipment? Will these physical conditions affect the layout and design of the instructions? What potential safety issues might the users encounter? See also <u>layout and design</u> (Tab 6).

Assessing Context

Each time you write, the context needs to be clearly in your mind so that your document will achieve its <u>purpose</u>. The following questions are starting points to help you become aware of the context, how it will influence your approach and your readers' interpretation of what you have written, and how it will affect the decisions you need to make during the writing process. See also "Five Steps to Successful Writing" (pages xxix–xxxvi).

- What is your professional relationship with your readers, and how might that affect the tone, style, and <u>scope</u> of your writing? See also Tab 10, "Style and Clarity."
- What is "the story" behind the immediate reason you are writing; that is, what series of events or perhaps previous documents led to your need to write?
- What is the preferred medium of your readers? (Is it e-mail? letter? memo?) See also <u>selecting the medium</u> (Tab 2).
- What specific factors (such as competition, finance, and regulation) are recognized within your organization or department as important?
- What is the corporate culture in which your readers work, and what are the key values that you might find in its mission statement?
- What are the professional relationships among the specific readers who will receive the document?
- What current events within or outside an organization or a department may influence how readers interpret your writing?
- What national cultural differences might affect your readers' expectations or interpretations of the document? See also <u>global communication</u>.

As these questions suggest, context is very specific each time you write and often involves, for example, the history of a specific organization or your past dealings with individual readers.

Signaling Context

Because context is so important, remind your reader in some way of the context for your writing, as in the following opening for a cover message to a proposal.

- During our meeting last week on improving quality, you mentioned that we have previously required usability testing only for documents going to high-profile clients because of the costs involved. The idea occurred to me that we might try less extensive usability testing for many of our other clients. Because you asked for suggestions, I have proposed in the attached document a method of limited usability testing for a broad range of clients in order to improve overall quality while keeping costs at a minimum.

Of course, as described in introductions, providing context for a reader may require only a brief background statement or short reminders.

- Several weeks ago, a financial adviser noticed a recurring problem in the software developed by Datacom Systems. Specifically, error messages repeatedly appeared when, in fact, no specific trouble . . .

- Jane, as I promised in my e-mail yesterday, I've attached the personnel budget estimates for the next fiscal year.

As the last example suggests, provide context for attachments that you send with e-mail (Tab 2).

defining terms

Defining key terms and concepts is often essential for clarity. Terms can be defined either formally or informally, depending on your purpose, your audience, and the context. A *formal definition* is a form of classification. You define a term by placing it in a category and then identifying the features that distinguish it from other members of the same category.

TERM	CATEGORY	DISTINGUISHING FEATURES
An *auction* is	a public sale	in which property passes to the highest bidder through successively increased offers.

An *informal definition* explains a term by giving a more familiar word or phrase as a synonym.

- Plants have a *symbiotic*, or *mutually beneficial*, relationship with certain kinds of bacteria.

State definitions in a positive way; focus on what the term *is* rather than on what it is not.

NEGATIVE   In a legal transaction, *real property* is not personal property.

POSITIVE   *Real property* is legal terminology for the right or interest a person has in land and the permanent structures on that land.

Avoid circular definitions, which merely restate the term to be defined.

CIRCULAR   *Spontaneous combustion* is fire that begins spontaneously.

CLEAR   *Spontaneous combustion* is the self-ignition of a flammable material through a chemical reaction.

In addition, avoid "is when" and "is where" definitions. Such definitions fail to include the category and are too indirect.

a binding agreement between two or more parties.
- A *contract* is ~~when two or more parties agree to something.~~

description

The key to effective description is the accurate presentation of details, whether for simple or complex descriptions. In Figure 1–2, notice that the simple description contained in the purchase order includes five specific details (in addition to the part number) structured logically.

Complex descriptions, of course, involve more details. In describing a mechanical device, for example, describe the whole device and its function before giving a detailed description of how each part works. The description should conclude with an explanation of how each part contributes to the functioning of the whole.

PURCHASE ORDER

PART NO.	DESCRIPTION	QUANTITY
IW 8421	Infectious-waste bags, 12″ × 14″, heavy-gauge polyethylene, red double closures with self-sealing adhesive strips	5 boxes containing 200 bags per box

---

FIGURE 1–2. Simple Description

1

In descriptions intended for readers who are unfamiliar with the topic, details are crucial. For such an <u>audience</u>, show or demonstrate (as opposed to "tell") primarily through the use of images and details. Notice the use of color, shapes, and images in the following description of a company's headquarters. The writer assumes that the reader knows such terms as *colonial design* and *haiku fountain*.

- Their corporate headquarters, which reminded me of a rural college campus, are located north of the city in a 90-acre lush green wooded area. The complex consists of five three-story buildings of red brick colonial design. The buildings are spaced about 50 feet apart and are built in a U shape surrounding a reflection pool that frames a striking haiku fountain.

You can also use analogy to explain unfamiliar concepts in terms of familiar ones, such as "U shape" in the previous example. See <u>figures of speech</u> (Tab 10).

Visuals can be powerful aids in descriptive writing. For a discussion of how to incorporate visual material into text, see Tab 6, "Design and Visuals."

ethics in writing

Ethics refers to the choices we make that affect others for good or ill. Ethical issues are inherent in writing and speaking because what we write and say can influence others. Further, how we express ideas affects our audience's perceptions of us and our organization's ethical stance. See also <u>audience</u>.

✚ ETHICS NOTE Obviously, no book can describe how to act ethically in every situation, but this entry describes some typical ethical lapses to watch for during <u>revision</u>.* In other entries throughout this book, ethical issues are highlighted using the symbols surrounding this paragraph. ✦

Avoid language that attempts to evade responsibility. Some writers use the passive <u>voice</u> (Tab 11) because they hope to avoid responsibility or obscure an issue: "It has been decided" (*Who* has decided?) or "Several mistakes were made" (*Who* made them?).

Avoid deceptive language. Do not use words with more than one meaning in an effort to circumvent the truth. Consider the company document that stated, "A nominal charge will be assessed for using our facilities." When clients objected that the charge was actually very high,

---

*Adapted from Brenda R. Sims, "Linking Ethics and Language in the Technical Communication Classroom," *Technical Communication Quarterly* 2, no. 3 (Summer 1993): 285–99.

the writer pointed out that the word *nominal* means "the named amount" as well as "very small." In that situation, clients had a strong case in charging that the company was attempting to be deceptive. Various abstract words (Tab 10), euphemisms (Tab 10), and technical and legal jargon (Tab 10) are unethical when they are used to mislead readers or to hide a serious or dangerous situation, even though technical or legal experts could interpret those words or terms as accurate. See also word choice (Tab 10).

Do not deemphasize or suppress important information. Not including information that a reader would want to have, such as potential safety hazards or hidden costs for which a customer might be responsible, is unethical and possibly illegal. Likewise, do not hide information in dense paragraphs with small type and little white space, as is common in credit-card contracts. Use layout and design (Tab 6) features such as type size, bullets, lists, and footnotes to highlight information that is important to readers.

Do not mislead readers with partial or self-serving information. For example, avoid the temptation to highlight a feature or service that readers would find attractive but that is available only with some product models or at extra cost. (See also logic errors, Tab 10, and positive writing, Tab 10.) Readers could justifiably object that you have given them a false impression to sell them a product or service, especially if you also deemphasize the extra cost or other special conditions.

In general, treat others—individuals, companies, and groups—with fairness and with respect. Avoid using language that is biased, racist, or sexist or that perpetuates stereotypes. See also biased language (Tab 10).

Finally, be aware that both plagiarism (Tab 3) and violations of copyright (Tab 3) not only are unethical but also can have serious professional and legal consequences for you in the classroom and on the job.

Writer's Checklist: Writing Ethically

Ask yourself the following questions:

- [✓] *Am I willing to take responsibility, publicly and privately, for what I have written?* Make sure you can stand behind what you have written.

- [✓] *Is the document or message honest and truthful?* Scrutinize findings and conclusions carefully. Make sure that the data support them.

- [✓] *Am I acting in my employer's, my client's, the public's, or my own best long-term interest?* Have someone outside your company review and comment on what you have written.

- [✓] *Does the document or message violate anyone's rights?* If information is confidential and you have serious concerns, consider a review by the company's legal staff or an attorney.

Writer's Checklist: Writing Ethically (continued)

☑ *Am I ethically consistent in my writing?* Apply consistently the principles outlined here and those you have assimilated throughout your life to meet this standard.

☑ *What if everybody acted or communicated in this way?* If you were the intended reader, consider whether the message would be acceptable and respectful.

If the answers to these questions do not come easily, consider asking a trusted colleague to review and comment on what you have written.

global communication

The prevalence of global communication technology and international markets means that the ability to communicate with <u>audiences</u> from varied cultural backgrounds is essential. The audiences for such communications include clients and customers as well as business partners and colleagues.

Many entries in this book, such as <u>résumés</u> (Tab 8) and <u>meetings</u> (Tab 9) are based on U.S. cultural patterns. The treatment of such topics might be very different in other countries and cultures where leadership styles, persuasive strategies, and even legal constraints differ. As illustrated in <u>international correspondence</u> (Tab 7), organizational patterns, forms of courtesy, and ideas about efficiency can vary significantly from culture to culture. What might be seen as direct and efficient in the United States could be considered blunt and even impolite in other cultures. The reasons behind these differing ways of viewing communication are complex. Researchers have found various ways to measure cultural differences through such concepts as the importance of saving face, perceptions of time, and individual versus group orientation.

Anthropologist Edward T. Hall, a pioneer in cross-cultural research, developed the concept of "contexting" to assess the predominant communication style of a culture.* By contexting, Hall means how much or how little an individual assumes another person understands about a subject under discussion. In a very low-context communication, the participants assume they share little knowledge and must communicate in great detail. Low-context cultures tend to assume little prior knowledge on the part of those with whom they communicate; thus, thorough documentation is important—written agreements (contracts) are expected, and rules are explicitly defined.

*Edward T. Hall and Mildred Reed Hall, *Understanding Cultural Differences: Germans, French and Americans* (Yarmouth, ME: Intercultural Press, 1990).

In a high-context communication, the participants assume they understand the <u>context</u> and thus depend on shared history (context) to communicate with each other. Thus, communications such as written contracts are not so important, while communication that relies on personal relationships and shared history is paramount. Of course, no culture is entirely high or low context; rather, these concepts can help you communicate more effectively to those in a particular culture.*

Writer's Checklist: Communicating Globally

☑ Acknowledge diversity within your organization. Discussing the differing cultures within your company or region will reinforce the idea that people can interpret verbal and nonverbal communications differently.

☑ Invite global and intercultural communication experts to speak at your workplace. Companies in your area may have employees who could be resources for cultural discussions.

☑ Understand that the key to effective communication with global audiences is recognizing that cultural differences, despite the challenges they may present, offer opportunities for growth for both you and your organization.

☑ Consult with someone from your intended audience's culture. Many phrases, gestures, and visual elements are so subtle that only someone who is very familiar with the culture can explain the effect they may have on others from that culture. See also <u>global graphics</u> (Tab 6).

 WEB LINK INTERCULTURAL RESOURCES

Intercultural Press publishes "books and training materials that help professionals, businesspeople, travelers, and scholars understand the meaning and diversity of culture." (See *www.interculturalpress.com.*) For other resources for global communication, see *bedfordstmartins.com/alred*, and select *Links Library*.

---

introductions

Every document must have either an opening or an introduction. An opening usually simply focuses the reader's attention on your topic and then proceeds to the body of your document. A formal introduction, however, sets the stage by providing necessary information to understand

---

*For an example of how contexting functions in a particular culture, see Gerald J. Alred, "Teaching in Germany and the Rhetoric of Culture," *Journal of Business and Technical Communication* 11, no. 3 (July 1997): 353–78.

the discussion that follows in the body. In general, <u>correspondence</u> (Tab 7) and routine <u>reports</u> (Tab 4) need only an opening; more complex reports and other longer documents need an introduction. Introductions are required for such documents as <u>formal reports</u> (Tab 5) and major <u>proposals</u> (Tab 4). For a discussion of comparable sections for Web sites, see <u>Web design</u> (Tab 2) and <u>writing for the Web</u> (Tab 2). See also <u>conclusions</u>.

Routine Openings

When your <u>audience</u> is familiar with your topic or if what you are writing is brief or routine, then a simple opening will provide adequate <u>context</u>, as shown in the following examples.

LETTER

Dear Mr. Ignatowski:
   You will be happy to know that we have corrected the error in your bank balance. The new balance shows . . .

MEMO

To date, 18 of the 20 specimens your department submitted for analysis have been examined.
   Our preliminary analysis indicates . . .

E-MAIL

Jane, as I promised in my e-mail yesterday, I've attached the human resources budget estimates for fiscal year 2011.

Opening Strategies

Opening strategies are aimed at focusing the readers' attention and motivating them to read the entire document.

Objective.   In reporting on a project, you might open with a statement of the project's objective so that the readers have a basis for judging the results.

- The primary goal of this project was to develop new techniques to solve the problem of waste disposal. Our first step was to investigate . . .

Problem Statement.   One way to give readers the perspective of your report is to present a brief account of the problem that led to the study or project being reported.

- Several weeks ago a financial adviser noticed a recurring problem in the software developed by Datacom Systems. Specifically, error messages repeatedly appeared when, in fact, no specific trouble. . . . After an extensive investigation, we found that Datacom Systems . . .

For proposals or formal reports, of course, problem statements may be more elaborate and a part of the full-scale introduction, which is discussed later in this entry.

Scope.   You may want to present the scope of your document in your opening. By providing the parameters of your material, the limitations of the subject, or the amount of detail to be presented, you enable your readers to determine whether they want or need to read your document.

- This pamphlet provides a review of the requirements for obtaining a private pilot's license. It is not intended as a textbook to prepare you for the examination itself; rather, it outlines the steps you need to take and the costs involved.

Background.   The background or history of a subject may be interesting and lend perspective and insight to a subject. Consider the following example from a newsletter describing the process of oil drilling:

- From the bamboo poles the Chinese used when the pyramids were young to today's giant rigs drilling in hundreds of feet of water, there has been considerable progress in the search for oil. But whether in ancient China or a modern city, a mountaintop or underwater, the objective of drilling has always been the same—to manufacture a hole in the ground, inch by inch.

Summary.   You can provide a summary opening by describing in abbreviated form the results, conclusions, or recommendations of your article or report. Be concise: Do not begin a summary by writing "This report summarizes . . ."

CHANGE   This report summarizes the advantages offered by the photon as a means of examining the structural features of the atom.

TO   As a means of examining the structure of the atom, the photon offers several advantages.

Interesting Detail.   Often an interesting detail will attract the readers' attention and pique their curiosity. Readers of an annual report for a manufacturer of telescopes and scientific instruments, for example, may be persuaded to invest if they believe that the company is developing innovative, cutting-edge products.

- The rings of Saturn have puzzled astronomers ever since they were discovered by Galileo in 1610 using the first telescope. Recently, even more rings have been discovered. . . .
  Our company's Scientific Instrument Division designs and manufactures research-quality, computer-controlled telescopes

The Writing Process

that promise to solve the puzzles of Saturn's rings by enabling scientists to use multicolor differential photometry to determine the rings' origins and compositions.

Definition.   Although a definition can be useful as an opening, do not define something with which your audience is familiar or provide a definition that is obviously a contrived opening (such as "Webster defines technology as . . ."). A definition should be used as an opening only if it offers insight into what follows.

- *Risk* is often a loosely defined term. In this report, risk refers to a qualitative combination of the probability of an event and the severity of the consequences of that event. In fact, . . .

Anecdote.   An anecdote can be used to attract and build interest in a subject that may otherwise be mundane; however, this strategy is best suited to longer documents and presentations (Tab 9).

- In his poem "The Calf Path" (1895), Sam Walter Foss tells of a wandering, wobbly calf trying to find its way home at night through the lonesome woods. It made a crooked path, which was taken up the next day by a lone dog. Then "a bellwether sheep pursued the trail over vale and steep, drawing behind him the flock, too, as all good bellwethers do." This forest path became a country lane that bent and turned and turned again. The lane became a village street, and at last the main street of a flourishing city. The poet ends by saying, "A hundred thousand men were led by a calf near three centuries dead."

  Many companies today follow a "calf path" because they react to events rather than planning. . . .

Quotation.   Occasionally, you can use a quotation to stimulate interest in your subject. To be effective, however, the quotation must be pertinent—not some loosely related remark selected from a book of quotations.

- Richard Smith, founder of PCS Corporation, recently said, "I believe that managers need to be more 'people smart' than ever before. The management style of today involves much more than just managing the operations of a department—it requires understanding the personalities that comprise a corporation." His statement represents a growing feeling among corporate leaders that . . .

Forecast.   Sometimes you can use a forecast of a new development or trend to gain the audience's attention and interest.

- In the not-too-distant future, we may be able to use a handheld medical diagnostic device similar to those in science fiction to assess the complete physical condition of accident victims. This project and others are now being developed at The Seldi Group, Inc.

Persuasive Hook. Although all opening strategies contain persuasive elements, the hook uses <u>persuasion</u> most overtly. A brochure touting the newest innovation in tax-preparation software might address readers as follows:

- Welcome to the newest way to do your taxes! TaxPro EZ ends the headache of last-minute tax preparation with its unique Web-Link feature.

Full-Scale Introductions

The purpose of a full-scale introduction is to give readers enough general information about the subject to enable them to understand the details in the body of the document. An introduction should accomplish any or all of the following:

- *State the subject.* Provide background information, such as definition, history, or theory, to provide context for your readers.
- *State the purpose.* Make your readers aware of why the document exists and whether the material provides a new perspective or clarifies an existing perspective.
- *State the scope.* Tell readers the amount of detail you plan to cover.
- *Preview the development of the subject.* Especially in a longer document, outline how you plan to develop the subject. Providing such information allows readers to anticipate how the subject will be presented and helps them evaluate your conclusions or recommendations.

Consider writing an opening or introduction last. Many writers find that it is only when they have drafted the body of the document that they have a full enough perspective on the subject to introduce it adequately.

organization

A well-organized document enables your readers to grasp how the pieces of your subject fit together as a coherent whole. An organized document or presentation is based on an effective outline produced from a method of development that suits your subject, fulfills your <u>purpose</u>, and satisfies the needs of your <u>audience</u> for shape and structure. Following are the most common methods of developing any document—from an e-mail to a formal report to a Web page. See also <u>outlining</u>.

- *Cause-and-effect development* begins with either the cause or the effect of an event. For example, if you were reporting on the cause of the financial crisis in a company, you might start your report with the causes (perhaps investment decisions) and lead into the current financial circumstances. Conversely, you might start with a description of the financial crisis and trace the events back to the causes. This approach can also be used to develop a report that offers a solution to a problem, beginning with the problem and moving on to the solution, or vice versa.
- *Chronological development* emphasizes the time element of a sequence. For example, a Federal Aviation Administration (FAA) report on an airplane crash might begin with takeoff and proceed in segments of time to the eventual crash.
- *Comparison* is useful when writing about a new topic that is in many ways similar to another, more familiar topic. For example, an online tutorial for a new operating system might compare that system to one that is familiar to the users.
- *Division* separates a whole into component parts and discusses each part separately. Division could be used, for example, to report on a multinational organization by describing its various operations.
- *Classification* groups parts into categories that clarify the relationship of the parts. For example, you might discuss local retail businesses by grouping them according to common demographic features of their target customers (such as age, household income, occupation).
- *General and specific development* proceeds either from general information to specific details or from specific information to a general conclusion. If you are writing about a new software product, for example, you might begin with a general statement of the function of the total software package, then explain the functions of the major routines in the package, and finally describe the functions of the various subroutines. Conversely, you might describe a software problem in a minor application and then trace it to a larger, more global problem with the software.
- *Order-of-importance development* presents information in either decreasing order of importance, as in a proposal that begins with the most important point, or increasing order of importance, as in a presentation that ends with your most important point.
- *Sequential development* emphasizes the order of elements in a process and is particularly useful when writing step-by-step instructions.

- *Spatial development* describes the physical appearance of an object or area (such as a room) from top to bottom, inside to outside, front to back, and so on. A crime-scene report might start at the site of the crime and proceed in concentric areas from that point.

Documents often blend methods of development. For example, in a report that describes the organization of a company, you might use elements from three methods of development. You could divide the larger topic (the company) into operations (division and classification), arrange the operations according to what you see as their impact within the company (order of importance), and present their manufacturing operations in the order they occur (sequential). As this example illustrates, when outlining a document, you may base your major division on one primary method of development appropriate to your purpose and then subordinate other methods to it.

During this step in the writing process, consider a design and layout that will be helpful to your reader and a format appropriate to your subject and purpose. If you intend to include visuals, plan them as you complete your outline, especially if they need to be prepared by someone else while you are writing and revising the draft. See also Tab 4, "Business Writing Documents and Elements," and Tab 6, "Design and Visuals."

outlining

An outline—the skeleton of the document you are going to write—structures your writing by ensuring that it has a beginning (introduction), a middle (main body), and an end (conclusion). An outline provides the foundation for <u>coherence</u> (Tab 10) so that relationships between ideas are clear and one part flows smoothly into the next. An outline also helps with <u>collaborative writing</u> by enabling a team to refine a project's scope, divide responsibilities, and maintain focus.

Types of Outlines

Two types of outlines are most common: short topic outlines and lengthy sentence outlines. A *topic outline* consists of short phrases arranged to reflect your primary method of development. A topic outline is especially useful for short documents such as e-mails, letters, or memos. See Tab 7, "Correspondence."

For a large writing project, create a topic outline first, and then use it as a basis for creating a sentence outline. A *sentence outline* summarizes each idea in a complete sentence that may become the topic sentence for a paragraph in the rough draft. If most of your notes can be shaped into topic sentences for paragraphs in your rough draft, you can

be relatively sure that your document will be well organized. See also
<u>note-taking</u> (Tab 3) and <u>research</u> (Tab 3).

Creating an Outline

When you are outlining large and complex subjects with many pieces of
information, the first step is to group related notes into categories. Sort
the notes by major and minor division headings. Use an appropriate
method of development to arrange items and label them with Roman
numerals. For example, the major divisions for this discussion of outlining could be shown as follows:

    I. Advantages of outlining
   II. Types of outlines
  III. Creating an outline

The second step is to establish your minor divisions within each major
division. Arrange your minor points using a method of development
under their major division and label them with capital letters.

   II. Types of outlines
      A. Topic outlines   **Division and Classification**
      B. Sentence outlines
  III. Creating an outline
      A. Establish major and minor divisions.
      B. Sort notes by major and minor divisions.   **Sequential**
      C. Complete the sentence outline.

You will sometimes need more than two levels of headings. If your
subject is complicated, you may need three or four levels of headings to
better organize all of your ideas in proper relationship to one another.
In that event, use the following numbering scheme:

  I. First-level heading
    A. Second-level heading
      1. Third-level heading
        a. Fourth-level heading

The third step is to mark each of your notes with the appropriate Roman
numeral and capital letter. Arrange the notes logically within each minor
heading, and mark each with the appropriate, sequential Arabic number. As you do, make sure your organization is logical and your headings have <u>parallel structure</u> (Tab 10). For example, all the second-level
headings under "III. Creating an outline" are complete sentences in the
active <u>voice</u> (Tab 11).

    Treat visuals as an integral part of your outline, and plan approxi-
mately where each should appear. Either include a rough sketch of the
visual or write "illustration of . . ." at each place. As with other information

in an outline, freely move, delete, or add visuals as needed. See also Tab 6, "Design and Visuals."

The outline samples shown earlier use a combination of numbers and letters to differentiate the various levels of information. You could also use a decimal numbering system, such as the following, for your outline.

1. FIRST-LEVEL HEADING
    1.1   Second-level heading
    1.2   Second-level heading
        1.2.1   Third-level heading
        1.2.2   Third-level heading
            1.2.2.1   Fourth-level heading
            1.2.2.2   Fourth-level heading
    1.3   Second-level heading
2. FIRST-LEVEL HEADING

This system should not go beyond the fourth level because the numbers get too cumbersome beyond that point. In many documents, such as policies and procedures, the decimal numbering system is carried over from the outline to the final version of the document for ease of cross-referencing sections.

Create your draft by converting your notes into complete sentences and paragraphs. If you have a sentence outline, the most difficult part of the writing job is over. However, whether you have a topic or a sentence outline, remember that an outline is flexible; it may need to change as you write the draft, but it should always be your point of departure and return. See writing a draft.

paragraphs

A paragraph performs three functions: (1) It develops the unit of thought stated in the topic sentence; (2) it provides a logical break in the material; and (3) it creates a visual break on the page, which signals a new topic.

Topic Sentence

A topic sentence states the paragraph's main idea; the rest of the paragraph supports and develops that statement with related details. The topic sentence is often the first sentence because it tells the reader what the paragraph is about.

- *The cost of training new employees is high.* In addition to the cost of classroom facilities and instructors, an organization must pay employees their regular salary while they sit in the classroom. For the companies to break even on this investment in their professional employees, those employees must stay in the job for which they have been trained for at least one year.

The topic sentence is usually most effective early in the paragraph, but a paragraph can lead to the topic sentence, which is sometimes done to achieve <u>emphasis</u> (Tab 10).

- Energy does far more than simply make our daily lives more comfortable and convenient. Suppose someone wanted to stop—and reverse—the economic progress of this nation. What would be the surest and quickest way to do it? Simply block the nation's ability to produce energy! The nation would face a devastating economic crisis. *Our economy, in short, is energy-based.*

On rare occasions, the topic sentence may logically fall in the middle of a paragraph.

- . . . [It] is time to insist that science does not progress by carefully designed steps called "experiments," each of which has a well-defined beginning and end. *Science is a continuous and often a disorderly and accidental process.* We shall not do the young psychologist any favor if we agree to reconstruct our practices to fit the pattern demanded by current scientific methodology.
                   —B. F. Skinner, "A Case History in Scientific Method"

Paragraph Length

A paragraph should be just long enough to deal adequately with the subject of its topic sentence. A new paragraph should begin whenever the subject changes significantly. A series of short, undeveloped paragraphs can indicate poor <u>organization</u> and can sacrifice unity by breaking a single idea into several pieces. A series of long paragraphs, however, can fail to provide the reader with manageable subdivisions of thought. Paragraph length should aid the reader's understanding of ideas.

Occasionally, a one-sentence paragraph is acceptable if it is used as a <u>transition</u> (Tab 10) between longer paragraphs or as a one-sentence <u>introduction</u> or <u>conclusion</u> in <u>correspondence</u> (Tab 7).

Writing Paragraphs

Careful paragraphing reflects the writer's logical organization and helps the reader follow the writer's thoughts. A good working outline makes it easy to group ideas into appropriate paragraphs. (See also <u>outlining</u>.)

The following partial topic outline plots the course of the subsequent paragraphs:

TOPIC OUTLINE (PARTIAL)

I. Advantages of Chicago as location for new facility
  A. Transport infrastructure
    1. Rail
    2. Air
    3. Truck
    4. Sea (except in winter)
  B. Labor supply
    1. Engineering and scientific personnel
      a. Similar companies in area
      b. Major universities
    2. Technical and manufacturing personnel
      a. Community college programs
      b. Custom programs

RESULTING PARAGRAPHS

Probably the greatest advantage of Chicago as a location for our new facility is its excellent transport facilities. The city is served by three major railroads. Both domestic and international air-cargo service are available at O'Hare International Airport; Midway Airport's convenient location adds flexibility for domestic air-cargo service. Chicago is a major hub of the trucking industry, and most of the nation's large freight carriers have terminals there. Finally, except in the winter months when the Great Lakes are frozen, Chicago is a seaport, accessible through the St. Lawrence Seaway.

Chicago's second advantage is its abundant labor force. An ample supply of engineering and scientific staff is assured not only by the presence of many companies engaged in activities similar to ours but also by the presence of several major universities in the metropolitan area. Similarly, technicians and manufacturing personnel are in abundant supply. The colleges in the Chicago City College system, as well as half a dozen other two-year colleges in the outlying areas, produce graduates with associate's degrees in a wide variety of technical specialties appropriate to our needs. Moreover, three of the outlying colleges have expressed an interest in developing off-campus courses attuned specifically to our requirements.

Paragraph Unity and Coherence

A good paragraph has unity (Tab 10) and coherence (Tab 10) as well as adequate development. *Unity* is singleness of purpose, based on a topic sentence that states the core idea of the paragraph. When every sentence in the paragraph develops the core idea, the paragraph has unity. *Coherence* is holding to one point of view, one attitude, one tense; it is the joining of sentences into a logical pattern. A careful choice of transitional words ties ideas together and thus contributes to coherence in a paragraph. Notice how the boldfaced italicized words tie together the ideas in the following paragraph.

TOPIC SENTENCE	*Over the past several months, I have heard complaints about the Merit Award Program.* **Specifically,** many employees feel that this program should be linked to annual **salary increases**. They believe that **salary increases** would provide a much better incentive than the current $500 to $700 cash awards for exceptional service. **In addition**, these **employees believe** that their supervisors consider the cash awards a satisfactory alternative to salary increases. Although I don't think this practice is widespread, the fact that the **employees believe** that it is justifies a reevaluation of the Merit Award Program.

Simple enumeration (*first, second, then, next,* and so on) also provides effective transition within paragraphs. Notice how the boldfaced italicized words and phrases give coherence to the instructions in the following paragraph.

- Most adjustable office chairs have nylon tubes that hold metal spindle rods. To keep the chair operational, lubricate the spindle rods occasionally. **First,** loosen the set screw in the adjustable bell. **Then** lift the chair from the base. **Next,** apply the lubricant to the spindle rod and the nylon washer. **When you have finished**, replace the chair and tighten the set screw.

persuasion

Persuasive writing attempts to convince an <u>audience</u> to adopt the writer's point of view or to take a particular action. Workplace writing often uses persuasion to reinforce ideas that readers already have, to convince readers to change their current ideas, or to lobby for a particular suggestion or policy (as in Figure 1–3). You may find yourself advocating for safer working conditions, justifying the expense of a new program, or writing a <u>proposal</u> (Tab 4) for a large purchase. See also <u>context</u> and <u>purpose</u>.

In persuasive writing, the way you present your ideas is as important as the ideas themselves. You must support your appeal with logic

---

Interoffice Memo

TO:	Marketing Staff
FROM:	Harold Kawenski, MIS Administrator *HK*
DATE:	April 21, 2011
SUBJECT:	Plans for the Changeover to the NRT/R4 System

As you all know, the merger with Datacom has resulted in dramatic growth in our workload — a 30-percent increase in our customer support services during the last several months. To cope with this expansion, we will soon install the NRT/R4 server and QCS Enterprise software with Web-based applications.

Let me briefly describe the benefits of this system and the ways we plan to help you cope with the changeover.

The QCS system will help us access up-to-date marketing and product information when we need it. This system will speed processing dramatically and give us access to all relevant companywide databases. Because we anticipate that our workload will increase another 30 percent in the next several months, we need to get the QCS system online and working smoothly as soon as possible.

The changeover to this system, unfortunately, will cause some disruption at first. We will need to transfer many of our legacy programs and software applications to the new system. In addition, all of us will need to learn to navigate in the R4 and QCS environments. Once we have made these adjustments, however, I believe we will welcome the changes.

To help everyone cope with the changeover, we will offer training sessions that will begin next week. I have attached a sign-up form with specific class times. We will also provide a technical support hotline at extension 4040, which will be available during business hours; e-mail support at qcs-support@conco.com; and online help documentation.

I would like to urge you to help us make a smooth transition to the QCS system. Please e-mail me with your suggestions or questions about the impact of the changeover on your department. I look forward to working with you to make this system a success.

Enclosure: Training Session Schedule

FIGURE 1–3. Persuasive Memo

and a sound presentation of facts, statistics, and examples. See also logic errors (Tab 10).

A writer also gains credibility, and thus persuasiveness, through the readers' impressions of the document's appearance. For this reason, consider carefully a document's layout and design (Tab 6). See also résumés (Tab 8).

The Writing Process

1

■ ETHICS NOTE Avoid ambiguity: Do not wander from your main point and, above all, never make false claims. You should also acknowledge any real or potentially conflicting opinions; doing so allows you to anticipate and overcome objections and builds your credibility. See also ethics in writing and promotional writing. ✦

The memo shown in Figure 1–3 was written to persuade the marketing staff to accept and participate in a change to a new computer system. Notice that not everything in this memo is presented in a positive light. Change brings disruption, and the writer acknowledges that fact.

A persuasive technique that places the focus on your reader's interest and perspective is discussed in the entry "you" viewpoint (Tab 10).

point of view

Point of view is the writer's relation to the information presented, as reflected in the use of grammatical person (Tab 11). The writer usually expresses point of view in first-, second-, or third-person personal pronouns (Tab 11). Use of first person indicates that the writer is a participant or an observer. Use of second or third person indicates that the writer is giving directions, instructions, or advice, or is writing about other people or something impersonal.

FIRST PERSON	*I* scrolled down to find the settings option.
SECOND PERSON	*You* need to scroll down to find the settings option. [*You* is explicitly stated.] Scroll down to find the settings option. [*You* is understood in such an instruction.]
THIRD PERSON	*He* scrolled down to find the settings option.

Consider the following sentence, revised from an impersonal to a more personal point of view. Although the meaning of the sentence does not change, the revision indicates that people are involved in the communication.

- *I regret* *we cannot accept*
  It is regrettable that the equipment shipped on Friday is unacceptable.

Some people think they should avoid the pronoun *I* in business writing. Such practice, however, often leads to awkward sentences, with people referring to themselves in the third person as *one* or as *the writer* instead of as *I*.

- *I believe*
  The writer believes that this project will be completed by July.

However, do not use the personal point of view when an impersonal point of view would be more appropriate or more effective because you need to emphasize the subject matter over the writer or the reader. In the following example, it does not help to personalize the situation; in fact, the impersonal version may be more tactful.

PERSONAL	I received objections to my proposal from several of your managers.
IMPERSONAL	Several managers have raised objections to the proposal.

Whether you adopt a personal or an impersonal point of view depends on the <u>purpose</u> and the <u>audience</u> of the document. For example, in an informal e-mail to an associate, you would most likely adopt a personal point of view. However, in a report to a large group, you would probably emphasize the subject by using an impersonal point of view.

 ETHICS NOTE In company <u>correspondence</u> (Tab 7), use of the pronoun *we* may be interpreted as reflecting company policy, whereas *I* clearly reflects personal opinion. Which pronoun to use should be decided according to whether you are speaking for yourself (*I*) or for the company (*we*).

- *I* understand your frustration with the price increase, but *we* must now add the import tax to the sales price. ✦

> **ESL TIP FOR STATING AN OPINION**
>
> In some cultures, stating an opinion in writing is considered impolite or unnecessary, but in the United States, readers expect to see a writer's opinion stated clearly and explicitly. The opinion should be followed by specific examples to help the reader understand the writer's point of view.

preparation

The preparation stage of the writing process is essential. By determining the needs of your <u>audience</u>, your <u>purpose</u>, the <u>context</u>, and the <u>scope</u> of coverage, you understand the information you will need to gather during <u>research</u> (Tab 3). See also <u>collaborative writing</u> and "Five Steps to Successful Writing" (pages xxix–xxxvi).

Writer's Checklist: Preparing to Write

- ☑ Determine who your readers are and learn certain key facts about them—their knowledge, attitudes, and needs relative to your subject.

- ☑ Determine the document's primary purpose. What exactly do you want your readers to know, to believe, or to be able to do when they have finished reading your document?

- ☑ Consider the context of your message and how it should affect your writing.

- ☑ Establish the scope of your document—the type and amount of detail you must include—not only by understanding your readers' needs and purpose but also by considering any external constraints, such as word limits for trade journal articles or the space limitations of Web pages. See also writing for the Web (Tab 2).

- ☑ Select the medium appropriate to your readers and purpose. See also selecting the medium (Tab 2).

process explanation

A process explanation may describe the steps in a process, an operation, or a procedure, such as the steps involved in starting a small business. The introduction often presents a brief overview of the process or lets readers know why it is important for them to become familiar with the process you are explaining. Be sure to define terms that readers might not understand and provide visuals (Tab 6) to clarify the process. See also defining terms.

In describing a process, use transitional words and phrases to create unity within paragraphs, and select headings to provide transition (Tab 10) from one step to the next. Notice in the following example how a company tuition refund policy is described as a step-by-step process.

Tuition Refund Policy

1. PROCEDURES
   1.1 Tuition Reimbursement Approval
       1.1.1 An employee who meets school requirements and is interested in receiving tuition reimbursement should obtain the approval of his or her manager and submit the request to the Human Resources (HR) Department. Human Resources may ask the manager to justify, in writing, the benefits of the academic work, if the reason is not obvious.

1.1.2 After reaching an agreement, the employee should complete Sections I and II of Form F-6970. After HR has obtained two levels of management approval—from the employee's supervisor and the head of the department—it approves the employee's enrollment in the course or degree program.

1.1.3 The employee who has been granted approval must submit to HR proof of enrollment and payment of appropriate fees to receive tuition reimbursement.

promotional writing

Promotional writing is vital to the success of any company or organization; high-quality, state-of-the-art products or services are of little value if customers and clients do not know they exist.

Although you may not be a marketing or public relations specialist, you may be asked to prepare promotional (or marketing) materials, especially if you work for a small organization or are self-employed. Even at a large company, you may help prepare a brochure, a Web page, or a department newsletter. (See also collaborative writing.) Several elements are central to promotional writing:

- *Understanding your audience.* Analyzing the needs, interests, concerns, and makeup of your audience is crucial.
- *Understanding your product or service.* Conduct adequate research (Tab 3), especially by talking with those with firsthand knowledge of the product or service. (See interviewing for information, Tab 3).
- *Understanding the principles of persuasion.* Good promotional writing uses persuasion to gain attention, build interest, reduce resistance, and motivate readers to act.
- *Making information both easy to find and visually appealing.* Make the most effective use of organization, layout and design (Tab 6), and appropriate visuals (Tab 6) that are well integrated with the text.
- *Using good writing style.* Write with clarity, coherence, and conciseness to help your readers understand the message and to achieve your purpose. See also Tab 10, "Style and Clarity."

⬧ ETHICS NOTE Because readers are persuaded only if they believe the source is credible, be careful not to overstate claims and to avoid possible logic errors (Tab 10). See also ethics in writing. ✦

1

The Writing Process

WEB LINK WRITING PROMOTIONAL CASE HISTORIES

One popular form of promotional writing is the case history, an informative story in a feature-article format that describes how a product or service solved a problem for a customer. Marketers use case histories to provide real-life examples of their products and services, adding credibility by mentioning real companies and references. For sites that provide advice on writing case histories, see *bedfordstmartins.com/alred*, and select *Links Library*.

The specific types of promotional writing discussed in this book include writing for the Web (Tab 2), proposals (Tab 4), and sales letters (Tab 7). (See also Web design, Tab 2.) Many other documents described in this book often include the additional or secondary purpose of promoting an organization. For example, adjustment letters, which are usually concerned with resolving a specific problem, offer opportunities to promote your organization. (See adjustments, Tab 7.) Likewise, progress and activity reports (Tab 4) provide an opportunity to promote the value of your work in an organization.

proofreading

Proofreading is essential whether you are writing a brief e-mail or a résumé. Grammar checkers and spell checkers are important aids to proofreading, but they can make writers overconfident. If a typographical error results in a legitimate English word (for example, *coarse* instead of *course*), the spell checker will not flag the misspelling. You may find some of the tactics discussed in revision useful when proofreading; in fact, you may find passages during proofreading that will require further revision.

■ PROFESSIONALISM NOTE Proofreading not only demonstrates that you respect your readers, who can be distracted, irritated, or misled by errors in writing but also reflects that you are professional in the way you approach all your work. ✦

Whether the material you proofread is your own writing or that of someone else, consider proofreading in several stages. Although you need to tailor the stages to the specific document and to your own problem areas, the following *Writer's Checklist* should provide a useful starting point for proofreading. Consider using standard proofreader's marks (shown on the facing inside back cover) for proofreading someone else's document.

1
The Writing Process

Writer's Checklist: Proofreading in Stages

FIRST-STAGE REVIEW

☑ Appropriate format, as for reports or correspondence

☑ Consistent style, including headings, terminology, spacing, fonts

☑ Correct numbering of figures and tables

SECOND-STAGE REVIEW

☑ Specific grammar and usage problems

☑ Appropriate punctuation

☑ Correct abbreviations and capitalization

☑ Correct spelling (especially names and places)

☑ Complete Web or e-mail addresses

☑ Accurate data in tables and lists

☑ Cut-and-paste errors; for example, a result of moved or deleted text and numbers

FINAL-STAGE REVIEW

☑ Survey of your overall goals: audience needs and purpose

☑ Appearance of the document (see **layout and design**, Tab 6)

☑ Review by a trusted colleague, especially for crucial documents (see **collaborative writing**)

See also Tab 11, "Grammar," and Tab 12, "Punctuation and Mechanics."

 DIGITAL TIP **PROOFREADING FOR FORMAT CONSISTENCY**

Viewing whole pages on-screen is an effective way to check formatting, spacing, and typographical consistency, as well as the general appearance of documents. For comparing layouts, view multiple pages or "tile" separate documents side by side. For instructions, see *bedfordstmartins.com/alred*, and select *Digital Tips*, "Proofreading for Format Consistency."

---

purpose

What do you want your readers to know, to believe, or to do when they have read your document? When you answer that question about your **audience**, you have determined the primary purpose, or objective, of your document. Be careful not to state a purpose too broadly. A statement of purpose such as "to explain continuing-education standards" is too general to be helpful during the writing process. In contrast, "to explain to Critical-Care Nurse Society (CCNS) members how to determine if a continuing-education course meets CCNS professional standards" is a specific purpose that will help you focus on what you need your document to accomplish. Often the <u>context</u> will help you focus your purpose.

The writer's primary purpose is often more complex than simply "to explain" something, as shown in the previous paragraph. To fully understand this complexity, you need to ask yourself not only *why* you are writing the document but *what* you want to influence your reader to believe or to do after reading it. Suppose a writer for a newsletter has been assigned to write an article about cardiopulmonary resuscitation (CPR). In answer to the question *what?* the writer could state the purpose as "to emphasize the importance of CPR." To the question *why?* the writer might respond, "to encourage employees to sign up for evening CPR classes." Putting the answers to the two questions together, the writer's purpose might be stated as, "To write an article that will emphasize the importance of CPR and encourage employees to sign up for evening CPR classes." Note that the primary purpose of this document is to persuade the readers of the importance of CPR, and the secondary goal is to motivate them to register for a class. Secondary goals often involve such abstract notions as to motivate, to persuade, to reassure, or to inspire your reader. See also <u>persuasion</u>.

If you answer the questions *what?* and *why?* and put the answers into writing as a stated purpose that includes both primary and secondary goals, you will simplify your writing task and more likely achieve your purpose. For a <u>collaborative writing</u> project, it is especially important to collectively write a statement of your purpose to ensure that the document achieves its goals. Do not lose sight of that purpose as you become engrossed in the other steps of the writing process. See also "Five Steps to Successful Writing" (pages xxix–xxxvi).

readers

The first rule of effective writing is *to help your readers*. If you overlook this commitment, your writing will not achieve its <u>purpose</u>, either for you or for your business or organization. For meeting the needs of both individual and multiple readers, see <u>audience</u>.

revision

When you revise your draft, read and evaluate it primarily from the point of view of your <u>audience</u>. In fact, revising requires a different frame of mind than <u>writing a draft</u>. To achieve that frame of mind, experienced writers have developed the following tactics:

- Allow a "cooling period" between writing the draft and revision to be able to evaluate the draft objectively.
- Print out your draft and mark up the paper copy; it is often difficult to revise on-screen.
- Read your draft aloud; often, hearing the text will enable you to spot problem areas that need improvement.
- Revise in passes by reading through your draft several times, each time searching for and correcting a different set of problems.

When you can no longer spot improvements, you may wish to give the draft to a colleague for review—especially for projects that are crucial for you or your organization as well as for collaborative projects, as described in <u>collaborative writing</u>.

Writer's Checklist: Revising Your Draft

☑ *Completeness.* Does the document achieve its primary <u>purpose</u>? Will it fulfill the readers' needs? Your writing should give readers exactly what they need but not overwhelm them.

☑ *Appropriate introduction and conclusion.* Check to see that your <u>introduction</u> frames the rest of the document and your <u>conclusion</u> ties the main ideas together. Both should account for revisions to the content of the document.

☑ *Accuracy.* Look for any inaccuracies that may have crept into your draft.

☑ *Unity and coherence.* Check to see that sentences and ideas are closely tied together (<u>coherence</u>, Tab 10) and contribute directly to the main idea expressed in the topic sentence of each <u>paragraph</u> (<u>unity</u>, Tab 10). Provide <u>transitions</u> (Tab 10) where they are missing and strengthen those that are weak.

☑ *Consistency.* Make sure that layout and design, visuals, and use of language are consistent. (See Tab 6, "Design and Visuals.") Do not call the same item by one term on one page and a different term on another page.

☑ *Conciseness.* Tighten your writing so that it says exactly what you mean. Prune unnecessary words, phrases, sentences, and even paragraphs. See <u>conciseness</u> (Tab 10).

Writer's Checklist: Revising Your Draft (continued)

☑ *Awkwardness.* Look for <u>awkwardness</u> (Tab 10) in sentence construction—especially any <u>garbled sentences</u> (Tab 10).

☑ *Ethical writing.* Check for <u>ethics in writing</u> and eliminate <u>biased language</u> (Tab 10).

☑ *Active voice.* Use the active <u>voice</u> (Tab 11) unless the passive voice is more appropriate.

☑ *Word choice.* Delete or replace <u>vague words</u> (Tab 10) and unnecessary <u>intensifiers</u> (Tab 10). Check for <u>affectation</u> (Tab 10) and unclear <u>pronoun references</u> (Tab 11). See also <u>word choice</u> (Tab 10).

☑ *Jargon.* If you have any doubt that all your readers will understand any <u>jargon</u> (Tab 10) or special terms you have used, eliminate or define them.

☑ *Clichés.* Replace <u>clichés</u> (Tab 10) with fresh <u>figures of speech</u> (Tab 10) or direct statements.

☑ *Grammar.* Check your draft for grammatical errors. Use computer grammar checkers with caution. Because they are not always accurate, treat their recommendations only as *suggestions.* See Tab 11, "Grammar."

☑ *Typographical errors.* Check your final draft for typographical errors both with your spell checker and with thorough <u>proofreading</u> because spell checkers do not catch all errors.

☑ *Wordy phrases.* Use the search-and-replace command to find and revise wordy phrases, such as *that is, there are, the fact that,* and *to be,* and unnecessary helping <u>verbs</u> (Tab 11) such as *will.*

 DIGITAL TIP INCORPORATING TRACKED CHANGES

When colleagues review your document, they can track changes and insert comments within the document itself. Tracking and commenting vary with types and versions of word-processing programs, but in most programs you can view the tracked changes on a single draft or review the multiple drafts of your reviewers' versions. For more on this topic, see *bedfordstmartins.com/ alred,* and select *Digital Tips,* "Tracked Changes."

---

scope

Scope is the depth and breadth of detail you include in a document as defined by your audience's needs, your <u>purpose</u>, and the <u>context</u>. (See also <u>audience</u>.) For example, if you write a trip report about a routine visit to a company facility, your readers may need to know only the basic details and any unusual findings. However, if you prepare a trip report about a visit to a division that has experienced problems and your purpose is to suggest ways to solve those problems, your report will contain many more details, observations, and even recommendations.

You should determine the scope of a document during the <u>preparation</u> stage of the writing process, even though you may refine it later. Defining your scope will expedite your <u>research</u> (Tab 3) and can help determine team members' responsibilities in <u>collaborative writing</u>.

Your scope will also be affected by the type of document you are writing as well as the medium you select for your message. For example, funding organizations often prescribe the general content and length for grant proposals, and some businesses may set informal limits for the length of memos and e-mails. See <u>selecting the medium</u> (Tab 2) and "Five Steps to Successful Writing" (pages xxix–xxxvi).

selecting the medium (*see* Tab 2)

writing a draft

You are well prepared to write a rough draft when you have established your <u>purpose</u> and readers' needs, considered the <u>context</u>, defined your <u>scope</u>, completed adequate <u>research</u> (Tab 3), and prepared an outline (whether rough or developed). (See also <u>audience</u> and <u>outlining</u>.) Writing a draft is simply transcribing and expanding the notes from your outline into paragraphs, without worrying about grammar, refinements of language, or spelling. Refinement will come with <u>revision</u> and <u>proofreading</u>. See also "Five Steps to Successful Writing" (pages xxix–xxxvi). Writing and revising are different activities. Do not let worrying about a good opening slow you down. Instead, concentrate on getting your ideas on paper—now is not the time to polish or revise. Do not wait for inspiration—treat writing a draft as you would any other on-the-job task.

Writer's Checklist: Writing a Rough Draft

- ☑ Set up your writing area with whatever supplies you need (laptop, notepads, reference material, and so on). Avoid distractions.
- ☑ Resist the temptation of writing first drafts on the computer without planning.
- ☑ Use an outline (rough or developed) as a springboard to start and to write quickly.

The Writing Process

1

Writer's Checklist: Writing a Rough Draft (continued)

☑ Give yourself a set time in which you write continuously, regardless of how good or bad your writing seems to be. But don't stop if you are rolling along easily—keep your momentum.

☑ Start with the section that seems easiest. Your readers will neither know nor care that the middle section of the document was the first section you wrote.

☑ Keep in mind your readers' needs, expectations, and knowledge of the subject. Doing so will help you write directly to your readers and suggest which ideas need further development.

☑ When you come to something difficult to explain, try to relate the new concept to something with which the readers are familiar, as discussed in **figures of speech** (Tab 10).

☑ Routinely save to your hard drive and create a backup copy of your documents on separate disks or on the company network.

☑ Give yourself a small reward—a short walk, a soft drink, a brief chat with a friend, an easy task—after you have finished a section.

☑ Reread what you have written when you return to your writing. Seeing what you have already written can return you to a productive frame of mind.

writing for the Web (*see* **Tab 2**)

2

Workplace Technology

Preview

This section presents an overview of the technologies that are integral to workplace writing and offers guidelines for making the most effective use of these media. The first entry, **adapting to new technologies**, covers how to learn and make the best use of new technologies as they continue to evolve. The entry **selecting the medium** covers how to select from among currently available communication technologies.

The **e-mail** and **instant messaging** entries focus on proven techniques for managing these media, on the evolving set of online manners (netiquette), and on the privacy and confidentiality issues that must be considered before you send a message.

The **Web design** entry provides an overview that will help you understand how to prepare attractive and useful Web sites. The entries **blogs and forums**, **FAQs (frequently asked questions)**, **repurposing**, and **writing for the Web** will help you develop and adapt content to be useful for those who visit your Web site.

2

Workplace Technology

adapting to new technologies

Technology constantly evolves and, whether you are in the classroom or in the workplace, the devices and software tools that are familiar and comfortable to you today will be out-of-date all too quickly. Imagine, for example, that you have spent months learning to use your employer's preferred word-processing software and, just when you've finally mastered it, your employer announces that a new version of the software is being acquired. Although the new software promises more features and improved efficiency, it also promises to make much of your hard work obsolete. This entry is designed to help you cope with such a situation by providing useful approaches to working with new technologies. See also selecting the medium.

Technology You Need to Know

The question you should ask when faced with a new technology is "how much do I *need* to know about the specific technology or device to do my work?" That is, you must determine the *level of knowledge* you need to accomplish your goals for making effective use of a technology, new application, or device.

What you need to learn will depend on your workplace context. For many circumstances, you may need only a basic level that will enable you to accomplish specific and limited tasks, such as navigating a software program to open, modify, save, and print files. For technologies directly related to your work, however, you may need a thorough knowledge so that you can adapt the technology to many situations and can assess its effectiveness for the benefit of colleagues, clients, or others. In other cases, you may need to gain just enough knowledge to allow you to work well with technical specialists with expert knowledge and to ask the right questions.

Strategies for Learning a New Technology

Because of the flood of new technologies, it is important to develop methods for quickly mastering new technological tools to the level you need. The following are suggestions for navigating the functions and operations of devices and programs with which you are unfamiliar:

* *Experimentation.* Often, the best way to acquaint yourself with a new tool is simply to begin using it, even if you don't fully understand what the tool does or why you might want to learn it. This approach, in which you "play" with a new tool until it becomes familiar, will help you develop greater confidence with new technologies and will rarely have negative consequences. Most software programs cannot be "broken" merely by experimenting with them and doing so is good preparation for more formal learning.

- *IT staff and trusted colleagues.* Many organizations employ information technology (IT) specialists and trainers whose primary task is helping other employees use technology more effectively. Don't be afraid to call on them as you begin to use a new tool. If you can't rely on a dedicated IT staff to train you, seek out tech-savvy individuals who seem to have a high level of technological knowledge. You may be able to return the favor by sharing your expertise in another area.
- *Built-in help.* Most modern software programs come equipped with built-in tutorials and searchable help files. In the past, many help menus were less than helpful, but trends in technical documentation have led to greatly improved help files. Many built-in help documents today are thorough and written in plain, easy-to-understand language.
- *Official help manuals* (in digital or book format). Upon acquiring a new technological tool, such as a cell phone or camera, you may be inclined to skip the instruction manual that came in the box, but often these manuals contain a good overview of the device's features and hidden gems of information that you would otherwise miss.
- *Third-party help manuals.* Many publishers offer how-to guides for computer software and hardware. With full-color printing; plenty of photos; and a casual, friendly tone, these books attempt to simplify information that may seem overwhelming or confusing in the tool's official documentation.
- *Online tutorials.* Sometimes the easiest way to learn a new technology is by watching someone use it. Video tutorial sites such as Lynda.com offer precise, professional guidance for a fee, while many amateur technology enthusiasts upload tutorials of their own to free video-sharing Web sites.
- *Careful Internet searches.* When you encounter a problem with a technological tool, chances are someone else has dealt with it before. You may find helpful advice on an Internet message board or on the Web site of the company that developed the tool. Search for the issue by using precise terminology, including the name of the tool and several additional keywords that describe your specific problem.

 DIGITAL TIP ASSESSING HARDWARE AND SOFTWARE

When individuals or organizations consider adopting a new technology, they need to ask a number of questions to assess the value of the technology for them. For a list of such questions, see *bedfordstmartins.com/alred*, and select *Digital Tips*, "Assessing Hardware and Software," in *Links Library*.

blogs and forums

A *blog* (from *Web log*) is a Web-based journal in which an individual or group of "bloggers" can post entries (displayed from the most recent to the initial posting) that document experiences, express opinions, provide information, and respond to other bloggers on subjects of mutual interest. Although blogs may allow readers to post comments, a *forum* typically fosters a wider "conversation" in which contributors can not only respond to the posts of others but also begin new topics or discussion threads. Blogs and forums may overlap or combine features. If your Web site features a blog or forum, keep it current in order to build an audience (Tab 1) and to maintain the credibility of your site.

Organizational Uses

Organizations create blogs and forums to help meet such goals as attracting and retaining clients or customers, promoting goodwill, obtaining valuable feedback on their products and services, and even developing a sense of community among their customers and employees. They can be both external and internal.

External sites are publicly available on the Internet both for an organization's customers or clients and for executives, spokespeople, or employees to share their views. Blogs and forums can help to build loyalty for a company because customers can make a direct connection with an organization's representatives or can exchange current information that may not be available in published documents and on Web sites. *Internal sites* are usually created for an organization's employees and can be accessed only through its intranet. Internal blogs may serve as interactive newsletters that help build a sense of community within an organization. See also Web design.

Writing Style

Write blog or forum entries in an informal, conversational style that uses contractions, first person, and active voice. (See Tab 10, "Style and Clarity.")

BLOG POSTING	"Check out the latest concept for our new dashboards—we've added enough space to hold your Starbucks and iPod by moving the air ducts to. . . . Tell us what you think." [Blog posting could be a paragraph or more.]
FORUM POSTING	"I'm new, but I'm surprised no one's discussed the issue of repair costs. Have I missed something?" [Forum postings tend to be briefer than blogs.]

2

Workplace Technology

Keep your sentences and paragraphs concise, as in <u>writing for the Web</u>. Use bulleted lists, italics, and other design elements, such as boldface and white space if possible. Doing so can help readers scan the postings to find information that is interesting or relevant to them. (See Tab 6, "Design and Visuals.") Keep headlines short and direct to catch attention and increase the visual appeal and readability. When blogs expand or forums become popular, you may need to organize them using *categories* (links to discussion topics) or *tags* (searchable labels for postings).

 WEB LINK DEVELOPING BLOGS AND FORUMS

Google Blogger (*www.blogger.com*) and Google Groups (*groups.google.com*) provide help in finding and developing blogs and forums. For more examples of blogs and forums, see *bedfordstmartins.com/alred*, and select *Links Library*.

⬧ ETHICS NOTE Because organizations expect employees to assume full responsibility for the content they post on a company blog or forum, you must maintain high ethical standards.

- Do not post information that is confidential, proprietary, or sensitive to your employer.
- Do not attack competitors or other individuals (such as employees, other participants, or shareholders).
- Do not post content that is profane, libelous, or harassing, or that violates the privacy of others. See also <u>biased language</u> (Tab 10).
- Obtain permission before using any material that is protected by <u>copyright</u> (Tab 3), and identify sources for <u>quotations</u> (Tab 3). See also <u>plagiarism</u> (Tab 3). ✦

e-mail

DIRECTORY

E-mail (or *email*) functions in the workplace as a medium to exchange information and share electronic files with colleagues, clients, and customers. Although e-mail messages may take the form of informal notes, you should follow the writing strategy and style described in correspondence (Tab 7) because e-mail messages often function as business letters to those outside organizations and memos to those within organizations. Of course, memos and letters can also be attached to e-mails. This entry reviews topics that are specifically related to the medium of e-mail. See also selecting the medium.

Review and Confidentiality

E-mail is such a quick and easy way to communicate that you need to avoid the temptation of sending a first draft without revision. As with all correspondence, your message should include all crucial details and be free of grammatical or factual errors, ambiguities, or unintended implications. See proofreading (Tab 1) and spelling (Tab 12).

Keep in mind that e-mail can be intercepted by someone other than the intended recipient and that e-mail messages are never truly deleted. Most companies back up and save all their e-mails and are legally entitled to monitor e-mail use. Companies can be compelled, depending on circumstances, to provide e-mail and instant messaging logs in a court of law. Consider the content of all your messages in the light of these possibilities, and carefully review your text before you click "Send."

◆ PROFESSIONALISM NOTE Be especially careful when sending messages to superiors in your organization or to people outside the organization. Spending extra time reviewing your e-mail message before you click "Send" can save you the embarrassment of misunderstandings caused by a careless message. One helpful strategy is to write the draft and revise your e-mail before filling in the "To" line with the address of your recipient. Be careful as well to observe the rules of netiquette (Inter*net* + *etiquette*) in the *Writer's Checklist* that follows. ✦

Writer's Checklist: Observing Workplace Netiquette

☑ Review your organization's policy regarding the appropriate use of e-mail.

☑ Maintain a high level of professionalism in your use of e-mail.

- Do not forward jokes or spam, discuss office gossip, or use biased language (Tab 10).
- Do not send flames (e-mails that contain abusive, obscene, or derogatory language) to attack someone.
- Do not use an e-mail account with a clever or hobby-related address (yogalover@gja.com); e-mail addresses based on your last name are more professional (jones23@gja.com).

2

Workplace Technology

Writer's Checklist: Observing Workplace Netiquette (continued)

☑ Provide a subject line that describes the topic and focus of your message (as described on page 197) to help recipients manage their e-mail.

☑ Adapt forwarded messages: Revise the subject line to reflect the current content and cut irrelevant previous text, based on your purpose and context.

☑ Use the "cc:" (courtesy copy) and "bcc:" (blind courtesy copy) address lines thoughtfully and consider your organization's practice or protocol.

☑ Include a cover message for all e-mails with attachments. ("Attached is a copy of my report for your review. . . .")

☑ Send a courtesy response informing someone when you need a few days or longer to reply to a request.

☑ Do not write in ALL UPPERCASE LETTERS or in all lowercase letters.

☑ Avoid abbreviations (BTW for *by the way*, for example) that are used in personal e-mail, chat rooms, and text messages.

☑ Do not use emoticons (keyboard characters used for conveying emotions) for business and professional e-mail.

☑ Always sign the e-mail or use a signature block (see Figure 2–1) or both; doing so not only is polite but also avoids possible confusion.

Design Considerations

Some e-mail systems allow you to use typographical features, such as various fonts and bullets. These options increase your e-mail file size and may display unpredictably in other e-mail systems. Unless you are sure your recipient's software will display your formatted message correctly, set your e-mail software to send messages in "plain text" and use alternative highlighting devices. For example, capital letters or asterisks, used sparingly, can substitute for boldface, italics, and underlines as emphasis.

- Dr. Wilhoit's suggestions benefit doctors AND patients.

- Although the proposal is sound in *theory*, it will never work in *practice*.

Intermittent underlining can replace solid underlining or italics when referring to published works in an e-mail message.

- My report follows the format given in _The Business Writer's Companion_.

If you find that you need many such substitutions, consider preparing a document that you attach to an e-mail. Doing so will allow you to use formatted elements, such as bulleted <u>lists</u> (Tab 6) and <u>tables</u> (Tab 6) that do not transmit well in e-mails. Keep in mind the following additional design considerations when sending e-mail:

- Use short paragraphs to avoid dense blocks of text.
- Provide a brief paragraph overview at the top of messages that run longer than a screen of text.
- Place your response to someone else's message at the beginning (or top) of the e-mail window so that recipients can see your response immediately.
- When replying to a message, quote only relevant parts. If your system does not distinguish the quoted text, note it with a greater-than symbol (>).

 DIGITAL TIP SENDING AN ATTACHMENT

Large graphics and other files attached to e-mails can slow the transmission speed of messages, and the recipient's software or Internet provider may not be able to accept large attachments. Consider using compression software, such as WinZip at *http://winzip.com*, which can reduce the file size by 80 percent or more. *Caution:* Viruses can be embedded in e-mail attachments, so regularly update your virus-scanning software and do not open attachments from anyone you do not know. See *bedfordstmartins .com/alred*, and select *Digital Tips*, "Sending an E-mail Attachment."

Salutations, Closings, and Signature Blocks

An e-mail can function as a letter, memo, or personal note; therefore, you must adapt your salutation and complimentary closing to your <u>audience</u> (Tab 1). Unless your employer requires certain forms, use the following guidelines:

- When e-mail functions as a traditional letter, use the standard letter salutation (*Dear Ms. Tucker:* or *Dear Docuform Customer:*) and closing (*Sincerely,* or *Best wishes,*).
- When you send e-mail to individuals or small groups inside an organization, you may wish to adopt a more personal greeting (*Dear Andy,* or *Dear Project Colleagues,*).
- When e-mail functions as a personal note to a friend or close colleague, you can use an informal greeting or only a first name (*Hi Mike,* or *Hello Jenny,* or *Bill,*) and a closing (*Take care,* or *Best,*).

Be aware that, in some cultures, business correspondents do not use first names as freely as do business correspondents in the United States. See <u>international correspondence</u> (Tab 7).

Because e-mail does not provide letterhead with standard addresses and contact information, many companies and individual writers include signature blocks (also called *signatures*) at the bottom of their messages. Signature blocks, which writers can set to appear on every e-mail they send, supply information that company letterhead usually provides as well as appropriate links to Web sites. If your organization requires a certain format, adhere to that standard. Otherwise, use the pattern shown in Figure 2–1. For signature blocks, consider as well the following guidelines:

- Keep line length to 60 characters or fewer to avoid unpredictable line wraps.
- Test your signature block in plain-text e-mail systems to verify your format.
- Use highlighting cues, such as hyphens, equal signs, and white space, to separate the signature from the message.
- Avoid using quotations, aphorisms, proverbs, or other sayings from popular culture, religion, or poetry in signatures to maintain a professional image.

```
================================
Gene Marting, Manager              ←   Name and Title
Sales Division, Building Systems, Inc.   ←   Division/Company
3555 South 47th Street, Boise, ID 83703  ←   Address
Off: 208-719-6620 Fax: 208-719-5500      ←   Phone and Fax
http://www.building/sys/com              ←   Web Address
e-mail: gmarting@secsystems.com          ←   E-mail Address
================================
```

FIGURE 2–1. E-mail Signature Block

 DIGITAL TIP **LEAVING AN AWAY-FROM-DESK MESSAGE**

Most e-mail systems allow you to create an away-from-desk automatic response. Your message should inform senders when you are expected back and, if necessary, whom they can contact in your absence. To learn how to set up an automatic response, see *bedfordstmartins.com/alred,* and select *Digital Tips,* "Leaving an Away-from-Desk Message."

Writer's Checklist: Managing Your E-mail and Reducing Overload

Given the high volume of e-mail in business, you need to manage your e-mail strategically.*

☑ Avoid becoming involved in an e-mail exchange if a phone call or meeting would be more efficient.

☑ Consider whether an e-mail message could prompt an unnecessary response from the recipient and make clear to the recipient whether you expect a response.

☑ Send a copy ("cc:") of an e-mail only when the person copied, in fact, needs or wants the information.

☑ Review all messages on a subject before responding to avoid dealing with issues that are no longer relevant.

☑ Set priorities for reading e-mail by skimming sender names and subject lines as well as where you appear in a "cc:" and "bcc:" address line.

☑ Check e-mail addresses before sending an e-mail and keep your addresses current.

☑ Check your in-box regularly and try to clear it by the end of each day.

☑ Create e-mail folders using key topics and personal names to file messages.

☑ Copy yourself or save sent copies of important e-mail messages in your folders.

☑ Use the search command to find particular subjects and personal names.

☑ Print copies of messages or attachments that you need for meetings, files, or similar purposes.

*For understanding the causes of e-mail overload, see Gail Fann Thomas and Cynthia L. King, "Reconceptualizing E-mail Overload," *Journal of Business and Technical Communication* 20, no. 3 (July 2006): 252–87.

FAQs (frequently asked questions)

FAQs are <u>lists</u> (Tab 6) of questions, paired with their answers, that readers will likely ask about products, services, or other information presented on a Web site or in customer-oriented documents. By presenting commonly sought information in one place, FAQs save readers from searching through an entire Web site or document to find what they need.

A good FAQ list can help create a positive impression with customers or clients because you are acknowledging that their time is valuable. An FAQ list also helps a company spend less time answering phone calls and <u>e-mail</u> questions by anticipating customer needs and providing important information in a simple, a logical, and an organized format. However, an FAQ list is not a substitute for solving problems with a product or service.

◆ ETHICS NOTE If customers are experiencing numerous problems because of a product design or programming flaw, you need to work with your company's product developers to correct the problem rather than try to skirt it within an FAQ. ✦

Questions to Include

Develop the list of questions and their answers by brainstorming with colleagues who regularly are in contact with customers. If customers frequently ask about company stock information and request annual reports, for example, your FAQ list could include the question "How do I obtain a copy of your latest annual report?" This question can be followed with a brief answer that includes the name, phone number, and e-mail address of the person who distributes the annual reports. For a Web site, you can also provide a link to a copy of the current annual report that can be downloaded. See also <u>writing for the Web</u>.

Organization

Organize the list so that readers can find the information they need quickly and easily. Study other FAQs that your readers might review for products or services similar to yours. Use these FAQs to find answers to questions: Can you find answers quickly, or do you need to scroll through many pages to find them? Consider how the questions are organized: Are they separated into logical categories or listed in random order? Is it easy to differentiate the question from the answer? Do the answers provide too little or too much information?*

List your questions in decreasing order of importance for your readers so that they can obtain the most important information first. (See <u>organization</u>, Tab 1.) If you have a number of questions that are related to a specific topic, such as investor relations, product returns, or completing forms, group them into categories and identify each category with a heading, such as "Investor Relations," "Shipping," and "Forms." You may also want to create a table of contents at the top of the FAQ page so that readers can find quickly the topics relevant to their interests.

---

*For up-to-date information on designing online forms, see *www.stcsig.org/usability/ topics/forms.html.*

Placement

The location of your FAQ list should enable readers to find answers quickly. For Web sites, an FAQ page is usually linked from the homepage either in a directory or with a text link for easy access. In small printed documents, such as brochures, FAQs are usually highlighted and placed after the standard information in the body of the document.

Writer's Checklist: Developing an FAQ List

☑ *Focus on your reader.* Write your questions and answers from a <u>"you"</u> <u>viewpoint</u> (Tab 10) and with a positive, conversational tone.

☑ *Separate long FAQ lists.* Group related questions under topic <u>headings</u> (Tab 6). For long online FAQs, consider listing only questions with links to separate pages, each containing an individual question and answer.

☑ *Distinguish questions from answers.* Use boldface for questions and use white space to separate questions from answers. Use sparingly multiple colors, italics, or other formatting styles that can make the list difficult to read.

☑ *Keep questions and answers concise.* If a question has a long answer, add a link to a separate Web page or refer to an appropriate page number in a printed document.

☑ *Keep the list updated.* Review and update FAQs at least monthly—or more frequently if your content changes often. Make it possible for your customers to submit questions they would like to see added to the FAQ list.

---

instant messaging

Instant messaging (IM) is a text-based communications medium that fills a niche between the telephone and <u>e-mail</u>. It allows both real-time communications, like a phone call, and the transfer of text or other files, like an e-mail. It is especially useful to those who are working at sites without access to e-mail. See also <u>selecting the medium</u>.

To set up routine IM exchanges, add to your contact list the user names of those with whom you regularly exchange messages. Choose a screen name that your colleagues will recognize. If you use IM routinely as part of your job, create an "away" message that signals when you are not available for IM interactions.

When writing instant messages, keep them simple and to the point, covering only one subject in each message to prevent confusion and inappropriate responses. Because screen space is often limited and speed is essential, many who send instant messages use abbreviations and shortened spellings ("u" for "you"). Be sure that your reader will understand such abbreviations; when in doubt, avoid them.*

In Figure 2–2, the manager of a software-development company in Maine ("Diane") is exchanging instant messages with a business

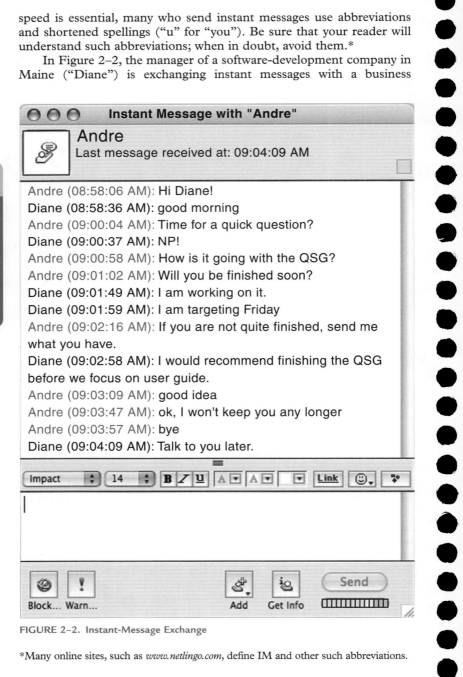

FIGURE 2–2. Instant-Message Exchange

*Many online sites, such as *www.netlingo.com*, define IM and other such abbreviations.

Workplace Technology

partner in the Netherlands ("Andre"). Notice that the correspondents use an informal style that includes personal and professional abbreviations with which both are familiar ("NP" for "no problem" and "QSG" for "Quick Start Guide"). These messages demonstrate how instant messaging can not only help exchange information quickly but also build rapport among distant colleagues and team members. The exchange also demonstrates why IM is not generally appropriate for many complex messages or for more formal circumstances, such as when establishing new professional relationships.

◼ ETHICS NOTE Be sure to follow your employer's IM policies, such as any limitations on sending personal messages during work hours or requirements concerning confidentiality. If no specific policy exists, assume that personal use of IM is not appropriate in your workplace. ✦

Writer's Checklist: Instant Messaging Privacy and Security

☑ Restrict contact lists on professional IM accounts to business associates to avoid inadvertently sending a personal message to an associate.

☑ Learn the options, capabilities, and security limitations of your IM system and set the preferences that best suit your use of the system.

☑ Be especially alert to the possibilities of virus infections and security risks with messages, attachments, contact lists, and other privacy issues.

☑ Save significant IM exchanges (or logs) for your future reference.

☑ Be aware that instant messages can be saved by your recipients and may be archived by your employer. (See the Professionalism Note on page 45.)

☑ Do not use professional IM for gossip or inappropriate exchanges.

repurposing

Repurposing is the copying or converting of existing content, such as written text and visuals, from one document or medium into another for a different purpose (Tab 1).* For example, if you are preparing a promotional brochure, you may be able to reuse material from a product description that is currently published on your organization's Web site.

---

*The reuse of standard texts or content in technical publications is often referred to as "single-source publishing" or simply "single sourcing." See *www.stcsig.org/ss/*. Traditionally, such reuse of standard texts has been referred to as "boilerplate."

2

Workplace Technology

The brochure may then be printed or even placed on the Web site where it can be downloaded. See also selecting the medium.

In the workplace, this process saves time because content that often requires substantial effort to develop need not be re-created for each new application. The process of repurposing may be as simple as copying and pasting content from one document into another or as complex as distributing content and updates through a system of content management.

Content can be repurposed exactly as it is written only if it fits the scope (Tab 1), audience (Tab 1), and purpose of the new document. If the content alters these areas, you must adapt the content to fit its new context (Tab 1), as described in the following sections.

Repurpose for the Context

Staying focused on the purpose of your new document is critical, especially when repurposing content between different media. If you are writing a sales proposal, for example, and you only need to describe the specifications for a product, it may be useful to repurpose the specification list from your organization's Web site. However, the purpose of the Web-site content may be *to inform* customers about your products, whereas the purpose of a proposal is *to persuade* customers to buy your products. To effectively use the repurposed content in your proposal, you may need to adapt the tense, voice, tone, grammar, and point of view (Tab 1) to make the repurposed content more persuasive and fit within the context of a sales proposal. See Tab 10, "Style and Clarity," and Tab 11, "Grammar."

Repurpose for the Medium

The proper style and format of content written for a specific medium, such as a brochure or fact sheet, may not work as effectively when repurposed for a different medium, such as a Web site. Solid blocks of text may be easy to read in a brochure, but Web readers often need blocks of text to be separated into bulleted lists or very short paragraphs because readers process information differently when reading on a computer monitor. Adapt the layout and design of the repurposed content as appropriate to accommodate your reader's needs for the medium. See also writing for the Web and Tab 6, "Design and Visuals."

⚡ ETHICS NOTE In the workplace, repurposing content within an organization does not violate copyright (Tab 3) because an organization owns the information it creates and can share it across the company. Likewise, a writer in an organization may use and repurpose material in the public domain and, with some limitations, content that is licensed under Creative Commons (see *http://creativecommons.org/about/*). See also blogs and forums and *Digital Tip: Collaborative Writing Software* on page 4.

In the classroom, of course, the use of content or someone else's unique ideas without acknowledgment or the use of someone else's exact words without <u>quotation marks</u> (Tab 12) and appropriate credit is <u>plagiarism</u> (Tab 3). ✦

selecting the medium

With so many media and forms of communication available, selecting the most appropriate medium can be challenging. Which electronic or paper medium (or *channel*) is best depends on a wide range of factors related to your <u>audience</u> (Tab 1), your <u>purpose</u> (Tab 1), and the <u>context</u> (Tab 1) of the communication. Those factors include the following:

- the audience's preferences and expectations
- your own most effective communication style
- how widely information needs to be distributed
- what kind of record you need to keep
- the urgency of the communication
- the sensitivity or confidentiality required
- the technological resources available
- the organizational practices or regulations

As this list suggests, choosing the best medium may involve personal considerations or the essential functions of the medium. If you need to collaborate with someone to solve a problem, for example, you may find e-mail exchanges less effective than a phone call or face-to-face meeting. If you need precise wording or a record of a complex or sensitive message, however, using a written medium is often essential.

Keep in mind that many of the following media and forms of communication evolve and overlap as technology develops. Understanding their basic functions will help you select the most appropriate medium for your needs. See <u>adapting to new technologies</u> for advice on how to learn and make the best use of new technologies as they continue to evolve.

E-mail

<u>E-mail</u> (or *email*) functions in the workplace as a primary medium to communicate and share electronic files with colleagues, clients, and customers. Although e-mail messages may function as informal notes, they should follow the writing strategy and style described in <u>correspondence</u> (Tab 7). Because recipients can easily forward messages and attachments to others and because e-mail messages are subject to legal disclosure, e-mail requires writers to review their messages carefully before clicking the "Send" button.

2

Workplace Technology

Memos

Memos (Tab 7) are appropriate for internal communication among members of the same organization; they use a standard header and are sent on paper or as attachments to e-mails. Organizations may use memos printed on organizational stationery when they need to communicate with the formality and authority of business letters. Memos may also be used in manufacturing or service industries, for example, where employees do not have easy access to e-mail. In such cases, memos can be used to instruct employees, announce policies, report results, disseminate information, and delegate responsibilities.

Letters

Business letters (Tab 7) with handwritten signatures are often the most appropriate choice for formal communications with professional associates or customers outside an organization. Letters printed on organizational letterhead stationery communicate formality, respect, and authority. They may be especially effective for those people who receive a high volume of e-mail and other electronic correspondence. Letters are often used for job applications, for recommendations, and in other official and social contexts.

Faxes

A fax is used when the information—a drawing or signed contract, for example—must be viewed in its original form. Although scanning such documents and attaching them to e-mail is common, faxing is often used when scanning is not available or when a recipient prefers a faxed document. Fax machines in offices can be located in shared areas, so let the intended recipient know before you send confidential or sensitive messages. Consider using a cover sheet that says "confidential" and be sure to include the name of the person to whose attention the fax is being sent.

Text Messaging

Text messaging, or texting, refers to the exchange of brief written messages between mobile phones over cellular networks. Text messaging is effective for simple messages communicated between people on the move or in nontraditional workplaces. For the real-time message exchanges of brief messages, use the telephone or instant messaging.

Instant Messaging

Instant messaging (IM) on a computer or handheld device may be an efficient way to communicate in real time with coworkers, suppliers, and customers—especially those at sites without access to e-mail. Instant messaging often uses online slang and such shortened spellings as "u" for *you* to save time and screen space. Instant messaging may have limited application in the workplace because recipients must be ready and willing to participate in an online conversation. For ethical and security issues for both text and instant messaging, see pages 53 and 59.

Telephone and Conference Calls

Telephone calls are best used for exchanges that require substantial interaction and the ability of participants to interpret each other's tone of voice. They are useful for discussing sensitive issues and resolving misunderstandings, although they do not provide the visual cues possible during face-to-face meetings. Cell (or *mobile*) phones are useful for communicating away from an office, but users should follow appropriate etiquette and organizational policies, such as speaking in an appropriate tone and turning off the phone or switching it to the vibrate mode during meetings.

A teleconference, or conference call among three or more participants, is a less expensive alternative to face-to-face meetings requiring travel. Such conference calls work best when the person coordinating the call works from an agenda shared by all the participants and directs the discussion as if chairing a meeting. Participants can use the Web during conference calls to share and view common documents. Conference calls in which decisions have been reached should be followed with written confirmation.

Voice-Mail Messages

Voice-mail messages should be clear and brief. ("I got your package, so you don't need to call the distributor.") If the message is complicated or contains numerous details, use another medium, such as e-mail. If you want to discuss a subject at length, let the recipient know the subject so that he or she can prepare a response before returning your call. When you leave a message, give your name and contact information as well as the date and time of the call (if you are unsure whether the message will be time-stamped).

Face-to-Face Meetings

In-person meetings are most appropriate for initial or early contacts with associates and clients with whom you intend to develop an important, long-term relationship or need to establish rapport. Meetings may also be best for brainstorming, negotiating, interviewing someone on a complex topic, solving a technical problem, or handling a controversial issue. For advice on how to record discussions and decisions, see both meetings (Tab 9) and minutes of meetings (Tab 9).

2

Workplace Technology

Videoconferences

Videoconferences are particularly useful for meetings when travel is impractical. Unlike telephone conference calls, videoconferences have the advantage of allowing participants to see as well as to hear one another. They work best with participants who are at ease in front of the camera and when the facilities offer good production quality.

Web Communication

The Web can encompass many of the media and forms of communication described in this entry and include some other interactive capabilities.

Web Conferencing. The Web can be used to conduct meetings, which are often referred to as Web conferences. In such meetings, the participants' computers may be connected to other participants' computers through a downloaded application on each of the attendees' computers. In such a conference, a moderator can control the cursor on the participants' computers. Web cameras or conference phone connections can enrich these meetings.

Professional Networking. Using the model of social-networking sites, like Facebook.com, some professional organizations and businesses are creating their own networking sites to foster professional contacts. Other commercial networks, like LinkedIn.com, aim to connect professionals for business purposes. Many businesses place advertising on both professional and social-networking sites—and, if used with caution, both may be helpful for your professional advancement and job search (Tab 8).

Web-Site Postings. A public Internet or company intranet Web site is ideal for posting announcements or policies as well as for making available or exchanging documents and files with others. Your Web site can serve not only as a home base for resources but also as a place where ideas can be developed through, for example, discussion boards, blogs and forums, and wikis. See also collaborative writing (Tab 1), Web design, writing for the Web, and *Digital Tip: Collaborative Writing Software* on page 4.

text messaging

Text messaging, or texting, refers to the exchange of brief written messages between mobile phones over cellular networks. Text messaging is effective for simple messages communicated between people on the move or in nontraditional workplaces. Although text messaging is similar to e-mail, the screen and device size means that text messages are short. ("The client's backup servers are down.") Like e-mail, text messages can also include video and other digital files. Keep in mind that because texting can be less secure than other media, various policies often limit its use, especially in highly regulated industries like financial services. For the real-time message exchanges of brief messages, use the phone or <u>instant messaging</u>.

Web design

Web sites are often developed as team efforts among managers, designers, writers, and programmers. If you are involved with developing a Web site, you need to stay current with changes in Web design and technology. The best sources for helping you stay current are on the Web itself.* To find the many useful tutorials on the Web, use a search engine with the term *tutorial* along with other keywords such as *HTML, XHTML,* or *Web design.*

 WEB LINK WEB-DESIGN RESOURCES

For Mike Markel's helpful overview of the process and principles of designing Web sites, see *bedfordstmartins.com/alred*, and select *Tutorials*, "Designing for the Web." For links to more tutorials as well as sites that provide advice for improving accessibility for people with disabilities, select *Links for Business Writing*.

Audience and Purpose

Many of the principles covered throughout this book apply to designing Web sites. When planning a Web site and designing Web pages, for example, carefully consider your <u>purpose</u> (Tab 1) and <u>audience</u> (Tab 1). Most professional Web sites have well-defined goals, such as reference, marketing, education, publicity, or advocacy. One way to help you achieve your goals is to create a clear purpose statement, as shown in the following examples.

EXTERNAL SITE	The purpose of this site is to enable our customers to locate product information, place online orders, and contact our customer-service department.
INTERNAL SITE	The purpose of this site is to provide SNR Security Corporation employees, suppliers, and partner organizations with a single, consistent, and up-to-date resource for materials about SNR Security.

*Some useful sites include *www.w3.org, webmonkey.com*, and *trace.wisc.edu/world/web/*.

2

Workplace Technology

As these examples show, the two general kinds of sites are external and internal. External Web sites target an audience from the entire Internet. Internal Web sites are designed for audiences on either an intranet (a network within an organization) that is not accessible to audiences outside that organization or an extranet (a password-protected site) available exclusively to trusted partners and suppliers to provide them with common data and documents.

Access for People with Disabilities

Design elements such as colorful graphics, animation, and streaming video and audio can be barriers to people with impaired vision or hearing or those who are color-blind. Use the following strategies to meet the needs of such audiences.

- Avoid frames, complex tables, animation, JavaScript, and other design elements incompatible with text-only browsers and adaptive technologies, such as voice or large-print software.
- Provide HTML versions of pages and documents whenever possible because this format is most compatible with the current generation of screen readers.
- Include text-equivalent captions with graphic or audio elements.
- Design for the color-blind reader by making meaning independent of color. For example, rather than asking users to "Click on the green button for more information," label the button ("Click Here") or embed a link in a sentence: "See our catalog for more information."

You may want to consider offering different options for site visitors, such as full-graphics, light-graphics, and text-only versions.

 DIGITAL TIP TESTING YOUR WEB SITE

You might take advantage of Web sites that will test a limited sample of your site's features for free. (They also offer greatly expanded testing for a fee.) For more on this topic, see *bedfordstmartins.com/alred*, and select *Digital Tips*, "Testing Your Web Site."

Writer's Checklist: Designing Web Pages

Many of the guidelines on typography in **layout and design** (Tab 6) are applicable to Web pages; however, not all apply, so keep the following in mind:

☑   Work with the site administrator to optimize your site for speed of access and to maintain technical and design standards.

Writer's Checklist: Designing Web Pages (continued)

- ☑ Draft a navigation chart or map of your site early in the design process to make information logically accessible in the fewest possible steps (or clicks).
- ☑ Anchor links on relevant words in the sentence. ("For more information about employment opportunities, visit <u>Human Resources</u>.")
- ☑ Avoid overusing graphics and animation that clutter or slow access to your site. For large graphics, use thumbnails (images reduced to 10 to 15 percent of the original file size) that link to the original-size image.
- ☑ Use light colors for backgrounds and typeface colors that contrast (but do not clash) with background colors.
- ☑ Limit the number of typeface colors as well as styles; use underlined text only for links.
- ☑ Separate text from graphics with generous blank space (the equivalent of white space).
- ☑ Block-indent text sections that you expect viewers to read in detail.
- ☑ Keep lines between 50 and 70 characters (or between 10 and 12 words) within defined page sections.
- ☑ Test your design and load time by viewing it on other browsers and systems.
- ☑ Incorporate the name of your organization and its logo in a banner at the top of each page.
- ☑ Include a link to your site's Privacy Statement (see page 64).
- ☑ Check that all your links work, particularly after site changes.

For further advice on developing your site's content for online readers, see **writing for the Web**.

writing for the Web

In the workplace, those who write content for Web sites are not always the same people who design the sites. This entry provides guidelines only for those writing for an online <u>audience</u> (Tab 1); for more information on Web-site design, see <u>Web design</u>.

◆ ETHICS NOTE For questions about the appropriateness of content you plan to post on the Web, check with your webmaster or manager to determine if your content complies with your organization's Web policy. On campus, consult your instructor or campus computer-support staff about standards for posting Web content. See <u>ethics in writing</u> (Tab 1). ◆

Crafting Content for Web Pages

Because most readers scan Web pages for specific information, the way you write and organize your information will greatly affect your readers' understanding. State your important points first, before any detailed supporting information. (This method is called *inverted pyramid organization*.) Keep your writing style simple and straightforward, and avoid such directional cues as "as shown in the example below" that make sense on the printed page but not on a Web page. Use the following techniques to make your content more accessible to readers.

Headings.　Break up dense blocks of text with short <u>paragraphs</u> (Tab 1) that stand out and can be quickly read and absorbed. Use informative <u>headings</u> (Tab 6) to help readers identify topics and decide at a glance whether to read a passage. Headings also clarify text by highlighting structure and organization as well as providing transitions from one topic to the next.

Lists.　Use bulleted and numbered <u>lists</u> (Tab 6) to break up dense paragraphs, reduce text length, and highlight important content.

Keywords.　To help search engines and your audience find your site, use keywords in the first fifty or so words of your text.

WITHOUT KEYWORDS	We are proud to introduce a new commemorative coin honoring our bank's founder and president. The item will be available on this Web site after December 3, 2011, which is the hundredth anniversary of our first deposit.
WITH KEYWORDS	The new *Reynolds* commemorative *coin* features a portrait of *George G. Reynolds,* the founder and president of *Reynolds Bank*. The *coin* can be purchased after December 3, 2011, in honor of the hundredth anniversary of the first *Reynolds* deposit.

Graphics.　Graphics provide visual relief from text and make your site attractive and appealing. Use only <u>visuals</u> (Tab 6) that are appropriate for your audience and <u>purpose</u> (Tab 1), however, and use graphics that load quickly.

Hyperlinks.　Use internal hyperlinks to help readers navigate the information on your site. If a passage of text is longer than two or three screens, create a table of contents of hyperlinks for it at the top of the Web page and link each item to the relevant content further down the page. Use external hyperlinks to enrich coverage of your topic with information outside your site and to help reduce content on your page. When you do, consider placing an icon or a text label next to the hyperlink to inform users that they are leaving the host site. In general, avoid too many hyperlinks within text paragraphs because they can distract readers, make scanning the text difficult, and tempt readers to leave your site before reaching the end of your page.

Fonts.   Font sizes and styles affect screen legibility. Because computer screens display fonts at lower resolutions than does printed text, sans serif fonts work better for online text passages. Consult your webmaster (or your manager) about your organization's font preferences. Do not use all capital letters or boldface type for blocks of text because they slow the reader. For content that contains special characters (such as for mathematical or chemical content), consult your webmaster about the best way to submit the files for HTML (hypertext markup language) coding or post them as PDF files.

Writing for a Global Audience

When you write for public-access sites, eliminate expressions and refer-ences that make sense only to someone very familiar with American English. Express dates, clock times, and measurements consistent with international practices. For visuals, choose symbols and icons, colors, representations of human beings, and captions that can be easily under-stood, as described in global communication (Tab 1) and global graphics (Tab 6). See also biased language (Tab 10) and English as a second language (Tab 11).

Linking to Reputable Sites

Links to outside sites can expand your content. However, review such sites carefully before linking to them. Is the site's author or sponsoring organization reputable? Is its content accurate, current, and unbiased? Does the site date-stamp its content with notices such as "This page was last updated on January 1, 2011"? (For more advice on evaluating Web sites, see research, Tab 3.) Link directly to the page or specific area of an outside site that is relevant to your users, and be sure that you provide a clear context (Tab 1) for why you are sending your readers there.

Posting an Existing Document or File

If you post electronic files of existing paper documents to a Web site, try to retain the document's original sequence and page layout. If you shorten or revise the original document for posting to the Web, add a notice informing readers that it differs from the printed original.

Regardless of format or version used, be sure to follow these practices:

- Obtain permission from the copyright (Tab 3) holder for the use of copyrighted text, tables, or images. See also plagiarism (Tab 3).

2

Workplace Technology

- Ask the webmaster or site administrator about the preferred file format to submit for coding and posting. On campus, consult your instructor or campus computer-support staff.
- Request that the webmaster optimize any slow-loading graphics files for quick access.
- Review the document internally before it is posted to the public site: Is it the correct version? Is any information missing? Do all links work and go to the right places? See <u>proofreading</u> (Tab 1).
- Create a single-file version of the document (a version formatted as a single, long Web page) for readers who will print it to read offline.

◆ ETHICS NOTE Document sources of information—text, images, streaming video, and other multimedia material—or of help received. Seek prior approval before using any copyrighted information. Documenting your sources not only is required but also bolsters the credibility of your site. To document your sources, either provide links to your source or use a citation, as described in <u>documenting sources</u> (Tab 3). ✦

Protecting the Privacy of Users

Put a link on your Web page to the site's privacy statement, particularly if you solicit comments about your content or have an <u>e-mail</u> link for unsolicited comments for site users. A privacy statement informs site visitors about how the site sponsor handles solicited and unsolicited information from individuals, its policy on the use of cookies,* and legal action it takes against hackers. Inform users if you intend to use their information for marketing or to share their information with third parties, and give visitors the option of refusing you permission to use or share their information.

 DIGITAL TIP USING PDF FILES

Converting documents such as reports, articles, and brochures to PDF files allows you to retain the identical look of the printed documents. The PDF pages will display on-screen exactly as they appear on the printed page. Readers can read the document online, download and save it, or print it in whole or in part. For more on this topic, see *bedfordstmartins .com/alred*, and select *Digital Tips*, "Using PDF Files."

*"Cookies" are small files that are downloaded to your computer when you browse certain Web pages. Cookies hold information, such as your user name and password, so that you do not need to enter it each time you visit the site.

2

Workplace Technology

3

Research and Documentation

Preview

This section contains entries related to the process of <u>research</u> using both library and Internet sources, <u>interviewing for information</u>, and <u>note-taking</u>. Entries in this section provide help for incorporating research material into your document, as well as using <u>quotations</u>, <u>paraphrasing</u>, and avoiding <u>plagiarism</u>. The entry <u>documenting sources</u> provides not only examples of bibliographic citations in the two major systems, both American Psychological Association (APA) and Modern Language Association (MLA) styles, but also sample pages using those styles.

 WEB LINK RESEARCH AND DOCUMENTATION RESOURCES

For links to research-related resources—including library catalogs, databases, and guidelines for documenting sources—see *bedfordstmartins.com/alred*, and select *Diana Hacker's Research and Documentation Online* as well as *Links Library*.

3

Research and
Documentation

bibliographies

A bibliography is an alphabetical list of books, articles, Web sources, and other works that have been consulted in preparing a document or that are useful for reference purposes. A bibliography provides a convenient alphabetical listing of sources in a standardized form for readers interested in getting further information on the topic or in assessing the scope of the <u>research</u>.

Whereas a list of references or works cited refers to works actually cited in your text, a bibliography also may include works consulted for background information. For information on using various citation styles, see <u>documenting sources</u>.

Entries in a bibliography are listed alphabetically by the author's last name. If an author is unknown, the entry is alphabetized by the first word in the title (other than *A*, *An*, or *The*). Entries also can be arranged by subject and then ordered alphabetically within those categories.

An annotated bibliography includes complete bibliographic information about a work (author, title, place of publication, publisher, and publication date) followed by a brief description or evaluation of what the work contains.

copyright

Copyright establishes legal protection for literary, dramatic, musical, artistic, and other intellectual works in printed or electronic form; it gives the copyright owner exclusive rights to reproduce, distribute, perform, or display a work. Copyright protects all original works from the moment of their creation, regardless of whether they are published or contain a notice of copyright (©).

✦ ETHICS NOTE If you plan to reproduce copyrighted material in your own publication or on your Web site, you must obtain permission from the copyright holder. To do otherwise is a violation of U.S. law. ✦

Permissions

To seek permission to reproduce copyrighted material, you must write to the copyright holder. In some cases, it is the author; in other cases, it is the editor or publisher of the work. For Web sites, read the site's "terms-of-use" information (if available) and e-mail your request to the appropriate party. State specifically which portion of the work you wish to reproduce and how you plan to use it. The copyright holder has the right to charge a fee and specify conditions and limits of use.

Exceptions

Some print and Web material—including text, <u>visuals</u> (Tab 6), and other digital forms—may be reproduced without permission. The rules governing copyright can be complex, so it is prudent to check carefully the copyright status of anything you plan to reproduce.

- *Educational material.* A small amount of material from a copyrighted source may be used for educational purposes (such as classroom handouts) without permission or payment as long as the use satisfies the "fair-use" criteria, as described at the U.S. Copyright Office Web site, *www.copyright.gov/*.
- *Company boilerplate.* Employees often borrow material freely from in-house manuals, reports, and other company documents to save time and ensure consistency. Using such "boilerplate" or "repurposed" material is not a copyright violation because the company is considered the author of works prepared by its employees on the job. See also <u>repurposing</u> (Tab 2).
- *Public domain material.* Works created by or for the U.S. government and not classified or otherwise protected are in the public domain—that is, they are not copyrighted. The same is true for older written works when their copyright has lapsed or never existed. Be aware that some works in the public domain may include "value-added" features, such as introductions, visuals, and indexes, that are copyrighted separately from the original work.
- *Copyleft Web material.* Some public-access Web sites, such as *Wikipedia*, follow the "copyleft" principle and grant permission to freely copy, distribute, or modify material.*

⚡ ETHICS NOTE Even when you use material that may be reproduced without permission, you must give appropriate credit to the source from which the material is taken, as described in <u>documenting sources</u> and <u>plagiarism</u>. ✦

documenting sources

*"Copyleft" is a play on the word *copyright* and is the effort to free materials from many of the restrictions of copyright. See *http://en.wikipedia.org/wiki/Copyleft*.

Documenting sources achieves three important purposes:

- It allows readers to locate and consult the sources used and to find further information on the subject.
- It enables writers to support their assertions and arguments in such documents as proposals, reports, and trade journal articles.
- It helps writers to give proper credit to others and thus avoid plagiarism by identifying the sources of facts, ideas, visuals (Tab 6), quotations, and paraphrases. See also paraphrasing.

This entry shows citation models and sample pages for two principal documentation systems: American Psychological Association (APA) and Modern Language Association (MLA). The following examples compare these two styles for citing a book by one author: *Capital Ideas Evolving* by Peter L. Bernstein, which was published in 2007 by Wiley in Hoboken, New Jersey.

- The APA system of citation is often used in the social sciences. It is referred to as an author-date method of documentation because parenthetical in-text citations and a reference list (at the end of the paper) in APA style emphasize the author(s) and date of publication so that the currency of the research is clear.

APA IN-TEXT CITATION

(Author's Last Name, Year)

(Bernstein, 2007)

APA REFERENCES ENTRY

Author's Last Name, Initials. (Year). *Title in italics*. Place of Publication: Publisher.

Bernstein, P. L. (2007). *Capital ideas evolving*. Hoboken, NJ: Wiley.

- The MLA system is used in literature and the humanities. MLA style uses parenthetical in-text citations and a list of works cited and places greater importance on the pages on which cited information can be found than on the publication date.

MLA IN-TEXT CITATION

(Author's Last Name Page Number)

(Bernstein 162)

MLA WORKS-CITED ENTRY

Author's Last Name, First Name. *Title Italicized*. Place of Publication: Publisher, Date of Publication. Medium of Publication.

Bernstein, Peter L. *Capital Ideas Evolving*. Hoboken: Wiley, 2007. Print.

3

Research and Documentation

APA

These systems are described in full detail in the following style manuals:

> American Psychological Association. *Publication Manual of the American Psychological Association.* 6th ed. Washington, DC: APA, 2010. See also *www.apastyle.org.*
>
> Modern Language Association. *MLA Handbook for Writers of Research Papers.* 7th ed. New York: MLA, 2009. See also *www.mla.org/style.*

For additional bibliographic advice and documentation models for types of sources not included in this entry, consult these style manuals or those listed in "Web Link: Other Style Manuals and Documentation Systems" on page 83. See also <u>bibliographies</u> and <u>research</u>.

APA Documentation

APA In-Text Citations.   Within the text of a paper, APA parenthetical documentation gives a brief citation—in parentheses—of the author, year of publication, and a relevant page number if it helps locate a passage in a lengthy document.

- Technology has the potential to produce a transformational impact on human life that will enable the human brain to reach beyond its current limitations (Kurzweil, 2006).

- According to Kurzweil (2006), we will witness a "pace of technological change that will be so rapid, its impact so deep, that human life will be irreversibly transformed" (p. 7).

When APA parenthetical citations are needed midsentence, place them after the closing quotation marks and continue with the rest of the sentence.

- In short, "the Singularity" (Kurzweil, 2006, p. 9) is a blending of human biology and technology that will help us develop beyond our human limitations.

If the APA parenthetical citation follows a block quotation, place it after the final punctuation mark.

- . . . a close collaboration with the marketing staff and the development group is essential. (Thompson, 2010)

When a work has two authors, cite both names joined by an ampersand: (Hinduja & Nguyen, 2008). For the first citation of a work with three, four, or five authors, include all names. For subsequent

3

Research and Documentation

APA

citations and for works with more than five authors, include only the last name of the first author followed by et al. (not italicized and with a period after al.). When two or more works by different authors are cited in the same parentheses, list the citations alphabetically and use semicolons to separate them: (Hinduja & Nguyen, 2008; Townsend, 2007).

APA Documentation Models.   In reference lists, APA requires that the first word of book and article titles be capitalized and all subsequent words be lowercased. Exceptions include the first word after a colon or dash and proper nouns.

PRINTED BOOKS
Single Author

Taleb, N. N. (2007). *The black swan: The impact of the highly improbable.* New York, NY: Random House.

Multiple Authors

Jones, E., Haenfler, R., & Johnson, B. (2007). *The better world handbook: Small changes that make a big difference.* Gabriola Island, British Columbia, Canada: New Society.

Corporate Author

Standard and Poor's. (2009). *Standard and Poor's 500 guide.* New York, NY: McGraw-Hill.

Edition Other Than First

Kouzes, J. M., & Posner, B. Z. (2007). *The leadership challenge* (4th ed.). New York, NY: Wiley.

Multivolume Work

Edgar, C., & Padgett, R. (Eds.). (2007). *Educating the imagination: Essays and ideas for teachers and writers* (Vols. 1–2). New York, NY: Teachers & Writers Collaborative.

Work in an Edited Collection

Sen, A. (2007). Education and standards of living. In R. Curren (Ed.), *Philosophy of education: An anthology* (pp. 95–101). Malden, MA: Blackwell.

Encyclopedia or Dictionary Entry

Wah, B. W. (Ed.). (2009). Agent technology. In *Wiley Encyclopedia of computer science and engineering.* Boston, MA: Wiley.

3

Research and
Documentation

APA

ARTICLES IN PRINTED PERIODICALS
Magazine Article

McGirt, E. (2007, November). Facebook opens up. *Fast Company, 120,*
54–89.

Journal Article

Moriarty, J. (2010). Participation in the workplace: Are employees special? *Journal of Business Ethics, 92*(3), 373–384.

Newspaper Article

Spors, K. K. (2008, October 13). Top small businesses 2008. *Wall Street
Journal,* p. R1.

Article with an Unknown Author

What sold, for how much, and why? (Fall 2009). *Modern, 1*(2), 22.

ELECTRONIC SOURCES
Entire Web Site

The APA recommends that a reference to a Web site should provide
an author (whenever possible), a site title or description, the date
of publication or update (use "(n.d.)" if no date is available), and a
URL. If the content could change or be deleted, such as on a Web
site, include the retrieval date also. (The retrieval date is not necessary for content with a fixed publication date, such as a journal
article.) If you need to break a URL at the end of a line, break it
after a double slash, but *before* other punctuation marks. Do not add
a hyphen. No periods follow URLs.

Association for Business Communication. (2009). Retrieved from
http://www.businesscommunication.org

Short Work from a Web Site, with an Author

Marshall, R. (2009, August 18). *IBM bolsters green sensor portfolio.*
Retrieved from http://www.businessgreen.com/business-green
/news/2248007/ibm-bolsters-smart-grid

Short Work from a Web Site, with a Corporate or an Organizational Author

General Motors. (2009). *Company profile.* Retrieved August 18, 2009,
from http://www.gm.com/corporate/about/company.jsp

Short Work from a Web Site, with an Unknown Author

Women owned businesses. (2009, July 20). Retrieved from
http://www.business.gov/start/woman-owned/

Article or Other Work from a Database

Gaston, N., & Kishi, T. (2007). Part-time workers doing full-time work in
Japan. *Journal of the Japanese and International Economies, 21*(4), 434–454.
doi:10.1016/j.jjie.2006.04.001

3

Research and
Documentation

APA

Article in an Online Periodical

Kapadia, R. (2009, August 17). Put your cash to work. *SmartMoney*. Retrieved from http://www.smartmoney.com/investing/economy /put-your-cash-to-work/

Article Posted on a Wiki

Hispanic marketing resources. (2008, January 30). Retrieved August 18, 2009, from http://www.library.ohiou.edu/subjects/bizwiki/index .php/Latino_Marketing

E-mail Message

E-mail messages are not cited in an APA reference list. They can be cited in the text as follows: "According to A. Kalil (personal communication, January 12, 2010), Web pages need to reflect. . . ."

Online Posting (Lists, Forums, Discussion Boards)

Electronic discussion sources, including postings to electronic mailing lists, online forums, or discussion groups, are seldom cited in formal publications because they are difficult to retrieve and not considered scholarly material. If you do include one of these sources, provide the real name of an author if given; otherwise, provide the screen name. Follow the name with the date of the posting, the subject line of the message, and any identifiers for the message in brackets after the title.

seniorscholar. (2009, March 15). Re: Surviving the job search [online forum comment]. Retrieved from http://chronicle.com/forums /index.php/topic,40486.msg1221730.html#msg1221730

Blog Entry

Chang, J. (2009, August 17). Sharing with Google groups [Web log post]. Retrieved from http://googleblog.blogspot.com/2009/08 /sharing-with-google-groups.html

Publication on CD-ROM

Tapscott, D., & Williams, A. D. (2007). *Wikinomics: How mass collaboration changes everything* [CD-ROM]. Old Saybrook, CT: Tantor.

MULTIMEDIA SOURCES (Electronic and Print)
Film or Video

Iowa Public Television. (2008, December 12). National debt impact on national security [Video file]. Retrieved from http://www.youtube .com/watch?v=hW1UCvqWY2E

3

Research and
Documentation

APA

Radio or Television Program

Winkler, A. (Producer). (2009, February 11). Battle brewing over electronic books [Radio program]. In *All things considered*. Boston, MA: WGBH. Retrieved from http://www.npr.org/templates/story/story.php?storyId=100584020

Bettag, T. (Producer). (2009, February 28). The fast lane [Television series episode]. In *Koppel: People's Republic of Capitalism*. Washington, DC: Discovery Channel.

Podcast

Hirsch, P. (2009, February 10). Write-downs [Audio podcast]. In *APM: Marketplace Whiteboard*. Retrieved from http://marketplace.publicradio.org/RSS/

OTHER SOURCES

Published Interview

Barro, R. (2009, February 5). An interview with Robert Barro [Interview by C. Clarke]. Retrieved from http://www.theatlantic.com/

Personal Communications

Personal communications such as lectures, letters, interviews, and e-mail messages are generally not cited in an APA reference list. They can be cited in the text as follows: "According to Elizabeth Andersen (personal communication, October 2, 2010), Web pages need to reflect. . . ."

Brochure or Pamphlet

Library of Congress, U.S. Copyright Office. (2007). *Copyright basics* [Brochure]. Washington, DC: Government Printing Office.

Government Document

U.S. Department of Labor, Bureau of Labor Statistics. (2009). *Highlights of women's earnings in 2008*. Washington, DC: Department of Labor.

Report

Ditch, W. (2007). *XML-based office document standards*. Bristol, England: Higher Education Funding Council for England.

3

Research and Documentation

APA

APA Sample Pages

Shortened title and page number.

This report examines the nature and disposition of the 3,458 ethics cases handled companywide by CGF's ethics officers and managers during 2010. The purpose of such reports is to provide the Ethics and Business Conduct Committee with the information necessary for assessing the effectiveness of the first year of CGF's Ethics Program (Davis, Marks, & Tegge, 2004). According to Matthias Jonas (2004), recommendations are given for consideration "in planning for the second year of the Ethics Program" (p. 152).

One-inch margins. Text double-spaced.

The Office of Ethics and Business Conduct was created to administer the Ethics Program. The director of the Office of Ethics and Business Conduct, along with seven ethics officers throughout CGF, was given the responsibility for the following objectives, as described by Rossouw (2000):

Long quote indented one-half-inch, double-spaced, without quotation marks.

Communicate the values, standards, and goals of CGF's Program to employees. Provide companywide channels for employee education and guidance in resolving ethics concerns. Implement companywide programs in ethics awareness and recognition. Employee accessibility to ethics information and guidance is the immediate goal of the Office of Business Conduct in its first year. (p. 1543)

The purpose of the Ethics Program, established by the Committee, is to "promote ethical business conduct through open communication and compliance with company ethics standards" (Jonas, 2006, p. 89). To accomplish this purpose, any ethics policy must ensure confidentiality and anonymity for employees who raise genuine ethics concerns. The procedure developed at CGF guarantees that employees can

In-text citation gives name, date, and page number.

FIGURE 3–1. APA Sample Page

3

Research and Documentation

APA

ETHICS CASES   21

References   Heading centered.

First word
of title
capitalized
and
subsequent
words
lowercased.

Davis, W. C., Marks, R., & Tegge, D. (2004). *Working in
    the system: Five new management principles*. New
    York, NY: St. Martin's Press.

Jonas, M. (2004). The Internet and ethical communication:
    Toward a new paradigm. *Journal of Ethics and
    Communication, 32*, 147–177.

List
alphabetized
by authors'
last names
and double-
spaced.

Jonas, M. (2006). Ethics in organizational communication:
    A review of the literature. *Journal of Ethics and
    Communication, 29*, 79–99.

National Science Foundation. (2007). *Conflicts of interest
    and standards of ethical conduct*. Arlington, VA:
    Author.

Rossouw, G. J. (2000). Business ethics in South Africa.
    Journal of Business Ethics, 16, 1539–1547.

Schipper, F. (2007). Transparency and integrity: Contrary
    concepts? In K. Homann, P. Koslowski, and
    C. Luetge (Eds.), *Globalisation and business ethics*
    (pp. 101–118). Burlington, VT: Ashgate.

Hanging-
indent style
used for
entries.

Smith, T. (Reporter), & Lehrer, J. (Host). (2006). *NewsHour
    business ethics anthology* [DVD]. Encino, CA:
    Business Training Media.

FIGURE 3–2. APA Sample List of References

MLA Documentation

MLA In-Text Citations.   The MLA parenthetical citation within the text of a paper gives a brief citation — in parentheses — of the author and relevant page number(s), separated only by a space. When citing Web sites where no author or page reference is available, provide a short title of the work in parentheses.

- Achieving results is one thing while maintaining results is another because "like marathon runners, companies hit a performance wall" (Studer 3).

- As Studer writes, the poor performance of a few employees will ultimately affect the performance — and the morale — of all of the employees (8).
  [If the author is cited in the text, include only the page number(s) in parentheses.]

- In 1810, Peter Durand invented the can, which was later used to provide soldiers and explorers canned rations and ultimately "saved legions from sure starvation" ("Forgotten Inventors").

If the parenthetical citation refers to a long, indented quotation, place it outside the punctuation of the last sentence.

- . . . a close collaboration with the marketing staff and the develop-ment group is essential. (Thompson 37)

If no author is named or if you are using more than one work by the same author, give a shortened version of the title in the parenthetical citation, unless you name the title in the text (a "signal phrase"). A citation for Quint Studer's book *Results That Last: Hardwiring Behaviors That Will Take Your Company to the Top* would appear as (Studer, *Results* 93).

MLA Documentation Models

PRINTED BOOKS
Single Author
Taleb, Nassim Nicholas. *The Black Swan: The Impact of the Highly Improbable.* New York: Random, 2007. Print.

Multiple Authors
Jones, Ellis, Ross Haenfler, and Brett Johnson. *The Better World Handbook: Small Changes That Make a Big Difference.* Gabriola Island: New Society, 2007. Print.

Corporate Author
Standard and Poor's. *Standard and Poor's 500 Guide.* New York: McGraw, 2009. Print.

3

Research and
Documentation

MLA

Edition Other Than First

Kouzes, James M., and Barry Z. Posner. *The Leadership Challenge*. 4th ed.
New York: Wiley, 2007. Print.

Multivolume Work

Edgar, Christopher, and Ron Padgett, eds. *Educating the Imagination*.
2 vols. New York: Teachers & Writers Collaborative, 2007.
Print.

Work in an Edited Collection

Sen, Amartya. "Education and Standards of Living." *Philosophy of
Education: An Anthology*. Ed. Randall Curren. Malden: Blackwell,
2007. 95–101. Print.

Encyclopedia or Dictionary Entry

Wah, Benjamin W., ed. "Agent Technology." *Wiley Encyclopedia of
Computer Science and Engineering*. Boston: Wiley, 2009. Print.

ARTICLES IN PRINTED PERIODICALS (*See also* Electronic Sources)
Magazine Article

McGirt, Ellen. "Facebook Opens Up." *Fast Company* Nov. 2007: 54–89.
Print.

Journal Article

Moriarty, Jeffrey. "Participation in the Workplace: Are Employees
Special?" *Journal of Business Ethics* 92.3 (2010): 373–84. Print.

Newspaper Article

Spors, Kelly K. "Top Small Businesses 2008." *Wall Street Journal* 13 Oct.
2008: R1. Print.

Article with an Unknown Author

"What Sold, for How Much, and Why?" *Modern* 1.2 (Fall 2009): 22.
Print.

ELECTRONIC SOURCES
Entire Web Site

The MLA recommends that a reference to a Web site should provide the author's name (whenever possible), the title of the site
(italicized), the name of the sponsoring organization, a publication
date (posted or updated), the medium of publication ("Web"), and
a retrieval date. If there is no title, use a description, such as
"Homepage," as a substitute.

Association for Business Communication. Assn. for Business Communication,
2009. Web. 18 Oct. 2009.

3

Research and
Documentation

MLA

Short Work from a Web Site, with an Author

Marshall, Rosalie. "IBM Bolsters Green Sensor Portfolio." *BusinessGreen .com*. Incisive Media, 18 Aug. 2009. Web. 23 Aug. 2009.

Short Work from a Web Site, with a Corporate or an Organizational Author

General Motors. "Company Profile." *General Motors*. General Motors, 2009. Web. 18 Aug. 2009.

Short Work from a Web Site, with an Unknown Author

"Women Owned Businesses." *Business.gov*. US Government, 20 July 2009. Web. 18 Aug. 2009.

Article or Other Work from a Database

Gaston, Noel, and Tomoka Kishi. "Part-Time Workers Doing Full-Time Work in Japan." *Journal of the Japanese and International Economies* 21.4 (2007): 435–54. *Business Source Premier*. Web. 25 Nov. 2007.

Article in an Online Periodical

Kapadia, Reshma. "Put Your Cash to Work." *SmartMoney.com*. SmartMoney, 17 Aug. 2009. Web. 19 Aug. 2009.

Article Posted on a Wiki

"Hispanic Marketing Resources." *The Biz Wiki*. Ohio Libs., 10 Sept. 2007. Web. 9 Dec. 2007.

E-mail Message

Kalil, Ari. "Customer Satisfaction Survey." Message to the author. 12 Jan. 2010. E-mail.

Online Posting (Lists, Forums, Discussion Boards)

seniorscholar. "Surviving the Job Search." *Chronicle Forums*. N.p., 15 Mar. 2009. Web. 19 Aug. 2009.

Blog Entry

Chang, Jeffery. "Sharing with Google Groups." *Google Blog*. Google, 17 Aug. 2009. Web. 19 Aug. 2009.

Publication on CD-ROM

Tapscott, Don, and Anthony D. Williams. "Wikinomics." *Wikinomics: How Mass Collaboration Changes Everything*. Old Saybrook: Tantor, 2007. CD-ROM.

MULTIMEDIA SOURCES (Electronic and Print)
Film or Video

"National Debt Impact on National Security." *Des Moines Register Republican Presidential Debate*. 12 Dec. 2007. Iptv.org. Web.

3

Research and
Documentation

MLA

Radio or Television Program

"Battle Brewing over Electronic Books." *All Things Considered*.
  Narr. Lynn Neary. Natl. Public Radio. *NPR.org*. 11 Feb. 2009.
  Web.

Koppel, Ted, narr. "Koppel: People's Republic of Capitalism." *The Fast
  Lane*. The Discovery Channel. 28 Feb. 2009. Television.

Podcast

Hirsch, Paddy. "Write-Downs." *APM: Marketplace Whiteboard*. Amer.
  Public Media, 10 Feb. 2009. MP3 file.

OTHER SOURCES
Published Interview

Barro, Robert. "An Interview with Robert Barro." *The Atlantic*. The
  Atlantic Monthly Group, 5 Feb. 2009. Web.

Personal Interview

Andersen, Elizabeth. Personal interview. 29 Nov. 2010.

Brochure or Pamphlet

Library of Congress. US Copyright Office. *Copyright Basics*. Washington:
  GPO, 2007. Print.

Government Document

United States. Dept. of Labor. Bureau of Labor Statistics. *Highlights of
  Women's Earnings in 2008*. Rept. 1000. Washington: US Dept. of
  Labor, 2009. Print.

Report

Ditch, Walter. *XML-Based Office Document Standards*. Bristol, Eng.:
  Higher Educ. Funding Council for England, 2007. Print.

3

Research and
Documentation

MLA

MLA Sample Pages

Author's last name and page number.

This report examines the nature and disposition of the 3,458 ethics cases handled companywide by CGF's ethics officers and managers during 2010. The purpose of such reports is to provide the Ethics and Business Conduct Committee with the information necessary for assessing the effectiveness of the first year of CGF's Ethics Program (Davis, Marks, and Tegge 142). According to Matthias Jonas, recommendations are given for consideration "in planning for the second year of the Ethics Program" ("Internet" 152).

One-inch margins. Text double-spaced.

The Office of Ethics and Business Conduct was created to administer the Ethics Program. The director of the Office of Ethics and Business Conduct, along with seven ethics officers throughout CGF, was given the responsibility for the following objectives, as described by Rossouw:

> Communicate the values, standards, and goals of CGF's Program to employees. Provide companywide channels for employee education and guidance in resolving ethics concerns. Implement companywide programs in ethics awareness and recognition. Employee accessibility to ethics information and guidance is the immediate goal of the Office of Business Conduct in its first year. (1543)

Long quote indented one inch (or 10 spaces), double-spaced, without quotation marks.

The purpose of the Ethics Program, according to Jonas, is to "promote ethical business conduct through open communication and compliance with company ethics standards" ("Ethics" 89). To accomplish this purpose, any ethics policy must ensure confidentiality for anyone

In-text citations give author name and page number. Title used when multiple works by same author cited.

3

Research and Documentation

MLA

FIGURE 3–3. MLA Sample Page

Litzinger 21

Works Cited

Davis, W. C., Roland Marks, and Diane Tegge. *Working in the*
    System: Five New Management Principles. New York:
    St. Martin's, 2004. Print.

International Business Ethics Institute. Inter. Business
    Ethics Inst., 14 Jan. 2008. Web. 19 June 2008.

Jonas, Matthias. "Ethics in Organizational Communication: A
    Review of the Literature." *Journal of Ethics and*
    Communication 29 (2006): 79–99. Print.

- - -. "The Internet and Ethical Communication: Toward a New
    Paradigm." *Journal of Ethics and Communication* 32
    (2004): 147–77. Print.

Rossouw, George J. "Business Ethics in South Africa." *Journal*
    of Business Ethics 16 (2000): 1539–47. Print.

Sariolgholam, Mahmood. Personal interview. 29 Jan. 2008.

Schipper, Fritz. "Transparency and Integrity: Contrary
    Concepts?" *Globalisation and Business Ethics.* Ed. Karl
    Homann, Peter Koslowski, and Christoph Luetge.
    Burlington: Ashgate, 2007. 101–18. Print.

Smith, Terrence. "Legislating Ethics." *NewsHour Business Ethics*
    Anthology. Host Jim Lehrer. Encino: Business Training
    Media, 2006. DVD.

United States. Natl. Science Foundation. *Conflicts of Interest and*
    Standards of Ethical Conduct. NSF Manual No. 15.
    Arlington: Natl. Science Foundation, 2007. Print.

Heading
centered.

List
alphabetized
by authors'
last names
or title and
double-spaced.

Hanging-
indent style
used for
entries.

3

Research and
Documentation

MLA

FIGURE 3–4. MLA Sample List of Works Cited

✦ ETHICS NOTE Visuals under copyright require permission from copyright owners before they can be reproduced. Contact the publisher to find out what needs permission, how best to obtain it, and what information copyright owners require in source lines and reference entries. Source lines almost always require mention of permission from the copyright owner to reproduce. ✦

 WEB LINK **OTHER STYLE MANUALS AND DOCUMENTATION SYSTEMS**

Many professional societies, publishing companies, and other organizations publish manuals that prescribe bibliographic reference formats for their publications or for publications in their fields. For example, the American Medical Association (AMA) publishes the *American Medical Association Manual of Style*. For links to style manuals and other documentation resources, see *bedfordstmartins.com/alred*, and select *Links Library*.

---

interviewing for information

The process of interviewing for information includes determining the proper person to interview, preparing for the interview, conducting the interview, and expanding your notes soon after the interview. See also research.

Determining the Proper Person to Interview

Many times, your subject or purpose (Tab 1) logically points to the proper person to interview for information. For example, if you were writing about using the Web to market a software-development business, you would want to interview someone with extensive experience in Web marketing as well as someone who has built a successful business developing software. The following sources can help you determine the appropriate person to interview: (1) workplace colleagues or faculty in appropriate academic departments, (2) local chapters of professional societies, (3) information from "contact" or "about" links at company or organization Web sites, and (4) targeted Internet searches, such as using relevant domains (.edu, .gov, and .org).

Preparing for the Interview

Before the interview, learn as much as possible about the person you are going to interview and the organization for which he or she works.

✦ PROFESSIONALISM NOTE When you contact the prospective interviewee, explain who you are, why you would like an interview, the

3

Research and
Documentation

subject and purpose of the interview, and generally how much time it will take. You should also ask permission if you plan to record the interview and let your interviewee know that you will allow him or her to review your draft. ✦

After you have made the appointment, prepare a list of questions to ask your interviewee. Avoid vague, general questions. A question such as "Do you think the Web would be useful for you?" is too general to elicit useful information. It is more helpful to ask specific but open-ended questions, such as the following: "Many physicians in your specialty are using the Web to answer routine patient questions. How might providing such information on your Web site affect your relationship with your patients?"

Conducting the Interview

Arrive promptly for the interview and be prepared to guide the discussion. During the interview, take only memory-jogging notes that will help you recall the conversation later; do not ask your interviewee to slow down so that you can take detailed notes. As the interview is reaching a close, take a few minutes to skim your notes and ask the interviewee to clarify anything that is ambiguous.

Writer's Checklist: Interviewing Successfully

- ☑ Be pleasant but purposeful. You are there to get information, so don't be timid about asking leading questions on the subject.
- ☑ Use the list of questions you have prepared, starting with the less complex and difficult aspects of the topic to get the conversation started and then going on to the more challenging aspects.
- ☑ Let your interviewee do most of the talking. Remember that the interviewee is the expert. See also <u>listening</u> (Tab 9).
- ☑ Be objective. Don't offer your opinions on the subject. You are there to get information, not to debate.
- ☑ Ask additional questions as they arise.
- ☑ Don't get sidetracked. If the interviewee strays too far from the subject, ask a specific question to direct the conversation back on track.
- ☑ If you use an audiocassette or a digital voice recorder, do not let it lure you into relaxing so that you neglect to ask crucial questions.
- ☑ After thanking the interviewee, ask permission to contact him or her again to clarify a point or two as you complete your interview notes.

Expanding Your Notes Soon After the Interview

Immediately after leaving the interview, use your memory-jogging notes to help you mentally review the interview and expand those notes. Do not postpone this step. No matter how good your memory is, you will forget some important points if you do not complete this step at once. See also note-taking.

Interviewing by Phone or E-mail

When an interviewee is not available for a face-to-face meeting, consider a telephone interview. Most of the principles for conducting face-to-face interviews apply also to phone interviews; be aware, however, that phone calls do not offer the important nonverbal cues of face-to-face meetings. Further, taking notes can be challenging while speaking on a phone, although a phone headset or a high-quality speakerphone can alleviate that problem.

As an alternative to a face-to-face or phone interview, consider an e-mail interview. Such an "interview," however, lacks the spontaneity and the immediacy of an in-person or a phone conversation. If e-mail is the only option, the interviewing principles in this entry can help you obtain useful responses. Before you send any questions, make sure that your contact is willing to participate and respond to follow-up requests for clarification. As a courtesy, give the respondent a general idea of the number of questions you plan to ask and the level of detail you expect. When you send the questions, ask for a reasonable deadline from the interviewee ("Would you be able to send your response by . . . ?"). See also selecting the medium (Tab 2).

note-taking

The purpose of note-taking is to summarize and record information you extract during research. The challenge in taking notes is to condense someone else's thoughts into your own words without distorting the original thinking. As you extract information, let your knowledge of the audience (Tab 1) and the purpose (Tab 1) of your writing guide you.

⬛ ETHICS NOTE Resist copying your source word for word as you take notes; instead, paraphrase the author's idea or concept. If you only change a few words from a source and incorporate that text into your document, you will be guilty of plagiarism. See also paraphrasing. ✦

On occasion, when an expert source states something that is especially precise, striking, or noteworthy or that reinforces your point, you can justifiably quote the source directly and incorporate it into your document. If you use a direct quote, enclose the material in quotation marks in your notes. In your finished writing, document the source of your quotation. Normally, you will rarely need to quote anything longer than a paragraph. See also documenting sources and quotations.

When taking notes on abstract ideas, as opposed to factual data, do not sacrifice clarity for brevity—notes expressing concepts can lose their meaning if they are too brief. The critical test is whether you can understand the note a week later and recall the significant ideas of the passage.

Writer's Checklist: Taking Notes

- ☑ Ask yourself the following questions: What information do I need to fulfill my purpose? What are the needs of my audience?

- ☑ Record only the most important ideas and concepts. Be sure to record all vital names, dates, and definitions.

- ☑ When in doubt about whether to take a note, consider the difficulty of finding the source again should you want it later.

- ☑ Use direct or indirect quotations when sources state something that is precise, striking, or noteworthy or that succinctly reinforces a point you are making.

- ☑ Give proper credit. Record the author; title; publisher; place; page number; URL; and date of publication, posting, or retrieval. (On subsequent notes from the same source, include only the author and page number or URL.)

- ☑ Use your own shorthand and record notes in a way that you find efficient, whether in an electronic document or on index cards.

- ☑ Photocopy or download pages and highlight passages that you intend to quote.

- ☑ Check your notes for accuracy against the original material before moving on to another source.

3

Research and Documentation

paraphrasing

Paraphrasing is restating or rewriting in your own words the essential ideas of another writer. The following example is an original passage explaining the concept of *object blur*. The paraphrased version restates the essential information of the passage in a form appropriate for a report.

ORIGINAL   One of the major visual cues used by pilots in maintaining precision ground reference during low-level flight is that of object blur. We are acquainted with the object-blur phenomenon experienced when driving an automobile. Objects in the foreground appear to be rushing toward us, while objects in the background appear to recede slightly.
— Wesley E. Woodson and Donald W. Conover, *Human Engineering Guide for Equipment Designers*

| PARAPHRASED | Object blur refers to the phenomenon by which observers in a moving vehicle report that foreground objects appear to rush at them, while background objects appear to recede slightly (Woodson & Conover, 1964). |

◆ ETHICS NOTE Because paraphrasing does not quote a source word for word, quotation marks are not used. However, paraphrased material should be credited because the *ideas* are taken from someone else. See also ethics in writing (Tab 1), note-taking, plagiarism, and quotations. ✦

plagiarism

Plagiarism is the use of someone else's unique ideas without acknowledgment or the use of someone else's exact words without quotation marks and appropriate credit. Plagiarism is considered to be the theft of someone else's creative and intellectual property and is not accepted in business, science, journalism, academia, or any other field. See also ethics in writing (Tab 1) and research.

Citing Sources

Quoting a passage—including cutting and pasting a passage from an Internet source into your work—is permissible only if you enclose the passage in quotation marks and properly cite the source. For detailed advice on quoting correctly, see quotations. If you intend to publish, reproduce, or distribute material that includes quotations from published works, including Web sites, you may need to obtain written permission from the copyright holders of those works.

Even Web sites that grant permission to copy, distribute, or modify material under the "copyleft" principle, such as *Wikipedia*, nonetheless caution that you must give appropriate credit to the source from which material is taken (see *http://en.wikipedia.org/wiki/Wikipedia :Citing_Wikipedia*).

Paraphrasing the words and ideas of another *also requires that you cite your source*, even though you do not enclose paraphrased ideas or materials in quotation marks. (See also documenting sources.) Paraphrasing a passage without citing the source is permissible only when the information paraphrased is common knowledge.

Common Knowledge

Common knowledge generally refers to information that is widely known and readily available in handbooks, manuals, atlases, and other

3

Research and Documentation

references. For example, the "law of supply and demand" is common knowledge and is found in virtually every economics and business textbook.

Common knowledge also refers to information within a specific field that is generally known and understood by most others in that field—even though it is not widely known by those outside the field. For examples, see the Web Link at the end of this entry.

An indication that something is common knowledge is whether it is repeated in multiple sources without citation. However, when in doubt, cite the source.

◆ ETHICS NOTE In the workplace, employees often borrow material freely from in-house manuals, reports, and other company documents. Using or <u>repurposing</u> (Tab 2) such material is neither plagiarism nor a violation of copyright. For information on the use of public domain and government material, see <u>copyright</u>. ✦

 WEB LINK **AVOIDING PLAGIARISM**

For a tutorial on using sources correctly, see *bedfordstmartins.com/alred*, and select *Tutorials*, "Avoiding Plagiarism." For links to other helpful resources, select *Links for Business Writing*.

---

quotations

Using direct and indirect quotations is an effective way to make or support a point. However, avoid the temptation to overquote during the <u>note-taking</u> phase of your <u>research</u>; concentrate on summarizing what you read.

◆ ETHICS NOTE When you use a quotation (or an idea of another writer), cite your source properly. If you do not, you will be guilty of <u>plagiarism</u>. For specific details on citation systems, see <u>documenting sources</u>. ✦

Direct Quotations

A direct quotation is a word-for-word copy of the text of an original source. Choose direct quotations (which can be of a word, a phrase, a sentence, or, occasionally, a paragraph) carefully and use them sparingly. Enclose direct quotations in <u>quotation marks</u> (Tab 12) and separate them from the rest of the sentence by a <u>comma</u> (Tab 12) or <u>colon</u>

(Tab 12). Use the initial capital letter of a quotation if the quoted material originally began with a capital letter.

- The economist stated, "Regulation cannot supply the dynamic stimulus that in other industries is supplied by competition."

When dividing a quotation, set off the material that interrupts the quotation with commas, and use quotation marks around each part of the quotation.

- "Regulation," the economist said in a recent interview, "cannot supply the dynamic stimulus that in other industries is supplied by competition."

Indirect Quotations

An indirect quotation is a paraphrased version of an original text. It is usually introduced by the word *that* and is not set off from the rest of the sentence by punctuation marks. See also <u>paraphrasing</u>.

- In a recent interview, he said *that* regulation does not stimulate the industry as well as competition does.

Deletions or Omissions

Deletions or omissions from quoted material are indicated by three ellipsis points (. . .) within a sentence and a period plus three ellipsis points (. . . .) at the end of a sentence. See <u>ellipses</u> (Tab 12).

- "If monopolies could be made to respond . . . we would be able to enjoy the benefits of . . . large-scale efficiency. . . ."

When a quoted passage begins in the middle of a sentence rather than at the beginning, ellipsis points are not necessary; the fact that the first letter of the quoted material is not capitalized tells the reader that the quotation begins in midsentence.

- Rivero goes on to conclude that "coordination may lessen competition within a region."

Inserting Material into Quotations

When it is necessary to insert a clarifying comment within quoted material, use <u>brackets</u> (Tab 12).

- "The industry is an integrated system that serves an extensive [geographic] area, with divisions existing as islands within the larger system's sphere of influence."

3

Research and
Documentation

When quoted material contains an obvious error or might be questioned in some other way, insert the expression *sic* (Latin for "thus") in italic type and enclose it in brackets ([*sic*]) following the questionable material to indicate that the writer has quoted the material *exactly as it appeared in the original.*

- The company considers the Baker Foundation to be a "guilt-edged [*sic*] investment."

Incorporating Quotations into Text

Quote word for word only when a source with particular expertise states something that is especially precise, striking, or noteworthy, or that may reinforce a point you are making.

Quotations must also logically, grammatically, and syntactically match the rest of the sentence and surrounding text. Notice in Figure 3–5 that the quotation blends with the content of the surrounding text, which uses <u>transition</u> (Tab 10) to introduce and comment on the quotation.

> According to Alred (2006), academics and workplace professionals might not value the same book or article because they do not share the same goals:
>
> > Generally, the goals of workplace professionals demand that they think in specific, practical, and immediately applicable ways; those of us in the academy must think in terms that are more abstract, conceptual, and long-term. It is understandable, then, that works that might be highly valued by either practitioners or academics can seem entirely irrelevant to the other. (p. 82)
>
> The works that seem irrelevant to practitioners, then, often do not give practical advice on accomplishing tasks. However, academics often find . . .

FIGURE 3–5. Long Quotation (APA Style)

Depending on the citation system, the style of incorporating quotations varies. For examples of two different styles, see <u>documenting sources</u>. Figure 3–5 shows APA style for a long quotation.

Do not rely too heavily on the use of quotations in the final version of your document. In general, avoid quoting anything that is longer than one paragraph.

research

Research is the process of investigation—the discovery of information. To be focused, research must be preceded by <u>preparation</u> (Tab 1), especially consideration of your <u>audience</u> (Tab 1), <u>purpose</u> (Tab 1), and <u>scope</u> (Tab 1). During your research, effective <u>note-taking</u> is essential for integrating your own ideas, supporting facts, and any well-selected <u>quotations</u> during <u>organization</u> (Tab 1) into an effective draft and final document. See also <u>documenting sources</u> and "Five Steps to Successful Writing" (pages xxix–xxxvi).

In an academic setting, your preparatory resources include conversations with your peers, instructors, and, especially, a reference librarian. On the job, your main resources are your own knowledge and experience and that of your colleagues. In business, the most important sources of information may also include market research, questionnaires and surveys, focus groups, shareholder meetings, and the like. In this setting, begin by brainstorming with colleagues about what sources will be most useful to your topic and how you can find them.

Primary Research

Primary research is the gathering of raw data from such sources as firsthand experience, interviews, direct observation, surveys and questionnaires, focus groups, <u>meetings</u> (Tab 9), and the like. In fact, direct observation and interaction are the only ways to obtain certain kinds of information, such as about human behavior and the functioning of organizations. You can also conduct primary research on the Internet by participating in discussion groups and newsgroups and by using <u>e-mail</u> (Tab 2) to request information from specific audiences. See also <u>interviewing for information</u> and <u>listening</u> (Tab 9).

■ ETHICS NOTE If you conduct research that involves observation or a questionnaire at your university or college, ask your instructor whether your methods or questions are appropriate and whether you may need to file an application with your school's Institutional Review Board (IRB). For an observation, be sure to obtain permission in advance and remain as unobtrusive as possible during your observation. Keep accurate, complete records that indicate date, time of day, duration of the observation, and so on. Save interpretations of your observations for future analysis. ✦

Secondary Research

Secondary research is the gathering of information that has been previously analyzed, assessed, evaluated, compiled, or otherwise organized into accessible form. Sources include books and articles as well as reports (Tab 4), Web documents, audio and video recordings, podcasts, correspondence, minutes of meetings, brochures, annual reports, and so forth. The following two sections—Library Research Strategies and Internet Research Strategies—provide methods for finding secondary sources.

As you seek information, keep in mind that in most cases the more recent the information, the better. Recently published periodicals and newspapers—as well as academic (.edu), organizational (.org), and government (.gov) Web sites—can be good sources of current information and can include published interviews, articles, papers, and conference proceedings. See *Writer's Checklist: Evaluating Print and Online Sources* on page 97.

When a resource seems useful, read it carefully and take notes that include any additional questions about your topic. Some of your questions may eventually be answered in other sources; those that remain unanswered can guide you to further primary research. For example, you may discover that you need to interview an expert. Not only can someone skilled in a field answer many of your questions, but he or she can also suggest further sources of information. See paraphrasing and plagiarism.

Library Research Strategies

The library provides organized paths into scholarship and the Internet as well as specialized resources—such as licensed online databases, indexes, catalogs, and directories—that are not accessible through standard Web searches. The first step in using library resources, either in an academic institution or in a workplace, is to develop a search strategy appropriate to the information needed for your topic. You may want to begin by asking a reference librarian for help (in person, by phone, by live chat, or by e-mail) to find the best print or online resources for your topic—a brief conversation can focus your research and save you time. In addition, use your library's homepage for access to its catalogs, databases of articles, subject directories to the Web, and more.

Your search strategy depends on the kind of information you are seeking. For example, if you need the latest data offered by government research, check the Web, as described later in this entry. Likewise, if you need a current scholarly article on a topic, search an online database (such as EBSCOhost's Academic Search Premier) subscribed to by your library. For an overview of a subject, you might turn to an encyclopedia; for historical background, your best resources are books, journals, and primary documents (such as a labor contract).

 DIGITAL TIP **STORING SEARCH RESULTS**

Databases offer various ways to save your results. You may be able to save your searches and results within the database itself by creating a personal account, send selected references and full-text articles to an e-mail account, or export them to citation-management software such as RefWorks, EndNote, or Zotero. These programs allow you to build your own database of references from multiple sources, sort them into folders, and generate bibliographies in the format of your choice. Database search tools will vary from library to library, so contact a reference librarian for usage guidance at your library.

Online Catalogs (Locating Books).   An online catalog—accessed through library research terminals and through the Internet—allows you to search a library's book collection, indicates a book's location and availability, and may allow you to arrange an interlibrary loan if a book is in another library.

You can search a library's online catalog by author, title, keyword, or subject. The most common ways of searching for a specific topic are by subject or by keyword. If your search turns up too many results, you can usually narrow it by using the "limit search" or "advanced search" option.

Online Databases and Indexes (Locating Articles).   Most libraries subscribe to online databases, such as the following, which are usually available through a library's Web site:

- *EBSCOhost's Academic Search Premier*: a large multidisciplinary database, providing full text for nearly 4,500 periodicals, including more than 3,700 peer-reviewed journals
- *Expanded Academic ASAP*: a large database, covering general-interest and scholarly journals, plus business, law, and health-care publications (many in full text)

- *ERIC (Education Resources Information Center)*: a U.S. Department of Education database providing access to journals and reports in education
- *JSTOR*: a full-text, archival collection of journals in humanities, social sciences, and sciences
- *Lexis/Nexis Academic*: a collection of databases that is particularly strong for news, business, legal, and corporate and financial information (most articles in full text), as well as congressional, statistical, and governmental resources

These databases, sometimes called *periodical indexes*, are excellent resources for articles published within the last 10 to 20 years. Many include descriptive abstracts and full texts of articles. To find older articles, you may need to consult a print index, such as the *Readers' Guide to Periodical Literature* and the *New York Times Index*, both of which have been digitized and may be available in some libraries.

To locate articles in a database, conduct a keyword search. If your search turns up too many results, refine your search by connecting two search terms with AND—"communication AND management"—or use other options offered by the database, such as a limited, a modified, or an advanced search.

Reference Works.   In addition to articles, books, and Web sources, you may want to consult reference works such as encyclopedias, dictionaries, and atlases for a brief overview of your subject. Ask your reference librarian to recommend works and <u>bibliographies</u> that are most relevant to your topic. Many are available online and can be accessed through your library's homepage.

ENCYCLOPEDIAS.   Encyclopedias are comprehensive, multivolume collections of articles arranged alphabetically. Some cover a wide range of subjects, while others—such as *The Encyclopedia of Careers & Vocational Guidance*, 13th ed., edited by William Hopke (Chicago: Ferguson, 2005)—focus on specific areas. The free online encyclopedia *Wikipedia* at *www.wikipedia.org* should be used only as a starting point for your research because users continuously update entries (with varying degrees of expert oversight).

DICTIONARIES.   Specialized dictionaries define terms used in a particular field, such as business, computers, architecture, or consumer affairs, and they offer detailed definitions of field-specific terms, usually written in straightforward language.

HANDBOOKS AND MANUALS.   Handbooks and manuals are typically one-volume compilations of frequently used information in a particular field. They offer brief definitions of terms or concepts, standards for presenting information, procedures for documenting sources, and <u>visuals</u> (Tab 6) to illustrate principles.

BIBLIOGRAPHIES.   Bibliographies list books, periodicals, and other research materials published in areas such as business, medicine, the humanities, and the social sciences.

GENERAL GUIDES.   The annotated *Guide to Reference Books*, 12th ed., by Robert Balay (Chicago: American Library Association, 2008), can help you locate reference books, indexes, and other research materials.

OTHER LIBRARY RESOURCES.   Many libraries offer special kinds of research information. For example, a library may provide access to data that can be downloaded into statistical packages, such as SPSS (statistical package for the social sciences) for manipulation. Others offer GIS (geographic information systems) software that links data to spatial information, allowing the researcher to create detailed maps that show factors such as income, ethnicity, or purchasing habits.

Internet Research Strategies

The Web varies widely in its completeness and accuracy, so you need to evaluate Internet sources critically by following the advice in *Writer's Checklist: Evaluating Print and Online Sources* on page 97.

As comprehensive as search engines and directories may seem, none is complete or objective, and they carry only a preselected range of content. Many, for example, do not index Adobe PDF files or Usenet newsgroups, and many cannot index databases and other non-HTML–based content. Search engines rank the sites they believe will be relevant to your research based on a number of different strategies. Almost all major search engines now sell high rankings to advertisers with the highest bids, so your results may not highlight the pages most relevant to your search. Your best strategy is to research how your favorite search engines work; nearly all provide detailed methodologies on their help pages.

3

Research and
Documentation

Search Engines.   A search engine locates information based on words or combinations of words that you specify. The software engine then lists for you the documents or files that contain one or more of these words in their titles, descriptions, or text. The following search engines are used widely:

Google	*www.google.com*
Bing	*www.bing.com*
Yahoo!	*www.yahoo.com*

Also available are metasearch engines—tools that do not maintain an internal database but instead launch your query to multiple databases of various Web-based resources (other search engines or subject directories).

Dogpile	*www.dogpile.com*
Metacrawler	*www.metacrawler.com*

Many search engines allow advanced searches with options that provide more selective results. Although search engines vary in what and how they search, you can use some basic strategies, described in the following *Writer's Checklist*.

Writer's Checklist: Using Search Engines and Keywords

☑ Enter keywords and phrases that are as specific to your topic as possible. For example, if you are looking for information about *nuclear power* and enter only the term *nuclear*, the search will also yield listings for *nuclear* family, *nuclear* medicine, and hundreds of others not related to your topic.

☑ Use Boolean operators (AND, OR, NOT) to narrow your search. For example, if you are searching for information on breast cancer and are finding references to nothing but prostate cancer, try "breast AND cancer NOT prostate."

☑ Check any search tips available at the engine you use. For example, some engines allow you to use an advanced search that narrows your search by combining phrases with double quotation marks: "usability testing" will return only pages that have the full compound phrase.

☑ Try several search engines to get more varied results and remember that high rankings may be based on marketing by advertisers.

Web Subject Directories.   A subject directory (also known as an index) organizes information by broad subject categories (business, entertainment, health, sports) and related subtopics (marketing, finance, investing). One such directory is *http://directory.google.com/*. A subject-directory search eventually produces a list of specific sites that contain information about the topics you request.

In addition to the subject directories offered by many search engines, the following directories will help you to conduct selective, scholarly research on the Web:

Infomine	*http://infomine.ucr.edu*
The Internet Public Library	*www.ipl.org*
The WWW Virtual Library	*www.vlib.org*

The Internet includes numerous directories and sites devoted to specific subject areas. Following are some suggested resources for researching a business topic.

CIO's Resource Centers	*www.cio.com/solutions/research-and-analysis*
GlobalEDGE	*http://globaledge.msu.edu/*
Inc.com Articles by Topic	*www.inc.com* (use search function)
LSU Libraries Federal Agencies Directory	*www.lib.lsu.edu/gov/*
FedStats	*www.fedstats.gov*

Some sites combine search engines with directories; for example, Google operates both a standard search engine and directory and a special contributor-generated directory referred to as an "Open Directory" (*http://dmoz.org*).

Evaluating Sources

The easiest way to ensure that information is valid is to obtain it from a reputable source. For Internet sources, be especially concerned about the validity of the information provided. Because anyone can publish on the Web, it is sometimes difficult to determine authorship of a document, and frequently a person's qualifications for speaking on a topic are absent or questionable. The Internet versions of established, reputable journals in medicine, management, engineering, computer software, and the like merit the same level of trust as the printed versions. Consider the domain abbreviation when evaluating the reliability of Internet sites: .edu (college or university), .gov (federal government), and .mil (U.S. military). As you move away from established, reputable sites, exercise more caution. Be especially wary of unmoderated, public Web forums. Collectively generated Web sites, such as *Wikipedia*, often make no guarantee of the validity of information on their sites (see *http://en.wikipedia.org/wiki/Wikipedia:General_disclaimer*).

Writer's Checklist: Evaluating Print and Online Sources

Keep in mind the following four criteria when evaluating Internet sources: authority, accuracy, bias, and currency.*

FOR ALL SOURCES

☑ Is the resource recent enough and relevant to your topic? Is it readily available?

☑ Who is the intended audience? Is it the mainstream public? a small group of professionals?

☑ Who is the author(s)? Is the author(s) an authority on the subject?

☑ Does the author(s) provide enough supporting evidence and document sources so that you can verify the information's accuracy?

*For more details, see Leigh Ryan, *The Bedford Guide for Writing Tutors*, 4th ed. (Boston: Bedford/St. Martin's, 2006).

3

Research and Documentation

Writer's Checklist: Evaluating Print and Online Sources (continued)

☑ Is the information presented in an objective, unbiased way? Are any biases made clear? Are opinions clearly labeled? Are viewpoints balanced, or are opposing opinions acknowledged?

☑ Are the language, tone, and style appropriate and cogent?

FOR A BOOK

☑ Does the preface or introduction indicate the author's or book's purpose?

☑ Does the table of contents relate to your topic? Does the index contain terms related to your topic?

☑ Are the chapters useful? Skim through one chapter that seems related to your topic—notice especially the introduction, headings, and closing.

FOR AN ARTICLE

☑ Is the publisher of the magazine or other periodical well known?

☑ What is the article's purpose? For a journal article, read the abstract; for a newspaper article, read the headline and lead sentences.

☑ Does the article contain informative diagrams or other visuals that indicate its scope?

FOR A WEB SITE

☑ Does a reputable group or organization sponsor or maintain the site?

☑ Are the purpose and scope of the site clearly stated? Check the "Mission Statement" or "About Us" pages. Are there any disclaimers?

☑ Is the site updated, thus current? Are the links functional and up-to-date?

☑ Is the documentation authoritative and credible? Check the links to other sources and cross-check facts at other reputable Web sites, such as academic ones.

☑ Is the site well designed? Is the material well written and error free?

 WEB LINK **EVALUATING ONLINE SOURCES**

For a tutorial on evaluating information online, see *bedfordstmartins.com/ alred*, and select *Tutorials*, "Evaluating Online Sources." For links to additional related resources, select *Links for Business Writing*.

3

Research and Documentation

4

Business Writing Documents and Elements

Preview

This section contains entries on various forms of business documents, including **proposals** and such frequently written **reports** as **progress and activity reports**, **trip reports**, and **trouble reports**. Because of their size and complexity, **formal reports** and related parts are covered separately in Tab 5, "Formal Reports," which includes a sample formal report (pages 136–152).

4

Business Writing
Documents
and Elements

feasibility reports

When organizations consider a new project—developing a new product or service, expanding a customer base, purchasing equipment, or moving operations—they first try to determine the project's chances for success. A feasibility report presents evidence about the practicality of a proposed project based on specific criteria. It answers such questions as the following: Is new construction or development necessary? Is sufficient staff available? What are the costs? Is funding available? What are the legal ramifications? Based on the findings of this analysis, the report offers logical conclusions and recommends whether the project should be carried out. When feasibility reports stress specific steps that should be taken as a result of a study of a problem or an issue, they are often referred to as *recommendation reports*.

Before beginning to write a feasibility report, analyze the needs of the audience as well as the context and purpose of the study. Then write a purpose statement, such as "The purpose of this study is to determine the feasibility of expanding our Pacific Rim operations," to guide you or a collaborative team. See <u>audience</u> (Tab 1), <u>context</u> (Tab 1), and <u>purpose</u> (Tab 1).

Report Sections

Every feasibility report should contain an introduction, a body, a conclusion, and a recommendation. See also <u>proposals</u> and <u>formal reports</u> (Tab 5).

Introduction.   The introduction states the purpose of the report, describes why the report was necessary, and includes any pertinent background information. It may also discuss the scope of the report, any procedures or methods used in the analysis of alternatives, and any limitations of the study. See <u>introductions</u> (Tab 1).

Body.   The body of the report presents a detailed review of the alternatives for achieving the goals of the project. Examine each option according to specific criteria, such as cost and financing, availability of staff, and other relevant requirements, identifying the subsections with <u>headings</u> (Tab 6) to guide readers.

Conclusion.   The conclusion interprets the available options and leads to one option as the best or most feasible. See <u>conclusions</u> (Tab 1).

Recommendation.   The recommendation section clearly presents the writer's (or team's) opinion on which alternative best meets the criteria as summarized in the conclusion.

4

Business Writing Documents and Elements

> ### 🌀 WEB LINK FEASIBILITY REPORTS
>
> For links to an example of a feasibility report, see *bedfordstmartins.com/ alred,* and select *Links Library*.

investigative reports

An investigative <u>report</u> offers a precise analysis of a workplace problem or an issue in response to a need for information. The investigative report shown in Figure 4–1, for example, evaluates whether a company should adopt a program called *Basic English* to train and prepare documentation for non–English-speaking readers.

Open an investigative report with a statement of its primary and (if any) secondary purposes, then define the scope of your investigation. (See also <u>purpose</u>, Tab 1, and <u>scope</u>, Tab 1.) If the report includes a survey of opinions, for example, indicate the number of people surveyed and other identifying information, such as income categories and occupations. Include any information that is pertinent in defining the extent of the investigation. Then report your findings and discuss their significance with your <u>conclusions</u> (Tab 1).

Sometimes the person requesting the investigative report may ask you to make recommendations as a result of your findings. In that case, the report may be referred to as a *recommendation report*. See also <u>feasibility reports</u> and <u>trouble reports</u>.

progress and activity reports

Progress reports provide details on the status of tasks involved in major workplace projects, whereas *activity reports* focus on the ongoing work of individual employees. Both are sometimes called *status reports*. Although many organizations use standardized forms for these reports, the content and structure shown in Figures 4–2 and 4–3 are typical.

Progress Reports

A progress report provides information to decision makers about the status of a project—whether it is on schedule and within budget. Progress reports are often submitted by a contracting company to a client company, as shown in Figure 4–2. They are used mainly for projects that involve many steps over a period of time and are issued at regular intervals to describe what has been done and what remains to be done. Progress

Memo

To: Noreen Rinaldo, Training Manager

From: Charles Lapinski, Senior Instructor   *CL*

Date: February 10, 2011

Subject: Adler's Basic English Program

As requested, I have investigated Adler Medical Instruments' (AMI's) Basic English Program to determine whether we might adopt a similar program.

The purpose of AMI's program is to teach medical technologists outside the United States who do not speak or read English to understand procedures written in a special 800-word vocabulary called *Basic English*. This program eliminates the need for AMI to translate its documentation into a number of different languages. The Basic English Program does not attempt to teach the medical technologists to be fluent in English but, rather, to recognize the 800 basic words that appear in Adler's documentation.

Course Analysis

The course teaches technologists a basic medical vocabulary in English; it does not provide training in medical terminology. Students must already know, in their own language, the meaning of medical vocabulary (e.g., the meaning of the word *hemostat*). Students must also have basic knowledge of their specialty, must be able to identify a part in an illustrated parts book, must have used AMI products for at least one year, and must be able to read and write in their own language.

Students are given an instruction manual, an illustrated book of equipment with parts and their English names, and pocket references containing the 800 words of the Basic English vocabulary plus the English names of parts. Students can write the corresponding word in their language beside the English word and then use the pocket reference as a bilingual dictionary. The course consists of 30 two-hour lessons, each lesson introducing approximately 27 words. No effort is made to teach pronunciation; the course teaches only recognition of the 800 words, which include 450 nouns; 70 verbs; 180 adjectives and adverbs; and 100 articles, prepositions, conjunctions, and pronouns.

Course Success

The 800-word vocabulary enables the writers of documentation to provide medical technologists with any information that might be required because the subject areas are strictly limited to usage, troubleshooting, safety, and operation of AMI medical equipment. All nonessential words (*apple*, *father*, *mountain*, and so on) are eliminated, as are most synonyms (for example, *under* appears, but *beneath* does not).

Conclusions and Recommendations

AMI's program appears to be quite successful, and a similar approach could also be appropriate for us. I see two possible ways in which we could use some or all of the elements of AMI's program: (1) in the preparation of our student manuals or (2) as AMI uses the program.

I think it would be unnecessary to use the Basic English methods in the preparation of manuals for *all* of our students. Most of our students are English speakers to whom an unrestricted vocabulary presents no problem.

As for our initiating a program similar to AMI's, we could create our own version of the Basic English vocabulary and write our instructional materials in it. Because our product lines are much broader than AMI's, however, we would need to create illustrated parts books for each of the different product lines.

FIGURE 4–1. Investigative Report

4

Business Writing
Documents
and Elements

Hobard Construction Company
9032 Salem Avenue
Lubbock, TX 79409

www.hobardcc.com
(808) 769-0832
Fax: (808) 769-5327

August 15, 2011

Walter M. Wazuski
County Administrator
109 Grand Avenue
Manchester, NH 03103

Dear Mr. Wazuski:

Subject: Progress Report 8 for July 29, 2011

The renovation of the County Courthouse is progressing on schedule and within budget. Although the cost of certain materials is higher than our original bid indicated, we expect to complete the project without exceeding the estimated costs because the speed with which the project is being completed will reduce overall labor expenses.

Costs
Materials used to date have cost $178,600, and labor costs have been $293,000 (including some subcontracted plumbing). Our estimate for the remainder of the materials is $159,000; remaining labor costs should not exceed $400,000.

Work Completed
As of July 29, we finished the installation of the circuit-breaker panels and meters, the level-one service outlets, and all the subfloor wiring. The upgrading of the courtroom, the upgrading of the records-storage room, and the replacement of the air-conditioning units are in the preliminary stages.

Work Scheduled
We have scheduled the upgrading of the courtroom to take place from August 29 to October 7, the upgrading of the records-storage room from October 10 to November 14, and the replacement of the air-conditioning units from November 21 to December 16. We see no difficulty in having the job finished by the scheduled date of December 23.

Sincerely yours,

Tran Nuguélen

Tran Nuguélen
ntran@hobardcc.com

FIGURE 4–2. Progress Report

reports help projects run smoothly by helping managers assign work, adjust schedules, allocate budgets, and order supplies and equipment. All progress reports for a particular project should have the same format.

The introduction to the first progress report should identify the project, methods used, necessary materials, expenditures, and completion date. Subsequent reports summarize the progress achieved since the preceding report and list the steps that remain to be taken. The body of the progress report should describe the project's status, including details such as schedules and costs, a statement of the work completed, and perhaps an estimate of future progress. The report ends with conclusions and recommendations about changes in the schedule, materials, techniques, and other information important to the project.

Activity Reports

Within an organization, employees often submit activity reports to managers on the status of ongoing projects. Managers may combine the activity reports of several individuals or teams into larger activity reports and, in turn, submit those larger reports to their own managers. The activity report shown in Figure 4–3 was submitted by a manager (Wayne Tribinski) who supervises 11 employees; the reader of the report (Kathryn Hunter) is Tribinski's manager.

Because the activity report is issued periodically (usually monthly) and contains material familiar to its readers, it normally needs no introduction or conclusion, although it may need a brief opening to provide context (Tab 1). Although the format varies from company to company, the following sections are typical: Current Projects, Current Problems, Plans for the Next Period, and Current Staffing Level (for managers).

proposals

4

Business Writing Documents and Elements

INTEROFFICE MEMO

Date: June 8, 2011

To: Kathryn Hunter, Director of IT

From: Wayne Tribinski, Manager, Applications Programs   *WT*

Subject: Activity Report for May 2011

We are dealing with the following projects and problems, as of May 31.

Projects

1. For the *Software Training Mailing Campaign*, we anticipate producing a set of labels for mailing software training information to customers by June 13.
2. The *Search Project* is on hold until the PL/I training has been completed, probably by the end of June.
3. The project to provide a database for the *Information Management System* has been expanded in scope to provide a database for all training activities. We are rescheduling the project to take the new scope into account.

Problems

The *Information Management System* has been delayed. The original schedule was based on the assumption that a systems analyst who was familiar with the system would work on this project. Instead, the project was assigned to a newly hired systems analyst who was inexperienced and required much more learning time than expected.

Bill Michaels, whose activity report is attached, is correcting a problem in the *CNG Software*. This correction may take a week.

Plans for Next Month

- Complete the *Software Training Mailing Campaign*.
- Resume the *Search Project*.
- Restart the project to provide a database on information management with a schedule that reflects its new scope.
- Write a report to justify the addition of two software developers to my department.
- Congratulate publicly the recipients of Meritorious Achievement Awards: Bill Thomasson and Nancy O'Rourke.

Current Staffing Level

Current staff: 11
Open requisitions: 0

Attachment

FIGURE 4–3. Activity Report

A proposal is a document written to persuade readers that what is proposed will benefit them by solving a problem or fulfilling a need. When you write a proposal, therefore, you must convince readers that they need what you are proposing, that it is practical and appropriate, and that you are the right person or organization to provide the proposed product or service. See also <u>persuasion</u> (Tab 1) and <u>"you" viewpoint</u> (Tab 10).

Proposal Strategies

For any proposal, support your assertions with relevant facts, statistics, and examples. Your supporting evidence must lead logically to your proposed plan of action or solution. Cite relevant sources of information that provide strong credibility to your argument. Avoid ambiguity, do not wander from your main point, and never make false claims. See <u>ethics in writing</u> (Tab 1).

Audience and Purpose.   Proposals often require more than one level of approval, so take into account all the readers in your <u>audience</u> (Tab 1). Consider especially their levels of technical knowledge of the subject. For example, if your primary reader is an expert on your subject but a supervisor who must also approve the proposal is not, provide an <u>executive summary</u> (Tab 5) written in nontechnical language for the supervisor. You might also include a <u>glossary</u> (Tab 5) of terms used in the body of the proposal or an <u>appendix</u> (Tab 5) that explains highly detailed information in nontechnical language. If your primary reader is not an expert but a supervisor is, write the proposal with the nonexpert in mind and include an appendix that contains the technical details.

Writing a persuasive proposal can be simplified by composing a concise statement of <u>purpose</u> (Tab 1)—the exact problem or opportunity that your proposal is designed to address and how you plan to persuade your readers to accept what you propose. Composing a purpose statement before outlining and writing your proposal will also help you and any collaborators understand the direction, scope, and goals of your proposal.

Project Management.   Proposal writers are often faced with writing high-quality, persuasive proposals under tight organizational deadlines. Dividing the task into manageable parts is the key to accomplishing your goals, especially when proposals involve substantial <u>collaborative writing</u> (Tab 1). For example, you might set deadlines for completing various proposal sections or stages of the writing process.*

*For help with project management, a good source is JoAnn T. Hackos, *Information Development: Managing Your Documentation Projects, Portfolio, and People* (Indianapolis, IN: Wiley, 2007).

4

Business Writing
Documents
and Elements

Writer's Checklist: Writing Persuasive Proposals

☑ Analyze your audience carefully to determine how to best meet your readers' needs or requirements.

☑ Write a concise purpose statement at the outset to clarify your proposal's goals.

☑ Divide the writing task into manageable segments and develop a timeline for completing tasks.

☑ Review the descriptions of proposal contexts, structure, and types in this entry.

☑ Focus on the proposal's benefits to readers and anticipate their questions or objections.

☑ Incorporate evidence to support the claims of your proposal.

☑ Select an appropriate, visually appealing format. See <u>layout and design</u> (Tab 6).

☑ Use a confident, positive <u>tone</u> (Tab 10) throughout the proposal.

Proposal Context and Types.   Proposals are written within a specific <u>context</u> (Tab 1). As that entry describes, understanding the context will help you determine the most appropriate writing strategy. In general, to persuade those within your organization to make a change or an improvement or perhaps to fund a project, you would write an *internal proposal.* To persuade those outside your company to agree to a plan or take a course of action, you would write an *external proposal,* such as a sales or grant proposal. A *sales proposal* seeks to convince a potential customer to purchase your products or services. A *grant proposal* requests funding for projects solicited by government agencies, research foundations, educational institutions, and other nonprofit organizations.

Internal Proposals

The purpose of an internal proposal is to suggest a change or an improvement within an organization. Often in memo format, it is addressed to a superior within the organization who has the authority to accept or reject the proposal. These proposals are typically reviewed by one or more departments for cost, practicality, and potential benefits, so take account of all relevant audience members. Two common types of internal proposals—informal and formal—are often distinguished from each other by the frequency with which they are written and by the degree of change they propose.

Informal Internal Proposals.   Informal internal proposals are the most frequent type of proposal and typically include small spending requests, requests for permission to hire new employees or increase salaries, and requests to attend conferences or purchase new equipment. In writing informal or routine proposals, highlight any key benefits to be realized.

 WEB LINK **INTERNAL PROPOSALS**

For examples of brief solicited and unsolicited proposals, see *bedfordstmartins.com/alred*, and select *ModelDoc Central*.

Formal Internal Proposals.   Formal internal proposals usually involve requests to commit relatively large sums of money. They are usually organized into sections that describe a problem, propose a solution and recommendation, and offer to implement the recommendation. The body, in turn, is further divided into sections to reflect the subject matter. The proposal may begin with a section describing the background or history of an issue and go on to discuss options for addressing the issue in separate sections.

The *introduction* of your internal proposal should establish that a problem exists and needs a solution. This section is sometimes called a "problem statement." If the audience is not convinced that there is a problem, your proposal will not succeed. After you identify the problem, summarize your proposed solution and indicate its benefits and estimated total cost. Notice how the introduction in Figure 4–4 states the problem directly and then summarizes the writer's proposed solution.

 WEB LINK **COMPLETE INTERNAL PROPOSAL**

For a complete version of Figure 4–4 with annotations, see *bedfordstmartins.com/alred*, and select *ModelDoc Central*.

The *body* of your internal proposal should offer a practical solution to the problem and provide the details necessary to inform and to persuade your readers. In the body, itemize the problem you are addressing; the methodology of your proposed solution; information about equipment, materials, and staff; cost breakdowns; and a detailed schedule. Figure 4–4 provides a section from the body of an internal proposal.

The *conclusion* of your internal proposal should tie everything together, restate your recommendation, and close with a spirit of cooperation (offering to set up a meeting, supply additional information,

4

Business Writing Documents and Elements

ABO, Inc.
Interoffice Memo

To: Joan Marlow, Director, Human Resources Division

From: Leslie Galusha, Chief
           Employee Benefits Department   *LG*

Date: June 15, 2011

Subject: Employee Fitness and Health-Care Costs

Health-care and workers' compensation insurance costs at ABO, Inc., have risen 100 percent over the last five years. In 2005, costs were $5,675 per employee per year; in 2011, they have reached $11,560 per employee per year. This doubling of costs mirrors a national trend, with health-care costs anticipated to continue to rise at the same rate for the next ten years. Controlling these escalating expenses will be essential. They are eating into ABO's profit margin because the company currently pays 70 percent of the costs for employee coverage.

Healthy employees bring direct financial benefits to companies in the form of lower employee insurance costs, lower absenteeism rates, and reduced turnover. Regular physical exercise promotes fit, healthy people by reducing the risk of coronary heart disease, diabetes, osteoporosis, hypertension, and stress-related problems. I propose that to promote regular, vigorous physical exercise for our employees, ABO implement a health-care program that focuses on employee fitness. . . .

Problem of Health-Care Costs

The U.S. Department of Health and Human Services (HHS) recently estimated that health-care costs in the United States will triple by the year 2020. Corporate expenses for health care are rising at such a fast rate that, if unchecked, in seven years they will significantly erode corporate profits.

According to HHS, people who do not participate in a regular and vigorous exercise program incur double the health-care costs and are hospitalized 30 percent more days than people who exercise regularly. Nonexercisers are also 41 percent more likely to submit medical claims over $10,000 at some point during their careers than are those who exercise regularly.

These figures are further supported by data from independent studies. A model created by the National Institutes of Health (NIH) . . .

FIGURE 4–4. Special-Purpose Internal Proposal (Introduction and Body)

Joan Marlow   2   June 15, 2011

Proposed Solutions for ABO
The benefits of regular, vigorous physical activity for employees and companies
are compelling. To achieve these benefits at ABO, I propose that we choose
from one of two possible options: Build in-house fitness centers at our
warehouse facilities, or offer employees several options for membership at a
national fitness club. The following analysis compares . . .

Conclusion and Recommendation
I recommend that ABO, Inc., participate in the corporate membership
program at AeroFitness Clubs, Inc., by subsidizing employee memberships.
By subsidizing memberships, ABO shows its commitment to the importance
of a fit workforce. Club membership allows employees at all five ABO
warehouses to participate in the program. The more employees who
participate, the greater the long-term savings. . . .

Enrolling employees in the corporate program at AeroFitness would allow
them to receive a one-month free trial membership. Those interested
in continuing could then join the club and pay half of the one-time
membership fee. . . .

Implementing this program will help ABO, Inc., reduce its health-care
costs while building stronger employee relations by offering employees
a desirable benefit. If this proposal is adopted, I have some additional
thoughts about publicizing the program to encourage employee
participation. I look forward to discussing the details of this proposal
with you and answering any questions you may have.

FIGURE 4–4. Special-Purpose Internal Proposal (*continued*) (Conclusion)

or provide any other assistance that might be needed). Keep your
conclusion brief, as in Figure 4–4.

If your proposal cites information that you obtained through
research, such as published reports, government statistics, or interviews,
follow the conclusion with a works-cited list that provides complete
publication information for each source.

External Proposals

External proposals are prepared for clients and customers outside your
company. They are either submitted in response to a request for goods and
services from another organization (a *solicited proposal*) or sent to them
without a prior request (an *unsolicited proposal*). Grant proposals, a type of
external proposal, are usually submitted to nonprofit organizations to
request funding to support research that could benefit the funding organization. These include medical and research institutions, charitable foundations, and government agencies at all levels (local, state, federal).

Solicited Proposals.   To find the best method of meeting their needs and the most-qualified company to help reach that goal, procuring organizations commonly issue a request for proposal (RFP) or an invitation for bids (IFB) that asks competing companies such as yours to bid for a job.

An RFP often defines a need or problem and allows those who respond to propose possible solutions. The procuring organization generally distributes an RFP to several predetermined vendors. The RFP usually outlines the specific requirements for the ideal solution. For example, if an organization needs an accounting system, it may require the proposed system to create customized reports. The RFP also may contain specific formatting requirements, such as page length, font type and size, margin widths, <u>headings</u> (Tab 6), numbering systems, sections, and appendix items. When responding to RFPs, follow their requirements exactly—proposals that do not provide the required information, do not follow the required format, or miss the submittal deadline are usually considered "nonresponsive" and immediately rejected.

In contrast to an RFP, an IFB is commonly issued by federal, state, and local government agencies to solicit bids on clearly defined products or services. An IFB is restrictive, binding the bidder to produce an item or a service that meets the exact requirements of the organization issuing the IFB. The goods or services are defined in the IFB by references to performance standards stated in technical specifications. Bidders must be prepared to prove that their product will meet all requirements of the specifications. The procuring organization generally publishes its IFB on its Web site or in a specialized venue, such as Federal Business Opportunities at *www.fbo.gov*. Like RFPs, IFBs usually have specific format requirements; proposals that do not follow the required format can be rejected without review.

 WEB LINK **SAMPLE REQUEST FOR PROPOSAL**

To review a sample RFP, see *bedfordstmartins.com/alred*, and select *ModelDoc Central*.

Unsolicited Proposals.   Unsolicited proposals are those submitted to a company without a prior request for a proposal. Companies often operate for years with a problem they have never recognized (unnecessarily high maintenance costs, for example, or poor inventory-control methods). Many unsolicited proposals are preceded by a letter of inquiry that specifies the problem or unmet need to determine whether there is any potential interest. If you receive a positive response, you would conduct a detailed study of the prospective client's needs to determine whether you can be of help and, if so, exactly how. You would then prepare a formal proposal on the basis of your study. Many sales proposals note that the offer is valid for a limited period (often 90 days).

Sales Proposals.   The sales proposal, a major marketing tool for business and industry, is a company's offer to provide specific goods or services to a potential buyer within a specified period of time and for a specified price. The primary purpose of a sales proposal is to demonstrate that the prospective customer's purchase of the seller's products or services will solve a problem, improve operations, or offer other benefits.

Sales proposals vary greatly in length and sophistication. Some are a page or two written by one person, others are many pages written collaboratively by several people, and still others are hundreds of pages written by a proposal-writing team. See also <u>collaborative writing</u> (Tab 1).

Simple sales proposals typically follow the introduction-body-conclusion pattern. Long sales proposals must accommodate a greater variety of information and are organized to include some or all of the following sections specified in the RFP:

- Cover, or transmittal, letter
- Title page
- Executive or project summary
- General description of products
- Detailed solution or rationale
- Cost analysis
- Delivery schedule or work plan
- Site-preparation description
- Training requirements
- Statement of responsibilities
- Description of vendor
- Organizational sales pitch (optional)
- Conclusion (optional)
- Appendixes (optional)

A long sales proposal begins with a cover letter—sometimes called a *transmittal letter*—that expresses your appreciation for the opportunity to submit your proposal and for any assistance you may have received in studying the customer's requirements. The letter should acknowledge any previous positive association with the customer. Then it should summarize the recommendations offered in the proposal and express your confidence that they will satisfy the customer's needs. Transmittal letters often list the physical documents attached or enclosed to help readers keep the associated documents together.

A title page and an <u>executive summary</u> (Tab 5)—sometimes called a *project summary*—follow the cover letter. The title page contains the title of the proposal, the date of submission, the company to which it is being submitted, your company's name, and any symbol or logo that identifies your company. The executive summary is addressed to the decision maker who will ultimately accept or reject the proposal and should summarize in nontechnical language how you plan to approach the work.

If your proposal offers products as well as services, it should include a general description of the products. In many cases, product descriptions will already exist as company boilerplate; be sure to check your company's files or server for such information before drafting a description from scratch.

⚡ ETHICS NOTE In the workplace, employees often borrow material freely from in-house manuals, reports, and other company documents. Using such boilerplate is neither plagiarism nor a violation of copyright. ✦

Following the executive summary and the general description, explain exactly how you plan to do what you are proposing. This section, called the *detailed solution* or *rationale*, will be read by specialists who can understand and evaluate your plan. It usually begins with a statement of the customer's problem, follows with a statement of the solution, and concludes with a statement of the benefits to the customer. In some proposals, the headings "Problem" and "Solution" are used for this section.

In the following section, a cost analysis itemizes the estimated cost of all the products and services that you are offering, and the delivery schedule—also called a *work plan*—commits you to a specific timetable for providing those products and services.

If your recommendations include modifying your customer's physical facilities by moving walls, adding increased electrical capacity, and the like, include a site-preparation description that details the modifications required. In some proposals, the headings "Facilities" and "Equipment" are used for this section.

If the products and services you are proposing require training the customer's employees, specify the required training and its cost.

To prevent misunderstandings about what you and your customer's responsibilities will be, draw up a statement of responsibilities that explains in detail the tasks solely your responsibility and those solely the customer's responsibility. Also toward the end of the proposal include a description-of-vendor section, which gives a profile of your company, its history, and its present position in the industry. The description-of-vendor section typically includes a list of people or subcontractors and the duties they will perform. The résumés (Tab 8) of key personnel may also be placed here or in an appendix.

An organizational sales pitch usually follows the description-of-vendor section and is designed to sell the company and its general capability in the field. The sales pitch promotes the company and concludes the proposal on an upbeat note.

Some long sales proposals include a conclusions (Tab 1) section that summarizes the proposal's salient points, stresses your company's strengths, and includes information about whom the potential client can contact for further information. It may also end with a request for the date the work will begin should the proposal be accepted.

Some proposals include <u>appendixes</u> (Tab 5) made up of statistical analyses, maps, charts, tables, and résumés of the principal staff assigned to the project. Appendixes to proposals should contain only supplemental information; the primary information should appear in the body of the proposal.

 WEB LINK **SAMPLE SALES PROPOSAL**

For a complete annotated version of a sales proposal, as well as additional sample proposals and the RFP to which the sales proposal responded, see *bedfordstmartins.com/alred*, and select *Links Library*.

Grant Proposals.   Grant proposals are written to nonprofit and government organizations to request the approval of and funding for projects that solve a problem or fulfill a need. A scientist, for example, may write a grant to the National Institutes of Health (NIH) to request a specific sum of money to conduct research on a new cancer therapy, or the executive director of Habitat for Humanity may write a grant to a local government requesting funding to purchase supplies to construct new housing for disadvantaged families in the area. Granting organizations typically post opportunities, along with detailed application guidelines, on their Web sites, and usually specify their requirements for the format and content of proposals. Although application guidelines may differ from one organization to another, grant proposals generally require the following sections at a minimum:

- Cover letter
- Title page
- Application form
- Introduction/summary
- Literature review (research emphasis)
- Project narrative
  - *Project description*
- *Project outcomes*
- *Budget*
- *Delivery Schedule*
- Organization description
- Conclusion
- Attachments (appendixes)

 WEB LINK **SAMPLE GRANT PROPOSAL**

For samples of grant proposals, as well as the full text of this grant proposal, go to *bedfordstmartins.com/alred*, and select *ModelDoc Central*.

COVER LETTER. Usually one page long, the cover letter should identify who you are and your affiliation. It should specify the grant that you are applying for, summarize the proposed project, and include the amount of funding you are requesting. See <u>cover messages</u> (Tab 7).

TITLE PAGE. The title page is the grant-proposal cover. On a single page, show the <u>title</u> of the project, names of team members and their affiliations, date submitted, and the name of the recipient's organization.

APPLICATION FORM. Particularly in electronic grant applications, an application form may replace the cover letter and title page. This form, which may be one or more pages, may require you to check boxes, fill in blanks, or insert brief descriptions or other information into text boxes or blank spaces. A word or character limit (typically 250 to 400 words) may be imposed or enforced. An official signature is often required. This section may request detailed information about the applicant organization, such as staff or board of directors' demographic composition or its human resources policies.

INTRODUCTION. The introduction is your proposal at a glance—it briefly describes (within a given limit) the problem to be solved and sketches the expected outcomes of your grant proposal. If substantial research is involved, you may also describe your proposed research methods (interviews, questionnaires, videotapes, observations, etc.) in a separate paragraph. See also <u>research</u> (Tab 3) and <u>abstracts</u> (Tab 5).

LITERATURE REVIEW. The literature review lists the relevant research sources you consulted in preparing your proposal. Also called *References* or *Works Cited*, this section allows reviewers of your proposal to assess your familiarity with current research in the field. Is your research up-to-date? thorough? pertinent? Be selective: Include only relevant journal articles, books, interviews, broadcasts, <u>blogs and forums</u> (Tab 2), and other sources.

PROJECT NARRATIVE. The project narrative is the heart of the proposal. Describe in detail the scope of the work, expected outcomes, list of tasks, schedule from start to finish, and proposed cost. Be specific and thorough.

Project Description

The project description includes an overview of the project and details of how the research or program will be conducted (its methodology). In nonresearch proposals, include a succinct *statement of need*—also called a *case statement*—which presents the facts and evidence that support the need for the project. The information presented can come from authorities in the field, as well as from your agency's own experience or research.

A logical and persuasive statement of need demonstrates that your company or nonprofit organization sufficiently understands the situation and is therefore capable of addressing it satisfactorily. Emphasize the benefits of the proposed activities for the grant maker's intended constituency or target population and why your solution to the problem or plan to fulfill the need should be approved.

Project Outcomes

Having described the preparations for the program, the grant writer must describe the outcomes or deliverables of the proposal. In other words, what can the funding organization expect as a result of the time, labor, and funding they have invested in the program. Outcomes are stated as quantifiable objectives—improvements in reading scores, volume of carbon emission reductions, aerobic fitness measures, and so on. Grant proposals, especially those solicited by government agencies, also must provide detailed plans for collecting, analyzing, and interpreting data to evaluate the success or failure of the research or program in achieving the stated outcomes.

Project Budget

Next, include a budget narrative section that provides a detailed listing of costs for personnel, equipment, building renovations, and other grant-related expenses. This information must be clear, accurate, and in a format easily grasped by those evaluating the data (usually in a table, Tab 6). If your proposal is approved, you are being entrusted with funds belonging to someone else, and you are accountable for them. Your cost estimates may also be subject to changes over which you have no control, such as price increases for equipment, software, or consulting assistance. The project may also require ongoing funding following completion of the grant's tasks. Either estimate such costs or note that they will appear in a section called *Future Funding*.

Project Schedule

Prepare a schedule of tasks that need to be performed to complete the project. Arrange them as bulleted points in sequence from first to last with due dates for each, or present them in a table or graph (Tab 6).

ORGANIZATION DESCRIPTION. The organization description may follow the Introduction or it may be placed just prior to the Conclusion. Describe the applicant organization briefly in terms of mission, history, qualifications, and credibility (significant, related accomplishments), taking care to include all information requested in the RFP or grant guidelines. Grant makers consider not only the merits of the proposed program or research but also your organization's standing in the community and similar accomplishments.

4

Business Writing
Documents
and Elements

PROPOSAL CONCLUSION.   The conclusion, a brief wrap-up section, emphasizes the benefits or advantages of your project. This section provides one more opportunity for you to give the funding organization a reason why your proposal merits its approval. Also express your appreciation for the opportunity to submit the proposal. Finally, close with a statement of your willingness to provide further information. Emphasize the benefits of the research, program, or other activities for the grant maker's intended constituency or target population.

ATTACHMENTS.   Funding organizations request supporting information, such as nonprofit documentation, copies of legal documents, or lists of information that you may need to design and compose yourself. Follow all instructions from the grant maker meticulously because the failure to include requested information may be grounds for rejection or lack of review. Provide a comprehensive list of attachments and clearly label each item to guide the grant reviewer in evaluating the proposal package.

 WEB LINK RESOURCES FOR PREPARING GRANT PROPOSALS

For useful Web sources for preparing grant proposals, go to *bedfordstmartins .com/alred*, and select *Links Library*.

---

reports

A report is an organized presentation of factual information, often aimed at multiple audiences (Tab 1), that may present the results of an investigation, a trip, or a research project. For any report—whether formal or informal—assessing the readers' needs is essential. Following is a list of report entries in this book:

feasibility reports 101	trip reports 121
formal reports 130	trouble reports 122
investigative reports 102	
progress and activity reports 102	

Formal reports often present the results of long-term projects or those that involve multiple participants. (See also collaborative writing, Tab 1.) Such projects may be done either for your own organization or as a contractual requirement for another organization. Formal reports generally follow a precise format and include such elements as abstracts (Tab 5) and executive summaries (Tab 5). See also proposals.

Informal and short reports normally run from a few paragraphs to a few pages and ordinarily include only an introduction (Tab 1), a body, a conclusion (Tab 1), and (if necessary) recommendations. Because of their brevity, informal reports are customarily written as correspondence (Tab 7), including letters (Tab 7), memos (Tab 7), and e-mails (Tab 2).

The introduction announces the subject of the report, states its purpose (Tab 1), and gives any essential background information. It may also summarize the conclusions, findings, or recommendations made in the report. The body presents a clearly organized account of the report's subject—the results of a test, the status of a project, and other details readers may need. The amount of detail to include depends on your reader's knowledge, your scope (Tab 1), and the complexity of the subject.

The conclusion summarizes your findings and interprets their significance for readers. In some reports, a final, separate section gives recommendations; in others, the conclusions and the recommendations are combined into one section. This final section makes suggestions for a course of action based on the data you have presented. See also persuasion (Tab 1).

titles

Titles are important because many readers decide whether to read documents—such as reports, e-mails (Tab 2), and memos (Tab 7)—based on their titles. Titles are also crucial for filing and retrieving of documents. This entry discusses both creating titles and referring to them in your writing. For advice on titles for figures and tables, see visuals (Tab 6).

Reports and Long Documents

Titles for reports, proposals, articles, and similar documents should identify the document's topic, reflect its tone (Tab 10), and indicate its scope (Tab 1) and purpose (Tab 1) as in the following title of an academic article.

- "Using Chaos Theory to Evaluate Small Business Growth Patterns"

Such titles should be concise but not so short that they are not specific. For example, the title "Chaos Theory and Small Businesses" announces the topic and might be appropriate for a book, but it does not answer important questions that readers of an article would expect, such as "What does the article say about the relationship between chaos theory and small businesses?" and "What aspect of small businesses is related to chaos theory?"

Avoid titles with such redundancies as "Notes on," "Studies on," or "A Report on." However, works like annual reports or <u>feasibility reports</u> should be identified as such in the title because this information specifies the purpose and scope of the report. For titles of <u>progress and activity reports</u>, indicate the dates in a subtitle ("Quarterly Report on Hospital Admission Rates: January–March 2011"). Avoid using technical shorthand, such as chemical formulas, and other <u>abbreviations</u> (Tab 12) in your title unless the work is addressed exclusively to specialists in the field. For multivolume publications, repeat the series title on each volume and include the subtitle and number of each volume.

Titles should not use the sentence form, except for titles of articles in newsletters and magazines that ask a rhetorical question.

* "Is Online Learning Right for You?"

Memos, E-mail, and Internet Postings

Subject lines of memos, e-mail messages, and Internet postings function as titles and should concisely and accurately describe the topic of the message. Because recipients often use subject-line titles to prioritize and sort their <u>correspondence</u> (Tab 7), such titles must be specific.

| VAGUE | Subject: Tuition Reimbursement |
| SPECIFIC | Subject: Tuition Reimbursement for Time-Management Seminar |

Although the title in the subject line announces your topic, you should still include an opening that provides <u>context</u> (Tab 1) for the message.

Formatting Titles

Capitalization. Capitalize the initial letters of the first and last words of a title as well as all major words in the title. Do not capitalize articles (*a, an, the*), coordinating conjunctions (*and, but*), or short prepositions (*at, in, on, of*) unless they begin or end the title (*The Lives of a Cell*). Capitalize prepositions in titles if they contain five or more letters (*Between, Since, Until, After*).

Italics. Use <u>italics</u> (Tab 12) or underlining when referring to titles of separately published works, such as books, periodicals, newspapers, pamphlets, brochures, legal cases, movies, television programs, and Web sites.

* *Turning Workplace Conflict into Collaboration* [book] by Joyce Richards was reviewed in the *New York Times* [newspaper].
* We will include a link to *The Weather Channel* (*www.weather.com*).

Abbreviations of such titles are italicized if their spelled-out forms would be italicized.

- *NEJM* for the *New England Journal of Medicine*

Italicize the titles of compact and digital video discs, videotapes, plays, long poems, paintings, sculptures, and long musical works.

Quotation Marks.   Use quotation marks (Tab 12) when referring to parts of publications, such as chapters of books and articles or sections within periodicals.

- Her chapter titled "Effects of Government Regulations on Motorcycle Safety" in the book *Government Regulation and the Economy* was cited in a recent article, "No-Fault Insurance and Motorcycles," published in *American Motorcyclist* magazine.

Titles of reports, essays, short poems, short musical works (including songs), short stories, and single episodes of radio and television programs are also enclosed in quotation marks.

Special Cases.   Some titles, by convention, are not set off by quotation marks, underlining, or italics. Such titles follow standard practice for capitalization and the practice of the organization.

- Business Writing [college course title], Old Testament, Magna Carta, the Constitution, Lincoln's Gettysburg Address, the Lands' End Catalog

For citing titles in references and works cited, see documenting sources (Tab 3).

trip reports

A trip report provides a permanent record of a business trip and its accomplishments. It provides managers with essential information about the results of the trip and can enable other staff members to benefit from the information. See also reports.

A trip report is normally written as a memo (Tab 7) or an e-mail (Tab 2) and addressed to an immediate superior, as shown in Figure 4–5. The subject line identifies the destination and dates of the trip. The body of the report explains why you made the trip, whom you visited, and what you accomplished. The report should devote a brief section to each major activity and may include a heading (Tab 6) for each section. You need not give equal space to each activity—instead, elaborate on the more important ones. Follow the body of the report with the appropriate conclusions and recommendations. Finally, if required, attach a record of expenses to the trip report.

From: James D. Kerson <jdkerson@psys.com>
To: Roberto Camacho <rcamacho@psys.com>
Sent: Wed, 12 Jan 2011 12:16:30 EST
Subject: Trip to Smith Electric Co., Huntington, West Virginia,
                January 5–6, 2011

Attachments: 📄 Expense Report.xls (25 KB)

I visited the Smith Electric Company in Huntington, West Virginia, to determine the cause of a recurring failure in our Model 247 printer.

Problem
The printer stopped printing periodically for no apparent reason. Repeated efforts to bring it back online eventually succeeded, but the problem recurred at irregular intervals. Neither customer personnel operating the printer nor the local maintenance specialist was able to solve the problem.

Action
On January 5, I met with Ms. Ruth Bernardi, the Office Manager, who explained the problem. My troubleshooting did not reveal the cause of the problem then or on January 6.

Only when I tested the logic cable did I find that it contained a broken wire. I replaced the logic cable and then ran all the normal printer test patterns to make sure no other problems existed. All patterns were positive, so I turned the printer over to the customer.

Conclusion
There are over 12,000 of these printers in the field, and to my knowledge this is the first occurrence of a bad cable. I believe the logic cable problem found at Smith Electric Company reflects the recurring failures during 2010.

================================

James D. Kerson, Product Analyst
Printer Systems, Inc.
1366 Federal St., Allentown, PA 18101
(610) 747-9955 Fax: (610) 747-9956
jdkerson@psys.com
www.psys.com
================================

FIGURE 4–5. Trip Report Sent as E-mail (with Attachment)

trouble reports

The trouble report is used to analyze such events as accidents, equipment failures, or health emergencies. For example, the report shown in Figure 4–6 describes an accident involving personal injury. The report assesses the causes of the problem and suggests changes

Consolidated Energy, Inc.

To: Marvin Lundquist, Vice President
           Administrative Services

From: Kalo Katarlan, Safety Officer   *KK*
           Field Service Operations

Date: August 19, 2011

Subject: Field Service Employee Accident on August 3, 2011

The following is an initial report of an accident that occurred on Wednesday, August 3, 2011, involving John Markley, and that resulted in two days of lost time.

Accident Summary

John Markley stopped by a rewiring job on German Road. Chico Ruiz was working there, stringing new wire, and John was checking with Chico about the materials he wanted for framing a pole. Some tree trimming had been done in the area, and John offered to help remove some of the debris by loading it into the pickup truck he was driving. While John was loading branches into the bed of the truck, a piece broke off in his right hand and struck his right eye.

Accident Details

1. John's right eye was struck by a piece of tree branch. John had just undergone laser surgery on his right eye on Monday, August 1, to reattach his retina.
2. John immediately covered his right eye with his hand, and Chico Ruiz gave him a paper towel with ice to cover his eye and help ease the pain.

7. On Thursday, August 4, John returned to his eye surgeon. Although bruised, his eye was not damaged, and the surgically reattached retina was still in place.

Recommendations

To prevent a recurrence of such an accident, the Safety Department will require the following actions in the future:

- When working around and moving debris such as tree limbs or branches, all service-crew employees must wear safety eyewear with side shields.
- All service-crew employees must always consider the possibility of shock for an injured employee. If crew members cannot leave the job site to care for the injured employee, someone on the crew must call for assistance from the Service Center. The Service Center phone number is printed in each service-crew member's handbook.

4

Business Writing
Documents
and Elements

FIGURE 4–6. Trouble Report (Using Printed Memo)

necessary to prevent its recurrence. Because it is usually an internal document, a trouble report normally uses the format of a <u>memo</u> (Tab 7).

In the subject line of the memo, state the precise problem you are reporting. In the body of the memo, provide a detailed, precise description of the problem. What happened? Where and when did the problem occur? Was anybody hurt? Was there any property damage? Was there a work stoppage?

◆ ETHICS NOTE Because insurance claims, workers' compensation awards, and even lawsuits may hinge on the information contained in a trouble report, be sure to include precise times, dates, locations, treatment of injuries, names of any witnesses, and any other crucial information. (Notice the careful use of language and factual detail in Figure 4–6.) Be thorough and accurate in your analysis of the problem and support any judgments or conclusions with facts. Be objective: Always use a neutral <u>tone</u> (Tab 10) and avoid assigning blame. If you speculate about the cause of the problem, make it clear to your readers that you are speculating. See also <u>ethics in writing</u> (Tab 1). ✦

In your conclusion, state what has been or will be done to correct the conditions that led to the problem. That may include, for example, recommendations for training in safety practices, improved equipment, and protective clothing. See also <u>reports</u>.

Formal Reports

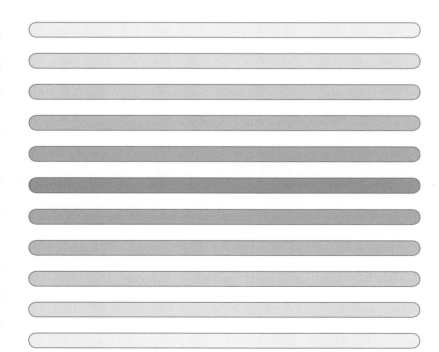

Preview

This section includes entries about the formal report and its components. Although the number and arrangement of elements in formal reports vary, the guidelines given in the **formal reports** entry follow the most common pattern. This section also includes entries that provide more detailed guidance for preparing key sections often included in formal reports. A sample formal report appears on pages 137–152. For specific types of reports and other documents that may be presented in formal-report form, see Tab 4, "Business Writing Documents and Elements."

abstracts

An abstract summarizes and highlights the major points of a formal report, trade journal article, dissertation, or other long work. Its primary purpose is to enable readers to decide whether to read the work in full. For a discussion of how summaries differ from abstracts, see executive summaries.

Although abstracts, typically 200 to 250 words long, are published with the longer works they condense, they can also be published separately in periodical indexes and by abstracting services (see research, Tab 3). For this reason, an abstract must be readable apart from the original document.

Types of Abstracts

Depending on the kind of information they contain, abstracts are often classified as descriptive or informative. A *descriptive abstract* summarizes the purpose, scope, and methods used to arrive at the reported findings. It is a slightly expanded table of contents in sentence and paragraph form. A descriptive abstract need not be longer than several sentences. An *informative abstract* is an expanded version of the descriptive abstract. In addition to information about the purpose, scope, and research methods used, the informative abstract summarizes any results, conclusions, and recommendations. The informative abstract retains the tone and essential scope of the original work, omitting its details. The first two paragraphs of the abstract shown in Figure 5–1 alone would be descriptive; with the addition of the paragraphs that detail the findings and conclusions of the report, the abstract becomes informative.

The type of abstract you should write depends on your audience (Tab 1) and the organization or publication for which you are writing. Informative abstracts work best for wide audiences that need to know conclusions and recommendations; descriptive abstracts work best for compilations, such as proceedings and progress reports, that do not contain conclusions or recommendations.

Writing Strategies

Write the abstract *after* finishing the report or document. Otherwise, the abstract may not accurately reflect the longer work. Begin with a topic sentence that announces the subject and scope of your original document. Then, using the major and minor headings of your outline or table of contents to distinguish primary ideas from secondary ones, decide what material is relevant to your abstract. (See outlining, Tab 1.) Write with clarity and conciseness (Tab 10), eliminating unnecessary words and ideas. Do not, however, become so terse that you

5

ABSTRACT

Purpose

This report investigates the long-term effects of long-distance running on the bones, joints, and general health of runners aged 50 to 72. The Sports Medicine Institute of Columbia Hospital sponsored this investigation, first to decide whether to add a geriatric unit to the Institute, and second to determine whether physicians should recommend long-distance running for their older patients.

Methods and scope

The investigation is based on recent studies conducted at Stanford University and the University of Florida. The Stanford study tested and compared male and female long-distance runners aged 50 to 72 with a control group of runners and nonrunners. The groups were matched by sex, race, education, and occupation. The Florida study used only male runners who had run at least 20 miles a week for five years and compared them with a group of runners and nonrunners. Both studies based findings on medical histories and on physical and X-ray examinations.

Descriptive section

Findings

Both studies conclude that long-distance running is not associated with increased degenerative joint disease. Control groups were more prone to spur formation, sclerosis, and joint-space narrowing and showed more joint degeneration than runners. Female long-distance runners exhibited somewhat more sclerosis in knee joints and the lumbar spine area than matched control subjects. Both studies support the role of exercise in retarding bone loss with aging. The investigation concludes that the health-risk factors are fewer for long-distance runners than for those less active aged 50 to 72.

Conclusions

The investigation recommends that the Sports Medicine Institute of Columbia Hospital consider the development of a geriatric unit a priority and that it inform physicians that an exercise program that includes long-distance running can be beneficial to their aging patients' health.

Recommendations

iii

FIGURE 5–1. Informative Abstract (from a Report)

omit articles (*a, an, the*) and important transitional words and phrases (*however, therefore, but, next*). Write complete sentences, but avoid stringing together a group of short sentences end to end; instead, combine ideas by using <u>subordination</u> (Tab 10) and <u>parallel structure</u> (Tab 10). Spell out all but the most common <u>abbreviations</u> (Tab 12). In a report, an abstract follows the title page and is numbered page iii.

appendixes

An appendix, located at the end of a <u>formal report</u>, <u>proposal</u> (Tab 4), or other long document, supplements or clarifies the information in the body of the document. Appendixes (or *appendices*) can provide information that is too detailed or lengthy for the primary <u>audience</u> (Tab 1) of the document. For example, an appendix could contain such material as maps, statistical analysis, <u>résumés</u> (Tab 8) of key personnel involved in a proposed project, or other documents needed by secondary readers.

A document may have more than one appendix, with each providing only one type of information. When you include more than one appendix, arrange them in the order they are mentioned in the body of the document. Begin each appendix on a new page, and identify each with a letter, starting with the letter *A* ("Appendix A: Sample Questionnaire"). If you have only one appendix, title it simply "Appendix." List the titles and beginning page numbers of the appendixes in the <u>table of contents</u>.

executive summaries

An executive summary consolidates the principal points of a report or proposal. Executive summaries differ from <u>abstracts</u> in that readers scan abstracts to decide whether to read the work in full. However, an executive summary may be the only section of a longer work read by many readers, so it must accurately and concisely represent the original document. It should restate the document's purpose, scope, methods, findings, conclusions, and recommendations, as well as summarize how results were obtained or the reasons for the recommendations. Executive summaries tend to be about 10 percent of the length of the documents they summarize and generally follow the same sequence.

Write the executive summary so that it can be read independently of the report or proposal. Executive summaries may occasionally include a figure, table, or footnote—if that information is essential to the summary. However, do not refer by number to figures, tables, or references contained elsewhere in the document. See Figure 5–2 (pages 140–141), which includes an executive summary of a report on the disposition of ethics cases in an aircraft corporation.

Writer's Checklist: Writing Executive Summaries

☑ Write the executive summary after you have completed the original document.

☑ Avoid or define terminology that may not be familiar to your intended <u>audience</u> (Tab 1).

☑ Spell out all uncommon symbols and <u>abbreviations</u> (Tab 12).

☑ Make the summary concise, but do not omit transitional words and phrases (*however, moreover, therefore, for example, next*).

☑ Include only information discussed in the original document.

☑ Place the executive summary at the very beginning of the body of the report, as described in <u>formal reports</u>.

formal reports

Formal reports are usually written accounts of major projects that require substantial <u>research</u> (Tab 3), and they often involve more than one writer. See also <u>collaborative writing</u> (Tab 1).

Most formal reports are divided into three primary parts—front matter, body, and back matter—each of which contains a number of elements. The number and arrangement of the elements may vary, depending on the subject, the length of the report, and the kinds of material covered. Further, many organizations have a preferred style for formal reports and furnish guidelines for report writers to follow. If you are not required to follow a specific style, use the format recommended in this entry. The following list includes most of the elements a formal report might contain, in the order they typically appear. (The items shown with page numbers appear in the sample formal report on pages 136–152.) Often, a <u>cover</u> letter (Tab 7) or <u>memo</u> (Tab 7) precedes the front matter and identifies the report by title, the person or persons to whom it is being sent, the reason it was written, the <u>scope</u> (Tab 1), and any information that the <u>audience</u> (Tab 1) considers important, as shown on page 136.

FRONT MATTER

Title Page (137)

Abstract (138)

Table of Contents (139)

List of Figures

List of Tables
Foreword
Preface
List of Abbreviations and Symbols

BODY

Executive Summary (140–141)
Introduction (142–144)
Text (including headings) (145–149)
Conclusions (150–151)
Recommendations (150–151)
Explanatory Notes
References (or Works Cited) (152)

BACK MATTER

Appendixes
Bibliography
Glossary
Index

 DIGITAL TIP **CREATING STYLES AND TEMPLATES**

Most word-processing programs enable you to create templates that automate text elements such as headings, paragraphs, and lists throughout a report. Once you specify your styles, save the template and use it each time you create a formal report. For step-by-step instructions, see *bedfordstmartins.com/alred*, and select *Digital Tips*, "Creating Styles and Templates."

Front Matter

The front matter serves several functions: It explains the writer's <u>purpose</u> (Tab 1), it describes the scope and type of information in the report, and it lists where specific information is covered in the report. Not all formal reports include every element of front matter described here. A title page and table of contents are usually mandatory, but the scope of the report and its <u>context</u> (Tab 1) as well as the intended audience determine whether the other elements are included.

Title Page.   Although the formats of title pages may vary, they often include the following items:

- *The full title of the report.* The title describes the topic, scope, and purpose of the report, as described in <u>titles</u> (Tab 4).
- *The name of the writer(s), principal investigator(s), or compiler(s).* Sometimes contributors identify themselves by their job title in the organization or by their tasks in contributing to the report ("Olivia Jones, Principal Investigator").
- *The date or dates of the report.* For one-time reports, the date shown is the date the report is distributed. For reports issued periodically (monthly, quarterly, or yearly), the subtitle shows the period that the report covers, and the distribution date is shown elsewhere on the title page, as shown in Figure 5–2.
- *The name of the organization for which the writer(s) works.*
- *The name of the organization to which the report is being submitted.* This information is included if the report is written for a customer or client.

The title page should not be numbered, as in the example in Figure 5–2, but it is considered page i. The back of the title page, which is left blank and unnumbered, is considered page ii, and the abstract falls on page iii. The body of the report begins with Arabic number 1, and a new chapter or large section typically begins on a new right-hand (odd-numbered) page. Reports with printing on only one side of each sheet can be numbered consecutively regardless of where new sections begin. Center page numbers at the bottom of each page throughout the report.

Abstract.   An <u>abstract</u>, which normally follows the title page, highlights the major points of the report, as shown on page 138, enabling readers to decide whether to read the report.

Table of Contents.   A <u>table of contents</u> lists all the major sections or <u>headings</u> (Tab 6) of the report in their order of appearance, as shown on page 139, along with their page numbers.

List of Figures.   All visuals contained in the report—drawings, photographs, maps, charts, and graphs—are labeled as figures. (See Tab 6, "Design and Visuals.") When a report contains more than five figures, list them, along with their page numbers, in a separate section, beginning on a new page immediately following the table of contents. Number figures consecutively with Arabic numbers.

List of Tables.   When a report contains more than five <u>tables</u> (Tab 6), list them, along with their titles and page numbers, in a separate section immediately following the list of figures (if there is one). Number tables consecutively with Arabic numbers.

Foreword.   A foreword is an optional introductory statement about a formal report or publication that is written by someone other than the author(s). The foreword author is usually an authority in the field or an executive of the organization sponsoring the report. That author's name and affiliation appear at the end of the foreword, along with the date it was written. The foreword generally provides background information about the publication's significance and places it in the context of other works in the field. The foreword precedes the preface when a work has both.

Preface.   The preface, another type of optional introductory statement, is written by the author(s) of the formal report. It may announce the work's purpose, scope, and context (including any special circumstances leading to the work). A preface may also specify the audience for a work, contain acknowledgments of those who helped in its preparation, and cite permission obtained for the use of copyrighted works. See also copyright (Tab 3).

List of Abbreviations and Symbols.   When the report uses numerous abbreviations (Tab 12) and symbols that readers may not be able to interpret, the front matter may include a section that lists symbols and abbreviations with their meanings.

Body

The body is the section of the report that provides context for the report, describes in detail the methods and procedures used to generate the report, demonstrates how results were obtained, describes the results, draws conclusions, and, if appropriate, makes recommendations.

Executive Summary.   The body of the report begins with the executive summary, which provides a more complete overview of the report than an abstract does. See an example on pages 140–141 and review the entry cross-referenced above.

Introduction.   The introduction (Tab 1) gives readers any general information, such as the report's purpose, scope, and context necessary to understand the detailed information in the rest of the report (see pages 142–144).

Text.   The text of the body presents, as appropriate, the details of how the topic was investigated, how a problem was solved, what alternatives were explored, and how the best choice among them was selected. This information is enhanced by the use of visuals, tables, and references that both clarify the text and persuade the reader. See also persuasion (Tab 1).

Conclusions.   The <u>conclusions</u> (Tab 1) section pulls together the results of the research and interprets the findings of the report, as shown on pages 150–151.

Recommendations.   Recommendations, which are sometimes combined with the conclusions, state what course of action should be taken based on the earlier arguments and conclusions of the study, as are shown on pages 150–151.

Explanatory Notes.   Occasionally, reports contain notes that amplify terms or points for some readers that might be a distraction for others. If such notes are not included as footnotes on the page where the term or point appears, they may appear in a "Notes" section at the end of the report.

References (or Works Cited).   A list of references or works cited appears in a separate section if the report refers to or quotes directly from printed or online research sources. If your employer has a preferred reference style, follow it; otherwise, use one of the guidelines provided in the entry <u>documenting sources</u> (Tab 3). For a relatively short report, place a references or works-cited section at the end of the body of the report, as shown on page 152. For a report with a number of sections or chapters, place a list of references or works cited at the end of each major section or chapter. In either case, title the reference or works-cited section as such and begin it on a new page. If a particular reference appears in more than one section or chapter, repeat it in full in each appropriate reference section.

■ ETHICS NOTE Always identify the sources of any facts, ideas, <u>quotations</u> (Tab 3), and paraphrases you include in a report. Even if unintentional, <u>plagiarism</u> (Tab 3) is unethical and may result in formal academic misconduct charges in a college course. On the job, it can result in legal actions or even dismissal. ✦

Back Matter

The back matter of a formal report contains supplementary material, such as where to find additional information about the topic (bibliography), and expands on certain subjects (appendixes). Other back-matter elements define special terms (glossary) and provide information on how to easily locate information in the report (index). For very large formal reports, back-matter sections may be individually lettered (Appendix A, Appendix B).

Appendixes.   An <u>appendix</u> clarifies or supplements the report with information that is too detailed or lengthy for the primary audience but is relevant to secondary audiences.

5

Bibliography. A <u>bibliography</u> (Tab 3) lists alphabetically all of the sources that were consulted to prepare the report—not just those cited—and suggests additional resources that readers might want to consult.

Glossary. A <u>glossary</u> is an alphabetical list of specialized terms used in the report and the definitions of those terms.

Index. An index is an alphabetical list of all the major topics and subtopics discussed in the report. It cites the page numbers where discussion of each topic can be found and allows readers to find information on topics quickly and easily. The index is always the final section of a report.

 DIGITAL TIP **CREATING AN INDEX**

Word-processing software can save you time when you are creating an index for your report. For step-by-step instructions on creating an index, see *bedfordstmartins.com/alred*, and select *Digital Tips*, "Creating an Index."

Sample Formal Report

Figure 5–2 shows the typical sections of a formal report. Keep in mind that the number and arrangement of the elements vary, depending on the context and on the requirements of an organization or a client.

glossaries

A glossary is an alphabetical list of definitions of specialized terms used in a <u>formal report</u>, a manual, or other long document. You may want to include a glossary if some readers in your <u>audience</u> (Tab 1) are not familiar with specialized or technical terms you use.

Keep glossary entries concise and be sure they are written in language that all your readers can understand.

- ***Amortize:*** To write off an expenditure by prorating it over a specific period of time.

Arrange the terms alphabetically, with each dictionary-like entry beginning on a new line. In a formal report, the glossary begins on a new page and appears after the appendix(es) and bibliography.

Including a glossary does not relieve you of the responsibility of <u>defining terms</u> (Tab 1) that your reader will not know when those terms are first mentioned in the text.

CGF Aircraft Corporation   _CGF_
Memo

To: Members of the Ethics and Business Conduct Committee

From: Susan Litzinger, Director of Ethics and Business Conduct *SL*

Date: March 4, 2011

Subject: Reported Ethics Cases, 2010

Identifies
topic

Enclosed is "Reported Ethics Cases: Annual Report, 2010." This report, required by CGF Policy CGF-EP-01, contains a review of the ethics cases handled by CGF ethics officers and managers during 2010, the first year of our Ethics Program.

Briefly
summarizes
content

The ethics cases reported are analyzed according to two categories: (1) major ethics cases, or those potentially involving serious violations of company policy or illegal conduct, and (2) minor ethics cases, or those that do not involve serious policy violations or illegal conduct. The report also examines the mode of contact in all of the reported cases and the disposition of the substantiated major ethics cases.

Offers
contact
information

It is my hope that this report will provide the Committee with the information needed to assess the effectiveness of the first year of CGF's Ethics Program and to plan for the coming year. Please let me know if you have any questions about this report or if you need any further information. I may be reached at (555) 211-2121 and by e-mail at sl@cgf.com.

Enc.

FIGURE 5–2. Formal Report (Cover Memo). Reprinted and adapted by permission of Susan Litzinger, a student at Pennsylvania State University, Altoona.

5

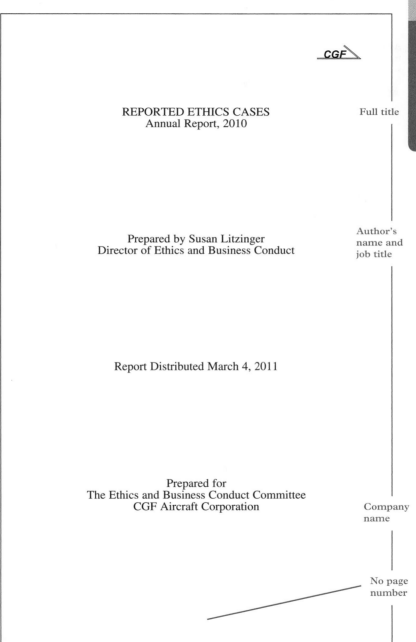

CGF

REPORTED ETHICS CASES
Annual Report, 2010

Full title

Prepared by Susan Litzinger
Director of Ethics and Business Conduct

Author's
name and
job title

Report Distributed March 4, 2011

Prepared for
The Ethics and Business Conduct Committee
CGF Aircraft Corporation

Company
name

No page
number

FIGURE 5–2. Formal Report (*continued*) (Title Page)

5

Formal Reports

Adapted
from MLA
style to fit
context

Reported Ethics Cases — 2010

ABSTRACT

This report examines the nature and disposition of 3,458 ethics
cases handled companywide by CGF Aircraft Corporation's
ethics officers and managers during 2010. The purpose of this
annual report is to provide the Ethics and Business Conduct
Committee with the information necessary for assessing the   Summarizes
effectiveness of the Ethics Program's first year of operation.   purpose
Records maintained by ethics officers and managers of all
contacts were compiled and categorized into two main types:
(1) major ethics cases, or cases involving serious violations of
company policies or illegal conduct, and (2) minor ethics cases,
or cases not involving serious policy violations or illegal conduct.
This report provides examples of the types of cases handled in
each category and analyzes the disposition of 30 substantiated
major ethics cases. Recommendations for planning for the second
year of the Ethics Program are (1) continuing the channels of
communication now available in the Ethics Program,
(2) increasing financial and technical support for the Ethics
Hotline, (3) disseminating the annual ethics report in some form
to employees to ensure employee awareness of the company's
commitment to uphold its Ethics Policies and Procedures, and
(4) implementing some measure of recognition for ethical
behavior to promote and reward ethical conduct.

Methods
and scope

Conclusions and
recommendations

Lowercase
Roman
numerals
used on
front-matter
pages

iii

FIGURE 5–2. Formal Report (*continued*) (Abstract)

Reported Ethics Cases — 2010

TABLE OF CONTENTS

Uniform
heading
styles

Indented
subheads

Page
number
for each
entry

iv

FIGURE 5-2. Formal Report (*continued*) (Table of Contents)

Reported Ethics Cases — 2010

EXECUTIVE SUMMARY

States purpose

This report examines the nature and disposition of the 3,458 ethics cases handled by the CGF Aircraft Corporation's ethics officers and managers during 2010. The purpose of this report is to provide CGF's Ethics and Business Conduct Committee with the information necessary for assessing the effectiveness of the first year of the company's Ethics Program.

Provides background information

Effective January 1, 2010, the Ethics and Business Conduct Committee (the Committee) implemented a policy and procedures for the administration of CGF's new Ethics Program. The purpose of the Ethics Program, established by the Committee, is to "promote ethical business conduct through open communication and compliance with company ethics standards." The Office of Ethics and Business Conduct was created to administer the Ethics Program. The director of the Office of Ethics and Business Conduct, along with seven ethics officers throughout the corporation, was given the responsibility for the following objectives:

- Communicate the values and standards for CGF's Ethics Program to employees.

- Inform employees about company policies regarding ethical business conduct.

- Establish companywide channels for employees to obtain information and guidance in resolving ethics concerns.

- Implement companywide ethics-awareness and education programs.

Employee accessibility to ethics information and guidance was available through managers, ethics officers, and an ethics hotline.

Describes scope

Major ethics cases were defined as those situations potentially involving serious violations of company policies or illegal conduct. Examples of major ethics cases included cover-up of defective workmanship or use of defective parts in products; discrimination in hiring and promotion; involvement in monetary or other kickbacks; sexual harassment; disclosure of proprietary or company information; theft; and use of corporate Internet resources for inappropriate purposes, such as conducting personal business, gambling, or access to pornography.

1

FIGURE 5–2. Formal Report (*continued*) (Executive Summary)

Reported Ethics Cases—2010

Minor ethics cases were defined as including all reported concerns not classified as major ethics cases. Minor ethics cases were classified as informational queries from employees, situations involving coworkers, and situations involving management.

The effectiveness of CGF's Ethics Program during the first year of implementation is most evidenced by (1) the active participation of employees in the program and the 3,458 contacts employees made regarding ethics concerns through the various channels available to them and (2) the action taken in the cases reported by employees, particularly the disposition of the 30 substantiated major ethics cases. Disseminating information about the disposition of ethics cases, particularly information about the severe disciplinary actions taken in major ethics violations, sends a message to employees that unethical or illegal conduct will not be tolerated.

Summarizes conclusions

Based on these conclusions, recommendations for planning the second year of the Ethics Program are (1) continuing the channels of communication now available in the Ethics Program, (2) increasing financial and technical support for the Ethics Hotline, the most highly used mode of contact in the ethics cases reported in 2010, (3) disseminating this report in some form to employees to ensure their awareness of CGF's commitment to uphold its Ethics Policies and Procedures, and (4) implementing some measure of recognition for ethical behavior, such as an "Ethics Employee of the Month" award to promote and reward ethical conduct.

Includes recommendations

Executive summary is about 10 percent of report length

2

FIGURE 5-2. Formal Report (*continued*) (Executive Summary)

5

Reported Ethics Cases — 2010

INTRODUCTION

Opening
states
purpose

This report examines the nature and disposition of the 3,458 ethics
cases handled companywide by CGF's ethics officers and managers
during 2010. The purpose of this report is to provide the Ethics and
Business Conduct Committee with the information necessary for
assessing the effectiveness of the first year of CGF's Ethics Program.
Recommendations are given for the Committee's consideration in
planning for the second year of the Ethics Program.

Subheads
signal shifts
in topic

Ethics and Business Conduct Policies and Procedures

Effective January 1, 2010, the Ethics and Business Conduct Committee
(the Committee) implemented Policy CGF-EP-01 and Procedure
CGF-EP-02 for the administration of CGF's new Ethics Program. The
purpose of the Ethics Program, established by the Committee, is to
"promote ethical business conduct through open communication and
compliance with company ethics standards" (CGF, "Ethics and
Conduct").

The Office of Ethics and Business Conduct was created to administer
the Ethics Program. The director of the Office of Ethics and
Business Conduct, along with seven ethics officers throughout
CGF, was given the responsibility for the following objectives:

- Communicate the values, standards, and goals of CGF's Ethics
  Program to employees.

List
identifies
key points

- Inform employees about company ethics policies.

- Provide companywide channels for employee education and
  guidance in resolving ethics concerns.

- Implement companywide programs in ethics awareness,
  education, and recognition.

- Ensure confidentiality in all ethics matters.

Employee accessibility to ethics information and guidance became
the immediate and key goal of the Office of Ethics and Business
Conduct in its first year of operation. The following channels for
contact were set in motion during 2010:

3

FIGURE 5-2. Formal Report (*continued*) (Introduction)

formal reports   143

5

Formal Reports

Reported Ethics Cases—2010

- Managers throughout CGF received intensive ethics training; in all ethics situations, employees were encouraged to go to their managers as the first point of contact.
- Ethics officers were available directly to employees through face-to-face or telephone contact, to managers, to callers using the ethics hotline, and by e-mail.
- The Ethics Hotline was available to all employees, 24 hours a day, seven days a week, to anonymously report ethics concerns.

Confidentiality Issues

CGF's Ethics Policy ensures confidentiality and anonymity for employees who raise genuine ethics concerns. Procedure CGF-EP-02 guarantees appropriate discipline, up to and including dismissal, for retaliation or retribution against any employee who properly reports any genuine ethics concern.

Documentation of Ethics Cases

The following requirements were established by the director of the Office of Ethics and Business Conduct as uniform guidelines for the documentation by managers and ethics officers of all reported ethics cases:

- Name, position, and department of individual initiating contact, if available
- Date and time of contact
- Name, position, and department of contact person
- Category of ethics case
- Mode of contact
- Resolution

Includes detailed methods

Managers and ethics officers entered the required information in each reported ethics case into an ACCESS database file, enabling efficient retrieval and analysis of the data.

4

FIGURE 5–2. Formal Report (*continued*) (Introduction)

                                          Reported Ethics Cases—2010

Major/Minor Category Definition and Examples

Major ethics cases were defined as those situations potentially
involving serious violations of company policies or illegal conduct.
Procedure CGF-EP-02 requires notification of the Internal Audit
and the Law departments in serious ethics cases. The staffs of the
Internal Audit and the Law departments assume primary responsibility
for managing major ethics cases and for working with the employees,
ethics officers, and managers involved in each case.

Examples of situations categorized as major ethics cases:

- Cover-up of defective workmanship or use of defective parts in
  products

Organized
by
decreasing
order of
importance

- Discrimination in hiring and promotion

- Involvement in monetary or other kickbacks from customers for
  preferred orders

- Sexual harassment

- Disclosure of proprietary customer or company information

- Theft

- Use of corporate Internet resources for inappropriate purposes,
  such as conducting private business, gambling, or gaining access
  to pornography

Minor ethics cases were defined as including all reported concerns
not classified as major ethics cases. Minor ethics cases were
classified as follows:

- Informational queries from employees

- Situations involving coworkers

- Situations involving management

5

FIGURE 5–2. Formal Report (*continued*) (Introduction)

Reported Ethics Cases—2010

ANALYSIS OF REPORTED ETHICS CASES

Reported Ethics Cases, by Major/Minor Category

CGF ethics officers and managers companywide handled a total of 3,458 ethics situations during 2010. Of these cases, only 172, or 5 percent, involved reported concerns of a serious enough nature to be classified as major ethics cases (see Fig. 1). Major ethics cases were defined as those situations potentially involving serious violations of company policy or illegal conduct.

Text introduces figure

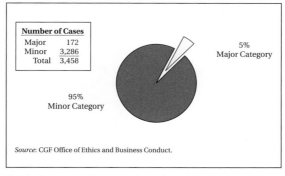

Fig. 1. Reported ethics cases, by major/minor category in 2010.

Number and title identify figure

Major Ethics Cases

Of the 172 major ethics cases reported during 2010, 57 percent, upon investigation, were found to involve unsubstantiated concerns. Incomplete information or misinformation most frequently was discovered to be the cause of the unfounded concerns of misconduct in 98 cases. Forty-four cases, or 26 percent of the total cases reported, involved incidents partly substantiated by ethics officers

6

FIGURE 5–2. Formal Report (*continued*) (Body)

5

Formal Reports

Reported Ethics Cases—2010

as serious misconduct; however, these cases were discovered to also involve inaccurate information or unfounded issues of misconduct.

Only 17 percent of the total number of major ethics cases, or 30 cases, were substantiated as major ethics situations involving serious ethical misconduct or illegal conduct (CGF, "2010 Ethics Hotline Results") (see Fig. 2).

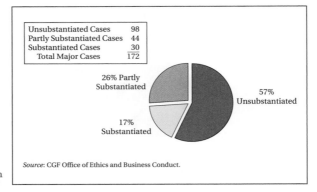

Unsubstantiated Cases	98
Partly Substantiated Cases	44
Substantiated Cases	30
Total Major Cases	172

26% Partly Substantiated

57% Unsubstantiated

17% Substantiated

Identifies
source of
information

Source: CGF Office of Ethics and Business Conduct.

Fig. 2. Major ethics cases in 2010.

Of the 30 substantiated major ethics cases, seven remain under investigation at this time, and two cases are currently in litigation. Disposition of the remainder of the 30 substantiated reported ethics cases included severe disciplinary action in five cases: the dismissal of two employees and the demotion of three employees. Seven employees were given written warnings, and nine employees received verbal warnings (see Fig. 3).

7

FIGURE 5-2. Formal Report (*continued*) (Body)

5

Reported Ethics Cases — 2010

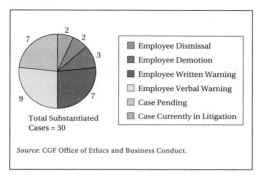

Source: CGF Office of Ethics and Business Conduct.

Fig. 3. Disposition of substantiated major ethics cases
in 2010.

Minor Ethics Cases

Minor ethics cases included those that did not involve serious
violations of company policy or illegal conduct. During 2010,
ethics officers and company managers handled 3,286 such cases.
Minor ethics cases were further classified as follows:

- Informational queries from employees
- Situations involving coworkers
- Situations involving management

Reports
findings in
detail

As might be expected during the initial year of the Ethics Program
implementation, the majority of contacts made by employees were
informational, involving questions about the new policies and
procedures. These informational contacts comprised 65 percent of
all contacts of a minor nature and numbered 2,148. Employees
made 989 contacts regarding ethics concerns involving coworkers
and 149 contacts regarding ethics concerns involving management
(see Fig. 4).

8

FIGURE 5–2. Formal Report (*continued*) (Body)

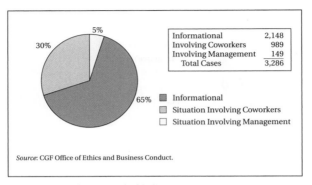

Reported Ethics Cases — 2010

Informational	2,148
Involving Coworkers	989
Involving Management	149
Total Cases	3,286

■ Informational
▨ Situation Involving Coworkers
□ Situation Involving Management

5%
30%
65%

Source: CGF Office of Ethics and Business Conduct.

Fig. 4. Minor ethics cases in 2010.

Mode of Contact

Assesses
findings

The effectiveness of the Ethics Program rested on the dissemination of information to employees and the provision of accessible channels through which employees could gain information, report concerns, and obtain guidance. Employees were encouraged to first go to their managers with any ethical concerns, because those managers would have the most direct knowledge of the immediate circumstances and individuals involved.

Other channels were put into operation, however, for any instance in which an employee did not feel able to go to his or her manager. The ethics officers companywide were available to employees through telephone conversations, face-to-face meetings, and e-mail contact. Ethics officers also served as contact points for managers in need of support and assistance in handling the ethics concerns reported to them by their subordinates.

The Ethics Hotline became operational in mid-January 2010 and offered employees assurance of anonymity and confidentiality. The Ethics Hotline was accessible to all employees on a 24-hour, 7-day basis. Ethics officers companywide took responsibility on a rotational basis for handling calls reported through the hotline.

9

FIGURE 5–2. Formal Report (*continued*) (Body)

5

Reported Ethics Cases—2010

In summary, ethics information and guidance were available to all employees during 2010 through the following channels:

- Employee to manager
- Employee telephone, face-to-face, and e-mail contact with ethics officer
- Manager to ethics officer
- Employee Hotline

The mode of contact in the 3,458 reported ethics cases was as follows (see Fig. 5):

Bulleted lists help organize and summarize information

- In 19 percent of the reported cases, or 657, employees went to managers with concerns.
- In 9 percent of the reported cases, or 311, employees contacted an ethics officer.
- In 5 percent of the reported cases, or 173, managers sought assistance from ethics officers.
- In 67 percent of the reported cases, or 2,317, contacts were made through the Ethics Hotline.

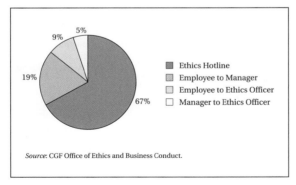

Source: CGF Office of Ethics and Business Conduct.

Fig. 5. Mode of contact in reported ethics cases in 2010.

10

FIGURE 5–2. Formal Report (*continued*) (Body)

5

Formal Reports

Reported Ethics Cases — 2010

CONCLUSIONS AND RECOMMENDATIONS

Pulls
together
findings

The effectiveness of CGF's Ethics Program during the first year of implementation is most evidenced by (1) the active participation of employees in the program and the 3,458 contacts employees made regarding ethics concerns through the various channels available to them, and (2) the action taken in the cases reported by employees, particularly the disposition of the 30 substantiated major ethics cases.

Uses
sources
for
support

One of the 12 steps to building a successful Ethics Program identified by Frank Navran in *Workforce* magazine is an ethics communication strategy. Navran explains that such a strategy is crucial in ensuring

> that employees have the information they need in a timely and usable fashion and that the organization is encouraging employee communication regarding the values, standards and the conduct of the organization and its members. (119)

The 3,458 contacts by employees during 2010 attest to the accessibility and effectiveness of the communication channels that exist in CGF's Ethics Program.

An equally important step in building a successful ethics program is listed by Navran as "Measurements and Rewards," which he explains as follows:

Long
quotation
in MLA
style

> In most organizations, employees know what's important by virtue of what the organization measures and rewards. If ethical conduct is assessed and rewarded, and if unethical conduct is identified and dissuaded, employees will believe that the organization's principals mean it when they say the values and code of ethics are important. (121)

Interprets
findings

Disseminating information about the disposition of ethics cases, particularly information about the severe disciplinary actions taken in major ethics violations, sends a message to employees that unethical or illegal conduct will not be tolerated. Making public such actions taken in cases of ethical misconduct provides "a golden opportunity to make other employees aware that the behavior is unacceptable and why" (Ferrell, Fraedrich, and Ferrell 129).

11

FIGURE 5–2. Formal Report (*continued*) (Conclusions and Recommendations)

Reported Ethics Cases — 2010

With these two points in mind, I offer the following recommendations for consideration for plans for the Ethics Program's second year:

- Continuation of the channels of communication now available in the Ethics Program
- Increased financial and technical support for the Ethics Hotline, the most highly used mode of contact in the reported ethics cases in 2010
- Dissemination of this report in some form to employees to ensure employees' awareness of CGF's commitment to uphold its Ethics Policy and Procedures
- Implementation of some measure of recognition for ethical behavior, such as an "Ethics Employee of the Month," to promote and reward ethical conduct

Recommends specific steps

To ensure that employees see the value of their continued participation in the Ethics Program, feedback is essential. The information in this annual review, in some form, should be provided to employees. Knowing that the concerns they reported were taken seriously and resulted in appropriate action by Ethics Program administrators would reinforce employee involvement in the program. While the negative consequences of ethical misconduct contained in this report send a powerful message, a means of communicating the *positive* rewards of ethical conduct at CGF should be implemented. Various options for recognition of employees exemplifying ethical conduct should be considered and approved. See MLogs. "Create and Evaluate a Code of Conduct." *Business Ethics Forum.* Management Logs, 12 Sept. 2006. Web. 19 Jan. 2010.

Continuation of the Ethics Program's successful 2010 operations, with the implementation of the above recommendations, should ensure the continued pursuit of the Ethics Program's purpose: "to promote a positive work environment that encourages open communication regarding ethics and compliance issues and concerns."

Links recommendations to company goal

12

FIGURE 5–2. Formal Report (*continued*) (Conclusions and Recommendations)

5

Formal Reports

Section begins on a new page

Reported Ethics Cases — 2010

WORKS CITED

CGF. "Ethics and Conduct at CGF Aircraft Corporation." *CGF Aircraft Corporation.* CGF, 1 Jan. 2010. Web. 11 Feb. 2011.

This report uses MLA style

---. "2010 Ethics Hotline Investigation Results." *CGF Aircraft Corporation.* CGF, 15 Jan. 2011. Web. 11 Feb. 2011.

Ferrell, O. C., John Fraedrich, and Linda Ferrell. *Business Ethics: Business Decision Making and Cases.* 7th ed. Boston: Houghton Mifflin, 2008. Print.

Navran, Frank. "12 Steps to Building a Best-Practices Ethics Program." *Workforce* 76.9 (1997): 117–22. Web. 10 Sept. 2009.

13

FIGURE 5-2. Formal Report (*continued*) (Works Cited)

5

tables of contents

A table of contents is typically included in a document longer than ten pages. It previews what the work contains and how it is organized, and it allows readers looking for specific information to locate sections by page number quickly and easily.

When creating a table of contents, use the major headings (Tab 6) and subheadings of your document exactly as they appear in the text, as shown in the entry formal reports. (See the table of contents in Figure 5–2 on page 139.) The table of contents is placed in the front matter following the title page and abstract, and precedes the list of tables or figures, the foreword, and the preface.

6

Design and Visuals

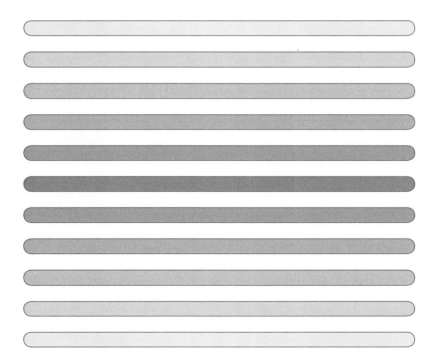

Preview

This section includes entries related to the physical appearance of a document, as discussed in <u>layout and design</u>, and entries concerning specific types of visuals, such as <u>drawings</u>, <u>graphs</u>, and <u>tables</u>. For an overview of creating and integrating specific types of illustrations into documents, read the entry <u>visuals</u>. Because many visuals are aimed at international audiences, this section includes the entry <u>global graphics</u>. See also <u>Web design</u> (Tab 2) and <u>writing for the Web</u> (Tab 2).

6

Design and Visuals

bulleted lists (*see* lists)

drawings

A drawing can depict an object's appearance and illustrate the steps in procedures or instructions. It can emphasize the significant parts or functions of a device or product, omit what is not significant, and focus on details or relationships that a photograph cannot reveal. Think about your need for drawings during your <u>preparation</u> (Tab 1) and <u>research</u> (Tab 3). Include them in your <u>outline</u> (Tab 1), indicating approximately where each should be placed. For advice on integrating drawings into your text, see <u>visuals</u>.

The types of drawings discussed in this entry are conventional line drawings and cutaway drawings. A conventional line drawing is appropriate if your <u>audience</u> (Tab 1) needs an overview of a series of steps or an understanding of an object's appearance or construction, as in Figure 6–1. A cutaway drawing, like the one in Figure 6–2, can be useful when you need to show the internal parts of a device or structure and illustrate their relationship to the whole.

6

Design and Visuals

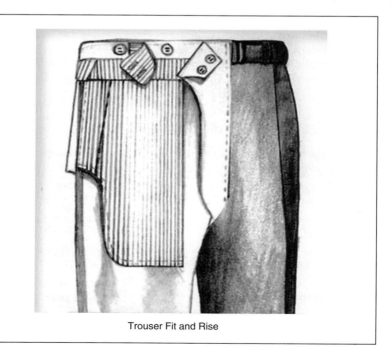

Trouser Fit and Rise

FIGURE 6–1. Conventional Line Drawing for a Retail Catalog

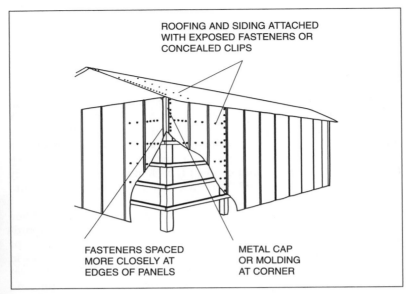

ROOFING AND SIDING ATTACHED
WITH EXPOSED FASTENERS OR
CONCEALED CLIPS

FASTENERS SPACED
MORE CLOSELY AT
EDGES OF PANELS

METAL CAP
OR MOLDING
AT CORNER

FIGURE 6–2. Cutaway Drawing

◆ ETHICS NOTE Do not use drawings from copyrighted sources without permission and proper documentation, especially from the Web—the same copyright laws that apply to printed material also apply to Web-based graphics. See also <u>copyright</u> (Tab 3), <u>documenting sources</u> (Tab 3), and <u>plagiarism</u> (Tab 3). ✦

Writer's Checklist: Creating and Using Drawings

☑ Seek the help of graphics specialists for drawings that require a high degree of accuracy and precision.

☑ Show equipment and other objects from the point of view of the person who will use them.

☑ When illustrating a subsystem, show its relationship to the larger system of which it is a part.

☑ Draw the parts of an object in proportion to one another and identify any parts that are enlarged or reduced.

☑ When a sequence of drawings is used to illustrate a process, arrange them from left to right or from top to bottom on the page.

☑ Label parts in the drawing so that the text references to them are clear and consistent.

☑ Depending on the complexity of what is shown, label the parts themselves, as in Figure 6-2, or use a letter/number key.

Design and Visuals

6

flowcharts

A flowchart is a diagram using symbols, words, or pictures to show the stages of a process in sequence from beginning to end. A flowchart provides an overview of a process and allows the reader to identify its essential steps quickly and easily. Flowcharts can take several forms. The steps might be represented by labeled blocks, as shown in Figure 6–3; pictorial symbols, as shown in Figure 6–4; or ISO (International Organization for Standardization) symbols, as shown in Figure 6–5.

Writer's Checklist: Creating Flowcharts

☑ Label each step in the process or identify each step with labeled blocks, pictorial representations, or standardized symbols.

☑ Follow the standard flow directions: left to right and top to bottom. Indicate any nonstandard flow directions with arrows.

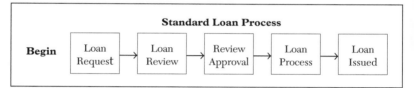

FIGURE 6–3. Flowchart Using Labeled Blocks

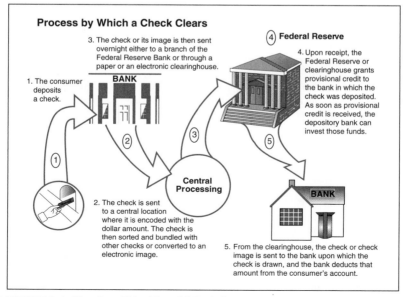

FIGURE 6–4. Flowchart Using Pictorial Symbols

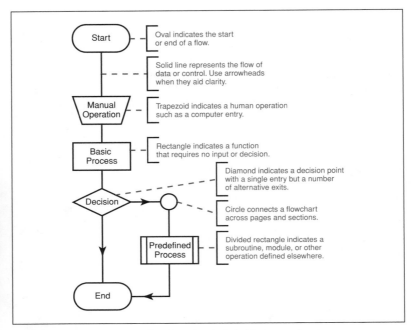

FIGURE 6–5. Common ISO Flowchart Symbols (with Annotations)

Writer's Checklist: Creating Flowcharts (continued)

☑   Include a key (or callouts) if the flowchart contains symbols your audience may not understand.

☑   Use standardized symbols for flowcharts that document computer programs and other information-processing procedures, as detailed in *Information Processing — Documentation Symbols and Conventions for Data, Program and System Flowcharts, Program Network Charts, and System Resources Charts*, ISO 5807-1985 (E).

For advice on integrating flowcharts into your text, see **visuals**. See also **global graphics**.

global graphics

In a global business and technological environment, **graphs** and other **visuals** require the same careful attention given to other aspects of **global communication** (Tab 1). The complex cultural connotations of visuals challenge writers to think beyond their own experience when they are aiming for audiences outside their own culture.

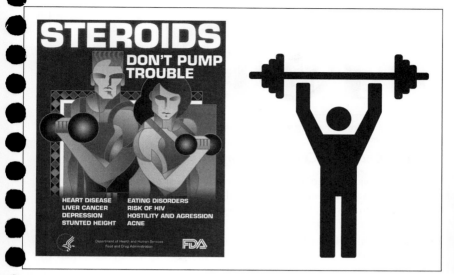

FIGURE 6-6. Graphics for U.S. (left) and Global (right) Audiences

6

Design and Visuals

Symbols, images, and even colors are not free from cultural associations—they depend on <u>context</u> (Tab 1), and context is culturally determined. For instance, in North America, a red cross is commonly used as a symbol for first aid or a hospital. In Muslim countries, however, a cross (red or otherwise) represents Christianity, whereas a crescent (usually green) signifies first aid or a hospital. A manual for use in Honduras could indicate "caution" by using a picture of a person touching a finger below the eye. In France, however, using that gesture would mean "You can't fool me."

Figure 6-6 shows two different graphics depicting weight lifters. The drawing at the left may be appropriate for U.S. audiences and others. However, that graphic would be highly inappropriate in many cultures where the image of a partially clothed man and woman in close proximity would be contrary to deeply held cultural beliefs and even laws about the public depiction of men and women. The drawing at the right in Figure 6-6, however, depicts a weight lifter with a neutral icon that avoids the connotations associated with more realistic images of people.

These examples suggest why the International Organization for Standardization (ISO) established agreed-upon symbols, such as those shown in Figure 6-7, designed for public signs, guidebooks, and manuals.

◆ PROFESSIONALISM NOTE Careful attention to the connotations that visual elements may have for a global <u>audience</u> (Tab 1) makes translations easier, prevents embarrassment, and earns respect for a company and its products and services. ✦

FIGURE 6–7. International Organization for Standardization Symbols

Writer's Checklist: Communicating with Global Graphics

☑ Consult with someone or test your use of graphics with people from your intended audience's country who understand the effect that visual elements will have on readers or listeners. See also **presentations** (Tab 9).

☑ Organize visual information for the intended audience. For example, North Americans read visuals from left to right in clockwise rotation. Middle Eastern readers typically read visuals from right to left in counterclockwise rotation.

☑ Be sure that the graphics have no unintended political or religious implications.

☑ Carefully consider how you depict people in visuals. Nudity in advertising, for example, may be acceptable in some cultures, but in others showing even isolated bare body parts can alienate audiences.

☑ Use outlines or neutral abstractions to represent human beings. For example, use stick figures and avoid representing men and women.

☑ Examine how you display body positions in signs and visuals. Body positioning can carry unintended cultural meanings very different from your own. For example, some Middle Eastern cultures regard the display of the soles of one's shoes to be disrespectful and offensive.

☑ Choose neutral colors (or those you know are appropriate) for your graphics; generally, black-and-white and gray-and-white illustrations work well. Colors can be problematic. For example, in North America, Europe, and Japan, red indicates danger. In China, however, red symbolizes good fortune and joy.

☑ Check your use of punctuation marks, which are as language specific as symbols. For example, in North America, the question mark generally represents the need for information or the help function in a computer manual or program. In many countries, that symbol has no meaning at all.

☑ Create simple visuals and use consistent labels for all visual items. In most cultures, simple shapes with fewer elements are easier to read.

graphs

A graph presents numerical or quantitative data in visual form and offers several advantages over presenting data within the text or in <u>tables</u>. Trends, movements, distributions, comparisons, and cycles are more readily apparent in graphs than they are in tables. However, although graphs present data in a more comprehensible form than tables do, they are less precise. For that reason, some <u>audiences</u> (Tab 1) may need graphs to be accompanied by tables that give exact data. The types of graphs described in this entry include line graphs, bar graphs, pie graphs, and picture graphs. For advice on integrating graphs within text, see <u>visuals;</u> for information about using presentation graphics, see <u>presentations</u> (Tab 9).

Line Graphs

A line graph shows the relationship between two variables or sets of numbers by plotting points in relation to two axes drawn at right angles. The vertical axis usually represents amounts, and the horizontal axis usually represents increments of time. Line graphs that portray more than one set of variables (double-line graphs) allow for comparisons between two sets of data for the same period of time. You can emphasize the difference between the two lines by shading the space between them, as shown in Figure 6–8.

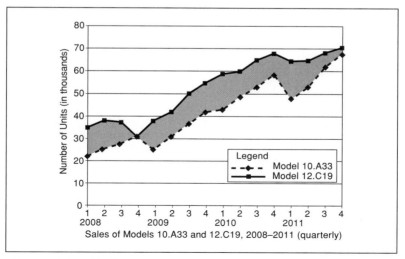

FIGURE 6–8. Double-Line Graph (with Shading)

6

Design and Visuals

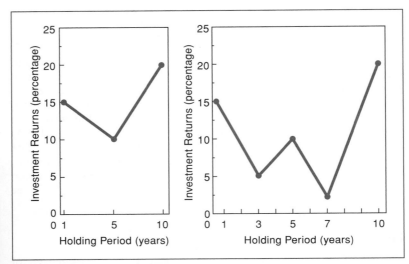

FIGURE 6–9. Distorted (left) and Distortion-Free (right) Expressions of Data

⬧ ETHICS NOTE Be especially careful to proportion the vertical and horizontal scales so that they give a precise presentation of the data that is free of visual distortion. To do otherwise is not only inaccurate but potentially unethical. (See <u>ethics in writing</u>, Tab 1.) In Figure 6–9, the graph on the left gives the appearance of a slight decline followed by a steady increase in investment returns because the scale is compressed, with some of the years selectively omitted. The graph on the right represents the trend more accurately because the years are evenly distributed without omissions. ✦

Bar Graphs

Bar graphs consist of horizontal or vertical bars of equal width, scaled in length to represent some quantity. They are commonly used to show (1) quantities of the same item at different times, (2) quantities of different items at the same time, and (3) quantities of the different parts of an item that make up a whole (in which case, the segments of the bar graph must total 100 percent). The horizontal bar graph in Figure 6–10 shows the quantities of different items for the same period of time.

Pie Graphs

A pie graph presents data as wedge-shaped sections of a circle. The circle equals 100 percent, or the whole, of some quantity, and the wedges

6

Design and Visuals

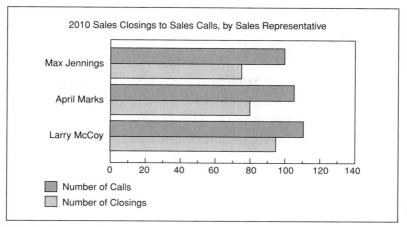

FIGURE 6–10. Bar Graph (Quantities of Different Items During a Fixed Period)

represent how the whole is divided. Figure 6–11 shows wedge-shaped sections that represent percentages of "Your Municipal Tax Dollar." Pie graphs provide a quicker way of presenting information that can be shown in a table; in fact, a table with a more-detailed breakdown of the same information often accompanies a pie graph.

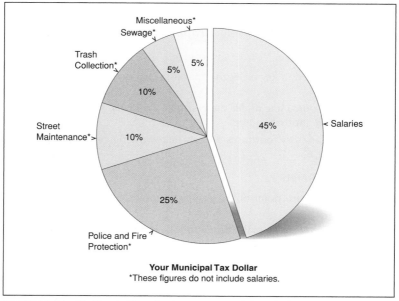

FIGURE 6–11. Pie Graph (Showing Percentages of the Whole)

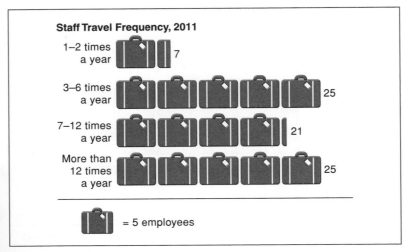

FIGURE 6–12. Picture Graph

Picture Graphs

Picture graphs are modified bar graphs that use pictorial symbols of the item portrayed. Each symbol corresponds to a specified quantity of the item, as shown in Figure 6–12. Note that, for precision and clarity, the picture graph includes the total quantity following the symbols.

Writer's Checklist: Creating Graphs

FOR ALL GRAPHS

☑ Use, as needed, a key or legend that lists and defines symbols (see Figure 6–8).

☑ Include a source line under the graph at the lower left when the data come from another source.

☑ Place explanatory footnotes directly below the figure caption or label (see Figure 6–11).

FOR LINE GRAPHS

☑ Indicate the zero point of the graph (the point where the two axes intersect).

☑ Insert a break in the scale if the range of data shown makes it inconvenient to begin at zero.

☑ Divide the vertical axis into equal portions, from the least amount at the bottom (or zero) to the greatest amount at the top.

☑ Divide the horizontal axis into equal units from left to right. If a label is necessary, center it directly beneath the scale.

6

Design and Visuals

Writer's Checklist: Creating Graphs (continued)

- ☑ Make all lettering read horizontally if possible, although the caption or label for the vertical axis is usually positioned vertically (see Figure 6–8).

FOR BAR GRAPHS

- ☑ Differentiate among the types of data each bar or part of a bar represents by color, shading, or crosshatching.
- ☑ Avoid three-dimensional graphs when they make bars seem larger than the amounts they represent.

FOR PIE GRAPHS

- ☑ Make sure that the complete circle is equivalent to 100 percent.
- ☑ Sequence the wedges clockwise from largest to smallest, beginning at the 12 o'clock position, whenever possible.
- ☑ Limit the number of items in the pie graph to avoid clutter and to ensure that the slices are thick enough to be clear.
- ☑ Give each wedge a distinctive color, pattern, shade, or texture.
- ☑ Label each wedge with its percentage value and keep all call-outs (labels that identify the wedges) horizontal.
- ☑ Detach a slice, as shown in Figure 6–11, if you wish to draw attention to a particular segment of the pie graph.

FOR PICTURE GRAPHS

- ☑ Indicate the zero point of the graph when appropriate.
- ☑ Use picture graphs to add interest to presentations and documents that are aimed at wide audiences.
- ☑ Choose symbols that are easily recognizable. See also **global graphics**.
- ☑ Let each symbol represent the same number of units.
- ☑ Indicate larger quantities by using more symbols, instead of larger symbols, because relative sizes are difficult to judge accurately.

6

Design and Visuals

headers and footers (*see* layout and design)

headings

Headings (also called *heads*) are titles or subtitles that highlight the main topics and signal topic changes within the body of a document. Headings help readers find information and divide the material into comprehensible segments. A report or proposal may need several levels

DISTRIBUTION CENTER LOCATION REPORT

First-level head

The committee initially considered 30 possible locations for the proposed new distribution center. Of these, 20 were eliminated almost immediately for one reason or another (unfavorable zoning regulations, inadequate transportation infrastructure, etc.). Of the remaining ten locations, the committee selected for intensive study the three that seemed most promising: Chicago, Minneapolis, and Salt Lake City. We have now visited these three cities, and our observations and recommendations follow.

Second-level head

CHICAGO

Of the three cities, Chicago presently seems to the committee to offer the greatest advantages, although we wish to examine these more carefully before making a final recommendation.

Third-level head

Selected Location

Though not at the geographic center of the United States, Chicago is the demographic center to more than three-quarters of the U.S. population. It is within easy reach of our corporate headquarters in New York. And it is close to several of our most important suppliers of components and raw materials—those, for example, in Columbus, Detroit, and St. Louis. Several factors were considered essential to the location, although some may not have had as great an impact on the selection. . . .

Fourth-level heads

Air Transportation. Chicago has two major airports (O'Hare and Midway) and is contemplating building a third. Both domestic and international air-cargo service are available. . . .

Sea Transportation. Except during the winter months when the Great Lakes are frozen, Chicago is an international seaport. . . .

Rail Transportation. Chicago is served by the following major railroads. . . .

FIGURE 6–13. Headings Used in a Document

of headings (as shown in Figure 6–13) to indicate major divisions, subdivisions, and even smaller units. If possible, avoid using more than four levels of headings. See also layout and design.

Headings typically represent the major topics of a document. In a short document, you can use the major divisions of your outline as headings; in a longer document, you may need to use both major and minor divisions.

No one format for headings is correct. Often an organization settles on a standard format, which everyone in that organization follows. Sometimes a client for whom a report or proposal is being prepared requires a particular format. In the absence of specific guidelines, follow the system illustrated in Figure 6–13. For an example of a different system (the decimal system of headings), see outlining (Tab 1).

Writer's Checklist: Using Headings

☑ Use headings to signal a new topic. Use a lower-level heading to indicate a new subtopic within the larger topic.

☑ Make headings concise but specific enough to be informative, as in Figure 6–13.

☑ Avoid too many or too few headings or levels of headings; too many clutter a document, and too few fail to provide recognizable structure.

☑ Ensure that headings at the same level are of relatively equal importance and have **parallel structure** (Tab 10).

☑ Subdivide sections only as needed; when you do, try to subdivide them into at least two lower-level headings.

☑ Do not leave a heading as the final line of a page. If two lines of text cannot fit below a heading, start the section at the top of the next page.

☑ Do not allow a heading to substitute for discussion; the text should read as if the heading were not there.

layout and design

The layout and design of a document can make even the most complex information accessible and give readers a favorable impression of the writer and the organization. To accomplish those goals, a design should help readers find information easily; offer a simple and uncluttered presentation; and highlight structure, hierarchy, and order. The design must also fit the **purpose** (Tab 1) of the document and its **context** (Tab 1). For example, if clients are paying a high price for consulting services, they may expect a sophisticated, polished design; if employees inside an organization expect management to be frugal, they may accept—even expect—an economical and standard company design.

Typography

Typography refers to the style and arrangement of type on a page. A complete set of all the letters, numbers, and symbols available in one typeface (or style) is called a *font*. The letters in a typeface have a number of distinctive characteristics, as shown in Figure 6–14.

Typeface and Type Size.   For most on-the-job writing, select a typeface primarily for its legibility. Avoid typefaces that may distract readers. Instead, choose popular typefaces with which readers are familiar, such as Times Roman, Garamond, or Gill Sans. Avoid using more than two typefaces in the text of a document. For certain documents,

6

Design and Visuals

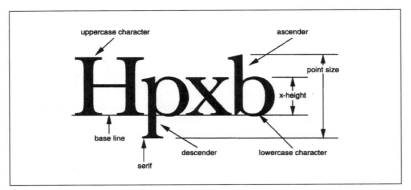

FIGURE 6–14. Primary Components of Letter Characters

however, such as newsletters, you may wish to use distinctively different typefaces for contrast among various elements such as headlines, headings, inset quotations (Tab 3), and sidebars. Experiment before making final decisions, keeping in mind your audience (Tab 1).

One way typefaces are characterized is by the presence or absence of serifs. Serif typefaces have projections, as shown in Figure 6–14; sans serif styles do not. (*Sans* is French for "without.") The text of this book is set in Sabon, a serif typeface. Although sans serif type has a smooth look, serif type is easier to read, especially in the smaller sizes. Sans serif, however, works well for headings and for Web sites and other documents read on-screen.

Ideal font sizes for the main text of paper documents range from 10 to 12 points.* However, for some elements or documents, you may wish to select typeface sizes that are smaller (as in footnotes) or larger (as in headlines for brochures). See Figure 6–15 for a comparison of type sizes in a serif typeface. Your readers and the distance from which they will read a document should help determine type size. For example, instructions that will rest on a table at which the reader stands require a larger typeface than a document that will be read up close. For

6 pt. This size might be used for dating a source.

8 pt. This size might be used for footnotes.

10 pt. This size might be used for figure captions.

12 pt. This size might be used for main text.

14 pt. This size might be used for headings.

FIGURE 6–15. Type Sizes (6- to 14-Point Type)

*A point is a unit of type size equal to 0.01384 inch, or approximately 1/72 of an inch.

<u>presentations</u> (Tab 9) and <u>writing for the Web</u> (Tab 2), preview your document to see the effectiveness of your choice of point sizes and typefaces.

Type Style and Emphasis.   One method of achieving emphasis through typography is to use capital letters. HOWEVER, LONG STRETCHES OF ALL UPPERCASE LETTERS ARE DIFFICULT TO READ. (See also <u>e-mail</u>, Tab 2.) Use all uppercase letters only in short spans, such as in headings. Likewise, use italics sparingly because *continuous italic type reduces legibility and thus slows readers*. Of course, italics are useful if your aim is to slow readers, as in cautions and warnings. **Boldface**, used in moderation, may be the best cuing device because it is visually different yet retains the customary shapes of letters and numbers.

Page-Design Elements

Thoughtfully used design elements can provide not only emphasis but also visual logic within a document by highlighting organization. Consistency and moderation are important—use the same technique to highlight a particular feature throughout your document and be careful not to overuse any single technique. The following typical elements can be used to make your document accessible and effective: justification, headings, headers and footers, lists, columns, white space, and color. For advice on design elements for Web pages, see <u>Web design</u> (Tab 2).

Justification.   Left-justified (ragged-right) margins are generally easier to read than full-justified margins, especially for text using wide margins on 8½ × 11" pages. Left justification is also better if full justification causes your word-processing or desktop-publishing software to insert irregular spaces between words, producing unwanted white space or unevenness in blocks of text. Full-justified text is more appropriate for publications aimed at a broad audience that expects a more formal, polished appearance. Full justification is also useful with narrow, multiple-column formats because the spaces between the columns (called *alleys*) need the definition that full justification provides.

Headings.   Headings reveal the organization of a document and help readers decide which sections they need to read. Provide typographic contrast between headings and the body text with either a different typeface or a different style (**bold**, *italic*, CAPS, and so on). Headings are often effective in boldface or in a sans serif typeface that contrasts with a body text in a serif typeface.

Headers and Footers.   A header in a report, letter, or other document appears at the top of each page (as in this book), and a footer appears at the bottom of each page. Document pages may have headers

6

Design and Visuals

or footers (or both) that include such elements as the topic or subtopic of a section, an identifying number, the date the document was written, the page number, and the document name. Keep your headers and footers concise because too much information in them can create visual clutter. However—at a minimum—a multipage document should include the page number in a header or footer. For more information on adding page numbers and laying out a page, see *Web Link: Designing Documents* on page 173. For headers used in letters and memos, see correspondence (Tab 7).

Lists. Vertically stacked words, phrases, and other items with numbers or bullets can effectively highlight such information as steps in sequence, materials or parts needed, key or concluding points, and recommendations. For further detail, see lists.

Columns. As you design pages, consider how columns may improve the readability of your document. A single-column format works well with larger typefaces, double-spacing, and left-justified margins. For smaller typefaces and single-spaced lines, the two-column structure keeps text columns narrow enough so that readers need not scan back and forth across the width of the entire page for every line. Avoid widows and orphans: A *widow* is a single word carried over to the top of a column or page; an *orphan* is a word on a line by itself at the end of a column.

White Space. White space visually frames information and breaks it into manageable chunks. For example, white space between paragraphs helps readers see the information in each paragraph as a unit. White space between sections can also serve as a visual cue to signal that one section is ending and another is beginning.

Color. Color and screening (shaded areas on a page) can distinguish one part of a document from another or unify a series of documents. They can set off sections within a document, highlight examples, or emphasize warnings. In tables, screening can highlight column titles or sets of data to which you want to draw the reader's attention.

Visuals

Readers notice visuals before they notice text, and they notice larger visuals before they notice smaller ones. Thus, the size of an illustration suggests its relative importance. For newsletter articles and publications aimed at wide audiences, consider especially the proportion of the visual to the text. Magazine designers often use the three-fifths rule: Page layout is more dramatic and appealing when the major element (photograph, drawing, or other visual) occupies three-fifths rather than one-half the available space. The same principle can be used to enhance the visual appeal of a report (Tab 4).

Visuals can be gathered in one place (for example, at the end of a report), but placing them in the text closer to their accompanying explanations makes them more effective. Illustrations in the text also provide visual relief. For advice on the placement of visuals, see the *Writer's Checklist: Creating and Integrating Visuals* (page 182).

Icons.   Icons are pictorial representations used to describe such abstract concepts as computer files, programs, or commands. Commonly used icons on the Web include the national flags to symbolize different language versions of a document. To be effective, icons must be simple and easily recognized without accompanying text. For using icons that are culturally appropriate, see also <u>global graphics</u>.

Captions.   Captions are titles that highlight or describe visuals, such as photographs. Captions usually appear below figures and above <u>tables</u>; they may be aligned with the visual to the left or they may be centered.

Rules.   Rules are vertical or horizontal lines used to box or divide one area of the page from another. For example, rules and boxes set off visuals from surrounding explanations or highlight warning statements from the steps in instructions.

Page Layout and Thumbnails

Page layout involves combining typography, design elements, and visuals on a page to make a coherent whole. The flexibility of your design is affected by your design software, your method of printing the document, your budget, and whether your employer or client requires you to use a template.

Before you spend time positioning actual text and visuals on a page, especially for documents such as brochures, you may want to create a thumbnail sketch, in which blocks of simulated text and visuals indicate the placement of elements. You can go further by roughly assembling all the thumbnail pages to show the size, shape, form, and general style of a large document. Such a mock-up, called a *dummy*, allows you to see how a finished document will look.

 WEB LINK DESIGNING DOCUMENTS

Word-processing and desktop-publishing programs offer many options for improving the layout-and-design elements of your document. For a tutorial on these options, see *bedfordstmartins.com/alred*, and select *Tutorials*, "Designing Documents with a Word Processor." For step-by-step instructions on how to create design elements, select *Digital Tips*, "Laying Out a Page" and "Creating Styles and Templates."

6

Design and Visuals

lists

Vertically stacked lists of words, phrases, and other items that are often highlighted with bullets, numbers, or letters can save readers time by allowing them to see at a glance specific items or key points in a document. Lists also help readers by breaking up complex statements and by focusing on such information as steps in sequence, materials or parts needed, questions or concluding points, and recommendations, as shown in Figure 6–16.

As Figure 6–16 also shows, you should provide context (Tab 1) for a list with an introductory sentence followed by a colon (or no punctuation for an incomplete sentence). Ensure coherence (Tab 10) by following the list with some reference to the list or the statement that introduced it.

Writer's Checklist: Using Lists

Follow the practices of your organization or use the guidelines below for consistency and formatting.

CONSISTENCY

☑ Do not overuse lists or create extended lists or **presentation** (Tab 9) slides that are dense with lists.

☑ List only comparable items, such as tasks or equipment, that are balanced in importance (as in Figure 6-16).

☑ Begin each listed item in the same way—whether with nouns, verbs, or other parts of speech—and maintain **parallel structure** (Tab 10) throughout.

Before we agree to hold the regional sales conference at the Brent Hotel, we need to make sure the hotel can provide the following resources:

- Business center with state-of-the-art digital and printing services
- Main exhibit area that can accommodate thirty 8-foot-by-15-foot booths
- Eight meeting rooms, each with a podium or table and seating for 25 people
- Broadband Internet access and digital projection in each room
- Ballroom dining facilities for 250 people with a dais for four speakers

To confirm that the Brent Hotel is our best choice, we should tour the facilities during our stay in Kansas City.

FIGURE 6–16. Bulleted List in a Paragraph

Writer's Checklist: Using Lists (continued)

FORMATTING

☑ Capitalize the first word in each listed item, unless doing so is visually awkward.

☑ Use periods or other ending punctuation when the listed items are complete sentences.

☑ Avoid commas or semicolons following items and do not use the conjunction *and* before the last item in a list.

☑ Use numbers to indicate sequence or rank.

☑ Follow each number with a period and start the item with a capital letter.

☑ Use bullets (round, square, arrow) when you do not wish to indicate rank or sequence.

☑ List bulleted items in a logical order, keeping your **audience** (Tab 1) and **purpose** (Tab 1) in mind.

☑ When lists need subdivisions, use letters with numbers. See also **outlining** (Tab 1).

6

Design and Visuals

organizational charts

An organizational chart shows how the various divisions or units of an organization are related to one another. This type of <u>visual</u> is useful when you want to give readers an overview of an organization or to display the lines of authority within it, as in Figure 6–17.

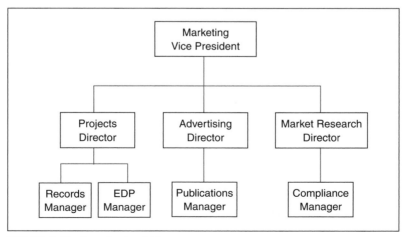

FIGURE 6–17. Organizational Chart

The title of each organizational component (office, section, division) is placed in a separate box. The boxes are then linked to a central authority. If readers need the information, include the name of the person and position title in each box. As with all visuals, place the organizational chart as close as possible to but not preceding the text that refers to it.

tables

6

Design and Visuals

A table organizes data, such as statistics, into parallel rows and columns that allow readers to make precise comparisons. Overall trends, however, are more easily conveyed in <u>graphs</u> and other <u>visuals</u>.

Table Elements

Tables typically include the elements shown in Figure 6–18.

Table Number.   Table numbers should be placed above tables and assigned sequentially throughout the document.

Table Title.   The title (or *caption*), which is normally placed just above the table, should describe concisely what the table represents.

Box Head.   The box head contains the column headings, which should be brief but descriptive. Units of measurement should be either specified as part of the heading or enclosed in parentheses beneath it. Standard abbreviations and symbols are acceptable. Avoid vertical or diagonal lettering.

Table 1. Estimated Emissions from Electric Power Generation (tons per gigawatthour)

Fuel	Sulphur Dioxide	Nitrogen Oxides	Particulate Matter	Carbon Dioxide	Volatile Organic Compounds
Eastern coal	1.74	2.90	0.10	1,000	0.06
Western coal	0.81	2.20	0.06	1,039	0.09
Gas	0.003	0.57	0.02	640	0.05
Biomass	0.06	1.25	0.11	0*	0.61
Oil	0.51	0.63	0.02	840	0.03
Wind	0	0	0	0	0
Geothermal	0	0	0	0	0
Hydro	0	0	0	0	0
Solar	0	0	0	0	0
Nuclear	0	0	0	0	0

*Net emissions.

SOURCE: Department of Energy

Labels in figure: Table number, Table title, Box head, Column headings, Stub, Body, Rule, Footnote, Source line

FIGURE 6–18. Elements of a Table

Stub.   The stub, the left vertical column of a table, lists the items about which information is given in the body of the table.

Body.   The body comprises the data below the column headings and to the right of the stub. Within the body, arrange columns so that the items to be compared appear in adjacent rows and columns. Align the numerical data in columns for ease of comparison, as shown in Figure 6–18. Where no information exists for a specific item, substitute a row of dots or a dash to acknowledge the gap.

Rules.   Rules are the lines (or *borders*) that separate the table into its various parts. Tables should include top and bottom borders. Tables often include right and left borders, although they may be open at the sides, as shown in Figure 6–18. Generally, include a horizontal rule between the column headings and the body of the table. Separate the columns with vertical rules within a table only when they aid clarity.

Footnotes.   Footnotes are used for explanations of individual items in the table. Symbols (such as * and †) or lowercase letters (sometimes in parentheses) rather than numbers are ordinarily used to key table footnotes because numbers might be mistaken for numerical data or could be confused with the numbering system for text footnotes.

Source Line.   The source line identifies where the data originated. When a source line is appropriate, it appears below the table. Many organizations place the source line below the footnotes. See also copyright (Tab 3) and plagiarism (Tab 3).

Continuing Tables.   When a table must be divided so that it can be continued on another page, repeat the column headings and the table number and title on the new page with a "continued" label (for example, "Table 3. [title], *continued*").

Informal Tables

To list relatively few items that would be easier for the reader to grasp in tabular form, you can use an informal table, as long as you introduce it properly, as shown in Figure 6–19. Although informal tables do not need titles or table numbers to identify them, they do require column headings that accurately describe the information listed.

6

Design and Visuals

Dear Customer:
To order replacement parts, use the following part numbers and prices:

Part	Part Number	Price ($)
Diverter valve	2-912	12.50
Gasket kit	2-776	0.95
Adapter	3-212	0.90

FIGURE 6–19. Informal Table

DIGITAL TIP **CREATING SIMPLE TABLES FOR A DOCUMENT**

Word-processing programs allow you to specify the number of rows and columns needed for your data, to define the style of the table elements, and to select vertical and horizontal rules. See *bedfordstmartins.com/alred*, and select *Digital Tips*, "Creating Tables."

visuals

Visuals can express ideas or convey information in ways that words alone cannot by making abstract concepts and relationships concrete. Visuals can show how things look (drawings, photographs, maps), represent numbers and quantities (graphs, tables), depict processes or relationships (flowcharts, schematic diagrams), and show hierarchical relationships (organizational charts). They also highlight important information and emphasize key concepts succinctly and clearly.

Many of the qualities of good writing—simplicity, clarity, conciseness, directness—are equally important when creating and using visuals. Presented with clarity and consistency, visuals can help readers focus on key portions of your document, presentation, or Web site. Be aware, though, that even the best visual will not be effective without context (Tab 1)—and most often context is provided by the text that introduces the visual and clarifies its purpose.

The following entries in this book are related to specific visuals and their use in printed and online documents, as well as in presentation graphics (see pages 263–65).

Design and Visuals

6

Selecting Visuals

Consider your audience (Tab 1) and your purpose (Tab 1) carefully in selecting visuals. You would need different illustrations for an automobile owner's manual or an auto dealer's Web site, for example, than you would for a technician's diagnostic guide. Figure 6–20 can help you select the most appropriate visuals, based on their purposes and special features. Jot down visual options when you are considering your scope (Tab 1) and organization (Tab 1).

❖ ETHICS NOTE Be aware that visuals have the potential of misleading readers when data are selectively omitted or distorted. For example, Figure 6–9 shows a graph that gives a misleading impression of investment returns because the scale is compressed, with some of the years selectively omitted. Visuals that mislead readers call the credibility of you and your organization into question at the least—and they are unethical. The use of misleading visuals can even subject you and your organization to lawsuits. ✦

Integrating Visuals with Text

Consider the best locations for visuals before you begin writing a draft (Tab 1). Your goal should be to use visuals where they will best advance your purpose, aid your readers, and integrate smoothly within your text. One way to use visuals wisely is to make their placement a part of your outlining (Tab 1) process. At appropriate points in your outline, either make a rough sketch of the visual, if you can, or write "illustration of . . . ," noting the source of the visual and enclosing each suggestion in a text box. You may also include sketches of visuals in your thumbnail pages, as discussed in layout and design.

When you write the draft, place visuals as close as possible to the text where they are discussed—in fact, no visual should precede its first text mention. Refer to graphics (such as drawings and photographs) as "figures" and to tables as "tables." Clarify for readers why each visual is included in the text. The amount of description you should provide will vary, depending on your readers' backgrounds. For example, non-experts may require lengthier explanations than experts need.

❖ ETHICS NOTE Obtain written permission to use copyrighted visuals—including images and multimedia material from Web sites—and acknowledge borrowed material in a source line below the caption for a

Design and Visuals

6

CHOOSING APPROPRIATE VISUALS

TO SHOW OBJECTS AND SPATIAL RELATIONSHIPS

DRAWINGS CAN . . .

- Depict real objects difficult to photograph
- Depict imaginary objects
- Highlight only parts viewers need to see
- Show internal parts of equipment in cutaway views
- Show how equipment parts fit together in exploded views

PHOTOGRAPHS CAN . . .

- Show actual physical images of subjects
- Record an event in process
- Record the development of phenomena over time
- Record the as-found condition of a situation for an investigation

TO DISPLAY GEOGRAPHIC INFORMATION

MAPS CAN . . .

- Show specific geographic features of an area
- Show distance, routes, or locations of sites
- Show the geographic distribution of information (e.g., populations by region)

TO SHOW NUMERICAL AND OTHER RELATIONSHIPS

TABLES CAN . . .

Divisions	Employees
Research	1,052
Marketing	2,782
Automotive	13,251
Consumer Products	2,227

- Organize information systematically in rows and columns
- Present large numerical quantities concisely
- Facilitate item-to-item comparisons
- Clarify trends and other graphical information with precise data

BAR & COLUMN GRAPHS CAN . . .

- Depict data in vertical or horizontal bars and columns for comparison
- Show quantities that make up a whole
- Visually represent data shown in tables

FIGURE 6–20. Chart for Choosing Appropriate Visuals

LINE GRAPHS CAN . . .	• Show trends over time in amounts, sizes, rates, and other measurements
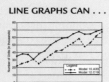	• Give an at-a-glance impression of trends, forecasts, and extrapolations of data
	• Compare more than one kind of data over the same time period
	• Visually represent data shown in tables

PICTURE GRAPHS CAN . . .	• Use recognizable images to represent specific quantities
	• Help nonexpert readers grasp the information
	• Visually represent data shown in tables

PIE GRAPHS CAN . . .	• Show quantities that make up a whole
	• Give an immediate visual impression of the parts and their significance
	• Visually represent data shown in tables or lists

TO SHOW STEPS IN A PROCESS OR RELATIONSHIPS IN A SYSTEM

FLOWCHARTS CAN . . .	• Show how the parts or steps in a process or system interact
	• Show the stages of an actual or a hypothetical process in the correct direction, including recursive steps

TO SHOW RELATIONSHIPS IN A HIERARCHY

ORGANIZATIONAL CHARTS CAN . . .	• Give an overview of an organization's departmental components
	• Show how the components relate to one another
	• Depict lines of authority within an organization

TO SUPPLEMENT OR REPLACE WORDS

SYMBOLS OR ICONS CAN . . .	• Convey ideas without words
	• Save space and add visual appeal
	• Transcend individual languages to communicate ideas effectively for international readers

FIGURE 6–20. Chart for Choosing Appropriate Visuals (*continued*)

6

Design and Visuals

figure and in a footnote at the bottom of a table. Use a Web site's "Contact Us" page to request approval. Acknowledge your use of any public (uncopyrighted) information, such as demographic or economic data from government publications and Web sites, with a source line. See also <u>copyright</u> (Tab 3), <u>documenting sources</u> (Tab 3), and <u>plagiarism</u> (Tab 3). ✦

Writer's Checklist: Creating and Integrating Visuals

CREATING VISUALS

☑ Keep visuals simple: Include only information needed for discussion in the text and eliminate unneeded labels, arrows, boxes, and lines.

☑ Position the lettering of any explanatory text or labels horizontally; allow adequate white space within and around the visual.

☑ Specify the units of measurement used, make sure relative sizes are clear, and indicate distance with a scale when appropriate.

☑ Use consistent terminology; for example, do not refer to the same information as a "proportion" in the text and a "percentage" in the visual.

☑ Define <u>abbreviations</u> (Tab 12) the first time they appear in the text and in figures and tables. If any symbols are not self-explanatory, include a key, as in Figure 6–12.

☑ Give each visual a caption or concise <u>title</u> (Tab 4) that clearly describes its content, and assign figure and table numbers if your document contains more than one illustration or table.

INTEGRATING VISUALS

☑ Clarify for readers why each visual is included in the text and provide an appropriate description.

☑ Place visuals as close as possible to the text where they are discussed, but always after their first text mention.

☑ Refer to visuals in the text of your document as "figures" or "tables" and by their figure or table numbers.

☑ Consider placing lengthy or detailed visuals in an <u>appendix</u> (Tab 5), which you refer to in the body of your document.

☑ In documents with more than five illustrations or tables, include a section following the table of contents titled "List of Figures" or "List of Tables" that identifies each by number, title, and page number.

☑ Check the editorial guidelines or recommended style manual when preparing visuals for a publication.

7

Correspondence

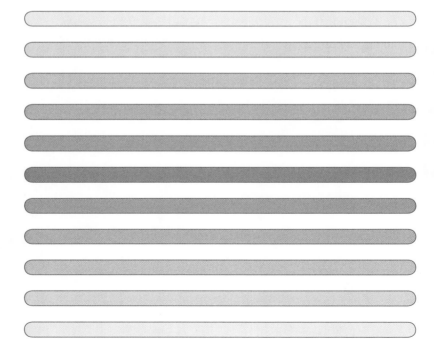

Preview

The process of writing business messages involves many of the same steps that go into most other on-the-job writing tasks, as described in "Five Steps to Successful Writing" (pages xxix–xxxvi). This section contains entries on the general principles of <u>correspondence</u> that will help you get the most out of specific entries on such forms as <u>e-mail</u> (Tab 2), <u>letters</u>, and <u>memos</u>. Other entries in this section cover specific situations, such as <u>complaints</u> and <u>adjustments</u>, as well as <u>international correspondence</u>. For choosing the best medium for corresponding, see <u>selecting the medium</u> (Tab 2).

7

Correspondence

acknowledgments

When a colleague or client sends you something or makes a request, you should acknowledge what was sent, respond to the request, or note that you cannot respond to the request immediately in a short, polite note. The message shown in Figure 7–1 could be sent as a letter or an e-mail (Tab 2). See also correspondence.

adjustments

An adjustment letter or e-mail (Tab 2) is written in response to a customer or client complaint and explains what your organization intends to do about the complaint. Although sent in response to a problem, an adjustment letter actually provides an excellent opportunity to build goodwill for your organization. An effective adjustment letter, such as the examples shown in Figures 7–2 and 7–3, can not only repair any damage done but also restore the customer's confidence in your company.

No matter how unreasonable the complaint, the tone (Tab 10) of your response should be positive and respectful. Avoid emphasizing the problem, but do take responsibility for it when appropriate. Focus your response on what you are doing to correct the problem. Settle such matters quickly and courteously, and lean toward giving the customer or client the benefit of the doubt at a reasonable cost to your organization. See also refusals.

7

Correspondence

Dear Ms. Stein:

I received your comprehensive report today. When I finish studying it in detail, I'll send you our cost estimate for the installation of the Checkout Reporting System.

Thank you for preparing such a thorough analysis.

Regards,

Wilbur Kohn

FIGURE 7–1. Acknowledgment

INTERNET SERVICES CORPORATION
10876 Crispen Way
Chicago, Illinois 60601

May 11, 2011

Mr. Jason Brandon
4319 Anglewood Street
Tacoma, WA 98402

Dear Mr. Brandon:

We are sorry that your experience with our customer support help
line did not go smoothly. We are eager to restore your confidence in
our ability to provide dependable, high-quality service. Your next
three months of Internet access will be complimentary as our sincere
apology for your unpleasant experience.

Providing dependable service is what is expected of us, and when our
staff doesn't provide quality service, it is easy to understand our
customers' disappointment. I truly wish we had performed better in
our guidance for setup and log-on procedures and that your experience
had been a positive one. To prevent similar problems in the future,
we plan to use your letter in training sessions with customer support
personnel.

We appreciate your taking the time to write us. It helps to receive
comments such as yours, and we conscientiously follow through to be
sure that proper procedures are being met.

Yours truly,

Inez Carlson

Inez Carlson, Vice President
Customer Support Services

www.isc.com

FIGURE 7–2. Adjustment Letter (When Company Is at Fault)

7

Correspondence

Dear Mr. Sanchez:

Enclosed is your Addison Laptop Computer, which you shipped to us on August 31.

Our technical staff reports that the laptop was damaged by exposure to high levels of humidity. You stated in your letter that you often use your laptop on a covered patio. Doing so in a high-humidity environment, as is typical in Louisiana, can result in damage to the internal circuitry of your computer — as described on page 32 of your Addison Owner's Manual.

We have replaced the damaged circuitry and thoroughly tested your laptop. To ensure that a repetition of your recent experience does not occur, we recommend you avoid leaving your laptop exposed to high humidity for extended periods.

If you should find that the problem recurs, please call us at 800-555-0990. We will be glad to work with you to find a solution.

Sincerely,

Customer Service Department

FIGURE 7-3. Partial Adjustment (Accompanying a Product)

Full Adjustments

Before granting an adjustment to a claim for which your company is at fault, first determine what happened and what you can do to satisfy the customer. Be certain that you are familiar with your company's adjustment policy—and be careful with word choice (Tab 10):

- We have just received your letter of May 7 about our defective gas grill.

Saying something is "defective" could be ruled in a court of law as an admission that the product is in fact defective. When you are in doubt, seek legal advice.

Grant adjustments graciously: A settlement made grudgingly will do more harm than good. Not only must you be gracious, but you must also acknowledge the error in such a way that the customer will not lose confidence in your company. Emphasize early what the reader will consider good news.

- Enclosed is a replacement for the damaged part.

- Yes, you were incorrectly billed for the delivery.

- Please accept our apologies for the error in your account.

◆ PROFESSIONALISM NOTE If an explanation will help restore your reader's confidence, describe what caused the problem. If appropriate, point out any steps you may be taking to prevent a recurrence of the problem. Explain that customer feedback helps your firm keep the quality of its product or service high. Close pleasantly, looking forward, not back. Avoid recalling the problem in your closing. (Do not write, "Again, we apologize. . . .") ◆

The adjustment letter in Figure 7–2, for example, begins by accepting responsibility and offers an apology for the customer's inconvenience (note the use of the pronouns *we* and *our*). The second paragraph expresses a desire to restore goodwill and describes specifically how the company intends to make the adjustment. The third paragraph expresses appreciation to the customer for calling attention to the problem and assures him that his complaint has been taken seriously.

Partial Adjustments

You may sometimes need to grant a partial adjustment—even when a claim is not justified—to regain the lost goodwill of a customer or client. If, for example, a customer incorrectly uses a product or service, you may need to help that person better understand the correct use of that product or service. In such a circumstance, remember that your customer or client believes that his or her claim is justified. Therefore, you should give the explanation before granting the claim—otherwise, your reader may never get to the explanation. If your explanation establishes customer responsibility, do so tactfully. Figure 7–3 is an example of a partial adjustment letter. See also correspondence.

complaints

A complaint letter (or e-mail) describes a problem that the writer requests the recipient to solve. The tone of a complaint letter or e-mail is important; the most effective ones do not sound complaining. If your message is shrill and belligerent, you may not be taken seriously. Assume that the recipient will be conscientious in correcting the problem. However, anticipate reader reactions or rebuttals. See audience (Tab 1), e-mail (Tab 2), and tone (Tab 10).

- I reviewed my user manual's "safe operating guidelines" carefully before I installed the device.
  [This assures readers you followed instructions.]

Subject: ST3 Diagnostic Scanners

On July 11, I ordered nine ST3 Diagnostic Scanners (order
ST3-1179R). The scanners were ordered from your customer
Web site.

On August 3, I received seven HL monitors from your parts warehouse in Newark, New Jersey. I immediately returned those monitors with a note indicating that a mistake had been made. However,
not only have I failed to receive the ST3 scanners that I ordered, but
I have also been billed repeatedly for the seven monitors.

I have enclosed a copy of my confirmation e-mail, the shipping
form, and the most recent bill. If you cannot send me the scanners I
ordered by November 2, please cancel my order.

Sincerely,

FIGURE 7–4. Complaint Letter

Without such explanations, readers may be tempted to dismiss your
complaint. Figure 7–4 shows a complaint letter that details a billing
problem. Although the circumstances and severity of the problem may
vary, effective complaint letters generally follow this pattern:

1. Identify the problem or faulty item(s) and include relevant
invoice numbers, part names, and dates. Include a copy of the
receipt, bill, or contract, and keep the original for your
records.
2. Explain logically, clearly, and specifically what went wrong, especially for a problem with a service. (Avoid guessing why you *think*
a problem occurred.)
3. State what you expect the reader to do to solve the problem.

Begin by checking to see if the company's Web site provides instructions for submitting a complaint. Otherwise, for large organizations,
you may address your complaint to Customer Service. In smaller
organizations, you might write to a vice president in charge of sales or
service or you might write directly to the owner. As a last resort, you
may find that sending copies of a complaint letter to more than one
person in the company will get faster results. See also adjustments and
refusals.

7

Correspondence

correspondence

Correspondence in the workplace—whether through <u>e-mail</u> (Tab 2), <u>letters</u>, or <u>memos</u> or another medium—requires many of the same steps that are described in "Five Steps to Successful Writing" (pages xxix–xxxvi). As you prepare an e-mail, for example, you might study previous messages ("research") and then list or arrange the points you wish to cover ("organization") in an order that is logical for your readers. See also <u>selecting the medium</u> (Tab 2).

Corresponding with others in the workplace also requires that you focus on both establishing or maintaining a positive working relationship with your readers and conveying a professional image of yourself and your organization. See also <u>audience</u> (Tab 1).

Audience and Writing Style

Effective correspondence uses an appropriate conversational style. To achieve that style, imagine your reader sitting across from you and write to the reader as if you were talking face to face. Take into account your reader's needs and feelings. Ask yourself, "How might I feel if I received this letter or e-mail?" and then tailor your message accordingly. Remember, an impersonal and unfriendly message to a customer or client can tarnish the image of you and your business, but a thoughtful and sincere one can enhance it.

Whether you use a formal or an informal writing style depends entirely on your reader and your <u>purpose</u> (Tab 1). You might use an informal (or a casual) style, for example, with a colleague you know well and a formal (or restrained) style with a client you do not know.

CASUAL   It worked! The new process is better than we had dreamed.

RESTRAINED   You will be pleased to know that the new process is more effective than we expected.

You will probably find yourself using the restrained style more frequently than the casual style. Remember that an overdone attempt to sound casual or friendly can sound insincere. However, do not adopt so formal a style that your writing reads like a legal contract. Affectation (Tab 10) not only will irritate and baffle readers but also can waste time and produce costly errors.

AFFECTED	Per yesterday's e-mail, we no longer possess an original copy of the brochure requested. Please be advised that a PDF copy is attached herewith to this e-mail.
IMPROVED	We are out of original copies of the brochure we discussed yesterday, so I am attaching a PDF copy to this e-mail.

The improved version is not only clearer and less stuffy but also more concise. See also business writing style (Tab 10) and conciseness (Tab 10).

Goodwill and the "You" Viewpoint

Write concisely, but do not be so blunt that you risk losing the reader's goodwill. Responding to a vague written request with "Your request was unclear" or "I don't understand" could offend your reader. Instead, establish goodwill to encourage your reader to provide the information you need.

- I will be glad to help, but I need additional information to locate the report you requested. Specifically, can you give me the report's title, release date, or number?

Although this version is a bit longer, it is more tactful and will elicit a helpful response. See also telegraphic style (Tab 10).

You can also build goodwill by emphasizing the reader's needs or benefits. Suppose you received a refund request from a customer who forgot to include the receipt with the request. In a response to that customer, you might write the following:

WEAK	We must receive the sales receipt before we can process a refund. [The writer's needs are emphasized: "*We* must."]

If you consider how to keep the customer's goodwill, you could word the request this way:

IMPROVED	Please send the sales receipt so that we can process your refund. [Although polite, the sentence focuses on the writer's needs: "so that *we* can process."]

7

Correspondence

You can put the reader's needs and interests foremost by writing from the reader's perspective. Often, doing so means using the words *you* and *your* rather than *we, our, I,* and *mine*—a technique called the <u>"you" viewpoint</u> (Tab 10). Consider the following revision:

EFFECTIVE	So that you can receive your refund promptly, please mail or fax the sales receipt. [The reader's needs are emphasized with *you* and *your*.]

This revision stresses the reader's benefit and interest. By emphasizing the reader's needs, the writer will be more likely to accomplish the purpose: to get the reader to act. See also <u>positive writing</u> (Tab 10).

If overdone, however, goodwill and the "you" viewpoint can produce writing that is fawning and insincere. Messages that are full of excessive praise and inflated language may be ignored—or even resented—by the reader.

EXCESSIVE PRAISE	You are just the kind of astute client that deserves the finest service that we can offer—and you deserve our best deal. Knowing how carefully you make decisions, I know you'll think about the advantages of using our consulting service.
REASONABLE	From our earlier correspondence, I understand your need for reliable service. We strive to give all our priority clients our full attention, and after you have reviewed our proposal, I am confident you will appreciate our "five-star" consulting option.

Writer's Checklist: Using Tone to Build Goodwill

Use the following guidelines to achieve a <u>tone</u> (Tab 10) that builds goodwill with your recipients.

☑ Be respectful, not demanding.

DEMANDING	Submit your answer in one week.
RESPECTFUL	I would appreciate your answer within one week.

☑ Be modest, not arrogant.

ARROGANT	My attached report is thorough, and I'm sure that you won't be able to continue without it.
MODEST	The attached report contains details of the refinancing options that I hope you will find useful.

Writer's Checklist: Using Tone to Build Goodwill (continued)

☑ Be polite, not sarcastic.

SARCASTIC	I just now received the shipment we ordered six months ago. I'm sending it back—we can't use it now. Thanks a lot!
POLITE	I am returning the shipment we ordered on March 14. Unfortunately, it arrived too late for us to be able to use it.

☑ Be positive and tactful, not negative and condescending.

NEGATIVE	Your complaint about our prices is way off target. Our prices are definitely not any higher than those of our competitors.
TACTFUL	Thank you for your suggestion concerning our prices. We believe, however, that our prices are comparable to or lower than those of our competitors.

Good-News and Bad-News Patterns

Although the relative directness of correspondence may vary, it is generally more effective to present good news directly and bad news indirectly, especially if the stakes are high.* This principle is based on the fact that readers form their impressions and attitudes very early and that you as the writer may want to subordinate the bad news to reasons that make the bad news understandable. Further, if you are writing international correspondence, consider that far more cultures are generally indirect in business messages than are direct.

Consider the thoughtlessness of the direct rejection in Figure 7–5. Although the message is concise and uses the pronouns *you* and *your*,

---

Dear Ms. Mauer:

Your application for the position of Records Administrator at Southtown Dental Center has been rejected. We have found someone more qualified than you.

Sincerely,

FIGURE 7–5. A Poor Bad-News Message

*Gerald J. Alred, "'We Regret to Inform You': Toward a New Theory of Negative Messages," in *Studies in Technical Communication*, ed. Brenda R. Sims (Denton: University of North Texas and NCTE, 1993), 17–36.

7

Correspondence

the writer does not consider how the recipient is likely to feel as she reads the rejection. Its pattern is (1) the bad news, (2) an explanation, and (3) the closing.

A better general pattern for bad news is (1) an opening that provides context (often called a "buffer"), (2) an explanation, (3) the bad news, and (4) a goodwill closing. (See also <u>context</u>, Tab 1, and <u>refusals</u>.) The opening introduces the subject and establishes a professional tone. The body provides an explanation by reviewing the facts that make the bad news understandable. Although bad news is never pleasant, information that either puts the bad news in perspective or makes it seem reasonable promotes not only understanding but also goodwill between the writer and the reader. The closing should reinforce a positive relationship through goodwill or helpful information. Consider, for example, the courteous rejection shown in Figure 7–6. It carries the same disappointing news as does the letter in Figure 7–5, but the writer is careful to thank the reader for her time and effort, explain why she was not accepted for the job, and offer her encouragement.

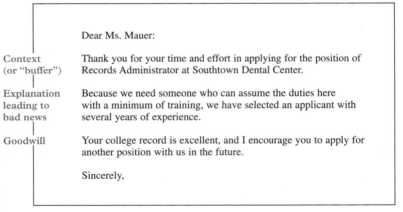

Dear Ms. Mauer:

Context (or "buffer")
Thank you for your time and effort in applying for the position of Records Administrator at Southtown Dental Center.

Explanation leading to bad news
Because we need someone who can assume the duties here with a minimum of training, we have selected an applicant with several years of experience.

Goodwill
Your college record is excellent, and I encourage you to apply for another position with us in the future.

Sincerely,

FIGURE 7–6. A Courteous Bad-News Message

This pattern can also be used in relatively short e-mail messages and memos. Consider the unintended secondary message the following notice conveys:

WEAK   It has been decided that the office will be open the day after Thanksgiving.

"It has been decided" not only sounds impersonal but also communicates an authoritarian, management-versus-employee tone. The passive voice also suggests that the decision maker does not want to say "I have decided" and thus accept responsibility. One solution is to remove the first part of the sentence.

IMPROVED   The office will be open the day after Thanksgiving.

The best solution, however, would be to suggest both that there is a good reason for the decision and that employees are privy to (if not a part of) the decision-making process.

EFFECTIVE   Because we must meet the December 15 deadline for submitting the Bradley Foundation proposal, the office will be open the day after Thanksgiving.

By describing the context of the bad news first (the need to meet the deadline), the writer focuses on the reasoning behind the decision to work. Employees may not necessarily like the message, but they will at least understand that the decision is not arbitrary and is tied to an important deadline.

Presenting good news is, of course, easier. Present good news in your opening, as in Figure 7–7. By doing so, you increase the likelihood that the reader will pay careful attention to details, and you achieve goodwill from the start. The pattern for good-news messages should be (1) a good-news opening, (2) an explanation of facts, and (3) a goodwill closing.

Dear Ms. Mauer:

We are pleased to offer you the position of Records Administrator at Southtown Dental Center at the salary of $54,300. Your qualifications fit our needs precisely, and we hope you will accept our offer.   Good news

If the terms we discussed in the interview are acceptable to you, please come to the main office at 9:30 a.m. on November 14. At that time, we will ask you to complete our benefits form, in addition to . . .   Explanation

I, as well as the others in the office, look forward to working with you. Everyone was favorably impressed with you during your interview.   Goodwill

Sincerely,

FIGURE 7–7. A Good-News Message

Openings and Closings

Although methods of development vary, the opening of any correspondence should identify the subject and often the main point of the message.

- Attached is the final installation report, which I hope you can review by Monday, December 5. You will notice that the report includes . . .

When your reader is not familiar with the subject or with the background of a problem, you may provide an introductory paragraph before stating the main point of the message. Doing so is especially important in correspondence that will serve as a record of crucial information. Generally, longer or complex subjects benefit most from more thorough introductions (Tab 1). However, even when you are writing a short message about a familiar subject, remind readers of the context. In the following example, words that provide context are shown in *italics*.

- *As Maria Lopez recommended,* I reviewed the office reorganization plan. I like most of the features; however, . . .

Do not state the main point first when (1) readers are likely to be highly skeptical or (2) key readers, such as managers or clients, may disagree with your position. In those cases, a more persuasive tactic is to state the problem or issue first, then present the specific points supporting your final recommendation, as discussed in the earlier section on bad-news messages. See also persuasion (Tab 1).

Your closing can accomplish many important tasks, such as building positive relationships with readers, encouraging colleagues and employees, and letting recipients know what you will do or what you expect of them.

- I will discuss the problem with the marketing consultant and let you know by Wednesday what we are able to change.

Routine statements are sometimes unavoidable. ("If you have further questions, please let me know.") However, try to make your closing work for you by providing specific prompts to which the reader can respond.

- Thanks again for the report, and let me know if you want me to send you a copy of the test results.

See also conclusions (Tab 1).

Clarity and Emphasis

A clear message is one that is adequately developed and emphasizes your main points. The following example illustrates how adequate development is crucial to the clarity of your message.

VAGUE   Be more careful on the loading dock.

DEVELOPED   To prevent accidents on the loading dock, follow these procedures:

1. Check . . . [followed by specific details]
2. Load only . . .
3. Replace . . .

Although the first version is concise, it is not as clear and specific as the "developed" revision. Do not assume your readers will know what you mean: Vague messages are easily misinterpreted.

Lists.   Vertically stacked words, phrases, and other items with numbers or bullets can effectively highlight such information as steps in sequence, materials or parts needed, key or concluding points, and recommendations. As described in the entry lists (Tab 6), make sure you provide context. Be careful not to overuse lists—a message that consists almost entirely of lists is difficult to understand because it forces readers to connect separate and disjointed items. Further, lists lose their effectiveness when they are overused.

Headings.   Headings (Tab 6) are particularly useful because they call attention to main topics, divide material into manageable segments, and signal a shift in topic. Readers can scan the headings and read only the section or sections appropriate to their needs.

Subject Lines.   Subject lines for e-mails, memos, and some letters announce the topic and focus of the correspondence. Because they also aid filing and later retrieval, they must be specific and accurate.

VAGUE   Subject: Tuition Reimbursement

VAGUE   Subject: Time-Management Seminar

SPECIFIC   Subject: Tuition Reimbursement for
Time-Management Seminar

Capitalize all major words in a subject line except articles, prepositions, and conjunctions with fewer than five letters (unless they are the first or last words). Remember that the subject line should not substitute for an opening that provides context for the message. See also titles (Tab 4).

Writer's Checklist: Correspondence and Accuracy

- ☑ Begin by establishing your purpose, analyzing your reader's needs, determining your scope (Tab 1), and considering the context.
- ☑ Prepare an outline, even if it is only a list of points to be covered in the order you want to cover them (see outlining, Tab 1).
- ☑ Write the first draft (see writing a draft, Tab 1).
- ☑ Allow for a cooling-off period prior to revision (Tab 1) or seek a colleague's advice, especially for correspondence that addresses a problem.

7
Correspondence

Writer's Checklist: Correspondence and Accuracy (continued)

☑ Revise the draft, checking for key problems in clarity and **coherence** (Tab 10).

☑ Use the appropriate or standard format, for example as in **letters** and **memos**.

☑ Check for accuracy: Make sure that all facts, figures, and dates are correct.

☑ Use effective **proofreading** (Tab 1) techniques to check your punctuation and usage (see the Appendix, "Usage"). See also Tab 12, "Punctuation and Mechanics."

☑ Consider who should receive a copy of the message and in what order the names or e-mail addresses should be listed (alphabetize if rank does not apply).

☑ Remember that when you sign a letter or send a message, you are accepting responsibility for it.

covers (or transmittals)

A cover **letter**, **memo**, or **e-mail** (Tab 2) accompanies a document, an electronic file, or other material. It identifies an item that is being sent, the person to whom it is being sent, the reason that it is being sent, and

---

Dear Mr. Hammersmith:

Attached is the report estimating our energy needs for the year as requested by John Brenan, Vice President, on September 5.

The report is a result of several meetings with the manager of plant operations and her staff and an extensive survey of all our employees. The survey was delayed by the transfer of key staff in Building A. We believe, however, that the report will provide the information you need in order to furnish us with a cost estimate for the installation of your Mark II Energy Saving System.

We would like to thank Diana Biel of ESI for her assistance in preparing the survey. If you need any more information, please let me know.

Sincerely,

FIGURE 7–8. Cover Message

any content that should be highlighted for readers. A cover letter provides a permanent record for both the writer and the reader. For cover letters to résumés, see application letters (Tab 8).

The example in Figure 7–8 is concise, but it also includes details such as how the information for the report was gathered.

e-mail (see Tab 2)

inquiries and responses

The purpose of writing an inquiry is to obtain responses to requests or specific questions, as in Figure 7–9, which shows a college student who is requesting information from an official at a power company. Inquiries may either benefit the reader (as in requests for information about a product that a company has advertised) or benefit the writer (as in the student's inquiry in Figure 7–9). Inquiries that primarily benefit the writer require the use of persuasion (Tab 1) and special consideration of the needs of your audience (Tab 1). See also correspondence.

7

Correspondence

Dear Ms. Metcalf:

I am an architecture student at the University of Dayton, and I am working with a team of students to design an energy-efficient house for a class project. I am writing to request information on heating systems based on the specifications of our design. To meet our deadline, we would appreciate any information you could provide by November 18.

The house we are designing contains 2,000 square feet of living space (17,600 cubic feet) and meets all the requirements in your brochure "Insulating for Efficiency." We need the following information, based on the southern Ohio climate:

• The proper-size heat pump for such a home.
• The wattage of the supplemental electrical heating units required.
• The estimated power consumption and rates for those units for one year.

We will be happy to send you our preliminary design report. If you have questions or suggestions, contact me at kparsons@fly.ud.edu or call 513-229-4598.

Thank you for your help.

FIGURE 7–9. Inquiry

Writing Inquiries

Inquiries need to be specific, clear, and concise in order to receive a prompt, helpful reply.

- Phrase your request so that the reader will immediately know the type of information you are seeking, why you need it, and how you will use it.
- If possible, present questions in a numbered or bulleted list (Tab 6) to make it easy for your reader to respond to them.
- Keep the number of questions to a minimum to improve your chances of receiving a prompt response.
- Offer some inducement for the reader to respond, such as promising to share the results of what you are doing. See also "you" viewpoint (Tab 10).
- Promise to keep responses confidential, when appropriate.
- Provide a date by which you need a response.

In the closing, thank the reader for taking the time to respond. In addition, make it convenient for the recipient to respond by providing your contact information, such as a phone number or an e-mail address, as shown in Figure 7–9.

Responding to Inquiries

When you receive an inquiry, determine whether you have both the information and the authority to respond. If you are the right person in your organization to respond and you understand your organization's policy about the issue, answer as promptly as you can, and be sure to answer every inquiry or question asked, as shown in Figure 7–10. How long and how detailed your response should be depends on the nature of the question and the information the writer provides.

If you have received an inquiry that you feel you cannot answer, find out who can and forward the inquiry to that person. Notify the writer that you have forwarded the inquiry. The person who replies to a forwarded inquiry should state in the first paragraph of the response who has forwarded the original inquiry, as shown in Figure 7–10.

instant messaging (*see* Tab 2)

international correspondence

Business correspondence varies among national cultures. Organizational patterns, persuasive strategies, forms of courtesy, formality, and ideas about efficiency differ from country to country. For example, in the

Dear Ms. Parsons:

Jane Metcalf forwarded to me your inquiry of October 14 about the house that your architecture team is designing. I can estimate the heating requirements of a typical home of 17,600 cubic feet as follows:

- For such a home, we would generally recommend a heat pump capable of delivering 40,000 BTUs, such as our model AL-42 (17 kilowatts).
- With the AL-42's efficiency, you don't need supplemental heating units.
- Depending on usage, the AL-42 unit averages between 1,000 and 1,500 kilowatt-hours from December through March. To determine the current rate for such usage, check with Dayton Power and Light Company.

I can give you an answer that would apply specifically to your house based on its particular design (such as number of stories, windows, and entrances). If you send me more details, I will be happy to provide more precise figures for your interesting project.

Sincerely,

FIGURE 7–10. **Response to an Inquiry**

United States, direct, concise correspondence usually demonstrates courtesy by not wasting the reader's time. In many other countries, however, such directness and brevity may seem rude to readers, suggesting that the writer wishes to spend as little time as possible corresponding with the reader. (See audience, Tab 1, and tone, Tab 10.) Likewise, where a U.S. writer might consider one brief letter or e-mail (Tab 2) sufficient to communicate a request, a writer in another country may expect an exchange of three or four longer letters to pave the way for action.

When you read correspondence from businesspeople in other cultures or countries, be alert to differences in such features as customary expressions, openings, and closings. Japanese business writers, for example, traditionally use indirect openings that reflect on the season, compliment the reader's success, and offer hopes for the reader's continued prosperity. Consider deeper issues as well, such as how writers from other cultures express bad news. Japanese writers traditionally express negative messages, such as refusals, indirectly to avoid embarrassing the recipient. Such cultural differences are often based on perceptions of time, face-saving, and traditions. The features and communication styles of specific national cultures are complex; the entry global communication (Tab 1) provides information and resources for cross-cultural study. See also global graphics (Tab 6).

> ### ⊛ WEB LINK SAMPLE INTERNATIONAL CORRESPONDENCE
>
> For an example of an inappropriate letter and an appropriate revised version for an international reader, see *bedfordstmartins.com/alred*, and select *ModelDoc Central*.

Writer's Checklist: Writing International Correspondence

- ☑ Observe the guidelines for courtesy, such as those in the *Writer's Checklist: Using Tone to Build Goodwill* on page 192.

- ☑ Write clear and complete sentences: Unusual word order or rambling sentences will frustrate and confuse readers. See **garbled sentences** (Tab 10).

- ☑ Avoid an overly simplified style that may offend or any affectation that may confuse the reader. See also **English as a second language** (Tab 11).

- ☑ Avoid humor, irony, and sarcasm; they are easily misunderstood outside their cultural **context** (Tab 1).

- ☑ Do not use **idioms** (Tab 10), **jargon** (Tab 10), slang expressions, unusual **figures of speech** (Tab 10), or allusions to events or attitudes particular to American life.

- ☑ Consider whether necessary technical terminology can be found in abbreviated English-language dictionaries; if it cannot, carefully define such terminology.

- ☑ Do not use contractions or abbreviations that may not be clear to international readers.

- ☑ Avoid inappropriate informality, such as using first names too quickly.

- ☑ Write out **dates** (Tab 12), whether in the month-day-year style (June 21, 2011, not 6/21/11) used in the United States or the day-month-year style (21 June 2011, not 21/6/11) used in many other parts of the world.

- ☑ Specify time zones or refer to international standards, such as Greenwich Mean Time (GMT) or Coordinated Universal Time (UTC).

- ☑ Use international measurement standards, such as the metric system (18°C, 14 cm, 45 kg, and so on) where possible.

- ☑ Ask someone from your intended audience's culture or with appropriate expertise to review your draft before you complete your final **proofreading** (Tab 1).

WEB LINK **GOOGLE'S INTERNATIONAL DIRECTORY**

Google's International Business and Trade Directory provides an excellent starting point for searching the Web for information related to customs, communication, and international standards. See *bedfordstmartins.com/ alred*, and select *Links Library*.

letters

Business letters—normally written for those outside an organization— are often the most appropriate choice for formal communications with professional associates or customers. Letters may be especially effective for those people who receive a high volume of e-mail and other electronic correspondence. Letters printed on organizational letterhead communicate formality, respect, and authority. See <u>correspondence</u> for advice on writing strategy and style. See also <u>selecting the medium</u> (Tab 2).

Although word-processing software includes templates for formatting business letters, the templates may not provide the appropriate dimensions and elements you need. The following sections offer specific advice on formatting and etiquette for business letters.*

Common Letter Styles

If your employer requires a particular format, use it. Otherwise, follow the guidelines provided here, and review the examples shown in Figures 7–11 and 7–12.

The two most common formats for business letters are the full-block style shown in Figure 7–11 and the modified-block style shown in Figure 7–12. In the *full-block style*, the entire letter is aligned at the left margin. In the *modified-block style*, the return address, date, and complimentary closing begin at the center of the page, and the other elements are aligned at the left margin. All other letter styles are variations of the full-block and modified-block styles.

To achieve a professional appearance, center the letter on the page vertically and horizontally. Although one-inch margins are the default standard in many word-processing programs, it is more important to establish a picture frame of blank space surrounding the page of text. When you use organizational letterhead stationery, consider the bottom of the letterhead as the top edge of the paper. The right margin should

7

Correspondence

*For additional details on letter formats and design, you may wish to consult a guide such as *The Gregg Reference Manual*, 11th ed., by William A. Sabin (New York: McGraw-Hill, 2010).

Letterhead	520 Niagara Street Braintree, MA 02184 Phone: (781) 787-1175 Fax: (781) 787-1213 EvansTE.com

EVANS
and Associates

Transportation Engineers

Date

May 16, 2011

Inside
address

Mr. George W. Nagel
Director of Operations
Boston Transit Authority
57 West City Avenue
Boston, MA 02210

Salutation

Dear Mr. Nagel:

Body

Enclosed is our final report evaluating the safety measures for the
Boston Intercity Transit System.

We believe that the report covers the issues you raised in our last
meeting and that you will be pleased with the results. However, if you
have any further questions, we would be happy to meet with you again
at your convenience.

We would also like to express our appreciation to Mr. L. K. Sullivan of
your committee for his generous help during our trips to Boston.

Compli-
mentary
closing

Sincerely,

Signature

Carolyn Brown

Writer's
signature
block

Carolyn Brown, Ph.D.
Director of Research
cbrown@evans.com

End
notations

CB/ls
Enclosure: Final Safety Report
cc: ITS Safety Committee Members

7

Correspondence

FIGURE 7–11. Full-Block-Style Letter (with Letterhead)

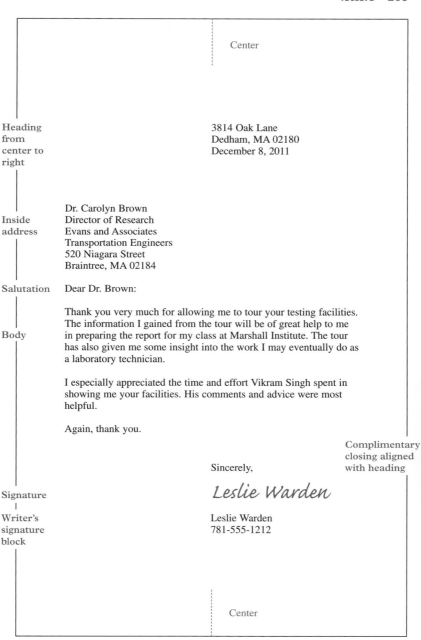

Center

Heading
from
center to
right

3814 Oak Lane
Dedham, MA 02180
December 8, 2011

Inside
address

Dr. Carolyn Brown
Director of Research
Evans and Associates
Transportation Engineers
520 Niagara Street
Braintree, MA 02184

Salutation

Dear Dr. Brown:

Body

Thank you very much for allowing me to tour your testing facilities.
The information I gained from the tour will be of great help to me
in preparing the report for my class at Marshall Institute. The tour
has also given me some insight into the work I may eventually do as
a laboratory technician.

I especially appreciated the time and effort Vikram Singh spent in
showing me your facilities. His comments and advice were most
helpful.

Again, thank you.

Complimentary
closing aligned
with heading

Sincerely,

Leslie Warden

Signature

Writer's
signature
block

Leslie Warden
781-555-1212

7

Correspondence

Center

FIGURE 7–12. Modified-Block-Style Letter (Without Letterhead)

be approximately as wide as the left margin. To give a fuller appearance to very short letters, increase both margins to about an inch and a half. Use your full-page or print-preview feature to check for proportion.

Heading

Unless you are using letterhead stationery, place your full return address and the date in the heading. Because your name appears at the end of the letter, it need not be included in the heading. Spell out words such as *street, avenue, first,* and *west* rather than abbreviating them. You may either spell out the name of the state in full or use the standard Postal Service abbreviation available at *usps.com.* The date usually goes directly beneath the last line of the return address. Do not abbreviate the name of the month. Begin the heading about two inches from the top of the page. If you are using letterhead that gives the company address, enter only the date, three lines below the last line of the letterhead.

Inside Address

Include the recipient's full name, title, and address in the inside address, two to six lines below the date, depending on the length of the letter. The inside address should be aligned with the left margin, and the left margin should be at least one-inch wide.

Salutation

Place the salutation, or greeting, two lines below the inside address and align it with the left margin. In most business letters, the salutation contains the recipient's personal title (such as *Mr., Ms., Dr.*) and last name, followed by a colon. If you are on a first-name basis with the recipient, use only the first name in the salutation.

Address women as *Ms.* unless they have expressed a preference for *Miss* or *Mrs.* However, professional titles (such as *Professor, Senator, Major*) take precedence over *Ms.* and similar courtesy titles.

When a person's first name could be either feminine or masculine, one solution is to use both the first and last names in the salutation (*Dear Pat Smith:*). Avoid "To Whom It May Concern" because it is impersonal and dated.

For multiple recipients, the following salutations are appropriate:

- Dear Professor Allen and Dr. Rivera:
  [two recipients]

- Dear Ms. Becham, Ms. Moore, and Mr. Stein:
  [three recipients]

- Dear Colleagues:
  [*Members*, or other suitable collective term]

If you are writing to a large company and do not know the name or title of the recipient, you may address a letter to an appropriate department or identify the subject in a subject line and use no salutation. (For information on creating subject lines, see page 197.)

- National Medical Supply Group
  501 West National Avenue
  Minneapolis, MN 55407

  Attention: Customer Service Department

- *Subject: Defective Cardio-100 Stethoscopes*

  I am returning six stethoscopes with damaged diaphragms that . . .

In other circumstances in which you do not know the recipient's name, use a title appropriate to the context of the letter, such as *Dear Customer* or *Dear IT Professional.*

Body

The body of the letter should begin two lines below the salutation (or any element that precedes the body, such as a subject or an attention line). Single-space within and double-space between paragraphs, as shown in Figures 7–11 and 7–12. To provide a fuller appearance to a very short letter, you can increase the side margins or increase the font size. You can also insert extra space above the inside address, the writer's signature block, and the initials of the person typing the letter—but do not exceed twice the recommended space for each of these elements.

Complimentary Closing

Type the complimentary closing two spaces below the body. Use a standard expression such as *Sincerely, Sincerely yours,* or *Yours truly.* If the recipient is a friend as well as a business associate, you can use a less formal closing, such as *Best wishes* or *Best regards* or, simply, *Best.* Capitalize only the initial letter of the first word, and follow the expression with a comma.

Writer's Signature Block

Type your full name four lines below and aligned with the complimentary closing. On the next line include your business title, if appropriate. The following lines may contain your individual contact information, such as a telephone number or an e-mail address, if not included in the letterhead or the body of your letter. Sign the letter in the space between the complimentary closing and your name.

7

Correspondence

End Notations

Business letters sometimes require additional information that is placed at the left margin, two spaces below the typed name and title of the writer in a long letter, four spaces below in a short letter.

Reference initials show the letter writer's initials in capital letters, followed by a slash mark (or colon), and then the initials of the person typing the letter in lowercase letters, as shown in Figure 7–11. When the writer is also the person typing the letter, no initials are needed.

Enclosure notations indicate that the writer is sending material along with the letter (an invoice, an article, and so on). Note that you should also mention the enclosure in the body of the letter. Enclosure notations may take several forms:

- Enclosure: Final Safety Report
- Enclosures (2)
- Enc. *or* Encs.

Copy notation ("cc:") tells the reader that a copy of the letter is being sent to the named recipient(s) (see Figure 7–11). Use a blind-copy notation ("bcc:") when you do not want the addressee to know that a copy is being sent to someone else. A blind-copy notation appears only on the copy, not on the original ("bcc: Dr. Brenda Shelton").

Continuing Pages

If a letter requires a second page (or, in rare cases, more), always carry at least two lines of the body text over to that page. Use plain (nonletterhead) paper of quality equivalent to that of the letterhead stationery for the second page. It should have a header with the recipient's name, the page number, and the date. Place the header in the upper left-hand corner or across the page, as shown in Figure 7–13.

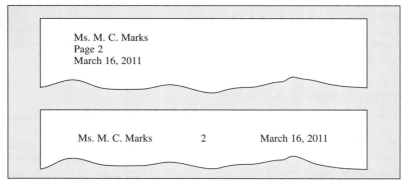

FIGURE 7–13. Headers for the Second Page of a Letter

memos

Memos are documents that use a standard form (*To:*, *From:*, *Date:*, *Subject:*) whether sent on paper or as attachments to e-mails. They are used within organizations to report results, instruct employees, announce policies, disseminate information, and delegate responsibilities.

Even in organizations where e-mail messages have largely taken the function of memos, a printed or an attached memo with organizational letterhead can communicate with formality and authority in addition to offering the full range of word-processing features. Paper memos are also useful in manufacturing and service industries, as well as in other businesses where employees do not have easy access to e-mail. For a discussion of writing strategies for memos, <u>e-mail</u> (Tab 2), and <u>letters</u>, see <u>correspondence</u>. See also <u>selecting the medium</u> (Tab 2).

Memo Format

The memo shown in Figure 7–14 illustrates that the memo format can be used not only for routine correspondence but also for short reports, proposals, and other internal documents.

Although memo formats and conventions vary, the format (*To:*, *From:*, *Date:*, *Subject:*) in Figure 7–14 is typical. As this example also illustrates, the use of <u>headings</u> (Tab 6) and <u>lists</u> (Tab 6) often fosters clarity and emphasizes important points in memos. For a discussion of subject lines, see page 197.

◆ PROFESSIONALISM NOTE As with e-mail, be alert to the practices of addressing and distributing memos in your organization. Consider who should receive or needs to be copied on a memo and in what order—senior managers, for example, take precedence over junior managers. If rank does not apply, alphabetizing recipients by last name is safe. ◆

Some organizations ask writers to initial or sign printed memos to verify that the writer accepts responsibility for a memo's contents. Electronic copies of memos do not need to include simulated initials.

 WEB LINK WRITING MEMOS

For links to articles about when to write memos and tips for following organization protocol, see *bedfordstmartins.com/alred*, and select *Links Library*.

7

Correspondence

Professional Publishing Services

MEMORANDUM

TO: Barbara Smith, Publications Manager

FROM: Hannah Kaufman, Vice President   *HK*

DATE: April 14, 2011

SUBJECT: Schedule for ACM Electronics Brochures

ACM Electronics has asked us to prepare a comprehensive set of
brochures for its Milwaukee office by August 10, 2011. We have worked
with similar firms in the past, so this job should be relatively easy to
prepare. My guess is that the job will take nearly two months. Ted Harris
has requested time and cost estimates for the project. Fred Moore in production will prepare the cost estimates, and I would like you to prepare a
tentative schedule for the project.

Additional Personnel
In preparing the schedule, check the status of the following:
- Production schedule for all staff writers
- Availability of freelance writers
- Availability of dependable graphic designers

Ordinarily, we would not need to depend on outside personnel; however,
because our bid for the *Wall Street Journal* special project is still under
consideration, we could be short of staff in June and July. Further, we have
to consider vacations that have already been approved.

Time Estimates
Please give me time estimates by April 18. A successful job done on time
will give us a good chance to obtain the contract to do ACM Electronics'
annual report for its stockholders' meeting this fall.

I have enclosed several brochures that may be helpful.

cc: Ted Harris, President
       Fred Moore, Production Editor

Enclosures: Sample Brochures

FIGURE 7–14. Typical Memo Format (Printed with Sender's Handwritten Initials)

Additional Pages

When memos require more than one page, use a second-page header and always carry at least two lines of the body text over to that page. The header should include either the recipient's name or an abbreviated subject line (if there are too many names to fit), the page number, and the date. Place the header in the upper left-hand corner or across the page, as shown in Figure 7–15.

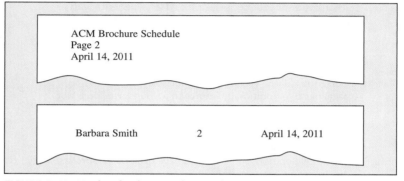

ACM Brochure Schedule
Page 2
April 14, 2011

Barbara Smith   2   April 14, 2011

FIGURE 7–15. Headers for the Second Page of Memos

refusals

A refusal delivers a negative message (or bad news) in the form of a letter, a memo, or an e-mail (Tab 2). The ideal refusal says "no" in such a way that you not only avoid antagonizing your reader but also maintain goodwill. See also audience (Tab 1).

When the stakes are high, you must convince your reader *before* you present the bad news that the reasons for your refusal are logical or understandable. (See also correspondence.) Stating a negative message in your opening may cause your reader to react too quickly and dismiss your explanation. The following pattern, used in the message shown in Figure 7–16, is an effective way to handle this problem:

1. Open with context (Tab 1) for the message (often called a "buffer").
2. Review the facts or details leading to the refusal or bad news.
3. Give the negative message based on the facts or details.
4. Close by establishing or reestablishing a positive relationship.

From: Nancy Nygaard <nn@bank21.com>
To: Marsha Coleman <mc2@ntr.com>
Sent: Monday, February 23, 2011 10:47 AM
Subject: NTR Check Sorter

Dear Ms. Coleman:

Context Thank you for your cooperation and your patience with us as we struggled to reach a decision. We believe our long involvement with your company indicates our confidence in your products.

Review of facts Based on our research, we found that the Winton Check Sorter has all the features that your sorter offers and, in fact, has two additional features that your sorter does not. The more important one is a backup feature that retains totals in its memory, even if the power fails. The second additional feature is stacked pockets, which are less space-consuming than the linear pockets on your sorter. After much deliberation, therefore, we have decided to purchase the Winton Check Sorter.

Refusal

Goodwill close Although we did not select your sorter, we were very favorably impressed with your system and your people. Perhaps we will be able to use other NTR products in the future.

Sincerely,

Nancy Nygaard

FIGURE 7–16. Refusal Letter (Sent as E-mail)

Your opening should provide an appropriate context and establish a professional <u>tone</u> (Tab 10), for example, by expressing appreciation for a reader's time, effort, or interest.

- The Screening Procedures Committee appreciates the time and effort you spent on your proposal for a new security-clearance procedure.

Next, review the circumstances of the situation sympathetically by placing yourself in the reader's position. Clearly detail the reasons you cannot do what the reader wants—even though you have not yet said you cannot do it. A good explanation should ideally detail the reasons for your refusal so thoroughly that the reader will accept the negative message as a logical conclusion as shown in the following example.

- We reviewed the potential effects of implementing your proposed security-clearance procedure companywide. We not only asked the Security Systems Department to review the data but also surveyed industry practices, sought the views of senior management, and submitted the idea to our legal staff. As a result of this process, we have reached the following conclusions:
  - The cost savings you project are correct only if the procedure could be required throughout the company.
  - The components of your procedure are legal, but most are not widely accepted by our industry.
  - Based on our survey, some components could alienate employees who would perceive them as violating an individual's rights.
  - Enforcing companywide use would prove costly and impractical.

Do not belabor the negative message—state your refusal quickly, clearly, and as positively as possible.

- For those reasons, the committee recommends that divisions continue their current security-screening procedures.

Close your message in a way that reestablishes goodwill—do not repeat the bad news. (Avoid writing "Again, we are sorry we cannot use your idea.") Ideally, provide an alternative, as in the following:

- Because some components of your procedure may apply in certain circumstances, we would like to feature your ideas in the next issue of *The Guardian*. I have asked the editor to contact you next week. On behalf of the committee, thank you for the thoughtful proposal.

If such an option is not possible or reasonable, offer a friendly remark that anticipates a positive future relationship, assure the reader of your high opinion of his or her product or service, or merely wish the reader success.

For responding to a complaint, see <u>adjustments</u>. For refusing a job offer, see <u>acceptance / refusals (for employment)</u> (Tab 8).

sales letters

A sales letter—a printed or an electronic message that promotes a product, service, or business—requires both a thorough knowledge of the product or service and an understanding of the potential customer's needs.

An effective sales letter (1) catches readers' attention, (2) arouses their interest, (3) convinces them that your product or service will fulfill a need or desire, and (4) confidently asks them to take the course of action you suggest. See also <u>persuasion</u> (Tab 1), <u>promotional writing</u> (Tab 1), <u>correspondence</u>, and <u>tone</u> (Tab 10).

Your first task in writing a sales letter is to determine to whom your message should be sent. One good source of names is a list of your customers; people who have at some time purchased a product or service from you may do so again. Other sources are lists of people who may be interested in similar products or services. Companies that specialize in marketing techniques compile such lists from the membership rolls of professional associations, lists of trade-show attendees, and the like. Because buying outside lists tends to be expensive, select them with care.

Once you determine who is to receive your sales letter, learn as much as you can about your readers so that you can effectively tell them how your product or service will satisfy their needs. Knowledge of your <u>audience</u> (Tab 1)—their gender, age, vocation, geographic location, educational level, financial status, and interests—will help determine your approach.

Analyze your product or service carefully to determine your strongest psychological sales points. Psychological selling involves stressing a product's benefits, which may be intangible, rather than its physical features. Select the most important psychological selling point about your product or service and build your sales message around it. Show how your product or service will make your readers' jobs easier, increase their status, make their personal lives more pleasant, and so on. Show how your product or service can satisfy your readers' needs or desires, which you identified in your opening. Then describe the physical features of your product in terms of their benefit to your readers. Help your readers imagine themselves using your product or service—and enjoying the benefits of doing so. See also <u>"you" viewpoint</u> (Tab 10).

⬛ ETHICS NOTE Be certain that any claim you make in a sales message is valid. To claim that a product is safe guarantees its absolute safety; therefore, say that the product is safe "provided that normal safety precautions are taken." Further, do not exaggerate or speak negatively about a competitor. For further ethical and legal guidelines, visit the Direct Marketing Association Web site at *www.the-dma.org*. See also <u>ethics in writing</u> (Tab 1). ✦

Writer's Checklist: Writing Sales Letters

☑ Attract your readers' attention and arouse their interest in the opening, for example, by describing a product's feature that would appeal strongly to their needs. See also <u>introductions</u> (Tab 1).

Writer's Checklist: Writing Sales Letters (continued)

☑ Convince readers that your product or service is everything you say it is through case histories, free-trial use, money-back guarantee, or testimonials and endorsements.*

☑ Suggest ways readers can make immediate use of the product or service.

☑ Minimize the negative effect price can have on readers.

- Mention the price along with a reminder of the benefits of the product.
- State the price in terms of units rather than sets ($20 per item, not $600 per set).
- Identify the daily, monthly, or even yearly cost based on the estimated life of the product.
- Suggest a series of payments rather than one total payment.
- Compare the cost of your product with that of something readers accept readily. ("This entire package costs no more than a DVD.")

☑ Make it easy and worthwhile for customers to respond: Include a brochure, a discount coupon, instructions for phone-in orders, information about free delivery, or a Web address or link where customers can view special discounts and order online.

*For detailed advice, see the FTC Guides Concerning Use of Endorsements and Testimonials in Advertising at *www.ftc.gov/opa/2009/10/endortest.shtm*.

 WEB LINK SALES-LETTER RESOURCES

For links to advice on writing sales letters as well as samples, see *bedfordstmartins.com/alred*, and select *Links Library*.

7

Correspondence

8

Job Search and Application

Preview

This section includes entries related to a successful <u>job search</u> — from the crucial <u>application letters</u> and <u>résumés</u> to job <u>acceptance / refusals</u>. The section also offers strategies for <u>interviewing for a job</u>.

8

Job Search and Application

acceptance / refusals (for employment)

When you decide to accept a job offer, you can notify your new employer by telephone or in a meeting—but to make your decision official, you need to send your acceptance in writing. What you include in your message and whether you send a <u>letter</u> (Tab 7) or an <u>e-mail</u> (Tab 2) depends on your previous conversations with your new employer. See also **correspondence** (Tab 7). Figure 8–1 shows an example of a job-acceptance letter written by a graduating student with substantial experience (see his <u>résumé</u> in Figure 8–9 on page 236).

Note that in the first paragraph of Figure 8–1, the writer identifies the job he is accepting and the salary he has been offered—doing so can avoid any misunderstandings about the job or the salary. In the second paragraph, the writer details his plans for relocating and reporting for work. Even if the writer discussed these arrangements during earlier conversations, he needs to confirm them, officially, in this written message. The writer concludes with a brief but enthusiastic statement that he looks forward to working for the new employer.

When you decide to reject a job offer, send a written job refusal to make that decision official, even if you have already notified the employer

---

Dear Ms. Castro:

I am pleased to accept your offer of $44,500 per year as a Graphic Designer with the Natural History Museum.

After graduation, I plan to leave Pittsburgh on Tuesday, June 7. I should be able to find living accommodations and be ready to report for work on Monday, June 20. If you need to reach me prior to this date, please call me at 412-555-1212 (cell) or contact me by e-mail at jgoodman@aol.com.

I look forward to joining the marketing team and working with the excellent support staff I met during the interview.

Sincerely,

Joshua S. Goodman

Joshua S. Goodman

FIGURE 8–1. Acceptance Letter (for Employment)

8
Job Search and Application

during a meeting or on the phone. Writing to an employer is an important goodwill gesture.

In Figure 8–2, an example of a job refusal, the applicant mentions something positive about his contact with the employer and refers to the specific job offered. He indicates his serious consideration of the offer, provides a logical reason for the refusal, and concludes on a pleasant note. (See his résumé in Figure 8–10 on page 237.) For further advice on handling refusals and negative messages generally, see <u>refusals</u> (Tab 7).

✦ PROFESSIONALISM NOTE Be especially tactful and courteous — the employer you are refusing has spent time and effort interviewing you and may have counted on your accepting the job. Remember, you may apply for another job at that company in the future. ✦

Dear Mr. Vallone:

I enjoyed talking with you about your opening for a manager of aerospace production at your Rockford facility, and I seriously considered your generous offer.

After giving the offer careful thought, however, I have decided to accept a management position with a research-and-development firm. I feel that the job I have chosen is better suited to my long-term goals.

I appreciate your consideration and the time you spent with me. I wish you success in filling the position.

Sincerely,

Robert Mandillo

Robert Mandillo

FIGURE 8–2. Refusal Letter (for Employment)

application letters

When applying for a job, you usually need to submit both an application letter (also referred to as a *cover letter*) and a <u>résumé</u>. Employers may ask you to submit a letter by standard mail, online form, fax, or <u>e-mail</u> (Tab 2). See also <u>job search</u> and <u>letters</u> (Tab 7).

The application letter is essentially a <u>sales letter</u> (Tab 7) in which you market your skills, abilities, and knowledge. Therefore, your application letter must be persuasive. The successful application letter accomplishes four tasks: (1) It catches the reader's attention favorably by describing how your skills can contribute to the organization, (2) it explains which particular job interests you and why, (3) it convinces the reader that you are qualified for the job by highlighting and interpreting the particularly impressive qualifications in your résumé, and (4) it requests an interview. See also persuasion (Tab 1), correspondence (Tab 7), and interviewing for a job.

The sample application letters shown in Figures 8–3 through 8–5 follow the structure described in this entry. Each sample's emphasis, tone, and style are tailored to fit the applicant's experience and the

---

From:	Marsha S. Parker <msparker@ubi.edu>
To:	Patrice C. Crandal <pcrandal@abel.com>
Sent:	Monday, February 7, 2011 10:47 AM
Subject:	Application for Summer Internship
Attachment:	📄 Parker_Resume.doc

Dear Ms. Crandal:

I have learned from your Web site that you are hiring undergraduates for summer internships. An internship with Abel's buyer training program interests me because I have learned that your program is one of the best in the industry.

The professional and analytical qualities that my attached résumé describes match the job description on your Web site. My experience with the Alumni Relations Program and the University Center Committee have enhanced my communication and persuasive abilities as well as my understanding of compromise and negotiation. For example, in the alumni program, I persuaded both uninvolved and active alumni to become more engaged with the direction of the university. On the University Center Committee, I balanced the students' demands with the financial and structural constraints of the administration. With these skills, I can ably assist the members of your department with their summer projects and successfully juggle multiple responsibilities.

I would appreciate the opportunity to meet with you to discuss your summer internship further. If you have questions or would like to speak with me, please contact me at (412) 863-2289 any weekday after 3 p.m., or you can e-mail me at <msparker@ubi.edu>. Thank you for your consideration.

Sincerely,

Marsha S. Parker

FIGURE 8–3. Application Letter Sent as E-mail (College Student Applying for an Internship)

222 Morewood Ave.
Pittsburgh, PA 15212
April 15, 2011

Ms. Judith Castro, Director
Human Resources
Natural History Museum
1201 South Figueroa Street
Los Angeles, CA 90015

Dear Ms. Castro:

I have recently learned from Jodi Hammel, a graphic designer at Dyer/Khan, that you are recruiting for a graphic designer in your Marketing Department. Your position interests me greatly because it offers me an opportunity both to fulfill my career goals and to promote the work of an internationally respected institution. Having participated in substantial volunteer activities at a local public museum, I am aware of the importance of your work.

I bring strong up-to-date academic and practical skills in multimedia tools and graphic arts production, as indicated in my enclosed résumé. Further, I have recent project management experience at Dyer/Khan, where I was responsible for the development of client brochures, newsletters, and posters. As project manager, I coordinated the project timelines, budgets, and production with clients, staff, and vendors.

My experience and contacts in the Los Angeles area media and entertainment community should help me make use of state-of-the-art design expertise. As you will see on my résumé, I have worked with the leading motion picture, television, and music companies — that experience should help me develop exciting marketing tools Museum visitors and patrons will find attractive. For example, I helped design an upgrade of the CGI logo for Paramount Pictures and was formally commended by the Director of Marketing.

Could we schedule a meeting at your convenience to discuss this position further? Call me any weekday morning at 412-555-1212 (cell) or e-mail me at <jgoodman@aol.com> if you have questions or need additional information. Thank you for your consideration.

Sincerely,

Joshua S. Goodman

Joshua S. Goodman

Enclosure: Résumé

FIGURE 8–4. Application Letter (Recent Graduate Applying for a Graphic Design Job)

Dear Ms. Smathers:

During the recent NOMAD convention in Washington, Karen Jarrett, Director of Operations, informed me of a possible opening at Aerospace Technologies for a manager of new product development. My extensive background in engineering exhibit design and management makes me an ideal candidate for the position she described.

I have been manager of the Exhibit Design Lab at Wright-Patterson Air Force Base for the past seven years. During that time, I received two Congressional Commendations for models of a space station laboratory and a docking/repair port. My experience in advanced exhibit design would give me a special advantage in helping develop AT's wind tunnel and aerospace models. Further, I have just learned this week that my exhibit design presented at NOMAD received a "Best of Show" Award.

As described on the enclosed résumé, I not only have workplace management experience but also have recently received an MBA from the University of Dayton. As a student in the MBA program, I won the Luson Scholarship to complete my coursework as well as the Jonas Outstanding Student Award.

I would be happy to discuss my qualifications in an interview at your convenience. Please telephone me at (937) 255-4137 or e-mail me at <mand@juno.com>. I look forward to talking with you.

Sincerely,

Robert Mandillo

FIGURE 8–5. Application Letter (Applicant with Years of Experience)

particular audience. Note that the letter shown in Figure 8–4 matches the résumé in Figure 8–9 ("Joshua S. Goodman") and the letter sent as an e-mail in Figure 8–5 matches the résumé in Figure 8–10 ("Robert Mandillo").

Opening

In the opening paragraph, provide <u>context</u> (Tab 1) by indicating how you heard about the position and name the specific job title or area. If you have been referred to a company by an employee, a career counselor, a professor, or someone else, be sure to say so. ("I have recently learned from Jodi Hammel, a graphic designer at Dyer/Khan, that you are recruiting. . . .") Show enthusiasm by explaining why you are interested in the job and demonstrate your initiative as well as your knowledge of the organization by relating your interest to some facet of the organization. ("An internship with Abel's buyer training program interests me because I have learned that your program is one of the best in the industry.")

Body

In the middle paragraphs, show through examples that you are qualified for the job. Limit each of these <u>paragraphs</u> (Tab 1) to just one basic point that is clearly stated in the topic sentence. For example, your second paragraph might focus on work experience and your third paragraph on educational achievements. Do not just *tell* readers that you are qualified—*show* them by including examples and details. ("I helped design an upgrade of the CGI logo for Paramount Pictures and was formally commended by the Director of Marketing.") Highlight your achievements and refer to your enclosed résumé, but do not simply summarize your résumé. Indicate how your talents can make valuable contributions to the company.

Closing

In the final paragraph, request an interview. Let the reader know how to reach you by including your phone number or e-mail address. End with a statement of goodwill, even if only a "thank you."

Proofread your letter *carefully*. Research indicates that if employers notice even one spelling, grammatical, or mechanical error, they often eliminate candidates from consideration immediately. Such errors give employers the impression that you lack writing skills or that you are careless in the way you present yourself professionally. See also <u>proofreading</u> (Tab 1).

interviewing for a job

Job interviews can take place in person, by phone, or by teleconference. They may last 30 minutes, an hour, or several hours. Sometimes, an initial job interview is followed by a series of additional interviews that can last a half or full day. Often, just one or two people conduct a job interview, but at times a group of four or more might do so. Because it is impossible to know exactly what to expect, it is important that you be well prepared.

Before the Interview

The interview is not a one-way communication. It presents you with an opportunity to ask questions of your potential employer. Before the interview, learn everything you can about the organization by answering for yourself such questions as the following:

- What kind of organization (profit, nonprofit, government) is it?
- How diversified are its activities or branches?
- Is it a locally owned business?
- Does it provide a product or service? If so, what kind?
- How large is the business? How large are its assets?
- Is the owner self-employed? Is the company a subsidiary of a larger operation? Is it expanding?
- How long has the company been in business?
- Where will I fit in?

You can obtain information from current employees, the Internet, the company's publications, and the business section of back issues of local newspapers. The company's Web site may help you learn about the company's size, sales volume, product line, credit rating, branch locations, subsidiary companies, new products and services, building programs, and similar information. You may also conduct research (Tab 3) using a company's annual reports and other publications, such as *Moody's Industrials*, *Dun and Bradstreet*, *Standard and Poor's*, and *Thomas' Register*, as well as other business reference sources a librarian might suggest. Ask your interviewer about what you cannot find through your own research. Doing so demonstrates your interest and allows you to learn more about your potential employer.

Try to anticipate the questions your interviewer might ask, and prepare your answers in advance. Be sure you understand a question before answering it, and avoid responding too quickly with a rehearsed answer—be prepared to answer in a natural and relaxed manner. Interviewers typically ask the following questions:

- What are your short-term and long-term occupational goals?
- Where do you see yourself five years from now?
- What are your major strengths and weaknesses?
- Do you work better with others or alone?
- What academic or career accomplishment are you particularly proud of? Describe it.
- Why are you leaving your current job?
- Why do you want to work for this organization?
- Why should I hire you?
- What salary and benefits do you expect?

Rather than such straightforward questions, some employers use behavioral interviews that focus on asking the candidate to provide examples or respond to hypothetical situations. Interviewers who use behavior-based questions are looking for specific examples from your experience. Prepare for the behavioral interview by recollecting challenging situations or problems that you successfully resolved. Examples of behavior-based questions include the following:

- Tell me about a time when you experienced conflict while on a team.
- If I were your boss and you disagreed with a decision I made, what would you do?
- How have you used your leadership skills to bring about change?
- Tell me about a time when you failed and what you learned from the experience.

◆ PROFESSIONALISM NOTE Arrive for your interview on time or even 10 or 15 minutes early—you may be asked to fill out an application or other paperwork before you meet your interviewer. Always bring extra copies of your résumé, samples of your work (if applicable), and a list of references and contact information. If you are asked to complete an application form, read it carefully before you write and proofread it when you are finished. The form provides a written record for company files and indicates to the company how well you follow directions and complete a task. ✦

During the Interview

The interview actually begins before you are seated: What you wear and how you act make a first impression. In general, dress simply and conservatively, avoid extremes in fragrance and cosmetics, and be well groomed.

Behavior. First, thank the interviewer for his or her time, express your pleasure at meeting him or her, and remain standing until you are offered a seat. Then sit up straight (good posture suggests self-assurance), look directly at the interviewer, and try to appear relaxed and confident. During the interview, you may find yourself feeling a little nervous. Use that nervous energy to your advantage by channeling it into the alertness that you will need to listen and respond effectively. Do not attempt to take extensive notes or use a laptop computer during the interview. You can jot down a few facts and figures on a small pad, but keep your focus on the interviewer. See also listening (Tab 9).

Responses. When you answer questions, do not ramble or stray from the subject. Say only what you must to answer each question properly and then stop, but avoid giving just yes or no answers—they usually do not allow the interviewer to learn enough about you. Some interviewers allow a silence to fall just to see how you will react. The burden of conducting the interview is the interviewer's, not yours—and he or she may interpret your rush to fill a void in the conversation as a sign of insecurity. If such a silence makes you uncomfortable, be ready to ask an intelligent question about the company.

If the interviewer overlooks important points, bring them up. However, let the interviewer mention salary first. Doing so yourself may indicate that you are more interested in the money than the work. However, make sure you are aware of prevailing salaries and benefits in your field.

Interviewers look for a degree of self-confidence and an applicant's understanding of the field, as well as genuine interest in the field, the company, and the job. Ask questions to communicate your interest in the job and company. Interviewers respond favorably to applicants who can communicate and present themselves well.

Conclusion.   At the conclusion of the interview, thank the interviewer for his or her time. Indicate that you are interested in the job (if true) and try to get an idea of the company's hiring time frame. Reaffirm friendly contact with a firm handshake.

After the Interview

After you leave the interview, jot down the pertinent information you obtained, as it may be helpful in comparing job offers. As soon as possible following a job interview, send the interviewer a note of thanks in a brief letter or e-mail. Such notes often include the following:

- Your thanks for the interview and to individuals or groups that gave you special help or attention during the interview
- The name of the specific job for which you interviewed
- Your impression that the job is attractive, if true
- Your confidence that you can perform the job well
- An offer to provide further information or answer further questions

Figure 8–6 shows a typical example of follow-up correspondence.

If you are offered a job you want, accept the offer verbally and write a brief letter of acceptance as soon as possible — certainly within a week. If you do not want the job, write a refusal letter or e-mail, as described in <u>acceptance / refusals</u>.

job search

Whether you are applying for your first job or want to change careers entirely, begin by assessing your skills, interests, and abilities, perhaps through brainstorming. Next, consider your career goals and values.*

*A good source for stimulating your thinking is the most recent edition of *What Color Is Your Parachute? A Practical Manual for Job-Hunters & Career-Changers* by Richard Nelson Bolles, published by Ten Speed Press.

8

Job Search and
Application

Dear Mr. Vallone:

Thank you for the informative and pleasant interview we had yesterday. Please extend my thanks to Mr. Wilson of the Media Group as well.

I came away from our meeting most favorably impressed with Adams Brokerage. I find the position of financial adviser to be an attractive one and feel confident that my qualifications would enable me to perform the duties to everyone's advantage.

If I can answer any further questions, please let me know.

Sincerely yours,

Elaine Treadwell

FIGURE 8–6. Follow-up Correspondence

For instance, do you prefer working independently or collaboratively? Do you enjoy public settings? Do you like meeting people? How important are career stability and location? What would you most like to be doing in the immediate future? in two years? in five years?

Once you have narrowed your goals and identified a professional area that is right for you, consider the following sources to locate the job you want. Of course, do not rely on any one source exclusively:

- Networking and informational interviews
- Campus career services
- Web resources
- Job advertisements
- Trade and professional journal listings
- Employment agencies (private, temporary, government)
- Internships
- Letters of inquiry

Keep a file during your job search of dated job ads, copies of <u>application letters</u> and <u>résumés</u>, and the names of important contacts. This collection can serve as a future resource and reminder.

Networking and Informational Interviews

Networking involves communicating with people who might provide useful advice or may know of potential jobs in your interest areas. They may include people already working in your chosen field, contacts in professional organizations, professors, family members, or friends.

Discussion groups and professional networking sites, such as LinkedIn .com, can be helpful in this process. Use your contacts to expand your network of contacts. Most career professionals estimate that between 60 and 80 percent of all open positions are filled through networking.

Informational interviews are appointments you schedule with working professionals who can give you "insider" views of an occupation or industry. These brief meetings (usually 20 to 30 minutes) also offer you the opportunity to learn about employment trends as well as leads for employment opportunities. Because you ask the questions, these interviews allow you to participate in an interview situation that is less stressful than the job interview itself. To make the most of informational interviews, prepare carefully and review both interviewing for information (Tab 3) and interviewing for a job.

Campus Career Services

A visit to the college career-development center is another good way to begin your job search. Government, business, and industry recruiters often visit campus career offices to interview prospective employees; recruiters also keep career counselors aware of their companies' current employment needs and submit job descriptions to them. Not only can career counselors help you select a career, but they can also put you in touch with the best and most current resources—identifying where to begin your search and saving you time. Career-development centers often hold workshops on résumé preparation and offer other job-finding resources on their Web sites.

Web Resources

In addition to professional networking sites mentioned earlier, the Web can enhance your job search in a number of ways. First, you can consult sites that give advice about careers, job seeking, and résumé preparation. Second, you can learn about businesses and organizations that may hire employees in your area by visiting their Web sites. Such sites often list job openings, provide instructions for applicants, and offer other information, such as employee benefits. Third, you can learn about jobs in your field and post your résumé for prospective employers at employment databases, such as Monster.com and Yahoo! hotjobs (*http://hotjobs.yahoo.com*). Fourth, you can post your résumé on your personal Web site. Although posting your résumé at an employment database will undoubtedly attract more potential employers, including your résumé on your own site has benefits. For example, you might provide a link to your site in e-mail correspondence or provide your Web site's URL in an inquiry letter to a prospective employer. If you use a personal Web site, however, it should contain only material that would be of interest to prospective employers, such as examples of your work, awards, and other professional items.

8

Job Search and Application

■ PROFESSIONALISM NOTE Be careful with the material that you post on such online social communities as MySpace, Facebook, and YouTube. Potential employers often conduct Web searches that could access content on such Web sites, so you need to be aware of how you present yourself in online public spaces. ✦

 WEB LINK FINDING A JOB

For job-hunting tips, sample documents, and links to the sites mentioned in this entry, see *bedfordstmartins.com/alred*, and select *Finding an Internship or Job* and *Links Library*.

Job Advertisements

Many employers advertise jobs in the classified sections of newspapers. Because job listings can differ, search in both the printed and Web editions of local and big-city newspapers under *employment* or *job market*. Use the search options they provide or the general strategies for database searches discussed in the entry <u>research</u> (Tab 3).

A human-relations specialist interested in training, for example, might find the specialty listed under "Human Resources" or "Consulting Services." Depending on a company's or government agency's needs, the listing could be even more specific, such as "Software Education Specialist" or "Learning and Development Coordinator."

As you read the ads, take notes on salary ranges, job locations, job duties and responsibilities, and even the terminology used in the ads to describe the work. A knowledge of keywords and key expressions that are generally used to describe a particular type of work can be helpful when you prepare your résumé and letters of application.

Trade and Professional Journal Listings

In many industries, trade and professional associations publish periodicals of interest to people working in the industry. Such periodicals (print and online) often contain job listings. To learn about such associations for your occupation, consult resources on the Web, such as Google's Directory of Professional Organizations or online resources offered by your library or campus career office. You may also consult the following references at a library: *Encyclopedia of Associations* and *Encyclopedia of Business Information Sources*.

Employment Agencies (Private, Temporary, Government)

Private employment agencies are profit-making organizations that are in business to help people find jobs—for a fee. Reputable agencies provide you with job leads, help you organize your job search, and supply information on companies doing the hiring. A staffing agency or temporary placement agency could match you with an appropriate temporary or permanent job in your field. Temporary work for an organization for which you might want to work permanently is an excellent way to build your network while continuing your job search.

Choose an employment or a temporary-placement agency carefully. Some are well established and reputable; others are not. Check with your local Better Business Bureau and your college career office before you sign an agreement with a private employment agency. Further, be sure you understand who is paying the agency's fee. Often the employer pays the agency's fee; however, if you have to pay, make sure you know exactly how much. As with any written agreement, read the fine print carefully.

Local, state, and federal government agencies also offer many free or low-cost employment services. Local government agencies are listed in telephone and Web directories under the name of your city, county, or state. For information on occupational trends, see the Occupational Outlook Handbook at *www.bls.gov/OCO* and, for information on jobs with the federal government, see the U.S. Office of Personnel Management Web site at *www.usajobs.gov*.

Internships

As you evaluate job options, consider taking an internship. An entry-level position lasting from six weeks to an entire semester, an internship provides you with the opportunity to gain experience in a field through a variety of career opportunities:

- Trying a position without making a permanent commitment
- Exploring a field to clarify your career goals while getting on-the-job experience
- Developing skills and gaining experience in a new field or industry
- Evaluating a prospective employer or firm
- Acquiring a mentor in the workplace
- Benefiting from networking contacts for future job opportunities
- Gaining access to professional references
- Becoming eligible for a job offer based on an employer's satisfaction with your work

To locate internship opportunities, begin with your campus career development office. Such offices usually post internship opportunities at their Web site, but you can also make appointments with counselors or take advantage of walk-in hours.

Direct Inquiries

If you would like to work for a particular firm, write or call to ask whether it has any openings for people with your qualifications. Normally, you can contact the department head, the director of human resources, or both; for a small firm, however, write to the head of the firm. Such contacts work best if you have networked as described earlier in this entry.

résumés

A résumé is the key tool of the job search that itemizes your qualifications and serves as a foundation for your application letter (often referred to as a *cover letter*). Limit your résumé* to one page—or two pages if you have substantial experience. On the basis of the information in the résumé and application letter, prospective employers decide whether to ask you to come in for an interview. If you are invited to an interview, the interviewer can base specific questions on the contents of your résumé. See also interviewing for a job.

◆ ETHICS NOTE Be truthful. The consequences of giving false information in your résumé are serious. In fact, the truthfulness of your résumé reflects not only on your own ethical stance but also on the integrity with which you would represent the organization. See also ethics in writing (Tab 1). ✦

Because résumés affect a potential employer's first impression, make sure that yours is well organized, carefully designed, consistently formatted, easy to read, and free of errors. Consider first an organization that highlights your strengths and fits your goals, as suggested by the examples shown in this entry. Proofreading (Tab 1) is essential—verify the accuracy of the information and have someone else review it.

 DIGITAL TIP FORMATTING THE RÉSUMÉ

The design of a résumé can highlight your qualifications and get you noticed. For specific advice on using your word-processing program to construct a well-designed résumé, see *bedfordstmartins.com/alred*, and select *Digital Tips*.

*A detailed résumé for someone in an academic and a scientific area is often called a *curriculum vitae* (also *vita* or *c.v.*). It may include education, publications, projects, grants, and awards as well as a full work history. Outside the United States, the term *curriculum vitae* is often used to mean *résumé*.

Sample Résumés

The sample résumés in this entry are provided to stimulate your thinking about how to tailor your résumé to your own job search. Before you design and write your résumé, look at as many samples as possible, and then organize and format your own to best suit your previous experience and your professional goals and to make the most persuasive case to your target employers. See also <u>persuasion</u> (Tab 1).

- Figure 8–7 presents a conventional student résumé for an entry-level position.
- Figure 8–8 shows a résumé with a variation of the conventional headings to highlight professional credentials.
- Figure 8–9 presents a student résumé with a format that is appropriately nonconventional because this student needs to demonstrate skills in graphic design for his potential audience. This résumé matches the letter in Figure 8–4.
- Figure 8–10 shows a résumé that focuses on the applicant's management experience. This résumé matches the letter in Figure 8–5.
- Figure 8–11 focuses on how the applicant advanced and was promoted within a single company.
- Figure 8–12 illustrates how an applicant can organize a résumé by combining functional and chronological elements.
- Figure 8–13 presents an electronic résumé in ASCII (American Standard Code for Information Interchange) format. Notice how this résumé emphasizes keywords so that potential employers searching a database for applicants will be able to find it easily.

 WEB LINK ANNOTATED SAMPLE RÉSUMÉS

For more examples of résumés with helpful annotations, see *bedfordstmartins .com/alred*, and select *ModelDoc Central*.

Analyzing Your Background

In preparing to write your résumé, determine what kind of job you are seeking. Then ask yourself what information about you and your background would be most important to a prospective employer. List the following:

- Schools you attended, degrees you hold, your major field of study, academic honors you were awarded, your grade point average, particular academic projects that reflect your best work
- Jobs you have held, your principal and secondary duties in each job, when and how long you held each job, promotions, skills you developed in your jobs that potential employers value and seek in

CAROL ANN WALKER

CAMPUS ADDRESS
148 University Drive
Bloomington, Indiana 47405
(812) 652-4781
caw2@iu.edu

HOME (after June 2011)
1436 West Schantz Avenue
Laurel, Pennsylvania 17322
(717) 399-2712
caw@yahoo.com

OBJECTIVE

Position in financial research, leading to management in corporate finance.

EDUCATION

Bachelor of Science in Business Administration, expected June 2011
Indiana University

Emphasis: Finance   Minor: Professional Writing
Grade Point Average: 3.88 out of possible 4.0
Senior Honor Society

FINANCIAL EXPERIENCE

FIRST BANK, INC., Bloomington, Indiana, 2010
Research Assistant, Summer and Fall Quarters
        Developed long-range planning models for the manager of corporate
        planning.

MARTIN FINANCIAL RESEARCH SERVICES, Bloomington, Indiana, 2009
Financial Audit Intern
        Created a design concept for in-house financial audits and provided
        research assistance to staff.
Associate Editor, *Martin Client Newsletter*, 2008–2009
        Wrote articles on financial planning with computer models;
        developed article ideas from survey of business periodicals; edited
        submissions.

COMPUTER SKILLS

Software: Microsoft Word, Excel, PowerPoint, InDesign, QuarkXPress
Hardware: Macintosh, IBM-PC
Languages: UNIX, JAVA, C++

REFERENCES

Available on request.

FIGURE 8–7. Student Résumé (for an Entry-Level Position)

CHRIS RENAULT, RN

3785 Raleigh Court, #46 • Phoenix, AZ 67903 •
(555) 467-1115 • chris@resumepower.com

Qualifications

➢ *Recent Honors Graduate of Approved Nursing Program*
➢ *Current Arizona Nursing Licensure and BLS Certification*
➢ *Presently Completing Clinical Nurse Internship Program*

Education & Licensure

ARIZONA STATE UNIVERSITY
  Tempe, AZ
Bachelor of Science in Nursing (BSN), 2011
Graduated summa cum laude (GPA: 4.0)

MOHAVE COMMUNITY COLLEGE
  Kingman, AZ
Associate Degree in Nursing (AN), 2009
Graduated cum laude (GPA: 3.5)

Coursework Highlights: Family and Community Nursing, Health-Care Delivery Models, Health Assessment, Pathology, Microbiology, Nursing Research, Nursing of Older Adults, Health-Care Ethics

Arizona RN License, 2011
BLS Certification, 2011

Clinical Internship

CAMELBACK MEDICAL CENTER—Phoenix, AZ
Nurse Intern, 2010 to Present

- Accepted into new graduate RN training program and completing in-depth, eight-month rotation working under a trained preceptor.
- Gaining valuable clinical experience to assume the role of a professional nurse within an acute-care setting. Rotating through all medical center areas, including Postsurgical, Orthopedics, Pediatrics, Oncology, Emergency Department, Psychiatric Nursing, Cardiac Telemetry, and Critical Care.
- Developing speed and skill in the day-to-day functions of a staff nurse. Participating in patient assessment, treatment, medication disbursement, and surgical preparation as a member of the health-care team.
- Earned written commendations from preceptor for *"excellent ability to interact with patients and their families, showing a high degree of empathy, medical knowledge, and concern for quality and continuity of patient care."*

Community Involvement

Active Volunteer and Fundraising Coordinator, The American Cancer Society—Scottsdale, AZ, Chapter (2009 to Present)
Participant, Annual AIDS Walkathon (2006–2009) and "Find the Cure" Breast Cancer Awareness Marathon (2008, 2009)

8
Job Search and Application

FIGURE 8–8. Résumé (Highlighting Professional Credentials). Prepared by Kim Isaacs, Advanced Career Systems, Inc.

Joshua S. Goodman
222 Morewood Avenue
Pittsburgh, PA 15212
cell: 412-555-1212
jgoodman@aol.com

OBJECTIVE

A position as a graphic designer with responsibilities in information design, packaging, and media presentations.

GRAPHIC DESIGN EXPERIENCE

Assistant Designer • Dyer/Khan, Los Angeles, California
Summer 2009, Summer 2010
Assistant Designer in a versatile design studio. Responsible for design, layout, comps, mechanicals, and project management.
Clients: Paramount Pictures, Mattel Electronics, and Motown Records.

Photo Editor • Paramount Pictures Corporation, Los Angeles, California
Summer 2008
Photo Editor for merchandising department. Established art files for movie and television properties. Edited images used in merchandising. Maintained archive and database.

Production Assistant • Grafis, Los Angeles, California
Summer 2007
Production assistant at fast-paced design firm. Assisted with comps, mechanicals, and miscellaneous studio work.
Clients: ABC Television, A&M Records, and Ortho Products Division.

EDUCATION

Carnegie Mellon University, Pittsburgh, Pennsylvania
BFA in Graphic Design—May 2011
   Graphic Design
   Corporate Identity
   Industrial Design
   Graphic Imaging Processes
   Color Theory
   Computer Graphics
   Typography
   Serigraphy
   Photography
   Video Production

COMPUTER SKILLS

XML, HTML, JavaScript, Forms, Macromedia Dreamweaver, Macromedia Flash Professional, Photoshop, Illustrator, Image Ready (Animated GIFs), CorelDRAW, DeepPaint, iGrafx Designer, MapEdit (Image Mapping), Scanning, Microsoft Access/Excel, QuarkXPress

ACTIVITIES

Member, Pittsburgh Graphic Design Society; Member, The Design Group

FIGURE 8–9. Student Résumé (for a Graphic Design Job)

ROBERT MANDILLO
7761 Shalamar Drive
Dayton, Ohio 45424
(937) 255-4137
mand@juno.com

OBJECTIVE

A management position in the aerospace industry with responsibility for developing new designs and products.

MANAGEMENT EXPERIENCE

MANAGER, EXHIBIT DESIGN LAB — May 2004–Present
Wright-Patterson Air Force Base, Dayton, Ohio

Supervise 11 technicians in support of engineering exhibit design and production. Develop, evaluate, and improve materials and equipment for the design and construction of exhibits. Write specifications, negotiate with vendors, and initiate procurement activities for exhibit design support.

SUPERVISOR, GRAPHICS ILLUSTRATORS — June 2001–April 2004
Henderson Advertising Agency, Cincinnati, Ohio

Supervised five illustrators and four drafting mechanics after promotion from Graphics Technician. Analyzed and approved work-order requirements. Selected appropriate media and techniques for orders. Rendered illustrations in pencil and ink. Converted department to CAD system.

EDUCATION

MASTER OF BUSINESS ADMINISTRATION, 2010
University of Dayton, Ohio

BACHELOR OF SCIENCE IN MECHANICAL ENGINEERING TECHNOLOGY, 2001
Edison State College, Wooster, Ohio

ASSOCIATE'S DEGREE IN MECHANICAL DRAFTING, 1999
Wooster Community College, Wooster, Ohio

PROFESSIONAL AFFILIATION

National Association of Mechanical Engineers

REFERENCES / WEB SITE

References, letters of recommendation, and a portfolio of original designs and drawings available online at <www.juno.com/mand>.

8
Job Search and
Application

FIGURE 8–10. Résumé (Applicant with Management Experience)

CAROL ANN WALKER
1436 West Schantz Avenue
Laurel, Pennsylvania 17322
(717) 399-2712
caw@yahoo.com

FINANCIAL EXPERIENCE

KERFHEIMER CORPORATION, Philadelphia, Pennsylvania

Senior Financial Analyst, June 2006–Present
Report to Senior Vice President for Corporate Financial Planning.
Develop manufacturing cost estimates totaling $30 million annually
for mining and construction equipment with Department of Defense.

Financial Analyst, November 2003–June 2006
Developed $50-million funding estimates for major Department of
Defense contracts for troop carriers and digging and earth-moving
machines. Researched funding options, resulting in savings of
$1.2 million.

FIRST BANK, INC., Bloomington, Indiana

Planning Analyst, September 1998–November 2003
Developed successful computer models for short- and long-range
planning.

EDUCATION

Ph.D. in Finance: expected, June 2011
The Wharton School of the University of Pennsylvania

M.S. in Business Administration, 2002
University of Wisconsin–Milwaukee
"Executive Curriculum" for employees identified as promising by their
employers.

B.S. in Business Administration (*magna cum laude*), 1998
Indiana University
Emphasis: Finance   Minor: Professional Writing

PUBLISHING AND MEMBERSHIP

Published "Developing Computer Models for Financial Planning," *Midwest
Finance Journal* 34.2 (2008): 126–36.

Association for Corporate Financial Planning, Senior Member.

REFERENCES

References and a portfolio of financial plans are available on request.

FIGURE 8–11. Advanced Résumé (Showing Promotion Within a Single Company)

CAROL ANN WALKER

1436 West Schantz Avenue • Laurel, PA 17322
(717) 399-2712 • caw@yahoo.com

Award-Winning Senior Financial Analyst

Astute senior analyst and corporate financial planner with 11 years of experience and proven success enhancing P&L scenarios by millions of dollars. Demonstrated ability to apply critical thinking and sound strategic/economic analysis to multidimensional business issues. Advanced computer skills include Hyperion, SQL, MS Office, and Crystal Reports.

Financial Analyst of the Year, 2009

Recipient of prestigious national award from the Association for Investment Management and Research (AIMR)

Areas of Expertise

- Financial Analysis & Planning
- Forecasting & Trend Projection
- Trend/Variance Analysis
- Comparative Analysis
- Expense Analysis
- Strategic Planning
- SEC & Financial Reporting
- Risk Assessment

Career Progression

KERFHEIMER CORPORATION—Philadelphia, PA   2003 to Present

Senior Financial Analyst, June 2006 to Present
Financial Analyst, November 2003 to June 2006

Rapidly promoted to lead team of 15 analysts in the management of financial/SEC reporting and analysis for publicly traded, $2.3-billion company. Develop financial/statistical models used to project and maximize corporate financial performance. Support nationwide sales team by providing financial metrics, trends, and forecasts.

Key Accomplishments:

- **Developed long-range funding requirements crucial to firm's subsequent capture of $1 billion** in government and military contracts.
- **Facilitated a 45% decrease in company's long-term debt** during several major building expansions through personally developed computer models for capital acquisition.
- **Jointly led large-scale systems conversion to Hyperion**, including personal upload of database in Essbase. Completed conversion without interrupting business operations.

FIGURE 8–12. Advanced Résumé (Combining Functional and Chronological Elements). Prepared by Kim Isaacs, Advanced Career Systems, Inc. (*continued on next page*)

—————————— CAROL ANN WALKER ——————————

Résumé • Page Two

Career Progression (*continued*)

FIRST BANK, INC.—Bloomington, IN   1998 to 2003

Planning Analyst, September 1998 to November 2003
Compiled and distributed weekly, monthly, quarterly, and annual closings/
financial reports, analyzing information for presentation to senior management. Prepared depreciation forecasts, actual-vs.-projected financial statements,
key-matrix reports, tax-reporting packages, auditor packages, and balance-
sheet reviews.

Key Accomplishments:

- **Devised strategies to acquire over $1 billion at 3% below market
rate.**
- **Analyzed financial performance for consistency to plans and forecasts**,
investigated trends and variances, and alerted senior management to areas
requiring action.
- **Achieved an average 23% return on all personally recommended
investments.** Applied critical thinking and sound financial and strategic
analysis in all funding options research.

Education

THE WHARTON SCHOOL of the UNIVERSITY OF PENNSYLVANIA
(Philadelphia)
Ph.D. in Finance Candidate, Expected June 2011

UNIVERSITY OF WISCONSIN–MILWAUKEE
M.S. in Business Administration, May 2002

INDIANA UNIVERSITY (Bloomington)
B.S. in Business Administration, Emphasis in Finance
(*magna cum laude*), May 1998

Affiliations

- Association for Investment Management and Research (AIMR), Member,
2005 to Present
- Association for Corporate Financial Planning (ACFP), Senior Member,
2003 to Present

Portfolio of Financial Plans Available on Request
(717) 399-2712 • caw@yahoo.com

FIGURE 8–12. Advanced Résumé (Combining Functional and Chronological
Elements) (*continued*)

DAVID B. EDWARDS
6819 Locustview Drive
Topeka, Kansas 66614
(913) 233-1552
dedwards@cpu.fairview.edu

JOB OBJECTIVE
Programmer with writing, editing, and training responsibilities,
leading to a career in information design management.

KEYWORDS
Programmer, Operating Systems, Unipro, Newsletter, Graphics,
Listserv, Professional Writer, Editor, Trainer, Instructor,
Technical Writer, Tutor, Designer, Manager, Information Design.

EDUCATION
** Fairview Community College, Topeka, Kansas
** Associate's Degree, Computer Science, June 2008
** Dean's Honor List Award (six quarters)

RELEVANT COURSE WORK
** Operating Systems Design
** Database Management
** Introduction to Cybernetics
** Technical Writing

EMPLOYMENT EXPERIENCE
** Computer Consultant: September 2008 to Present
Fairview Community College Computer Center: Advised and trained novice
users; wrote and maintained Unipro operating system documentation.
** Tutor: January 2007 to June 2008
Fairview Community College: Assisted students in mathematics and
computer programming.

SKILLS AND ACTIVITIES
** Unipro Operating System: Thorough knowledge of word-processing,
text-editing, and file-formatting programs.
** Writing and Editing Skills: Experience in documenting computer
programs for beginning programmers and users.
** Fairview Community Microcomputer Users Group: Cofounder and
editor of monthly newsletter ("Compuclub"); listserv manager.

FURTHER INFORMATION
** References, college transcripts, a portfolio of computer programs,
and writing samples available on request.

FIGURE 8-13. Electronic Résumé (in ASCII Format)

8
Job Search and
Application

ideal job candidates, projects or accomplishments that reflect your important contributions
- Other experiences and skills you have developed that would be of value in the kind of job you are seeking; extracurricular activities that have contributed to your learning experience; leadership, interpersonal, and communication skills you have developed; any collaborative work you have performed; computer skills you have acquired

Use this information to brainstorm any further key details. Then, based on all the details, decide which to include in your résumé and how you can most effectively present your qualifications.

Organizing Your Résumé (Sections)

A number of different organizational patterns can be used effectively. The following sections are typical—which you choose should depend on your experience and goals, the employer's needs, and any standard practices in your profession.

- Heading (name and contact information)
- Job Objective
- Qualifications Summary
- Education
- Employment Experience
- Related Skills and Abilities
- Honors and Activities
- References and Portfolios

Whether you place "education" before "employment experience" depends on the job you are seeking and on which credentials would strengthen your résumé the most. If you are a recent graduate without much work experience, list education first. If you have years of job experience, including jobs directly related to the kind of position you are seeking, list employment experience first. In your education and employment sections, use a reverse chronological sequence: List the most recent experience first, the next most recent experience second, and so on.

Heading.   At the top of your résumé, include your name, address, telephone number (home or cell), and a professional e-mail address.* Make sure that your name stands out on the page. If you have both a school address and a permanent home address, place your school address on the left side of the page and your permanent home address

*Do not use a clever or hobby-related e-mail address in employment correspondence; e-mail addresses that are based on your last name work well.

on the right side of the page. Place both underneath your name, as shown in Figure 8–7. Indicate the dates you can be reached at each address (but do not date the résumé itself).

Job Objective.   A job objective introduces the material in a résumé and helps the reader quickly understand your goal. If you decide to include an objective, use a heading such as "Objective," "Employment Objective," "Career Objective," or "Job Objective." State your immediate goal and, if you know that it will give you an advantage, the direction you hope your career will take. Try to write your objective in no more than three lines, and tailor it to the specific job for which you are applying, as illustrated in the following examples:

- A full-time computer-science position aimed at solving engineering problems and contributing to a management team.
- A position involving meeting the concerns of women, such as family planning, career counseling, or crisis management.
- Full-time management of a high-quality local restaurant.
- A summer research or programming position providing opportunities to use software-development and software-debugging skills.

Qualifications Summary.   You may wish to include a brief summary of your qualifications to persuade hiring managers to select you for an interview. Sometimes called a *summary statement* or *career summary*, a qualifications summary can include skills, achievements, experience, or personal qualities that make you especially well suited to the position. You may wish to give this section a heading such as "Profile," "Career Highlights," or, simply, "Qualifications." Or you may use a headline, as shown on the first page of the résumé in Figure 8–12 ("Award-Winning Senior Financial Analyst").

Education.   List the school(s) you have attended, the degree(s) you received and the dates you received them, your major field(s) of study, and any academic honors you have earned. Include your grade point average only if it is 3.0 or higher—or include your average in your major if that is more impressive. List courses only if they are unusually impressive or if your résumé is otherwise sparse (see Figures 8–8 and 8–9). Consider including the skills developed or projects completed in your course work. Mention your high school only if you want to call attention to special high school achievements, awards, projects, programs, internships, or study abroad.

Employment Experience.   Organize your employment experience in reverse chronological order, starting with your most recent job and working backward under a single major heading called "Experience," "Employment," "Professional Experience," or the like. You could also organize your experience functionally by clustering similar types of jobs into one or several sections with specific headings such as "Management Experience" or "Major Accomplishments."

One type of arrangement might be more persuasive than the other, depending on the situation. For example, if you are applying for an accounting job but have no specific background in accounting, you would probably do best to list past and present jobs in chronological order, from most to least recent. If you are applying for a supervisory position and have had three supervisory jobs in addition to two non-supervisory positions, you might choose to create a single section called "Supervisory Experience" and list only your three supervisory jobs. Or you could create two sections—"Supervisory Experience" and "Other Experience"—and include the three supervisory jobs in the first section and the nonsupervisory jobs in the second section.

The functional résumé groups work experience by types of workplace activities or skills rather than by jobs in chronological order. However, many employers are suspicious of functional résumés because they can be used to hide a poor work history, such as excessive job hopping or extended employment gaps. Functional elements can be combined with a chronological arrangement by using a qualifications summary or skills section, as shown in Figure 8–12.

In general, follow these conventions when working on the "Experience" section of your résumé:

- Include jobs or internships when they relate directly to the position you are seeking. Although some applicants choose to omit internships and temporary or part-time jobs, including such experiences can make a résumé more persuasive if they have helped you develop specific related skills.
- Include extracurricular experiences, such as taking on a leadership position in a college organization or directing a community-service project, if they demonstrate that you have developed skills valued by potential employers.
- List military service as a job; give the dates served, the duty specialty, and the rank at discharge. Discuss military duties if they relate to the job you are seeking.
- For each job or experience, list both the job and company titles. Throughout each section, consistently begin with either the job or the company name, depending on which will likely be more impressive to potential employers.
- Under each job or experience, provide a concise description of your primary and secondary duties. If a job is not directly relevant, provide only a job title and a brief description of duties that helped you develop skills valued in the position you are seeking. For example, if you were a lifeguard and now seek a management position, focus on supervisory experience or even experience in

averting disaster to highlight your management, decision-making, and crisis-control skills.

- Focus as much as possible on your achievements in your work history. ("Increased employee retention rate by 16 percent by developing a training program.") Employers want to hire doers and achievers.

- Use action verbs (for example, "managed" rather than "as the manager") and state ideas succinctly, as shown in Figure 8–10. Even though the résumé is about you, do not use "I" (for example, instead of "I was promoted to Section Leader," use "Promoted to Section Leader"). For electronic résumés that will be scanned for keywords, however, replace such verbs with nouns (instead of "managed" use *manager*, as in Figure 8–13).

Related Skills and Abilities.   Employers are interested in hiring applicants with a variety of skills or the ability to learn new ones quickly. Depending on the position, you might list in a skills section items such as fluency in foreign languages, writing and editing abilities, specialized technical knowledge, or computer skills (including knowledge of specific languages, software, and hardware).

Honors and Activities.   If you have room on your résumé, list any honors and unique activities near the end. Include items such as student or community activities, professional or club memberships, awards received, and published works. Be selective: Do not duplicate information given in other categories, and include only information that supports your employment objective. Provide a heading for this section that fits its contents, such as "Activities," "Honors," "Professional Affiliations," or "Publications and Memberships."

References and Portfolios.   Avoid listing references unless that is standard practice in your profession or your résumé is sparse. If you create a separate list of references for prospective employers, you can include a phrase such as "References available on request" to signal the end of a résumé, or write "Available on request" after the heading "References" as a design element to balance a page. Always seek permission from anyone you list as a reference.

A portfolio is a collection of samples in a binder or on the Web of your most impressive work and accomplishments. The portfolio can include documents you have written, articles, letters of praise from employers, and copies of awards and certificates. If you have developed a portfolio, you could also include the phrase "Portfolio available on request." If portfolios are standard in your profession, you might even include a small section that lists the contents of your portfolio.

8

Job Search and
Application

⬛ PROFESSIONALISM NOTE Avoid listing the salary you desire in the résumé. On the one hand, you may price yourself out of a job you want if the salary you list is higher than a potential employer is willing to pay. On the other hand, if you list a low salary, you may not get the best possible offer. ✦

Advice for Returning Job Seekers

If you are returning to the workplace after an absence, most career experts say that it is important to acknowledge the gap in your career. That is particularly true if, for example, you are reentering the work-force because you have devoted a full-time period to care for children or dependent adults. Do not undervalue such work. Although unpaid, it often provides experience that develops important time-management, problem-solving, organizational, and interpersonal skills. Although gaps in employment can be explained in the application letter, the following examples illustrate how you might reflect such experiences in a résumé. They would be especially appropriate for an applicant seeking employment in a field related to child or health care.

- **Primary Child–Care Provider, 2009 to 2011**
  Provided full-time care to three preschool children at home. Instructed in beginning academic skills, time management, basics of nutrition, arts, and swimming. Organized activities, managed household, and served as neighborhood-watch captain.

- **Home Caregiver, 2009 to 2011**
  Provided 60 hours per week in-home care to Alzheimer's patient. Coordinated medical care, developed exercise programs, completed and processed complex medical forms, administered medications, organized budget, and managed home environment.

If you have performed volunteer work during such a period, list that experience. Volunteer work often results in the same experience as does full-time, paid work, a fact that your résumé should reflect, as in the following example.

- **School Association Coordinator, 2009 to 2011**
  Managed special activities of the Briarwood High School Parent-Teacher Association. Planned and coordinated meetings, scheduled events, and supervised fund-drive operations. Raised $70,000 toward refurbishing the school auditorium.

Electronic Résumés

In addition to the traditional paper résumé, you can post a Web-based résumé. You may also need to submit a scannable, plain-text résumé through e-mail or an online form to a potential employer to be included in an organization's database. As Internet and database technologies converge, remain current with the forms and protocols that employers prefer by reviewing popular job-search sites, such as HotJobs at *http:// hotjobs.yahoo.com* and Monster.com at *www.monster.com.*

Web Résumés.   If you plan to post your résumé on your own Web site, keep the following points in mind.

- Follow the general advice for <u>Web design</u> (Tab 2), such as viewing your résumé on several browsers to see how it looks.
- Just below your name, you may wish to provide a series of internal page links to such important categories as "experience" and "education."
- Consider building a multipage site for displaying a work portfolio, publications, reference letters, and other related materials.
- If privacy is an issue, include an e-mail link ("mailto") at the top of the résumé rather than your home address and phone number.

The disadvantage of posting a résumé at your own Web site is that you must attract the attention of employers on your own. For that reason, commercial services may be a better option because they can attract recruiters with their large databases.

Scannable and Plain-Text Résumés.   A scannable résumé is normally mailed to an employer in paper form, scanned, and downloaded into a company's searchable database. Such a résumé can be well formatted, but it should not contain decorative fonts, underlining, shading, letters that touch each other, and other features that will not scan easily. Scan such a résumé yourself to make sure there are no problems.

Some employers request ASCII or plain-text résumés via e-mail, which can be added directly into the company's résumé database without scanning. The ASCII résumés also allow employers to read the file no matter what type of software they are using. You can copy and paste such a résumé directly into the body of the e-mail message.

 DIGITAL TIP PREPARING AN ASCII RÉSUMÉ

When preparing an ASCII document, proper formatting is critical. For example, you need to insert manual line breaks at 65 characters to prevent long, single lines when the documents are opened in various systems. Further, many word-processing elements such as bullets, underlining, and boldface are incompatible with ASCII, which is limited to letters, numbers, and basic punctuation. For more on this topic, see *bedfordstmartins.com/ alred*, and select *Digital Tips*, "Preparing an ASCII Résumé."

For résumés that will be downloaded into databases, it is better to use nouns than verbs to describe experience and skills (*designer* and *management* rather than *designed* and *managed*). You may also include a section in such a résumé titled "Keywords" (or perhaps give a descriptive name, such as "Areas of Expertise"). Keywords, also called *descriptors,* allow potential employers to search the database for qualified candidates. So be sure to use keywords that are the same as those used in the employer's descriptions of the jobs that best match your interests and qualifications. This section can follow the main heading or appear near the end of your résumé. Figure 8–13 is an example of an electronic résumé that demonstrates the use of keywords.

E-mail–Attached Résumés.   An employer may request, or you may prefer to submit, a résumé as an e-mail attachment to be printed out by the employer. If so, consider using a relatively plain design and sending the résumé as a rich text format (.rtf) document. Or, if precise design is important, send the résumé as a portable document format (PDF) file that will preserve the fonts, images, graphics, and layout. You can attach this file to an e-mail that will then serve as your application letter. See *Digital Tip: Using PDF Files* on page 64.

9

Presentations and Meetings

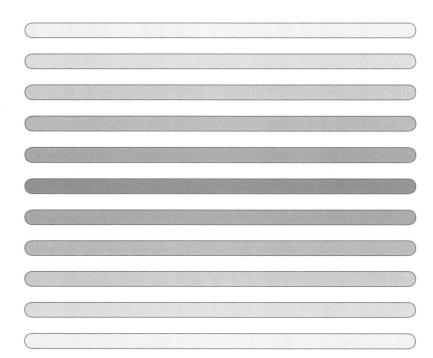

Preview

This section contains entries on the essential subjects of <u>listening</u> and <u>presentations</u> as well as entries on conducting <u>meetings</u> and recording <u>minutes of meetings</u>. Because preparing an oral presentation is much like preparing to write, review Tab 1, "The Writing Process," noting in particular the entries <u>audience</u>, <u>context</u>, <u>organization</u>, and <u>purpose</u>.

listening

Effective listening enables the listener to understand the directions of an instructor, the message in a speaker's <u>presentation</u>, the goals of a manager, and the needs and wants of customers. Above all, it lays the foundation for productive communication.

Fallacies About Listening

Most people assume that because they can hear, they know how to listen. In fact, *hearing* is passive, whereas *listening* is active. Hearing voices in a crowd or a ringing telephone requires no analysis and no active involvement—we have no choice but to hear them. But listening requires actively focusing on a speaker, interpreting the message, and assessing its worth. Listening also requires that you consider the <u>context</u> (Tab 1) of messages and the differences in meaning that may be the result of differences in the speaker's and the listener's occupation, education, culture, sex, race, or other factors. See also <u>global communication</u> (Tab 1), <u>biased language</u> (Tab 10), <u>connotation / denotation</u> (Tab 10), and <u>English as a second language</u> (Tab 11).

Active Listening

To become an active listener, you need to take the following steps:

Step 1: Make a Conscious Decision.   The first step to active listening is simply making up your mind to do so. Active listening requires a conscious effort, something that does not come naturally. The well-known precept offers good advice: "Seek first to understand and *then* to be understood."*

Step 2: Define Your Purpose.   Knowing why you are listening can go a long way toward managing the most common listening problems: drifting attention, formulating your response while the speaker is still talking, and interrupting the speaker. To help you define your purpose for listening, ask yourself these questions:

- What kind of information do I hope to get from this exchange, and how will I use it?
- What kind of message do I want to send while I am listening? (Do I want to portray understanding, determination, flexibility, competence, or patience?)

*Stephen R. Covey, *The 7 Habits of Highly Effective People: Powerful Lessons in Personal Change*, 15th ed. (New York: Free Press, 2004).

9

- What factors—boredom, daydreaming, anger, impatience—might interfere with listening during the interaction? How can I keep these factors from placing a barrier between the speaker and me?

Step 3: Take Specific Actions.   Becoming an active listener requires a willingness to become a responder rather than a reactor. *Responders* are listeners who slow down the communication to be certain that they are accurately receiving messages sent by speakers. *Reactors* simply say the first thing that comes to mind, without checking to make sure that they accurately understand a message. Take the following actions to help you become a responder and not a reactor.

- Make a conscious effort to be impartial when evaluating a message. For example, do not dismiss a message because you dislike the speaker or are distracted by the speaker's appearance, mannerisms, or accent.
- Slow down the communication by asking for more information or by <u>paraphrasing</u> (Tab 3) the message received before you offer your thoughts. Paraphrasing lets the speaker know you are listening, gives the speaker an opportunity to clear up any misunderstanding, and keeps you focused.
- Listen with empathy by putting yourself in the speaker's position. When people feel they are being listened to empathetically, they tend to respond with appreciation and cooperation, thereby improving the communication.
- Take notes, when possible, to help you stay focused on what a speaker is saying. <u>Note-taking</u> (Tab 3) not only communicates your attentiveness to the speaker but also reinforces the message and helps you remember it.

Step 4: Adapt to the Situation.   The requirements of active listening differ from one situation to another. For example, when you are listening to a lecture, you may be listening only for specific information. However, if you are on a team project that depends on everyone's contribution, you need to listen at the highest level so that you can gather information as well as pick up on nuances the other speakers may be communicating. See also <u>collaborative writing</u> (Tab 1).

meetings

Meetings allow people to share information and collaborate to produce better results than exchanges of e-mail messages or other means would allow. Like a <u>presentation</u>, a successful meeting requires planning and preparation. See also <u>selecting the medium</u> (Tab 2).

9

Planning a Meeting

As you plan a meeting, determine the focus of the meeting, decide who should attend, and choose the best time and place to hold it. Prepare an agenda for the meeting and determine who should take the minutes.

Determine the Purpose of the Meeting.   The first step in planning a meeting is to focus on the desired outcome by asking questions to help you determine the meeting's purpose (Tab 1): What should participants know, believe, do, or be able to do as a result of attending the meeting?

Once you have your desired outcome in focus, use the information to write a purpose statement for the meeting that answers the questions *what* and *why*.

• The purpose of this meeting is to gather ideas from the sales force [*what*] in order to create a successful sales campaign for our new scanner [*why*].

Decide Who Should Attend.   Determine first the key people who need to attend the meeting. If a meeting must be held without some key participants, ask those people for their contributions prior to the meeting or invite them to participate by speakerphone, videoconference, or such remote methods as described in *Digital Tip: Conducting Meetings from Remote Locations* (see page 254). Of course, the meeting minutes should be distributed to everyone, including appropriate nonattendees.

Choose the Meeting Time.   Schedule a meeting for a time when all or most of the key people can be present. Consider as well other factors, such as the time of day and the length of the meeting, that can influence its outcome:

• Monday morning is often used to prepare for the coming week's work.
• Friday afternoon is often focused on completing the current week's tasks.
• Long meetings may need to include breaks to allow participants to respond to messages and refresh themselves.
• Meetings held during the last 15 minutes of the day will be quick, but few people will remember what happened.
• Remote participants may need consideration for their time zones.

Choose the Meeting Location.   Having a meeting at your own location can give you an advantage: You feel more comfortable, which, along with your guests' newness to their surroundings, may give you an edge. Holding the meeting on someone else's premises, however, can signal cooperation. For balance, especially when people are meeting for the first

9

Sales Meeting Agenda

Purpose: To get input for a sales campaign for the CZX software
Date: Monday, May 9, 2011
Place: Conference Room E
Time: 9:30 a.m.–11:00 a.m.
Attendees: Advertising Manager, Sales Manager and Reps, Customer Service
           Manager

Topic	Presenter	Time
CZX Software	Bob Arbuckle	9:30–9:45
The Campaign	Maria Lopez	9:45–10:00
The Sales Strategy	Mary Winifred	10:00–10:15
Discussion	Led by Dave Grimes	10:15–11:00

FIGURE 9–1. Meeting Agenda

time or are discussing sensitive issues, meet at a neutral site where no one
gains an advantage and attendees may feel freer to participate.

Establish the Agenda.   A tool for focusing the group, the agenda is
an outline of what the meeting will address. Figure 9–1 shows a typical
agenda. Always prepare an agenda for a meeting, even if it is only an
informal list of main topics. Ideally, the agenda should be distributed
to attendees a day or two before the meeting. For a longer meeting in
which participants are required to make a presentation, try to distribute
the agenda a week or more in advance.

The agenda should list the attendees, the meeting time and place,
and the topics you plan to discuss. If the meeting includes presentations,
list the time allotted for each speaker. Finally, indicate an approximate
length for the meeting so that participants can plan the rest of their day.

 DIGITAL TIP **CONDUCTING MEETINGS FROM REMOTE
LOCATIONS**

When participants cannot meet face to face, consider holding a videoconference or Web conference. In such meetings, the participants' computers
are often connected to other participants' computers through a downloaded application on each of the attendees' computers. For links to Web
sites with information on various types of groupware and features that
allow sharing of texts, video, and graphics, see *bedfordstmartins.com/alred*,
and select *Links Library*.

9

If the agenda is distributed in advance of the meeting, it should be accompanied by a memo or an e-mail informing people of the following:

- The purpose of the meeting
- The date and place of the meeting
- The meeting start and stop times
- The names of the people invited to the meeting
- Instructions on how to prepare for the meeting

Figure 9–2 shows a cover message to accompany an agenda. See <u>covers</u> (Tab 7).

From: "S. McLaughlin" <smc@mscan.com>
To: "M. Lopez" <mlop@mscan.com>; "M. Winifred"
               <wini@mscan.com>; "B. Arbuckle" <arbu@mscan.com>;
               "D. Grimes" <dgri@mscan.com>; "Sales Reps"
               <sales-all@mscan.com>
Sent: Tues, 03 May 2011 13:30:12 EST
Subject: Sales Meeting (May 9 at 9:30 a.m.)
Attachments: 📄 Sales Meeting Agenda.doc (29 KB)

Purpose of the Meeting

The purpose of this meeting is to get your ideas for the upcoming introduction and sales campaign for our new CZX software.

Date, Time, and Location

Date: Monday, May 9, 2011
Time: 9:30 a.m.–11:00 a.m.
Place: Conference Room E (go to the ground floor, take a right off the elevator, third door on the left)

Attendees

Those addressed above

Meeting Preparation

Everyone should be prepared to offer suggestions on the following topics:

- Sales features of the new software
- Techniques for selling the software
- Customer profile of potential buyers
- FAQs—questions customers may ask
- Anticipated support services

Agenda

Please see the attached document.

FIGURE 9–2. E-mail to Accompany an Agenda

9

Assign the Minute-Taking.   Delegate the minute-taking to someone other than the leader. The minute-taker should record major decisions made and tasks assigned. To avoid misunderstandings, the minute-taker needs to record each assignment, the person responsible for it, and the date on which it is due.

For a standing committee, it is best to rotate the responsibility of taking minutes. See also minutes of meetings and note-taking (Tab 3).

Conducting the Meeting

Assign someone to write on a board or project a computer image of information that needs to be viewed by everyone present.

During the meeting, keep to your agenda; however, create a productive environment by allowing room for differing views and fostering an environment in which participants listen respectfully to one another.

- Consider the feelings, thoughts, ideas, and needs of others—do not let your own agenda blind you to other points of view.
- Help other participants feel valued and respected by listening to them and responding to what they say.
- Respond positively to the comments of others whenever possible.
- Consider communication styles and approaches that are different from your own, particularly those from other cultures. See also global communication (Tab 1).

Deal with Conflict.   Despite your best efforts, conflict is inevitable. However, conflict is potentially valuable; when managed positively, it can stimulate creative thinking by challenging complacency and showing ways to achieve goals more efficiently or economically. See collaborative writing (Tab 1).

Members of any group are likely to vary in their personalities and attitudes, and you may encounter people who approach meetings differently. Consider the following tactics for the interruptive, negative, rambling, overly quiet, and territorial personality types.

- The *interruptive person* rarely lets anyone finish a sentence and may intimidate the group's quieter members. Tell that person in a firm but nonhostile tone to let the others finish in the interest of getting everyone's input. By addressing the issue directly, you signal to the group the importance of putting common goals first.
- The *negative person* has difficulty accepting change and often considers a new idea or project from a negative point of view. Such negativity, if left unchecked, can demoralize the group and suppress enthusiasm for new ideas. If the negative person brings up a valid point, however, ask for the group's suggestions to

remedy the issue being raised. If the negative person's reactions are not valid or are outside the agenda, state the necessity of staying focused on the agenda and perhaps recommend a separate meeting to address those issues.

- The *rambling person* cannot collect his or her thoughts quickly enough to verbalize them succinctly. Restate or clarify this person's ideas. Try to strike a balance between providing your own interpretation and drawing out the person's intended meaning.
- The *overly quiet person* may be timid or may just be deep in thought. Ask for this person's thoughts, being careful not to embarrass the person. In some cases, you can have a quiet person jot down his or her thoughts and give them to you later.
- The *territorial person* fiercely defends his or her group against real or perceived threats and may refuse to cooperate with members of other departments, companies, and so on. Point out that although such concerns may be valid, everyone is working toward the same overall goal and that goal should take precedence.

Close the Meeting.   Just before closing the meeting, review all decisions and assignments. Paraphrase each to help the group focus on what they have agreed to do and to ensure that the minutes will be complete and accurate. Now is the time to raise questions and clarify any misunderstandings. Set a date by which everyone at the meeting can expect to receive copies of the minutes. Finally, thank everyone for participating, and close the meeting on a positive note.

Writer's Checklist: Planning and Conducting Meetings

☑ Develop a purpose statement for the meeting to focus your planning.

☑ Invite only those essential to fulfilling the purpose of the meeting.

☑ Select a time and place convenient to all those attending.

☑ Create an agenda and distribute it a day or two before the meeting.

☑ Assign someone to take meeting minutes.

☑ Ensure that the minutes record key decisions; assignments; due dates; and the date, time, and location of any follow-up meeting.

☑ Follow the agenda to keep everyone focused.

☑ Respect the views of others and how they are expressed.

☑ Use the strategies in this entry for handling conflict and attendees whose style of expression may prevent getting everyone's best thinking.

☑ Close the meeting by reviewing key decisions and assignments.

minutes of meetings

Organizations and committees that keep official records of their meetings refer to such records as *minutes*. Because minutes are often used to settle disputes, they must be accurate, complete, and clear. When approved, minutes of meetings are official and can be used as evidence in legal proceedings. A section from the minutes of a meeting is shown in Figure 9–3.

Keep your minutes brief and to the point. Except for recording formally presented motions, which must be transcribed word for word, summarize what occurs and paraphrase discussions. To keep the minutes concise, follow a set format, and use headings for each major point discussed. See also note-taking (Tab 3).

Avoid abstractions and generalities; always be specific. Refer to everyone in the same way—a lack of consistency in titles or names may suggest a deference to one person at the expense of another. Avoid adjectives and adverbs that suggest good or bad qualities, as in "Mr. Sturgess's *capable* assistant read the *comprehensive* report to the sub-committee." Minutes should be objective and impartial.

If a member of the committee is to follow up on something and report back to the committee at its next meeting, clearly state the person's name and the responsibility he or she has accepted.

NORTH TAMPA MEDICAL CENTER

Minutes of the Monthly Meeting
Medical Audit Committee

DATE: June 23, 2011

PRESENT: G. Miller (Chair), C. Bloom, J. Dades, K. Gilley,
             D. Ingoglia (Secretary), S. Ramirez

ABSENT: D. Rowan, C. Tsien, C. Voronski, R. Fautier, R. Wolf

Dr. Gail Miller called the meeting to order at 12:45 p.m. Dr. David Ingoglia made a motion that the June 2, 2011, minutes be approved as distributed. The motion was seconded and passed.

The committee discussed and took action on the following topics.

(1) TOPIC: Meeting Time

   Discussion: The most convenient time for the committee to meet.
   Action taken: The committee decided to meet on the fourth Tuesday of every month, at 12:30 p.m.

FIGURE 9–3. Minutes of a Meeting (partial section)

Writer's Checklist: Preparing Minutes of Meetings

Include the following in meeting minutes:

- ☑ The name of the group or committee holding the meeting
- ☑ The topic of the meeting
- ☑ The kind of meeting (a regular meeting or a special meeting called to discuss a specific subject or problem)
- ☑ The number of members present and, for committees or boards of ten or fewer members, the names of those present and absent
- ☑ The place, time, and date of the meeting
- ☑ A statement that the chair and the secretary were present or the names of any substitutes
- ☑ A statement that the minutes of the previous meeting were approved or revised
- ☑ A list of any reports that were read and approved
- ☑ All the main motions that were made, with statements as to whether they were carried, defeated, or tabled (vote postponed), and the names of those who made and seconded the motions (motions that were withdrawn are not mentioned)
- ☑ A full description of resolutions that were adopted and a simple statement of any that were rejected
- ☑ A record of all ballots with the number of votes cast for and against resolutions
- ☑ The time the meeting was adjourned (officially ended) and the place, time, and date of the next meeting
- ☑ The recording secretary's signature and typed name and, if desired, the signature of the chairperson

presentations

DIRECTORY

The steps required to prepare an effective presentation parallel the steps you follow to write a document. As with writing a document, determine your purpose (Tab 1) and analyze your audience (Tab 1). Then gather the facts that will support your point of view (Tab 1) or proposal (Tab 4) and logically organize that information. Presentations do, however, differ from written documents in a number of important ways. They are intended for listeners, not readers. Because you are speaking, your manner of delivery, the way you organize the material, and your supporting visuals (Tab 6) require as much attention as your content.

Determining Your Purpose

Every presentation is given for a purpose, even if it is only to share information. To determine the primary purpose of your presentation, use the following question as a guide: What do I want the audience to know, to believe, or to do when I have finished the presentation? Based on the answer to that question, write a purpose statement that answers the *what?* and *why?* questions.

- The purpose of my presentation is to convince my company's chief information officer of the need to improve the appearance, content, and customer use of our company's Web site [*what*] so that she will be persuaded to allocate additional funds for site-development work in the next fiscal year [*why*].

Analyzing Your Audience

Once you have determined the desired end result of the presentation, analyze your audience so that you can tailor your presentation to their needs. Ask yourself these questions about your audience:

- What is your audience's level of experience or knowledge about your topic?
- What is the general educational level and age of your audience?
- What is your audience's attitude toward the topic you are speaking about, and—based on that attitude—what concerns, fears, or objections might your audience have?
- Do any subgroups in the audience have different concerns or needs?
- What questions might your audience ask about this topic?

Gathering Information

Once you have focused the presentation, you need to find the facts and arguments that support your point of view or the action you propose. As you gather information, keep in mind that you should give the audience only what will accomplish your goals; too much detail will overwhelm your audience, and too little will not adequately inform your listeners or support your recommendations. For detailed guidance about gathering information, see <u>research</u> (Tab 3).

Structuring the Presentation

When structuring the presentation, focus on your audience. Listeners are freshest at the outset and refocus their attention near the end. Take advantage of that pattern. Begin with a brief overview of your presentation, use the body to develop your ideas, and end with a summary of what you covered and, if appropriate, a call to action. See also <u>organization</u> (Tab 1).

The Introduction.   Include in the <u>introduction</u> (Tab 1) an opening that focuses your audience's attention, as in the following examples:

- [*Definition of a problem*] "You have to write an important report, but you'd like to incorporate lengthy handwritten notes from several meetings you attended. Your scanner will not read these notes, and you will have to type many pages. You groan because that seems an incredible waste of time. Have I got a solution for you!"

- [*An attention-getting statement*] "As many as 50 million Americans have high blood pressure."

- [*A rhetorical question*] "Would you be interested in a full-sized computer keyboard that is waterproof and noiseless and can be rolled up like a rubber mat?"

- [*A personal experience*] "As I sat at my computer one morning, deleting my eighth spam message of the day, I decided that it was time to take action to eliminate this time-waster."

- [*An appropriate quotation*] "According to researchers at the Massachusetts Institute of Technology, 'Garlic and its cousin, the onion, confer major health benefits—including fighting cancer, infections, and heart disease.'"

Following your opening, use the introduction to set the stage for your audience by providing an overview of the presentation, which can include general or background information that will be needed to understand the detailed information in the body of your presentation. It can also show how you have organized the material.

- This presentation analyzes three high-volume, on-demand printers for us to consider purchasing. Based on a comparison of all three, I will recommend the one I believe best meets our needs. To do so, I'll discuss the following five points:

  1. Why we need a high-volume printer [*the problem*]
  2. The basics of on-demand technology [*general information*]

9

3. The criteria I used to compare the three printer models
   [*comparison*]
4. The printer models I compared and why [*possible solutions*]
5. The printer I propose we buy [*proposed solution*]

The Body.   If your goal is <u>persuasion</u> (Tab 1), present the evidence
that will persuade the audience to agree with your conclusions and act
on them. If you are discussing a problem, demonstrate that it exists
and offer a solution or range of possible solutions. For example, if your
introduction stated that the problem is low profits, high costs, outdated
technology, or high employee absenteeism, you could use the following
approach.

1. Prove your point.
   • Strategically organize the facts and data you need.
   • Present the information using easy-to-understand visuals.
2. Offer solutions.
   • Increase profits by lowering production costs.
   • Cut overhead to reduce costs, or abolish specific programs or
     product lines.
   • Replace outdated technology, or upgrade existing technology.
   • Offer employees more flexibility in their work schedules, or offer
     them other incentives.
3. Anticipate questions ("How much will it cost?") and objections
   ("We're too busy now—when would we have time to learn
   the new software?") and incorporate the answers into your
   presentation.

The Closing.   Fulfill the goals of your presentation in the closing. If
your purpose is to motivate the listeners to take action, ask them to do
what you want them to do; if your purpose is to get your audience to
think about something, summarize what you want them to think about.
Many presenters make the mistake of not actually closing—they simply
quit talking, shuffle papers, and then walk away.

Because your closing is what your audience is most likely to remember, use that time to be strong and persuasive. Consider the following
typical closing:

• Based on all the data, I believe that the Worthington TechLine
  5510 Production Printer best suits our needs. It produces
  40 pages per minute more than its closest competitor and
  provides modular systems that can be upgraded to support new
  applications. The Worthington is also compatible with our current
  computer network, and staff training at our site is included with
  our purchase. Although the initial cost is higher than that for the

other two models, the additional capabilities, compatibility with most standard environments, lower maintenance costs, and strong customer support services make it a better value.

    I recommend we allocate the funds necessary for this printer by the fifteenth of this month in order to be well prepared for the production of next quarter's customer publications.

This closing brings the presentation full circle and asks the audience to fulfill the purpose of the presentation—exactly what a <u>conclusion</u> (Tab 1) should do.

Transitions.   Planned <u>transitions</u> (Tab 10) should appear between the introduction and the body, between major points in the body, and between the body and the closing. Transitions are simply a sentence or two to let the audience know that you are moving from one topic to the next. They also prevent a choppy presentation and provide the audience with assurance that you know where you are going and how to get there.

- Before getting into the specifics of each printer I compared, I'd like to present the benefits of networked, on-demand printers in general. That information will provide you with the background you'll need to compare the differences among the printers and their capabilities discussed in this presentation.

It is also a good idea to pause for a moment after you have delivered a transition between topics to let your listeners shift gears with you. Remember, they do not know your plan.

Using Visuals

Well-planned visuals not only add interest and emphasis to your presentation but also clarify and simplify your message because they communicate clearly, quickly, and vividly. Charts, graphs, and illustrations can greatly increase audience understanding and retention of information, especially for complex issues and technical information that could otherwise be misunderstood or overlooked.

    ◼ ETHICS NOTE Be sure to provide credit for any visual taken from a print or an online source. You can include a citation either on an individual visual (such as a slide) or in a list of references or works cited that you distribute to your audience. For information on citing visuals from print or Web sources, see <u>documenting sources</u> (Tab 3). ✦

    You can create and present the visual components of your presentation by using a variety of media—flip charts, whiteboard or chalkboard, overhead transparencies, slides, or computer presentation software. See also <u>layout and design</u> (Tab 6).

Flip Charts.   Flip charts are ideal for smaller groups in a conference room or classroom and are also ideal for brainstorming with your audience.

Whiteboard or Chalkboard.   The whiteboard or chalkboard common to classrooms is convenient for creating sketches and for jotting notes during your presentation. If your presentation requires extensive notes or complex drawings, however, prepare handouts on which the audience can jot notes and which they can keep for future reference.

Overhead Transparencies.   With transparencies you can create a series of overlays to explain a complex device or system, adding (or removing) the overlays one at a time. You can also lay a sheet of paper over a list of items on a transparency, uncovering one item at a time as you discuss it, to focus audience attention on each point in the sequence.

Presentation Software.   Presentation software, such as Microsoft PowerPoint, Corel Presentations, and OpenOffice.org Impress, lets you create your presentation on your computer. You can develop charts and graphs with data from spreadsheet software or locate visuals on the Web and then import those files into your presentation. This software also offers standard templates and other features that help you design effective visuals and integrated text. Enhancements include a selection of typefaces, highlighting devices, background textures and colors, and clip-art images. Images can also be printed out for use as overhead transparencies or handouts. However, avoid using too many enhancements, which may distract viewers from your message. Figure 9–4 shows well-balanced slides for a presentation based on the sample formal report in Figure 5–2 on pages 137–152.

◼ PROFESSIONALISM NOTE Rehearse your presentation using your electronic slides, and practice your transitions from slide to slide. Also practice loading your presentation and anticipate any technical difficulties that might arise. Should you encounter a technical snag during the presentation, stay calm and give yourself time to solve the problem. If you cannot solve the problem, move on without the technology. As a backup, carry a printout of your electronic presentation as well as an extra electronic copy on a storage medium. ✦

 WEB LINK **PREPARING PRESENTATION SLIDES**

For a helpful tutorial on creating effective slides, see *bedfordstmartins.com/alred*, and select *Tutorials*, "Preparing Presentation Slides." For links to additional information and tutorials for using presentation software, select *Links Library*.

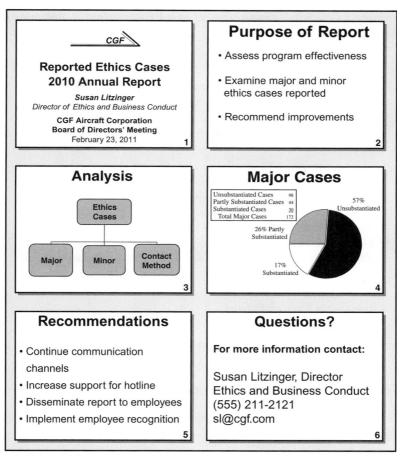

FIGURE 9–4. Slides for a Presentation

Writer's Checklist: Using Visuals in a Presentation

☑ Use text sparingly in visuals. Use bulleted or numbered <u>lists</u> (Tab 6), keeping them in **parallel structure** (Tab 10) and with balanced content. Use numbers if the sequence is important and bullets if it is not.

☑ Limit the number of bulleted or numbered items to no more than five or six per visual.

☑ Limit each visual to no more than 40 to 45 words. Any more will clutter the visual and force you to use a smaller font, which could impair the audience's ability to read it.

☑ Make your visuals consistent in type style, size, and spacing.

9

Writer's Checklist: Using Visuals in a Presentation (continued)

☑ Use a type size visible to members of the audience at the back of the room. Type should be boldface and no smaller than 30 points. For headings, 45- or 50-point type works even better.

☑ Use graphs and charts to show data trends. Use only one or two illustrations per visual to avoid clutter and confusion.

☑ Make the contrast between your text and the background sharp. Use light backgrounds with dark lettering and avoid textured or decorated backgrounds.

☑ Use no more than 12 visuals per presentation. Any more will tax the audience's concentration.

☑ Match your delivery of the content to your visuals. Do not put one set of words or images on the screen and talk about the previous visual or, even worse, the next one.

☑ Do not read the text on your visual word for word. Your audience can read the visuals; they look to you to provide the key points in detail.

Delivering a Presentation

Once you have outlined and drafted your presentation and prepared your visuals, you are ready to practice your presentation and delivery techniques.

Practice.   Familiarize yourself with the sequence of the material — major topics, notes, and visuals — in your outline. Once you feel comfortable with the content, you are ready to practice the presentation (in front of others if possible).

PRACTICE ON YOUR FEET AND OUT LOUD.   Try to practice in the room where you will give the presentation. Practicing on-site helps you get the feel of the room: the lighting, the arrangement of the chairs, the position of electrical outlets and switches, and so forth. Practice out loud to gauge the length of your presentation, to uncover problems such as awkward transitions, and to eliminate verbal tics (such as "um," "you know," and "like").

PRACTICE WITH YOUR VISUALS AND TEXT.   Integrate your visuals into your practice sessions to help your presentation go more smoothly. Operate the equipment (computer, slide projector, or overhead projector) until you are comfortable with it. Decide if you want to use a remote control or wireless mouse or if you want to have someone else advance your slides. Even if things go wrong, being prepared and practiced will give you the confidence and poise to continue.

Delivery Techniques That Work.   Your delivery is both audible and visual. In addition to your words and message, your nonverbal communication affects your audience. Be animated—your words have impact and staying power when they are delivered with physical and vocal animation. If you want listeners to share your point of view, show enthusiasm for your topic. The most common delivery techniques include making eye contact; using movement and gestures; and varying voice inflection, projection, and pace.

EYE CONTACT.   The best way to establish rapport with your audience is through eye contact. In a large audience, directly address those people who seem most responsive to you in different parts of the room. Doing that helps you establish rapport with your listeners by holding their attention and gives you important visual cues that let you know how your message is being received. Do the listeners seem engaged and actively listening? Based on your observations, you may need to adjust the pace of your presentation.

MOVEMENT.   Animate the presentation with physical movement. Take a step or two to one side after you have been talking for a minute or so. That type of movement is most effective at transitional points in your presentation between major topics or after pauses or emphases. Too much movement, however, can be distracting, so try not to pace.

Another way to integrate movement into your presentation is to walk to the screen and point to the visual as you discuss it. Touch the screen with the pointer and then turn back to the audience before beginning to speak (remember the three *t*'s: touch, turn, and talk).

GESTURES.   Gestures both animate your presentation and help communicate your message. Most people gesture naturally when they talk; nervousness, however, can inhibit gesturing during a presentation. Keep one hand free and use that hand to gesture.

VOICE.   Your voice can be an effective tool in communicating your sincerity, enthusiasm, and command of your topic. Use it to your advantage to project your credibility. *Vocal inflection* is the rise and fall of your voice at different times, such as the way your voice naturally rises at the end of a question. ("You want it *when*?") A conversational delivery and eye contact promote the feeling among members of the audience that you are addressing them directly. Use vocal inflection to highlight differences between key and subordinate points in your presentation.

PROJECTION.   Most presenters think they are speaking louder than they are. Remember that your presentation is ineffective for anyone in the audience who cannot hear you. If listeners must strain to hear you, they may give up trying to listen. Correct projection problems by practicing out loud with someone listening from the back of the room.

PACE.   Be aware of the speed at which you deliver your presentation. If you speak too fast, your words will run together, making it difficult for your audience to follow. If you speak too slowly, your listeners will become impatient and distracted.

Presentation Anxiety.   Everyone experiences nervousness before a presentation. Survey after survey reveals that for most people dread of public speaking ranks among their top five fears. Instead of letting fear inhibit you, focus on channeling your nervous energy into a helpful stimulant. Practice will help you, but the best way to master anxiety is to know your topic thoroughly—knowing what you are going to say and how you are going to say it will help you gain confidence and reduce anxiety as you become immersed in your subject.

Writer's Checklist: Preparing for and Delivering a Presentation

- ☑ Prepare a set of notes that will trigger your memory during the presentation.
- ☑ Make as much eye contact as possible with your audience to establish rapport and maximize opportunities for audience feedback.
- ☑ Animate your delivery by integrating movement, gestures, and vocal inflection into your presentation. However, keep your movements and speech patterns natural.
- ☑ Speak loudly and slowly enough to be heard and understood.
- ☑ Review the earlier checklist on using visuals as well as the advice on delivery in this entry.

For information and tips on communicating with cross-cultural audiences, see **global communication** (Tab 1), **global graphics** (Tab 6), and **international correspondence** (Tab 7).

10

Style and Clarity

Preview

The entries in this section are intended to help you develop a style that is clear and effective — and that follows the conventions of standard English. For a number of related entries, see Tab 1, "The Writing Process"; Tab 11, "Grammar"; and the Appendix, "Usage."

Some entries in this section — <u>awkwardness</u>, <u>coherence</u>, <u>parallel structure</u>, and <u>sentence variety</u> — will help you construct clear sentences and paragraphs. Other entries discuss such word-choice issues as <u>abstract / concrete words</u>, <u>idioms</u>, and <u>jargon</u>. Finally, this section covers the important subjects of <u>biased language</u>, <u>business writing style</u>, and the <u>"you" viewpoint</u>.

10

Style and Clarity

abstract / concrete words

Abstract words refer to general ideas, qualities, conditions, acts, or relationships — intangible things that cannot be detected by the five senses (sight, hearing, touch, taste, and smell), such as *learning, leadership,* and *technology. Concrete words* identify things that can be perceived by the five senses, such as *diploma, manager,* and *keyboard.*

Abstract words must frequently be further defined or described.

to develop its own customer database

- The marketing team needs freedom.
  ^

Abstract words are best used with concrete words to help make intangible concepts specific and vivid.

- *Transportation* [abstract] was limited to *buses* [concrete] and *commuter trains* [concrete].

See also <u>word choice</u>.

10

Style and Clarity

affectation

Affectation is the use of language that is more formal, technical, or showy than necessary to communicate information to the reader. Affectation is a widespread writing problem in the workplace because many people feel that affectation lends a degree of authority to their writing. In fact, affectation can alienate customers, clients, and colleagues because it forces readers to work harder to understand the writer's meaning.

Affected writing typically contains inappropriate abstract, highly technical, or foreign words and is often liberally sprinkled with trendy <u>buzzwords</u>.

◆ ETHICS NOTE <u>Jargon</u> and <u>euphemisms</u> can become affectation, especially if their purpose is to hide relevant facts or give a false impression of competence. See <u>ethics in writing</u> (Tab 1). ✦

Writers easily slip into affectation through the use of long variants — words created by adding prefixes and suffixes to simpler words (*orientate* for *orient; utilization* for *use*). Unnecessarily formal words (such as *penultimate* for *next to last*), created words using *-ese* (such as *managementese*), and outdated words (such as *aforesaid*) can produce affectation. Elegant variation — attempting to avoid repeating a word within a paragraph by substituting a pretentious synonym — is also a form of affectation. Either repeat the term or use a pronoun.

- The use of digital modules in our assembly process has increased
  production. ~~Modular digitization has also~~ cut costs.
  and

Another type of affectation is gobbledygook, which is wordy, round-about writing with many legal- and technical-sounding terms (such as *wherein* and *morphing*). See also <u>clichés</u>, <u>conciseness</u>, <u>nominalizations</u>, and <u>word choice</u>.

> **WEB LINK AFFECTED WRITING REVISED**
>
> For an example of regulations that are revised to eliminate various forms of affectation, see *bedfordstmartins.com/alred*, and select *ModelDoc Central*.

10

Style and Clarity

awkwardness

Any writing that strikes readers as awkward — that is, as forced or unnatural — impedes their understanding. The following checklist and the entries indicated will help you smooth out most awkward passages.

Writer's Checklist: Eliminating Awkwardness

☑ Strive for clarity and <u>coherence</u> during <u>revision</u> (Tab 1).

☑ Check for <u>organization</u> (Tab 1) to ensure your writing develops logically.

☑ Keep <u>sentence construction</u> (Tab 11) as direct and simple as possible.

☑ Use <u>subordination</u> appropriately and avoid needless <u>repetition</u>.

☑ Correct any <u>logic errors</u> within your sentences.

☑ Revise for <u>conciseness</u> and avoid <u>expletives</u> where possible.

☑ Use the active <u>voice</u> (Tab 11) unless you have a justifiable reason to use the passive voice.

☑ Eliminate jammed or misplaced <u>modifiers</u> (Tab 11) and, for particularly awkward constructions, apply the tactics in <u>garbled sentences</u>.

biased language

Biased language refers to words and expressions that offend because they make inappropriate assumptions or stereotypes about gender, ethnicity, physical or mental disability, age, or sexual orientation. Biased language, which is often used unintentionally, can defeat your purpose by damaging your credibility.

⬦ PROFESSIONALISM NOTE The easiest way to avoid bias is simply not to mention differences among people unless the differences are relevant to the discussion. Keep current with accepted usage and, if you are unsure of the appropriateness of an expression or the tone of a passage, have several colleagues review the material and give you their assessments. ✦

Sexist Language

Sexist language can be an outgrowth of sexism, the arbitrary stereotyping of men and women—it can breed and reinforce inequality. To avoid sexism in your writing, treat men and women equally and use nonsexist occupational descriptions.

INSTEAD OF	CONSIDER
chairman, chairwoman	chair, chairperson
foreman	supervisor, manager
man-hours	staff hours, worker hours
policeman, policewoman	police officer
salesman, saleswoman	salesperson

Use parallel terms to describe men and women.

INSTEAD OF	USE
ladies and men	ladies and gentlemen; women and men
man and wife	husband and wife
Ms. Jones and Bernard Weiss	Ms. Jones and Mr. Weiss; Mary Jones and Bernard Weiss

One common way of handling pronoun references (Tab 11) that could apply equally to a man or a woman is the use of the expression *his or her*. To avoid this awkward usage, try rewriting the sentence in the plural.

- *All employees* ~~Every employee~~ should submit *their* ~~his or her~~ expense *reports* ~~report~~ by Monday.

Another solution is to omit pronouns completely if they are not essential to the meaning of the sentence.

- Every employee should submit *an* ~~his or her~~ expense report by Monday.

Other Types of Biased Language

Identifying people by racial, ethnic, or religious categories is simply not relevant in most workplace writing. Telling readers that an accountant is Native American or an attorney is Jewish almost never conveys useful information.

Consider how you refer to people with disabilities. If you refer to "a disabled employee," you imply that the part (*disabled*) is as significant as the whole (*employee*). Use "an employee with a disability" instead. Similarly, the preferred usage is "a person who uses a wheelchair" rather than "a wheelchair-bound person," an expression that inappropriately equates the wheelchair with the person. Likewise, references to a person's age can be inappropriate, as in expressions like "middle-aged manager" or "young Web designer." See also ethics in writing (Tab 1).

business writing style

Business writing has evolved from a very formal and elaborate style to one that is more personal and direct. Business writing today varies from the conversational style you might use in a note sent by instant messaging (Tab 2) to the formal, legalistic style found in contracts. In most e-mails, letters, and memos, a style between those two extremes generally is appropriate. (See correspondence, Tab 7.) Writing that is too formal can alienate your audience. But an inappropriate attempt to be casual and informal may strike readers as insincere and unprofessional, especially to clients or those you do not know well.

> *Dear   :*
> • ~~Hey~~ Jane~~,~~
>
>   *Your proposal arrived today, and it looks good.*
>   ~~Just got your proposal. It's awesome!~~

The use of personal pronouns (Tab 11) is important in letters and memos. In fact, one way you can make your business writing natural and persuasive is to use the "you" viewpoint, which often (but not always) uses the pronoun *you* to place the readers' interest foremost.

✚ ETHICS NOTE Be careful when you use the pronoun *we* in a business letter that is written on company stationery because it commits your company to what you have written. In general, when a statement is your opinion, use *I*; when it is company policy, use *we*. Do not refer to yourself in the third person by using *one* or *the writer*. It is perfectly natural and appropriate to refer to yourself as *I* and to the reader as *you*. In a report, however, you may be writing to more than one reader and may not necessarily want to refer to collective readers as *you*. See also ethics in writing (Tab 1), persuasion (Tab 1), and point of view (Tab 1). ✦

The best writers strive to write in a style that is so clear that their message cannot be misunderstood. In fact, you cannot be persuasive without being clear. One way to achieve clarity, especially during <u>revision</u> (Tab 1), is to eliminate overuse of the passive <u>voice</u> (Tab 11), which plagues most poor business writing. Although the passive voice is sometimes necessary, often it makes your writing not only dull but also ambiguous, indirect, or overly impersonal.

You can also achieve clarity with <u>conciseness</u>. Proceed cautiously here, however, because business writing should not be an endless series of short, choppy sentences that are blunt or deliver too little information to be helpful to the reader. (See also <u>sentence variety</u> and <u>telegraphic style</u>.) Appropriate and effective <u>word choice</u> is also essential to clarity. Finally, the careful use of punctuation can promote clarity, as discussed in Tab 12, "Punctuation and Mechanics." See also "Five Steps to Successful Writing" (pages xxix–xxxvi).

buzzwords

Buzzwords are words or phrases that suddenly become popular and, because of an intense period of overuse, lose their freshness and preciseness. They may become popular through their association with technology, popular culture, or even sports. See also <u>jargon</u>.

- interface [as a verb]   win/win   F2F meeting
  impact [as a verb]   24/7   data dump
  cyberslackers   dot-com   action items

Obviously, the words in this example are appropriate when used in the right context.

- We must establish an *interface* between the computer and the satellite hardware.
  [*Interface* is appropriately used as a noun.]

When writers needlessly shift from the normal function of a word, however, they often create a buzzword that is imprecise.

- *cooperate*
  We must ~~interface~~ with the Human Resources Department.
  [*Interface* is inappropriately used as a verb; *cooperate* is more precise.]

We include such words in our vocabulary because they *seem* to give force and vitality to our language. Actually, buzzwords often sound like an <u>affectation</u> in business writing. See also <u>word choice</u>.

WEB LINK BUZZWORDS

Former newspaper editor John Walston offers BuzzWhack, a lighthearted site "dedicated to demystifying buzzwords." See *bedfordstmartins.com/alred*, and select *Links Library*.

clichés

Clichés are expressions that have been used for so long that they are no longer fresh but come to mind easily because they are so familiar. Clichés are often wordy as well as vague and can be confusing, especially to speakers of <u>English as a second language</u> (Tab 11). A better, more direct word or phrase is given for each of the following clichés.

INSTEAD OF	USE
all over the map	scattered; unfocused
the game plan	strategy; schedule
last but not least	last; finally

Some writers use clichés in a misguided attempt to appear casual or spontaneous, just as other writers try to impress readers with <u>buzzwords</u>. Although clichés may come to mind easily while you are writing a draft, eliminate them during revision. See also <u>affectation</u>, <u>conciseness</u>, and <u>international correspondence</u> (Tab 7).

coherence

Writing is coherent when the relationships among ideas are clear to readers. The major components of coherent writing are a logical sequence of related ideas and clear transitions between these ideas. See also <u>organization</u> (Tab 1).

Presenting ideas in a logical sequence is the most important requirement in achieving coherence. The key to achieving a logical sequence is the use of a good outline. (See <u>outlining</u>, Tab 1.) An outline forces you to establish a beginning, a middle, and an end. That structure contributes greatly to coherence by enabling you to experiment with sequences and to lay out the most direct route to your <u>purpose</u> (Tab 1) without digressing.

Thoughtful <u>transition</u> is also essential; without it, your writing cannot achieve the smooth flow of sentence to sentence and paragraph to paragraph that results in coherence.

Check your draft carefully for coherence during <u>revision</u> (Tab 1). If possible, have someone else review your draft for how well it expresses the relationships between ideas. See also <u>unity</u>.

compound words

A compound word is made from two or more words that function as a single concept. A compound may be hyphenated, written as one word, or written as separate words.

- high-energy   nevertheless   post office
  low-level   online   blood pressure

If you are not certain whether a compound word should use a <u>hyphen</u> (Tab 12), check a dictionary.

Be careful to distinguish between compound words (*greenhouse*) and words that simply appear together but do not constitute compound words (*green house*). For plurals of compound words, generally add *s* to the last letter (*bookcases* and *Web sites*). However, when the first word of the compound is more important to its meaning than the last, the first word takes the *s* (*editors in chief*). Possessives are formed by adding *'s* to the end of the compound word (the *editor in chief's* desk, the *pipeline's* diameter, the *post office's* hours). See also <u>possessive case</u> (Tab 11).

conciseness

Conciseness means that unnecessary words, phrases, clauses, and sentences have been removed from writing without sacrificing clarity or appropriate detail. Conciseness is not a synonym for brevity; a long report may be concise, while its <u>abstract</u> (Tab 5) may be brief and concise. Conciseness is always desirable, but brevity may or may not be desirable in a given passage, depending on the writer's purpose. Although concise sentences are not guaranteed to be effective, wordy sentences always sacrifice some of their readability and <u>coherence</u>.

Causes of Wordiness

<u>Modifiers</u> (Tab 11) that repeat an idea implicit or present in the word being modified contribute to wordiness by being redundant.

basic essentials   *completely* finished
final outcome   *present* status

Coordinated synonyms that merely repeat each other contribute to wordiness.

each and every   *basic and fundamental*
finally and for good   *first and foremost*

Excess qualification also contributes to wordiness.

perfectly clear   *completely* accurate

Expletives, relative pronouns, and relative adjectives, although they have legitimate purposes, often result in wordiness.

WORDY   *There are* [expletive] many Web designers *who* [relative pronoun] are planning to attend the conference, *which* [relative adjective] is scheduled for May 13–15.

CONCISE   Many Web designers plan to attend the conference scheduled for May 13–15.

Circumlocution (a long, indirect way of expressing things) is a leading cause of wordiness.

WORDY   The payment to which a subcontractor is entitled should be made promptly so that in the event of a subsequent contractual dispute we, as general contractors, may not be held in default of our contract by virtue of nonpayment.

CONCISE   Pay subcontractors promptly. Then, if a contractual dispute occurs, we cannot be held in default of our contract because of nonpayment.

When conciseness is overdone, writing can become choppy and ambiguous. (See also telegraphic style.) Too much conciseness can produce a style that is not only too brief but also too blunt, especially in correspondence (Tab 7).

Writer's Checklist: Achieving Conciseness

Wordiness is understandable when you are writing a draft (Tab 1), but it should not survive revision (Tab 1).

☑ Use subordination to achieve conciseness.

- The financial report was carefully documented, and it covered five pages.
  five-page

Writer's Checklist: Achieving Conciseness (continued)

☑ Avoid **affectation** by using simple words and phrases.

WORDY	It is the policy of the company to provide Internet access to enable employees to conduct the online communication necessary to discharge their responsibilities; such should not be utilized for personal communications or nonbusiness activities.
CONCISE	Employee Internet access should be used only for appropriate company business.

☑ Eliminate redundancy.

WORDY	Postinstallation testing, which is offered to all our customers at no further cost to them whatsoever, is available with each Line Scan System One purchased from this company.
CONCISE	Free postinstallation testing is offered with each Line Scan System One.

☑ Change the passive **voice** (Tab 11) to the active voice and the indicative **mood** (Tab 11) to the imperative mood whenever possible.

WORDY	Bar codes normally are used when an order is intended to be displayed on a monitor, and inventory numbers normally are used when an order is to be placed with the manufacturer.
CONCISE	Use bar codes to display the order on a monitor, and use inventory numbers to place the order with the manufacturer.

☑ Eliminate or replace wordy introductory phrases or pretentious words and phrases (*in the case of, it may be said that, it appears that, needless to say*).

REPLACE	WITH
in order to; with a view to	to
due to the fact that; for the reason that; owing to the fact that; the reason for	because
by means of; by using; in connection with; through the use of	by; with
at this time; at this point in time; at present; at the present	now; currently

☑ Do not overuse **intensifiers**, such as *very, more, most, best, quite, great, really,* and *especially*. Instead, provide specific and useful details.

☑ Use the search-and-replace command to find and revise wordy expressions, including *to be* and unnecessary helping **verbs** (Tab 11) such as *will*.

10

Style and Clarity

connotation / denotation

The *denotations* of a word are its literal meanings, as defined in a dictionary. The *connotations* of a word are its meanings and associations beyond its literal definitions. For example, the denotations of *Hollywood* are "a district of Los Angeles" and "the U.S. movie industry as a whole"; its connotations for many are "glamour, opulence, and superficiality."

Often words have particular connotations for <u>audiences</u> (Tab 1) within professional groups and organizations. Choose words with both the most accurate denotations and the most appropriate connotations for the <u>context</u> (Tab 1). See also <u>defining terms</u> (Tab 1) and <u>word choice</u>.

emphasis

Emphasis is the principle of stressing the most important ideas in your writing. You can achieve emphasis in your writing through one or more of the following techniques: position, climactic order, sentence length, sentence type, active <u>voice</u> (Tab 11), <u>repetition</u>, <u>intensifiers</u>, direct statements, long <u>dashes</u> (Tab 12), and typographical devices.

Achieving Emphasis

Position.   Place the idea in a conspicuous position. The first and last words of a sentence, paragraph, or document stand out in readers' minds.

- Moon craters are important to understanding the earth's history because they reflect geological history.

The term *moon craters* is emphasized because it appears at the beginning of the sentence, and *geological history* is emphasized because it appears at the end of the sentence. See also <u>subordination</u>.

Climactic Order.   List the ideas or facts within a sentence in sequence from least to most important, as in the following example. See also <u>lists</u> (Tab 6).

- The hostile takeover of the company will result in some employees being relocated to different cities, some being downgraded, and some being let go.

Sentence Length.   Vary sentence length strategically. A very short sentence that follows a very long sentence or a series of long sentences stands out in the reader's mind, as in the short sentence ("We must cut costs") that ends the following example paragraph.

- We have already reviewed the problem the accounting department has experienced during the past year. We could continue to examine the causes of our problems and point an accusing finger at all the culprits beyond our control, but in the end it all leads to one simple conclusion. We must cut costs.

See sentence construction (Tab 11).

Sentence Type.   Vary sentences by the strategic use of a compound sentence, a complex sentence, or a simple sentence.

- The report submitted by the committee was carefully illustrated, and it covered five pages of single-spaced copy.
  [This compound sentence carries no special emphasis; it contains two coordinate independent clauses.]
- The committee's report, which was carefully illustrated, covered five pages of single-spaced copy.
  [This complex sentence emphasizes the size of the report.]
- The carefully illustrated report submitted by the committee covered five pages of single-spaced copy.
  [This simple sentence emphasizes that the report was carefully illustrated.]

See sentence variety.

Active Voice.   Use the active voice to emphasize the performer of an action: Make the performer the subject of the verb.

- Our department designed the new system.
  [This sentence emphasizes *our department*, which is the performer and the subject of the verb, *designed*.]

Repetition.   Repeat key terms, as in the use of the word *remains* and the phrase *come and go* in the following sentence.

- Similarly, atoms *come and go* in a molecule, but the molecule *remains*; molecules *come and go* in a cell, but the cell *remains*; cells *come and go* in a body, but the body *remains*; persons *come and go* in an organization, but the organization *remains*.
  —Kenneth Boulding, *Beyond Economics*

Intensifiers.   Although you can use intensifiers (*most, much, very*) for emphasis, this technique is so easily abused that it should be used with caution.

- The final proposal is *much* more persuasive than the first one. [The intensifier *much* emphasizes the contrast.]

Direct Statements. Use direct statements, such as "most important," "foremost," or someone's name in a direct address.

- Most important, keep in mind that everything you do affects the company's bottom line.

- John, I believe we should rethink our plans.

Long Dashes. Use a dash to call attention to a particular word or statement.

- The job will be done—after we are under contract.

Typographical Devices. Use *italics*, **bold type**, underlining, and CAPITAL LETTERS—but use them sparingly because overuse can create visual clutter and cause readers to ignore truly important information. See also layout and design (Tab 6), capitalization (Tab 12), and italics (Tab 12).

euphemisms

A euphemism is an inoffensive substitute for a word or phrase that could be distasteful, offensive, or too blunt: *passed away* for *died*; *previously owned* or *preowned* for *used*; *lay off* or *restructure* for *fire* or *terminate* employees. Used judiciously, euphemisms can help you avoid embarrassing or offending someone.

⬛ ETHICS NOTE Euphemisms can also hide the facts of a situation (*incident* or *event* for *accident*) or be a form of affectation if used carelessly. Avoid them especially in international correspondence (Tab 7) and other forms of global communication (Tab 1) where their meanings could be not only confusing but also misleading. See also ethics in writing (Tab 1). ✦

expletives

An expletive is a word that fills the position of another word, phrase, or clause. *It* and *there* are common expletives.

- *It* is certain that he will be promoted.

In the example, the expletive *it* occupies the position of subject in place of the real subject, *that he will be promoted*. Expletives are sometimes necessary to avoid <u>awkwardness</u>, but they are commonly overused, and most sentences can be better stated without them.

> *Many*   *were*
> • ~~There were many~~ files lost when we converted to the new server.
>   ^   ^

In addition to its grammatical use, the word *expletive* means an exclamation or oath, especially one that is obscene.

figures of speech

A figure of speech is an imaginative expression that often compares two things that are basically not alike but have at least one thing in common. For example, if a device is cone-shaped and has an opening at the narrow end, you might say that it looks like a volcano.

Figures of speech can clarify the unfamiliar by relating a new concept to one with which readers are familiar. In that respect, they help establish understanding between the specialist and the nonspecialist. Figures of speech can help translate the abstract into the concrete; in the process of doing so, they can also make writing more colorful and graphic. (See also <u>abstract / concrete words</u>.) A figure of speech must make sense, however, to achieve the desired effect.

> **ILLOGICAL**   Without the fuel of tax incentives, our economic
>   engine would operate less efficiently.
>   [It would not operate at all without fuel.]

Figures of speech also must be consistent to be effective.

> • We must get our sales program *back on course*, and we are
>   *steer the effort.*
>   counting on you to ~~carry the ball.~~
>   ^

A figure of speech should not overshadow the point the writer is trying to make. In addition, it is better to use no figure of speech at all than to use a trite one. A surprise that comes "like a bolt out of the blue" seems stale and not much of a surprise. See also <u>clichés</u>.

garbled sentences

A garbled sentence is one that is so tangled with structural and grammatical problems that it cannot be repaired. Garbled sentences often result from an attempt to squeeze too many ideas into one sentence.

10

Style and Clarity

- My job objectives are accomplished by my having a diversified background which enables me to operate effectively and efficiently, consisting of a degree in computer science, along with twelve years of experience, including three years in Staff Engineering-Packaging sets a foundation for a strong background in areas of analyzing problems and assessing economical and reasonable solutions.

Do not try to patch such a sentence; rather, analyze the ideas it contains, list them in a logical sequence, and then construct one or more entirely new sentences. An analysis of the preceding example yields the following five ideas:

- My job requires that I analyze problems to find economical and workable solutions.
- My diversified background helps me accomplish my job.
- I have a computer-science degree.
- I have twelve years of job experience.
- Three of these years have been in Staff Engineering-Packaging.

Using those five ideas—together with parallel structure, sentence variety, subordination, and transition—the writer might have described the job as follows:

- My job requires that I analyze problems to find economical and workable solutions. Both my education and my experience help me achieve this goal. Specifically, I have a computer-science degree and twelve years of job experience, three of which have been in the Staff Engineering-Packaging Department.

See also mixed constructions (Tab 11) and sentence construction (Tab 11).

idioms

An idiom is a group of words that has a special meaning apart from its literal meaning. A candidate who "runs for political office" in the United States, for example, need not be an athlete. The same candidate would "stand for office" in the United Kingdom. Because such expressions are specific to a culture, nonnative speakers must memorize them.

Idioms are often constructed with prepositions that follow adjectives (*similar to*), nouns (*need for*), and verbs (*approve of*). Some idioms can change meaning slightly with the preposition used, as in *agree to* ("consent") and *agree with* ("in accord"). The following are typical idioms that give nonnative speakers trouble.

call off [cancel]	hand in [submit]
call on [visit a client]	hand out [distribute]
drop in on [visit unexpectedly]	look up [research a subject]
find out [discover information]	run into [meet by chance]
get through with [finish]	run out of [deplete supply]
give up [quit]	watch out for [be careful]

Idioms often provide helpful shortcuts. In fact, they can make writing more natural and lively. Avoid them, however, if your writing is to be translated into another language or read in other English-speaking countries. Because no language system can fully explain such usages, a reader must check dictionaries or usage guides to interpret the meaning of idioms. See also <u>international correspondence</u> (Tab 7) and <u>English as a second language</u> (Tab 11).

 WEB LINK PREPOSITIONAL IDIOMS

For links to helpful lists of common pairings of prepositions with nouns, verbs, and adjectives, see *bedfordstmartins.com/alred*, and select *Links Library*.

---

intensifiers

Intensifiers are <u>adverbs</u> (Tab 11) that emphasize degree, such as *very*, *quite*, *rather*, *such*, and *too*. (See also <u>emphasis</u>.) Although intensifiers serve a legitimate and necessary function, unnecessary intensifiers can weaken your writing. Eliminate those that do not make an obvious contribution or replace them with specific details.

- The team learned the ~~very~~ good news that it had been awarded a
  $10,000
  ~~rather substantial monetary~~ prize for its design.
  ^

Some words (such as *perfect*, *impossible*, and *final*) do not logically permit intensification because, by definition, they do not allow degrees of comparison. Although usage often ignores that logical restriction, avoid such comparisons in business writing. See also <u>adjectives</u> (Tab 11); <u>conciseness</u>; and the Appendix, "Usage."

jargon

Jargon is a specialized slang that is unique to an occupational or a professional group. For example, the *attending* is slang used by medical professionals to refer to "the attending physician" in a hospital. Jargon is at first understood only by insiders; over time, it may become known more widely and become a buzzword. If all your readers are members of a particular occupational group, jargon may provide an efficient means of communicating. However, if you have any doubt that your entire audience (Tab 1) is part of such a group, avoid jargon. See also affectation.

logic errors

Logic is essential to convincing an audience that your conclusions are valid. Errors in logic can undermine the point you are trying to communicate and your credibility. Some typical logic errors are described in this entry. See also persuasion (Tab 1).

◆ ETHICS NOTE   Many of the following errors in logic, when used to mislead readers, are unethical as well as illogical. See also ethics in writing (Tab 1). ✦

Lack of Reason

When a statement is contrary to the reader's common sense, that statement is not reasonable. If, for example, you stated, "New York City is a small town," your reader might immediately question your statement. However, if you stated, "Although New York City's population is over eight million, it is composed of neighborhoods that function as small towns," your reader could probably accept the statement as reasonable.

Sweeping Generalizations

Sweeping generalizations are statements that are too broad or all-inclusive to be supportable; they generally enlarge an observation about a small group to refer to an entire population. A flat statement such as "Management is never concerned about employees" ignores any evidence that management could be concerned for its employees. Using such generalizations weakens your credibility.

Non Sequiturs

A non sequitur is a statement that does not logically follow a previous statement.

- I cleared off my desk, and the report is due today.

The missing link in these statements is that the writer cleared his or her desk to make space for materials to help finish the report that is due today. In your own writing, be careful that you do not allow gaps in logic to produce non sequiturs.

False Cause

A false cause (also called *post hoc, ergo propter hoc*) refers to the logical fallacy that because one event followed another event, the first somehow caused the second.

- I didn't bring my umbrella today. No wonder it is now raining.
- Because we now have our board meetings at the Education Center, our management turnover rate has declined.

Such errors in reasoning can happen when the writer hastily concludes that two events are related without examining whether a causal connection between them, in fact, exists.

Biased or Suppressed Evidence

A conclusion reached as a result of biased or suppressed evidence— self-serving data, questionable sources, purposely omitted or incomplete facts—is both illogical and unethical. Suppose you are preparing a report on the acceptance of a new policy among employees. If you distribute questionnaires only to those likely to think the policy is effective, the resulting evidence will be biased. Intentionally ignoring relevant data that might not support your position not only produces inaccurate results but also is unethical.

Fact Versus Opinion

Distinguish between fact and opinion. Facts include verifiable data or statements, whereas opinions are personal conclusions that may or may not be based on facts. For example, it is verifiable that distilled water boils at 100°C; that it tastes better or worse than tap water is an opinion. Distinguish the facts from your opinions in your writing so that your readers can draw their own conclusions.

Loaded Arguments

When you include an opinion in a statement and then reach conclusions that are based on that statement, you are loading the argument. Consider the following opening for a memo:

- I have several suggestions to improve the poorly written policy manual. First, we should change . . .

10

Style and Clarity

Unless everyone agrees that the manual is poorly written, readers may reject a writer's entire message because they disagree with this loaded premise. Conclusions reached with such loaded statements are weak and can produce negative reactions in readers who detect the loading.

 WEB LINK UNDERSTANDING AN ARGUMENT

Dr. Frank Edler of Metropolitan Community College in Omaha, Nebraska, offers a tutorial in recognizing the logical components of an argument and thinking critically. See *bedfordstmartins.com/alred*, and select *Links Library*.

---

nominalizations

A nominalization is a noun form of a verb that is often combined with vague and general (or "weak") verbs like *make, do, give, perform,* and *provide.* Avoid nominalizations when you can use specific verbs that communicate the same idea more directly and concisely.

- The staff should ~~perform an evaluation of~~ *evaluate* the new software.

If you use nominalizations solely to make your writing sound more formal, the result will be <u>affectation</u>. You may occasionally have an appropriate use for a nominalization. For example, you might use a nominalization to slow the pace of your writing. See also <u>business writing style</u>, <u>conciseness</u>, and <u>verbs</u> (Tab 11).

parallel structure

Parallel structure requires that sentence elements that are alike in function be alike in grammatical form as well. This structure achieves an economy of words, clarifies meaning, expresses the equality of the ideas, and achieves <u>emphasis</u>. Parallel structure assists readers because it allows them to anticipate the meaning of a sentence element on the basis of its construction.

Parallel structure can be achieved with words, phrases, or clauses.

- If you want to benefit from the jobs training program, you must be *punctual, courteous,* and *conscientious.*
  [parallel words]

- If you want to benefit from the jobs training program, you must recognize the importance *of punctuality, of courtesy,* and *of conscientiousness.*
  [parallel phrases]

- If you want to benefit from the jobs training program, *you must arrive punctually, you must behave courteously,* and *you must study conscientiously.*
  [parallel clauses]

Correlative conjunctions *(either . . . or, neither . . . nor, not only . . . but also)* should always join elements that use parallel structure. Both parts of the pairs should be followed immediately by the same grammatical form: two similar words, two similar phrases, or two similar clauses.

- Viruses carry either *DNA* or *RNA*, never both.
  [parallel words]

- Clearly, neither *serological tests* nor *virus isolation studies* alone would have been adequate.
  [parallel phrases]

- Either *we must increase our production efficiency* or *we must decrease our production goals.*
  [parallel clauses]

To make a parallel construction clear and effective, it is often best to repeat an article, a pronoun, a helping verb, a preposition, a subordinating conjunction, or the mark of an infinitive (*to*).

- The association has *a* mission statement and *a* code of ethics.

- The software is popular *because* it is compatible across platforms and *because* it is easily customized.

Parallel structure is especially important in creating <u>lists</u> (Tab 6), outlines, <u>tables of contents</u> (Tab 5), and <u>headings</u> (Tab 6) because it lets readers know the relative value of each item in a table of contents and each heading in the body of a document. See also <u>outlining</u> (Tab 1).

Faulty Parallelism

Faulty parallelism results when joined elements are intended to serve equal grammatical functions but do not have equal grammatical form.

10

Style and Clarity

Faulty parallelism sometimes occurs because a writer tries to compare items that are not comparable.

NOT PARALLEL   The company offers special college training to help hourly employees move into professional careers like engineering management, software development, service technicians, and sales trainees. [Notice faulty comparison of occupations — *engineering management* and *software development* — to people — *service technicians* and *sales trainees*.]

To avoid faulty parallelism, make certain that each element in a series is similar in form and structure to all others in the same series.

PARALLEL   The company offers special college training to help hourly employees move into professional careers like *engineering management, software development, technical services*, and *sales*.

positive writing

Presenting positive information as though it were negative is confusing to readers.

NEGATIVE   If the error does *not* involve data transmission, the backup function will *not* be used.

In this sentence, the reader must reverse two negatives to understand the exception that is being stated. The following sentence presents the exception in a positive and straightforward manner.

POSITIVE   The backup function is used only when the error involves data transmission.

◆ ETHICS NOTE Negative facts or conclusions, however, should be stated negatively; stating a negative fact or conclusion positively is deceptive because it can mislead the reader.

DECEPTIVE   In the first quarter of this year, employee exposure to airborne lead averaged within 10 percent of acceptable state health standards.

ACCURATE   In the first quarter of this year, employee exposure to airborne lead averaged 10 percent below acceptable state health standards.

See also ethics in writing (Tab 1). ✦

10

Style and Clarity

Even if what you are saying is negative, do not state it more negatively than necessary.

NEGATIVE   We are withholding your shipment because we have not received your payment.

POSITIVE   We will forward your shipment as soon as we receive your payment.

See also <u>correspondence</u> (Tab 7) and <u>"you" viewpoint</u>.

repetition

The deliberate use of repetition to build a sustained effect or to emphasize a feeling or an idea can be a powerful device. See also <u>emphasis</u>.

- Similarly, atoms *come and go* in a molecule, but the molecule *remains*; molecules *come and go* in a cell, but the cell *remains*; cells *come and go* in a body, but the body *remains*; persons *come and go* in an organization, but the organization *remains*.
  —Kenneth Boulding, *Beyond Economics*

Repeating keywords from a previous sentence or paragraph can also be used effectively to achieve <u>transition</u>.

- For many years, *oil* has been a major industrial energy source. However, *oil* supplies are limited, and other sources of energy must be developed.

Be consistent in the word or phrase you use to refer to something. In business writing, it is generally better to repeat a word or use a clear pronoun reference (so readers know that you mean the same thing) than to use synonyms to avoid repetition. See also <u>affectation</u>.

SYNONYMS   Several recent *analyses* support our conclusion. These *studies* cast doubt on the feasibility of long-range forecasting. The *reports*, however, are strictly theoretical.

CONSISTENT TERMS   Several recent *studies* support our conclusion. These *studies* cast doubt on the feasibility of long-range forecasting. *They* are, however, strictly theoretical.

Purposeless repetition, however, makes a sentence awkward and hides its key ideas. See also <u>conciseness</u>.

- She said that the customer ~~said that he~~ was canceling the order.

sentence variety

Sentences can vary in length, structure, and complexity. As you revise, vary your sentences so that they do not become tiresomely alike. See also sentence construction (Tab 11).

Sentence Length

A series of sentences of the same length is monotonous, so varying sentence length makes writing less tedious to the reader. For example, avoid stringing together a number of short independent clauses. Either connect them with subordinating connectives, thereby making some dependent clauses, or make some clauses into separate sentences.

> **STRING**   The river is 63 miles long, and it averages 50 yards in width, and its depth averages 8 feet.
>
> **IMPROVED**   The river, which is 63 miles long and averages 50 yards in width, has an average depth of 8 feet.

You can often effectively combine short sentences by converting verbs into adjectives.

- The digital timer unit ~~failed. It~~ *failed* was pulled from the market.

Although too many short sentences make your writing sound choppy and immature, a short sentence can be effective following a long one.

- During the past two decades, many changes have occurred in American life—the extent, durability, and significance of which no one has yet measured. *No one can.*

In general, short sentences are good for emphatic, memorable statements. Long sentences are good for detailed explanations and support. Nothing is inherently wrong with a long sentence, or even with a complicated one, as long as its meaning is clear and direct. Sentence length becomes an element of style when varied for emphasis or contrast; a conspicuously short or long sentence can be used to good effect.

Word Order

When a series of sentences all begin in exactly the same way (usually with an article and a noun), the result is likely to be monotonous. You can make your sentences more interesting by occasionally starting with a modifying word, phrase, or clause.

- *To salvage the project*, she presented alternatives when existing policies failed to produce results.
  [modifying phrase]

However, overuse of this technique itself can be monotonous, so use it in moderation.

Inverted word order can be an effective way to achieve variety, but be careful not to create an awkward construction.

AWKWARD   Then occurred the event that gained us the contract.

EFFECTIVE   Never have sales been so good.

For variety, you can alter normal sentence order by inserting a phrase or clause.

- Titanium fills the gap, *both in weight and in strength*, between aluminum and steel.

The technique of inserting a phrase or clause is good for achieving emphasis, providing detail, breaking monotony, and regulating pace.

Loose and Periodic Sentences

A loose sentence makes its main point at the beginning and then adds subordinate phrases and clauses that develop or modify the point. A loose sentence could end at one or more points before it actually ends, as the periods in brackets illustrate in the following example:

- It went up[.], a great ball of fire about a mile in diameter[.], an elemental force freed from its bonds[.] after being chained for billions of years.

A periodic sentence delays its main idea until the end by presenting modifiers or subordinate ideas first, thus holding the readers' interest until the end.

- During the last century, the attitude of Americans toward technology underwent a profound change.

Experiment with shifts from loose sentences to periodic sentences in your own writing, especially during revision (Tab 1). Avoid the monotony of a long series of loose sentences, particularly a series containing coordinate clauses joined by conjunctions (Tab 11). Using subordination not only provides emphasis but also makes your sentences more interesting.

10

Style and Clarity

subordination

Use subordination to show, by the structure of a sentence, the appropriate relationship between ideas of unequal importance. Subordination allows you to emphasize your main idea by putting less important ideas in subordinate <u>clauses</u> (Tab 11) or <u>phrases</u> (Tab 11).

- Envirex Systems now employs 500 people. It was founded just three years ago.
  [The two ideas are equally important.]

- Envirex Systems, *which now employs 500 people*, was founded just three years ago.
  [The number of employees is subordinated; the founding date is emphasized.]

- Envirex Systems, *which was founded just three years ago*, now employs 500 people.
  [The founding date is subordinated; the number of employees is emphasized.]

Effective subordination can be used to achieve <u>conciseness</u>, <u>emphasis</u>, and <u>sentence variety</u>. For example, consider the following sentences.

DEPENDENT CLAUSE	The regional manager's report, *which covered five pages*, was carefully illustrated.
PHRASE	The regional manager's report, *covering five pages*, was carefully illustrated.
SINGLE MODIFIER	The regional manager's *five-page* report was carefully illustrated.

Subordinating conjunctions (*because, if, while, when, although*) achieve subordination effectively.

- An increase in local sales is unlikely *because* the local population has declined.

You may use a coordinating conjunction (*and, but, for, nor, or, so, yet*) to concede that an opposite or balancing fact is true; however, a subordinating conjunction can often make the point more smoothly.

- *Although* their bank has a lower interest rate on loans, ours provides a wider range of essential services.

The relationship between a conditional statement and a statement of consequences is clearer if the condition is expressed as a subordinate clause.

- *Because* the bill was incorrect, the customer was angry.

Relative pronouns (*who, whom, which, that*) can be used effectively to combine related ideas within sentences. See pronouns (Tab 11).

- OnlinePro, *which* protects computers from malicious programs, makes your system "invisible" to hackers.

Avoid overlapping subordinate constructions that depend on the preceding construction. Overlapping can make the relationship between a relative pronoun and its antecedent less clear.

OVERLAPPING	Shock, *which* often accompanies severe injuries and infections, is a failure of the circulation, *which* is marked by a fall in blood pressure *that* initially affects the skin (*which* explains pallor) and later the vital organs such as the kidneys and brain.
CLEAR	Shock often accompanies severe injuries and infections. Marked by a fall in blood pressure, it is a failure of the circulation, initially to the skin (thus producing pallor) and later to the vital organs like the kidneys and the brain.

telegraphic style

Telegraphic style condenses writing by omitting articles, pronouns, conjunctions, and transitions. Although conciseness is important, especially in instructions, writers sometimes try to achieve conciseness by omitting necessary words and thus produce misunderstandings. Compare the following two passages and notice how much easier the revised version reads (the added words are italicized).

TELEGRAPHIC	Per 5/21 e-mail, 12 booklets/questionnaires enclosed. Report can be complete when above materials received. July filling, so let's set date. Pls advise.
CLEAR	*As promised in my May 21* e-mail, enclosed *are* 12 *copies of the instruction* booklet *and the* questionnaire. *We* can complete *the* report when *we* receive *the questionnaires. Our* July *calendar is* filling *quickly,* so *please call me to* set *a meeting* date *as soon as possible.*

Telegraphic style can also produce ambiguity, as the following example demonstrates.

AMBIGUOUS	The director wants report written by New York office. [Does the director want a report that the New York office *wrote in the past*, or does the director want the New York office *to write a report in the future*?]
CLEAR	The director wants the report *that was* written by the New York office.
CLEAR	The director wants the report *to be* written by the New York office.

⬥ PROFESSIONALISM NOTE Although you may save yourself work by writing telegraphically, your readers will have to work that much harder to decipher your meaning. Professional courtesy requires that you help your <u>reader</u> (Tab 1). ✦

10

Style and Clarity

tone

Tone is the attitude a writer expresses toward the subject and his or her readers. In workplace writing, tone may range widely—depending on the purpose, situation, context, audience, and even the medium of a communication. For example, in an e-mail message to be read only by an associate who is also a friend, your tone might be casual.

- Your proposal to Smith and Kline is super. We'll just need to hammer out the schedule. If we get the contract, I owe you lunch!

In a message to your manager or superior, however, your tone might be more formal and respectful.

- I think your proposal to Smith and Kline is excellent. I have marked a couple of places where I'm concerned that we are committing ourselves to a schedule that we might not be able to keep. If I can help in any other way, please let me know.

In a message to numerous readers, the tone would be professional, without the more personal style that you would use with an individual reader.

- The Smith and Kline proposal appears complete and thorough, based on our department's evaluation. Several small revisions, however, would ensure that the company is not committing itself to an unrealistic schedule. These revisions are marked on the copy of the report attached to this message.

The <u>word choice</u>, the introduction, and even the title contribute to the overall tone of your document. For instance, a title such as "Ecological Consequences of Diminishing Water Resources in California" clearly sets a different tone from "What Happens When We've Drained California

Dry?" The first title would be appropriate for a report; the second title would be more appropriate for a popular magazine or newsletter article. See also <u>titles</u> (Tab 4), <u>correspondence</u> (Tab 7), and <u>business writing style</u>.

transition

Transition is the means of achieving a smooth flow of ideas from sentence to sentence, paragraph to paragraph, and subject to subject. Transition is a two-way indicator of what has been said and what will be said; it provides readers with guideposts for linking ideas and clarifying the relationship between them.

Transition can be obvious.

- *Having considered* the benefits of a new facility, *we move next* to the question of adequate staffing.

Transition can be subtle.

- *Even if* this facility can be built at a reasonable cost, there *still remains* the problem of adequate staffing.

Either way, you now have your readers' attention fastened on the problem of adequate staffing, exactly what you set out to do.

Methods of Transition

Transition can be achieved in many ways: (1) using transitional words and phrases, (2) repeating keywords or key ideas, (3) using <u>pronouns</u> (Tab 11) with clear antecedents, (4) using enumeration (1, 2, 3, or first, second, third), (5) summarizing a previous paragraph, (6) asking a question, and (7) using a transitional paragraph.

Certain words and phrases are inherently transitional. Consider the following terms and their functions:

FUNCTION	TERMS
Result	*therefore, as a result, consequently, thus, hence*
Example	*for example, for instance, specifically, as an illustration*
Comparison	*similarly, likewise, in comparison*
Contrast	*but, yet, still, however, nevertheless, on the other hand*
Addition	*moreover, furthermore, also, too, besides, in addition*
Time	*now, later, meanwhile, since then, after that, before that time*
Sequence	*first, second, third, initially, then, next, finally*

Within a paragraph, such transitional expressions clarify and smooth the movement from idea to idea. Conversely, the lack of transitional devices can make for disjointed reading. See also <u>telegraphic style</u>.

10

Style and Clarity

Transition Between Sentences

You can achieve effective transition between sentences by repeating key-words or key ideas from preceding sentences and by using pronouns that refer to antecedents in previous sentences. Consider the following short paragraph, which uses both of those means.

- Representative of many American university towns is Middletown. *This midwestern town*, formerly *a sleepy farming community*, is today the home of a large and vibrant *academic community*. Attracting students from all over the Midwest, *this university town* has grown very rapidly in the last ten years.

Enumeration is another device for achieving transition.

- The recommendation rests on *two conditions*. *First*, the department staff must be expanded to handle the increased workload. *Second*, sufficient time must be provided for training the new staff.

Transition Between Paragraphs

The means discussed so far for achieving transition between sentences can also be effective for achieving transition between paragraphs. For paragraphs, however, longer transitional elements are often required. One technique is to use an opening sentence that summarizes the preceding paragraph and then moves on to a new paragraph.

- One property of material considered for manufacturing processes is hardness. Hardness is the internal resistance of the material to the forcing apart or closing together of its molecules. Another property is ductility, the characteristic of material that permits it to be drawn into a wire. Material also may possess malleability, the property that makes it capable of being rolled or hammered into thin sheets of various shapes. Purchasing managers must consider these properties before selecting manufacturing materials for use in production.
  The requirements of hardness, ductility, and malleability account for the high cost of such materials. . . .

Another technique is to ask a question at the end of one paragraph and answer it at the beginning of the next.

- New technology was feared in the past because it often displaced some jobs. However, it invariably created many more jobs than it eliminated. Almost always, the jobs eliminated by technological advances were menial, unskilled jobs, and displaced workers were forced to increase their skills, which resulted in better and higher-paying jobs for them. *In view of this history, should we now uncritically embrace new technology?*
  Certainly technology has given us unparalleled access to information and created many new roles for employees. . . .

A purely transitional paragraph may be inserted to aid readability.

- The problem of inept management, therefore, was a key factor that caused the weak performance of the company.
    Two other setbacks to the company's fortunes also marked the company's decline: the loss of many skilled workers through the early retirement program and the intensification of the rate of employee turnover.
    The early retirement program resulted in engineering staff . . .

If you provide logical <u>organization</u> (Tab 1) and have prepared an outline, your transitional needs will easily be satisfied and your writing will have <u>unity</u> and <u>coherence</u>. During revision, look for places where transition is missing and add it. Look for places where it is weak and strengthen it.

unity

Unity is singleness of <u>purpose</u> (Tab 1) and focus; a unified <u>paragraph</u> (Tab 1) or document has a central idea and does not digress into unrelated topics.

The logical sequence provided through <u>outlining</u> (Tab 1) is essential to achieving unity. An outline enables you to lay out the most direct route from introduction to conclusion, and it enables you to build each paragraph around a topic sentence that expresses a single idea. Effective <u>transition</u> helps build unity as well as <u>coherence</u>, because transitional terms clarify the relationship of each part to what precedes it.

vague words

A vague word is one that is imprecise in the context in which it is used. Some words encompass such a broad range of meanings that there is no focus for their definition. Words such as *real, nice, important, good, bad, contact, thing,* and *fine* are often called "omnibus words" because they can have so many meanings and interpretations. In speech, our vocal inflections help make the meanings of such words clear. Because you cannot rely on vocal inflections when you are writing, avoid using vague words. Be concrete and specific. See also <u>abstract / concrete words</u> and <u>word choice</u>.

VAGUE	It was a *good* meeting. [Why was it good?]
SPECIFIC	The meeting resolved three questions: pay scales, fringe benefits, and workloads.

10

Style and Clarity

word choice

Mark Twain once said, "The difference between the right word and almost the right word is the difference between 'lightning' and 'lightning bug.'" The most important goal in choosing the right word in business writing is the preciseness implied by Twain's comment. Vague words and abstract words defeat preciseness because they do not convey the writer's meaning directly and clearly.

> **VAGUE**   It was a *productive* meeting.
>
> **PRECISE**   The meeting resulted in the approval of the health-care benefits package.

In the first sentence, *productive* sounds specific but conveys little information; the revised sentence says specifically what made the meeting "productive." Although abstract words may at times be appropriate to your topic, using them unnecessarily will make your writing difficult to understand. See also abstract / concrete words.

Being aware of the connotations and denotations of words will help you anticipate the reactions of your audience (Tab 1) to the words you choose. Understanding antonyms (*fresh / stale*) and synonyms (*notorious / infamous*) will increase your ability to choose the proper word. For help with some common usage decisions, see the Appendix, "Usage." See also connotations / denotations.

Although many of the entries throughout this book will help you improve your word choices and avoid impreciseness, the following entries should be particularly helpful:

affectation 271	euphemisms 282
biased language 272	idioms 284
buzzwords 275	jargon 286
clichés 276	logic errors 286
conciseness 277	vague words 299

A key to choosing the correct and precise word is to keep current in your reading and to be aware of new words in your profession and in the language. In your quest for the right word, remember that there is no substitute for an up-to-date dictionary. See also English as a second language (Tab 11).

 WEB LINK WISE WORD CHOICES

For online exercises on word choice, see *bedfordstmartins.com/alred*, and select *Exercise Central*.

"you" viewpoint

The "you" viewpoint places the reader's interest and perspective foremost. It is based on the principle that most readers are naturally more concerned about their own needs than they are about those of a writer or a writer's organization. See <u>audience</u> (Tab 1).

The "you" viewpoint often, but not always, means using the words *you* and *your* rather than *we, our, I,* and *mine.* Consider the following sentence that focuses on the needs of the writer and organization (*we*) rather than on those of the reader.

- *We must receive* your signed invoice before *we can process* your payment.

Even though the sentence uses *your* twice, the words in italics suggest that the <u>point of view</u> (Tab 1) centers on the writer's need to receive the invoice in order to process the payment. Consider the following revision, written with the "you" viewpoint.

- *So you can receive* your payment promptly, please send your signed invoice.

Because the benefit to the reader is stressed, the writer is more likely to motivate the reader to act. See also <u>persuasion</u> (Tab 1).

In some instances, as suggested earlier, you may need to avoid using the pronouns *you* and *your* to achieve a positive <u>tone</u> and maintain goodwill. Notice how the first of the following examples (with *your*) seems to accuse the reader. But the second (without *your*) uses <u>positive writing</u> to emphasize a goal that reader and writer share—meeting a client's needs.

ACCUSATORY   *Your* budget makes no allowance for setup costs.

POSITIVE   The budget should include an allowance for setup costs to meet all the concerns of our client.

As this example illustrates, the "you" viewpoint means more than using the pronouns *you* and *your* or adopting a particular writing style. By genuinely considering the readers' interests as you write, you can achieve your <u>purpose</u> (Tab 1) not only in <u>correspondence</u> (Tab 7) but also in <u>proposals</u> (Tab 4), many <u>reports</u> (Tab 4), and <u>presentations</u> (Tab 9).

11

Grammar

Preview

Grammar is the systematic description of the way words work together to form a coherent language. *Parts of speech* is a term used to describe the class of words to which a particular word belongs, according to its function in a sentence. For example, <u>nouns</u> and <u>pronouns</u> name things, <u>verbs</u> express action, <u>adjectives</u> and <u>adverbs</u> describe and modify, and <u>conjunctions</u> and <u>prepositions</u> join elements of sentences. The entries in this section are intended to help you understand grammar and parts of speech so that you can diagnose and correct problems that may occur in your writing.

However, to be an effective writer, you also need to know the conventions of usage that help writers select the appropriate word or expression, as well as know the principles of effective business writing style. Therefore, you may wish to consult Tab 10, "Style and Clarity"; Tab 12, "Punctuation and Mechanics"; and the Appendix, "Usage."

11

Grammar

 WEB LINK **GETTING HELP WITH GRAMMAR**

For helpful Web sites providing useful grammar tutorials and other resources, see *bedfordstmartins.com/alred*, and select *Links Library*. For online grammar exercises, select *Exercise Central*.

adjectives

An adjective is any word that modifies a <u>noun</u> or <u>pronoun</u>. *Descriptive adjectives* identify a quality of a noun or pronoun. *Limiting adjectives* impose boundaries on the noun or pronoun.

- *hot* surface
  [descriptive]

- *three* phone lines
  [limiting]

Limiting Adjectives

Limiting adjectives include the following categories:

- Articles (*a, an, the*)
- Demonstrative adjectives (*this, that, these, those*)
- Possessive adjectives (*my, your, his, her, its, our, their*)
- Numeral adjectives (*two, first*)
- Indefinite adjectives (*all, none, some, any*)

Articles.   Articles (*a, an, the*) are traditionally classified as adjectives because they modify nouns by either limiting them or making them more specific. See also <u>articles</u> and <u>English as a second language</u>.

Demonstrative Adjectives.   A demonstrative adjective points to the thing it modifies, specifying the object's position in space or time. *This* and *these* specify a closer position; *that* and *those* specify a more remote position.

- *This* report is more current than *that* report, which Human Resources distributed last month.

- *These* sales figures are more recent than *those* reported last week.

Demonstrative adjectives often cause problems when they modify the nouns *kind, type,* and *sort.* Demonstrative adjectives used with those nouns should agree with them in number.

- *this* kind, *these* kinds; *that* type, *those* types

Confusion often develops when the preposition *of* is added (*this kind of, these kinds of*) and the object of the preposition does not conform in number to the demonstrative adjective and its noun. See also <u>agreement</u> and <u>prepositions</u>.

11

Grammar

- *This kind of* human resources ~~policies are~~ standard.
  policy is
  ^

- *These kinds of* human resources ~~policy is~~ standard.
  policies are
  ^

Avoid using demonstrative adjectives with words like *kind*, *type*, and *sort* because doing so can easily lead to vagueness. Instead, be more specific.

Possessive Adjectives.   Because possessive adjectives (*my*, *your*, *his*, *her*, *its*, *our*, *their*) directly modify nouns, they function as adjectives, even though they are pronoun forms (*my* idea, *her* plans, *their* projects).

Numeral Adjectives.   Numeral adjectives identify quantity, degree, or place in a sequence. They always modify count nouns. Numeral adjectives are divided into two subclasses: cardinal and ordinal. A *cardinal adjective* expresses an exact quantity (*one* pencil, *two* computers); an *ordinal adjective* expresses degree or sequence (*first* quarter, *second* edition).

In most writing, an ordinal adjective should be spelled out if it is a single word (*tenth*) and written in figures if it is more than one word (*312th*). Ordinal numbers can also function as adverbs. ("John arrived *first*.") See also <u>numbers</u> (Tab 12).

Indefinite Adjectives.   Indefinite adjectives do not designate anything specific about the nouns they modify (*some* CD-ROMs, *all* designers). The articles *a* and *an* are included among the indefinite adjectives (*a* chair, *an* application).

Comparison of Adjectives

Most adjectives in the positive form show the comparative form with the suffix *-er* for two items and the superlative form with the suffix *-est* for three or more items.

- The first report is *long*.
  [positive form]

- The second report is *longer*.
  [comparative form]

- The third report is *longest*.
  [superlative form]

Many two-syllable adjectives and most three-syllable adjectives are preceded by the word *more* or *most* to form the comparative or the superlative.

- The new media center is *more* impressive than the old one. It is the *most* impressive in the county.

A few adjectives have irregular forms of comparison (*much, more, most; little, less, least*).

Some adjectives (*round, unique, exact, accurate*), often called *absolute words*, are not logically subject to comparison.

Placement of Adjectives

When limiting and descriptive adjectives appear together, the limiting adjectives precede the descriptive adjectives, with the articles usually in the first position.

- *The ten yellow* taxis were sold at auction.
  [article (*The*), limiting adjective (*ten*), descriptive adjective (*yellow*)]

Within a sentence, adjectives may appear before the nouns they modify (the attributive position) or after the nouns they modify (the predicative position).

- *The small* jobs are given priority.
  [attributive position]

- The exposure is *brief*.
  [predicative position]

Use of Adjectives

Nouns often function as adjectives to clarify the meaning of other nouns.

- The *accident* report prompted a *product* redesign.

When adjectives modifying the same noun can be reversed and still make sense or when they can be separated by *and* or *or*, they should be separated by commas.

- The company seeks *bright, energetic, creative* managers.

Notice that there is no comma after *creative*. Never use a comma between a final adjective and the noun it modifies. When an adjective modifies a phrase, no comma is required.

- We need an *updated Web page design*.
  [*Updated* modifies the phrase *Web page design*.]

Writers sometimes string together a series of nouns used as adjectives to form a unit modifier, thereby creating stacked (jammed) <u>modifiers</u>, which can confuse readers. See also <u>word choice</u> (Tab 10).

11
Grammar

TIP FOR USING ADJECTIVES

Do not add *-s* or *-es* to an adjective to make it plural.

- the *long* trip
- the *long* trips

Capitalize adjectives of origin (city, state, nation, continent).

- the *Venetian* canals
- the *Texas* longhorn steer
- the *French* government
- the *Indian* subcontinent

In English, verbs of feeling (for example, *bore, interest, surprise*) have two adjectival forms: the present participle (*-ing*) and the past participle (*-ed*). Use the present participle to describe what causes the feeling. Use the past participle to describe the person who experiences the feeling.

- We heard the *surprising* election results.
  [The *election results* cause the feeling.]
- Only the losing candidate was *surprised* by the election results.
  [The *candidate* experienced the feeling of surprise.]

Adjectives follow nouns in English in only two cases: when the adjective functions as a subjective complement

- That project is not *finished*.

and when an adjective phrase or clause modifies the noun.

- The project *that was suspended temporarily* . . .

In all other cases, adjectives are placed before the noun.

In a sentence with multiple adjectives, it is often difficult to know the right order. The guidelines illustrated in the following example would apply in most circumstances, but there are exceptions. (Normally do not use a phrase with so many stacked <u>modifiers</u>.) See also <u>articles</u>.

- The six extra-large rectangular brown cardboard take-out containers

determiner	number	comment	size	shape	color	material	qualifier	noun

adverbs

An adverb modifies the action or condition expressed by a <u>verb</u>.

- The wrecking ball hit the side of the building *hard*.
  [The adverb tells *how* the wrecking ball hit the building.]

An adverb also can modify an <u>adjective,</u> another adverb, or a <u>clause</u>.

- The brochure design used *remarkably* bright colors.
  [*Remarkably* modifies the adjective *bright*.]
- The redesigned brake pad lasted *much* longer.
  [*Much* modifies the adverb *longer*.]
- *Surprisingly*, the engine failed.
  [*Surprisingly* modifies the clause *the engine failed*.]

Types of Adverbs

A simple adverb can answer one of the following questions:

- *Where?* (adverb of place)
  - Move the display *forward* slightly.
- *When?* or *How often?* (adverb of time)
  - Replace the thermostat *immediately*.
  - I worked overtime *twice* this week.
- *How?* (adverb of manner)
  - Add the solvent *cautiously*.
- *How much?* (adverb of degree)
  - The *nearly* completed report was sent to the director.

An interrogative adverb can ask a question (*Where? When? Why? How?*):

- *How* many hours did you work last week?
- *Why* was the hard drive reformatted?

A conjunctive adverb can modify the clause that it introduces as well as join two independent clauses with a <u>semicolon</u> (Tab 12). The

11

Grammar

most common conjunctive adverbs are *however, nevertheless, moreover, therefore, further, then, consequently, besides, accordingly, also,* and *thus.*

- I rarely work on weekends; *however,* this weekend will be an exception.

In this example, note that a semicolon precedes and a comma follows *however.* The conjunctive adverb (*however*) introduces the independent clause (*this weekend will be an exception*) and indicates its relationship to the preceding independent clause (*I rarely work on weekends*). See also transition (Tab 10).

Comparison of Adverbs

Most one-syllable adverbs show comparison with the suffixes *-er* and *-est.*

- This copier is *fast.*
  [positive form]

- This copier is *faster* than the old one.
  [comparative form]

- This copier is the *fastest* of the three tested.
  [superlative form]

Most adverbs with two or more syllables end in *-ly,* and most adverbs ending in *-ly* are compared by inserting the comparative *more* or *less* or the superlative *most* or *least* in front of them.

- The patient recovered *more quickly* than the staff expected.

- *Most surprisingly,* the engine failed during the final test phase.

A few irregular adverbs require a change in form to indicate comparison (*well, better, best; badly, worse, worst; far, farther, farthest*).

- The training program functions *well.*

- Our training program functions *better* than most others in the industry.

- Many consider our training program the *best* in the industry.

Placement of Adverbs

An adverb usually should be placed in front of the verb it modifies.

- The pilot *methodically* performed the preflight check.

An adverb may, however, follow the verb (or the verb and its object) that it modifies.

- The system failed *unexpectedly.*
- They replaced the hard drive *quickly.*

An adverb may be placed between a helping verb and a main verb.

- In this temperature range, the pressure will *quickly* drop.

Adverbs such as *only, nearly, almost, just,* and *hardly* should be placed immediately before the words they limit. See also modifiers.

agreement

Grammatical agreement is the correspondence in form between different elements of a sentence to indicate number, person, gender, and case.

A subject and its verb must agree in number.

- The *design is* acceptable.
  [The singular subject, *design,* requires the singular verb, *is.*]
- The new *products are* going into production soon.
  [The plural subject, *products,* requires the plural verb, *are.*]

A subject and its verb must agree in person.

- *I am* the designer.
  [The first-person singular subject, *I,* requires the first-person singular verb, *am.*]
- *They are* the designers.
  [The third-person plural subject, *they,* requires the third-person plural verb, *are.*]

A pronoun and its antecedent must agree in person, number, gender, and case.

- The *employees* report that *they* are more efficient in the new facility.
  [The third-person plural subject, *employees,* requires the third-person plural pronoun, *they.*]
- *Kaye McGuire* will meet with the staff on Friday, when *she* will assign duties.
  [The third-person singular subject, *Kaye McGuire,* requires *she,* the third-person feminine pronoun, in the subjective case.]

See also sentence construction.

11

Grammar

appositives

An appositive is a <u>noun</u> or noun <u>phrase</u> that follows and amplifies another noun or noun phrase. It has the same grammatical function as the noun it complements.

- George Thomas, *the noted economist*, summarized the president's speech in a confidential memo.

- The noted economist *George Thomas* summarized the president's speech in a confidential memo.

For detailed information on the use of commas with appositives, see <u>restrictive and nonrestrictive elements</u>.

If you are in doubt about the case of an appositive, check it by substituting the appositive for the noun it modifies. See also <u>pronouns</u>.

- My boss gave the two of us, Jim and ~~I~~, the day off. *[me]*

[You would not say, "My boss gave *I* the day off."]

11 articles

Articles (*a, an, the*) function as <u>adjectives</u> because they modify the items they designate by either limiting them or making them more specific. Articles may be indefinite or definite.

The indefinite articles, *a* and *an*, denote an unspecified item.

- *A* package was delivered yesterday.
  [*not* a specific package]

The choice between *a* and *an* depends on the sound rather than on the letter following the article. Use *a* before words or abbreviations beginning with a consonant sound, including *y* or *w* (*a* person, *a* historic event, *a* year's salary, *a* one-page report, *a* DNR order).

The definite article, *the*, denotes a particular item.

- *The* package was delivered yesterday.
  [*one* specific package]

Do not omit all articles from your writing in an attempt to be concise. Eliminating them makes reading more difficult. (See also <u>telegraphic style</u>, Tab 10.) However, eliminate unnecessary articles.

Grammar

- I'll meet you in *a* half *an* hour.
  [Choose one article and eliminate the other.]

Do not capitalize articles in titles except when they are the first word. ("*The Economist* reviewed *Winning the Talent Wars.*")

 TIP FOR USING ARTICLES

Whether to use a definite or an indefinite article is determined by what you can safely assume about your audience's knowledge. In each of these sentences, you can safely assume that the reader can clearly identify the noun. Therefore, use a definite article.

- *The* sun rises in the east.
  [The Earth has only one *sun*.]

- Did you know that yesterday was *the* coldest day of the year so far?
  [The modified noun refers to *yesterday*.]

- *The* man who left his briefcase in the conference room was in a hurry.
  [The relative phrase *who left his briefcase in the conference room* restricts and, therefore, identifies the meaning of *man*.]

In the following sentence, however, you cannot assume that the reader can clearly identify the noun.

- *A* package is on the way.
  [It is impossible to identify specifically what package is meant.]

  A more important question for some nonnative speakers of English is when *not* to use articles. These generalizations will help. Do not use articles with the following:

- Singular proper nouns

  - Utah, Main Street, Harvard University, Mount Hood

- Plural nonspecific count nouns (when making generalizations)

  - *Helicopters* are the new choice of transportation for the rich and famous.

- Singular mass nouns

  - She loves *chocolate*.

- Plural count nouns used as complements

  - Those women are *physicians*.

See also <u>English as a second language</u>.

11

Grammar

clauses

A clause is a group of words that contains a subject and a predicate and that functions as a sentence or as part of a sentence. (See sentence construction.) Every subject-predicate word group in a sentence is a clause, and every sentence must contain at least one independent clause; otherwise, it is a sentence fragment.

A clause that could stand alone as a simple sentence is an *independent clause*. ("*The scaffolding fell* when the rope broke.") A clause that could not stand alone if the rest of the sentence were deleted is a *dependent* (or *subordinate*) *clause*. ("I was at the St. Louis branch *when the decision was made*.")

Dependent (or subordinate) clauses are useful in making the relationship between thoughts clearer and more succinct than if the ideas were presented in a series of simple sentences or compound sentences.

FRAGMENTED	The recycling facility is located between Millville and Darrtown. Both villages use it. [The two thoughts are of approximately equal importance.]
SUBORDINATED	The recycling facility, *which is located between Millville and Darrtown*, is used by both villages. [One thought is subordinated to the other.]

Subordinate clauses are especially effective for expressing thoughts that describe or explain another statement. Too much subordination (Tab 10), however, can be confusing and foster wordiness. See also conciseness (Tab 10).

- He selected instructors whose classes ~~had a slant that was~~ *were* specifically *accounting students.* designed for ~~students~~ *who intended to go into accounting.*

A clause can be connected with the rest of its sentence by a coordinating conjunction, a subordinating conjunction, a relative pronoun, or a conjunctive adverb.

- It was 500 miles to the facility, *so* we made arrangements to fly. [coordinating conjunction]

- Mission control will need to be alert *because* at launch the space shuttle could be damaged by flying debris. [subordinating conjunction]

- Robert M. Fano was the scientist *who* developed the earliest multiple-access computer system at MIT. [relative pronoun]

- We arrived in the evening; *nevertheless*, we began the tour of the facility.
  [conjunctive adverb]

complements

A complement is a word, phrase, or clause used in the predicate of a sentence to complete the meaning of the sentence.

- Pilots fly *airplanes*.
  [word]

- To invest is *to risk losses*.
  [phrase]

- John knew *that he would be late*.
  [clause]

The four types of complements are direct object, indirect object, objective complement, and subjective complement. See also sentence construction.

A *direct object* is a noun or noun equivalent that receives the action of a transitive verb; it answers the question *What?* or *Whom?* after the verb.

- I designed *a Web site*.
  [noun phrase]

- I like *to travel*.
  [verbal]

- I like *it*.
  [pronoun]

- I like *what I saw*.
  [noun clause]

An *indirect object* is a noun or noun equivalent that occurs with a direct object after certain kinds of transitive verbs such as *give, wish, cause*, and *tell*. It answers the question *To whom or what?* or *For whom or what?*

- We should buy the *office* a *scanner*.
  [*Scanner* is the direct object, and *office* is the indirect object.]

An *objective complement* completes the meaning of a sentence by revealing something about the object of its transitive verb. An objective complement may be either a noun or an adjective.

- They call him *a genius*.
  [noun phrase]

- We painted the building *white*.
  [adjective]

11

Grammar

A *subjective complement*, which follows a linking verb rather than a transitive verb, describes the subject. A subjective complement may be either a noun or an adjective.

- His sister is *a consultant.*
  [noun phrase follows linking verb *is*]

- His brother is *ill.*
  [adjective follows linking verb *is*]

conjunctions

A conjunction connects words, <u>phrases</u>, or <u>clauses</u> and can also indicate the relationship between the elements it connects.

A *coordinating conjunction* joins two sentence elements that have identical functions. The coordinating conjunctions are *and, but, or, for, nor, yet,* and *so.*

- Nature *and* technology affect petroleum prices.
  [joins two <u>nouns</u>]

- To hear *and* to listen are two different things.
  [joins two phrases]

- I would like to include the survey, *but* that would make the report too long.
  [joins two clauses]

Coordinating conjunctions in the titles of books, articles, plays, and movies should not be capitalized unless they are the first or last word in the title.

- Our library contains *Consulting and Financial Independence* as well as *So You Want to Improve Your Bottom Line?*

Occasionally, a conjunction may begin a sentence; in fact, conjunctions can be strong transitional words and at times can provide <u>emphasis</u> (Tab 10). See also <u>transition</u> (Tab 10).

- I realize that the project is more difficult than expected and that you have encountered staffing problems. *But* we must meet our deadline.

Correlative conjunctions are used in pairs. The correlative conjunctions are *either . . . or, neither . . . nor, not only . . . but also, both . . . and,* and *whether . . . or.*

- The auditor will arrive *either* on Wednesday *or* on Thursday.

A *subordinating conjunction* connects sentence elements of different relative importance, normally independent and dependent clauses.

Frequently used subordinating conjunctions are *so*, *although*, *after*, *because*, *if*, *where*, *than*, *since*, *as*, *unless*, *before*, *that*, *though*, and *when*.

* I left the office *after* finishing the report.

A *conjunctive adverb* functions as a conjunction because it joins two independent clauses. The most common conjunctive <u>adverbs</u> are *however*, *moreover*, *therefore*, *further*, *then*, *consequently*, *besides*, *accordingly*, *also*, and *thus*.

* The engine performed well in the laboratory; *however*, it failed under road conditions.

dangling modifiers

Phrases that do not clearly and logically refer to the correct <u>noun</u> or <u>pronoun</u> are called *dangling modifiers*. Dangling modifiers usually appear at the beginning of a sentence as an introductory <u>phrase</u>.

DANGLING   *While eating lunch*, the computer malfunctioned.
            [*Who* was eating lunch?]

CORRECT   While *I* was eating lunch, the computer malfunctioned.

Dangling modifiers can appear at the end of the sentence as well.

DANGLING   The program gains efficiency *by eliminating the superfluous instructions*.
            [*Who* eliminates the superfluous instructions?]

CORRECT   The program gains efficiency *when you* eliminate the superfluous instructions.

To correct a dangling modifier, add the appropriate subject to either the dangling modifier or the main <u>clause</u>.

DANGLING   After finishing the research, the proposal was easy to write.
            [The appropriate subject is *I*, but it is not stated in either the dangling phrase or the main clause.]

CORRECT   After *I* finished the research, the proposal was easy to write.
            [The pronoun *I* is now the subject of an introductory clause.]

CORRECT   After finishing the research, *I* found the proposal easy to write.
            [The pronoun *I* is now the subject of the main clause.]

For a discussion of misplaced modifiers, see <u>modifiers</u>.

English as a second language (ESL)

Learning to write well in a second language takes a great deal of effort and practice. The most effective way to improve your command of written English is to read widely beyond the reports and professional articles your job requires; you should read magazines, newspapers, articles, novels, biographies, and any other writing that interests you. In addition, listen carefully to native speakers on television, on radio, and in person. Do not hesitate to consult a native speaker of English, especially for important writing tasks, such as e-mails, memos, and reports. Focus on those particular areas of English that give you trouble. This entry focuses on several areas often confusing to nonnative speakers and writers of English. See also global communication (Tab 1).

Count and Mass Nouns

Count nouns refer to things that can be counted (tables, pencils, projects, reports). *Mass nouns* (also called *noncount nouns*) identify things that cannot be counted (electricity, air, loyalty, information). This distinction can be confusing with words like *electricity* and *water*. Although we can count kilowatt-hours of electricity and bottles of water, counting becomes inappropriate when we use the words *electricity* and *water* in a general sense, as in "*Water* is an essential resource." Following is a list of typical mass nouns.

anger	education	money	technology
biology	equipment	news	transportation
business	furniture	oil	water
clothing	health	precision	weather
coffee	honesty	research	work

The distinction between whether something can or cannot be counted determines the form of the noun to use (singular or plural), the kind of article that precedes it (*a, an, the,* or no article), and the kind of limiting adjective it requires (such as *fewer* or *less* and *much* or *many*). (See also fewer / less in the Appendix, "Usage.") Notice that count and mass nouns are always common nouns, not proper nouns, such as the names of people.

Articles and Modifiers

The general rule is that every count noun must be preceded by an article (*a, an, the*), a demonstrative adjective (*this, that, these, those*), a possessive adjective (*my, your, her, his, its, their*), or some expression of quantity (such as *one, two, several, many, a few, a lot of, some, no*). The article, adjective, or expression of quantity appears either directly in front of the noun or in front of the whole noun phrase.

- Beth read *a* report last week.
  [article]

- *Those* reports Beth read were long.
  [demonstrative adjective]

- *Their* report was long.
  [possessive adjective]

- *Some* reports Beth read were long.
  [indefinite adjective]

The articles *a* and *an* are used with count nouns that refer to one item of the whole class of like items.

- Matthew has *a* pen.
  [Matthew could have any pen.]

The article *the* is used with nouns that refer to a specific item that both the reader and the writer can identify.

- Matthew has *the* pen.
  [Matthew has a specific pen that is known to both the reader and the writer.]

When making generalizations with count nouns, writers can either use *a* or *an* with a singular count noun or use no article with a plural count noun. Consider the following generalization using an article.

- *An* egg is a good source of protein.
  [any egg, all eggs, eggs in general]

However, the following generalization uses a plural count noun with no article.

- *Eggs* are good sources of protein.
  [any egg, all eggs, eggs in general]

When you are making a generalization with a mass noun, do not use an article in front of the mass noun.

- *Sugar* is bad for your teeth.

Gerunds and Infinitives

Nonnative writers of English are often puzzled by which form of a verbal (a <u>verb</u> used as another part of speech) to use when it functions as the direct object of a verb—or a <u>complement</u>. No structural rule exists for distinguishing between the use of an infinitive and a gerund as the object of a verb. Any specific verb may take an infinitive as its object, others may take a gerund, and still others take either an infinitive or a gerund. At times, even the base form of the verb is used.

- He enjoys *working*.
  [gerund as a complement]

- She promised *to fulfill* her part of the contract.
  [infinitive as a complement]

- The president had the manager *assign* her staff to another project.
  [basic verb form as a complement]

To make such distinctions accurately, rely on what you hear native speakers use or what you read. You might also consult a reference book for ESL students.

Adjective Clauses

Because of the variety of ways adjective clauses are constructed in different languages, they can be particularly troublesome for nonnative writers of English. The following guidelines will help you form adjective clauses correctly.

Place an adjective clause directly after the noun it modifies.

- The tall woman is a vice president of the company ^ *who is standing across the room.*

The adjective clause *who is standing across the room* modifies *woman*, not *company*, and thus comes directly after *woman*.

Avoid using a relative pronoun with another pronoun in an adjective clause.

- The man who ~~he~~ sits at that desk is my boss.

Present-Perfect Verb Tense

In general, use the present-perfect <u>tense</u> to refer to events completed in the past that have some implication for the present.

PRESENT PERFECT   She *has revised* that report three times.
[She might revise it again.]

When a specific time is mentioned, however, use the simple past.

SIMPLE PAST   I *wrote* the letter yesterday morning.
[The action, *wrote*, does not affect the present.]

Use the present perfect with a *since* or *for* phrase to describe actions that began in the past and continue in the present.

- This company *has been* in business *for* seventeen years.
- This company *has been* in business *since* 1994.

Present-Progressive Verb Tense

The present-progressive tense is especially difficult for those whose native language does not use this tense. The present-progressive tense is used to describe some action or condition that is ongoing (or in progress) in the present and may continue into the future.

PRESENT PROGRESSIVE   I *am searching* for an error in the document. [The search is occurring now and may continue.]

In contrast, the simple present tense more often relates to habitual actions.

SIMPLE PRESENT   I *search* for errors in my documents. [I regularly search for errors, but I am not necessarily searching now.]

See *ESL Tip for Using the Progressive Form* in the entry <u>tense</u>.

ESL Entries

Most of the entries in Tabs 10 through 12 and the Appendix may interest writers of English as a second language; however, the entries listed in the index under English as a second language (ESL) skills address issues that often cause problems.

 WEB LINK ENGLISH AS A SECOND LANGUAGE

For Web sites and electronic grammar exercises intended for speakers of English as a second language, see *bedfordstmartins.com/alred*, and select *Links Library* and *Exercise Central*.

11

Grammar

---

mixed constructions

A mixed construction is a sentence in which the elements do not sensibly fit together. The problem may be a grammar error, a <u>logic error</u> (Tab 10), or both.

- Because the copier wouldn't start, ~~explains why~~ we called a technician.

The original sentence mixes a subordinate <u>clause</u> (*Because the copier wouldn't start*) with a <u>verb</u> (*explains*) that attempts to incorrectly use the subordinate clause as its subject. The revision correctly uses the <u>pronoun</u> *we* as the subject of the main clause. See also <u>sentence construction</u>.

modifiers

Modifiers are words, <u>phrases</u>, or <u>clauses</u> that expand, limit, or make otherwise more specific the meaning of other elements in a sentence. Although we can create sentences without modifiers, we often need the detail and clarification they provide.

WITHOUT MODIFIERS   Production decreased.

WITH MODIFIERS   *Glucose* production decreased *rapidly*.

Most modifiers function as <u>adjectives</u> or <u>adverbs</u>. Adjectives describe qualities or impose boundaries on the words they modify.

- *noisy* machinery, *ten* files, *this* printer, *a* workstation

An adverb modifies an adjective, another adverb, a <u>verb</u>, or an entire clause.

- Under test conditions, the brake pad showed *much* less wear than it did under actual conditions.
  [The adverb *much* modifies the adjective *less*.]
- The redesigned brake pad lasted *much* longer.
  [The adverb *much* modifies another adverb, *longer*.]
- The wrecking ball hit the wall of the building *hard*.
  [The adverb *hard* modifies the verb *hit*.]
- *Surprisingly*, the motor failed even after all the durability and performance tests it had passed.
  [The adverb *surprisingly* modifies an entire clause.]

Adverbs are <u>intensifiers</u> (Tab 10) when they increase the impact of adjectives (*very* fine, *too* high) or adverbs (*very* slowly, *rather* quickly). Be cautious using intensifiers; their overuse can lead to vagueness and a resulting lack of precision.

Stacked (Jammed) Modifiers

Stacked (or jammed) modifiers are strings of modifiers preceding <u>nouns</u> that make writing unclear or difficult to read.

- Your *staffing-level authorization reassessment* plan should result in a major improvement.

The noun *plan* is preceded by three long modifiers, a string that forces the reader to slow down to interpret its meaning. Stacked modifiers often result from a tendency to overuse <u>buzzwords</u> (Tab 10) or <u>jargon</u> (Tab 10). See how breaking up the stacked modifiers makes the sentence easier to read.

- Your plan for reassessing the staffing-level authorizations should result in a major improvement.

Misplaced Modifiers

A modifier is misplaced when it modifies the wrong word or phrase. A misplaced modifier can cause ambiguity.

- We *almost* lost all of the parts.
  [The parts were *almost* lost but were not.]

- We lost *almost* all of the parts.
  [Most of the parts were in fact lost.]

To avoid ambiguity, place modifiers as close as possible to the words they are intended to modify. Note the two meanings possible when the modifying phrase is shifted in the following sentences:

- The equipment *without the accessories* sold the best.
  [Different types of equipment were available, some with and some without accessories.]

- The equipment sold the best *without the accessories*.
  [One type of equipment was available, and the accessories were optional.]

Place clauses as close as possible to the words they modify.

REMOTE   We sent the brochure to several local firms *that had four-color art*.

CLOSE   We sent the brochure *that had four-color art* to several local firms.

Squinting Modifiers

A squinting modifier is one that can be interpreted as modifying either of two sentence elements simultaneously, thereby confusing readers about which is intended.

- We agreed *on the next day* to make the adjustments.
  [Did they agree *to make the adjustments* on the next day? Or *on the next day*, did they agree to make the adjustments?]

11

Grammar

A squinting modifier can sometimes be corrected simply by changing its position, but often it is better to rewrite the sentence.

- We agreed that *on the next day* we would make the adjustments. [The adjustments were to be made *on the next day*.]

- *On the next day*, we agreed that we would make the adjustments. [The agreement was made *on the next day*.]

See also <u>dangling modifiers</u>.

mood

The grammatical term *mood* refers to the <u>verb</u> functions that indicate whether the verb is intended to make a statement, ask a question, give a command, or express a hypothetical possibility.

The *indicative mood* states a fact, gives an opinion, or asks a question.

- The setting *is* correct.

- *Is* the setting correct?

The *imperative mood* expresses a command, suggestion, request, or plea. In the imperative mood, the implied subject *you* is not expressed. ("*Install* the system today.")

The *subjunctive mood* expresses something that is contrary to fact, conditional, hypothetical, or purely imaginative; it can also express a wish, a doubt, or a possibility. In the subjunctive mood, *were* is used instead of *was* in clauses that speculate about the present or future, and the base form (*be*) is used following certain verbs, such as *propose*, *request*, or *insist*. See also progressive <u>tense</u>.

- If we *were* to close the sale today, we would meet our monthly goal.

- The senior partner insisted that she [I, you, we, they] *be* the project leader.

The most common use of the subjunctive mood is to express clearly that the writer considers a condition to be contrary to fact. If the condition is not considered to be contrary to fact, use the indicative mood.

SUBJUNCTIVE	If I *were* president of the firm, I would change several hiring policies.
INDICATIVE	Although I *am* president of the firm, I don't control every aspect of its policies.

11

Grammar

TIP FOR DETERMINING MOOD

In written and especially in spoken English, the tendency increasingly is to use the indicative mood where the subjunctive traditionally has been used. Note the differences between traditional and contemporary usage in the following examples.

TRADITIONAL (FORMAL) USE OF THE SUBJUNCTIVE MOOD

- I wish he *were* here now.

- If I *were* going to the conference, I would travel with him.

- I requested that she *arrive* on time.

CONTEMPORARY (INFORMAL) USE OF THE INDICATIVE MOOD

- I wish he *was* here now.

- If I *was* going to the conference, I would travel with him.

- I requested that she *arrives* on time.

In professional writing, it is better to use the more traditional expressions.

nouns

A noun names a person, place, thing, concept, action, or quality.

Types of Nouns

The two basic types of nouns are proper nouns and common nouns. *Proper nouns,* which are capitalized, name specific people, places, and things (*H. G. Wells, Boston, United Nations, Nobel Prize*). See also capitalization (Tab 12).

Common nouns, which are not capitalized unless they begin sentences or appear in titles, name general classes or categories of persons, places, things, concepts, actions, and qualities (*writer, city, organization, award*). Common nouns include collective nouns, concrete nouns, abstract nouns, count nouns, and mass nouns.

Collective nouns are common nouns that indicate a group or collection. They are plural in meaning but singular in form (*audience, jury, brigade, staff, committee*). (See the subsection Collective Nouns on pages 326–27 for advice on using singular or plural forms with collective nouns.)

Concrete nouns are common nouns used to identify those things that can be discerned by the five senses (*paper, keyboard, glue, nail, grease*).

11

Grammar

Abstract nouns are common nouns that name ideas, qualities, or concepts that cannot be discerned by the five senses (*loyalty, pride, valor, peace, devotion*).

Count nouns are concrete nouns that identify things that can be separated into countable units (*desks, envelopes, printers, pencils, books*).

Mass nouns are concrete nouns that identify things that cannot be separated into countable units (*water, air, electricity, oil, cement*). See also **English as a second language**.

Noun Functions

Nouns function as subjects of **verbs,** direct and indirect objects of verbs and **prepositions,** subjective and objective **complements,** or **appositives.**

- The *metal* failed during the test.
  [subject]

- The bricklayer cemented the *blocks* efficiently.
  [direct object of a verb]

- The state presented our *department* a safety award.
  [indirect object]

- The event occurred within the *year*.
  [object of a preposition]

- A dynamo is a *generator*.
  [subjective complement]

- The regional manager was appointed *chairperson*.
  [objective complement]

- Philip Garcia, the *treasurer*, gave his report last.
  [appositive]

Words normally used as nouns can also be used as **adjectives** and **adverbs.**

- It is *company* policy.
  [adjective]

- He went *home*.
  [adverb]

Collective Nouns

When a collective noun refers to a group as a whole, it takes a singular verb and pronoun.

- The staff *was* divided on the issue and could not reach *its* decision until May 16.

When a collective noun refers to individuals within a group, it takes a plural verb and pronoun.

- The staff *have returned* to *their* offices after the conference.

A better way to emphasize the individuals on the staff would be to use the phrase *the staff members*.

- The staff members *have returned* to *their* offices after the conference.

Treat organization names and titles as singular.

- LRM Associates *has* grown 30 percent in the last three years; *it* will move to a new facility in January.

Plural Nouns

Most nouns form the plural by adding -*s* (dolphin/dolphins, pencil/pencils). Nouns ending in *ch*, *s*, *sh*, *x*, and *z* form the plural by adding -*es*.

- search/searches, glass/glasses, wish/wishes, six/sixes, buzz/buzzes

Nouns that end in a consonant plus *y* form the plural by changing the *y* to *ies* (delivery/deliveries). Some nouns ending in *o* add -*es* to form the plural, but others add only -*s* (tomato/tomatoes, dynamo/dynamos). Some nouns ending in *f* or *fe* add -*s* to form the plural; others change the *f* or *fe* to *ves*.

- cliff/cliffs, cafe/cafes, hoof/hooves, knife/knives

Some nouns require an internal change to form the plural.

- woman/women, man/men, mouse/mice, goose/geese

Some nouns do not change in the plural form.

- many *fish*, several *deer*, fifty *sheep*

Some nouns remain in the plural form whether singular or plural.

- headquarters, means, series, crossroads

Hyphenated and open compound nouns form the plural in the main word.

- sons-in-law, high schools, editors in chief

Compound nouns written as one word add -*s* to the end (two *tablespoonfuls*).

If you are unsure of the proper usage, check a dictionary. See possessive case for a discussion of how nouns form possessives.

11

Grammar

objects

Objects are <u>nouns</u> or noun equivalents: <u>pronouns,</u> verbals, and noun <u>phrases</u> or <u>clauses</u>. The three kinds of objects are direct objects, indirect objects, and objects of <u>prepositions</u>.

A *direct object* answers the question *what?* or *whom?* about a verb and its subject.

- We sent a *full report.*
  [We sent *what?*]

- Michelle e-mailed the *client.*
  [Michelle e-mailed *whom?*]

An *indirect object* is a noun or noun equivalent that occurs with a direct object after certain kinds of transitive verbs, such as *give, wish, cause,* and *tell.* The indirect object answers the question *to whom or what?* or *for whom or what?* The indirect object always precedes the direct object.

- We sent the *general manager* a full report.
  [*Report* is the direct object; the indirect object, *general manager,* answers the question, "We sent a full report *to whom?*"]

The *object of a preposition* is a noun or pronoun that is introduced by a preposition, forming a prepositional phrase.

- At the *meeting,* the district managers approved the contract.
  [*Meeting* is the object, and *at the meeting* is the prepositional phrase.]

(See also <u>complements</u> and <u>verbs</u>.)

person

Person refers to the form of a personal <u>pronoun</u> that indicates whether the pronoun represents the speaker, the person spoken to, or the person or thing spoken about. A pronoun representing the speaker is in the *first* person. ("*I* could not find the answer in the manual.") A pronoun that represents the person or people spoken to is in the *second* person. ("*You* will be a good manager.") A pronoun that represents the person or people spoken about is in the *third* person. ("*They* received the news quietly.") The following list shows first-, second-, and third-person pronouns.

PERSON	SINGULAR	PLURAL
First	I, me, my, mine	we, us, our, ours
Second	you, your, yours	you, your, yours
Third	he, him, his, she, her, hers, it, its	they, them, their, theirs

11

Grammar

phrases

A phrase is a meaningful group of words that cannot make a complete statement because it does not contain both a subject and a predicate, as <u>clauses</u> do. Phrases, which are based on <u>nouns</u>, nonfinite <u>verb</u> forms, or verb combinations, provide context within a clause or sentence in which they appear. See also <u>sentence construction</u>.

- She reassured her staff *by her calm confidence.*
  [phrase]

A phrase may function as an <u>adjective</u>, an <u>adverb</u>, a noun, or a verb.

- The subjects *on the agenda* were all discussed.
  [adjective]

- We discussed the project *with great enthusiasm.*
  [adverb]

- *Working hard* is her way of life.
  [noun]

- The human resources director *should have been notified.*
  [verb]

Even though phrases function as adjectives, adverbs, nouns, or verbs, they are normally named for the kind of word around which they are constructed—<u>preposition</u>, participle, infinitive, gerund, verb, or noun. A phrase that begins with a preposition is a *prepositional phrase,* a phrase that begins with a participle is a *participial phrase,* and so on. For typical verb phrases and prepositional phrases that can cause difficulty for speakers of <u>English as a second language</u>, see <u>idioms</u> (Tab 10).

possessive case

A <u>noun</u> or <u>pronoun</u> is in the possessive case when it represents a person, place, or thing that possesses something. Possession is generally expressed with an <u>apostrophe</u> (Tab 12) and an *s* ("the *report's* title"), with a prepositional <u>phrase</u> using *of* ("the title *of the report*"), or with the possessive form of a pronoun ("*our* report").

Practices vary for some possessive forms, but the following guidelines are widely used. Above all, be consistent.

Singular Nouns

Most singular nouns show the possessive case with *'s.*

- the *company's* stock value   the *witness's* testimony
  an *employee's* paycheck   the *bus's* schedule

When pronunciation with *'s* is difficult or when a multisyllable noun ends in a *z* sound, you may use only an apostrophe.

- *New Orleans'* convention hotels

Plural Nouns

Plural nouns that end in *-s* or *-es* show the possessive case with only an apostrophe.

- the *managers'* reports   the *witnesses'* testimony
  the *employees'* paychecks   the *buses'* schedules
  the *companies'* joint project

Plural nouns that do not end in *-s* show the possessive with *'s*.

- *children's* clothing, *women's* resources, *men's* room

Apostrophes are not always used in official names ("*Consumers* Union") or for words that may appear to be possessive nouns but function as <u>adjectives</u> ("a *computer peripherals* supplier").

Compound Nouns

Compound words form the possessive with *'s* following the final letter.

- the *attorney general's* decision, the *editor-in-chief's* desk, the *pipeline's* diameter

Plurals of some compound expressions are often best expressed with a prepositional phrase ("presentations *of the editors in chief*").

Coordinate Nouns

Coordinate nouns show joint possession with *'s* following the last noun.

- *Fischer and Goulet's* partnership was the foundation of their business.

Coordinate nouns show individual possession with *'s* following each noun.

- The difference between *Barker's* and *Washburne's* test results was not statistically significant.

Possessive Pronouns

The possessive pronouns (*its, whose, his, her, our, your, my, their*) are also used to show possession and do not require apostrophes. ("Even good systems have *their* flaws.") Only the possessive form of a pronoun should be used with a gerund (a noun formed from an *-ing* <u>verb</u>).

- The safety officer insisted on *our* wearing protective clothing. [*Wearing* is the gerund.]

Possessive pronouns are also used to replace nouns. ("The responsibility was *theirs*.") See also <u>its / it's</u> in the Appendix, "Usage."

Indefinite Pronouns

Some indefinite pronouns (*all, any, each, few, most, none, some*) form the possessive case with the <u>preposition</u> *of*.

- We tested both packages and found the bacteria on the surface *of each*.

Other indefinite pronouns (*everyone, someone, anyone, no one*), however, use *'s*.

- *Everyone's* contribution is welcome.

prepositions

A preposition is a word that links a <u>noun</u> or <u>pronoun</u> to another sentence element by expressing such relationships as direction (*to, into, across, toward*), location (*at, in, on, under, over, beside, among, by, between, through*), time (*before, after, during, until, since*), or position (*for, against, with*). Together, the preposition, its object (the noun or pronoun), and the object's <u>modifiers</u> form a prepositional <u>phrase</u> that acts as a modifier.

- Answer help-line questions *in a courteous manner*. [The prepositional phrase *in a courteous manner* modifies the <u>verb</u> *answer*.]

The object of a preposition (the word or phrase following the preposition) is always in the objective case. When the object is a compound, both nouns and pronouns should be in the objective case. For example, the phrase "between you and *me*" is frequently and incorrectly written as "between you and *I*." *Me* is the objective form of the pronoun, and *I* is the subjective form.

Many words that function as prepositions also function as <u>adverbs</u>. If the word takes an object and functions as a connective, it is a preposition; if it has no object and functions as a modifier, it is an adverb.

PREPOSITIONS	The manager sat *behind* the desk *in* her office.
ADVERBS	The customer lagged *behind*; then he came *in* and sat down.

11

Grammar

Certain verbs, adverbs, and adjectives are normally used with certain prepositions (interested *in*, aware *of*, equated *with*, adhere *to*, capable *of*, object *to*, infer *from*). See also idioms (Tab 10).

Prepositions at the End of a Sentence

A preposition at the end of a sentence can be an indication that the sentence is awkwardly constructed.

She was at the
- ~~The~~ branch office ~~is where she was at.~~

However, if a preposition falls naturally at the end of a sentence, leave it there. ("I don't remember which file name I saved it *under*.")

Prepositions in Titles

Capitalize prepositions in titles (Tab 4) when they are the first or last words, or when they contain five or more letters (unless you are following a style that recommends otherwise). See also capitalization (Tab 12).

- The newspaper column "*In* My Opinion" included a review of the article "New Concerns *About* Excellence in Education."

Preposition Errors

Do not use redundant prepositions, such as "off *of*," "in back *of*," "inside *of*," and "at *about*."

| EXACT | The client will arrive at ~~about~~ four o'clock. |
| APPROXIMATE | The client will arrive ~~at~~ about four o'clock. |

Avoid unnecessarily adding the preposition *up* to verbs.

to
- Call ~~up and~~ see if he is in his office.

Do not omit necessary prepositions.

to
- He was oblivious and not distracted by the view from his office window.

See also conciseness (Tab 10) and English as a second language.

pronoun reference

A pronoun should refer clearly to a specific antecedent. Avoid vague and uncertain references.

, which was a big one,
- We got the account after we wrote the proposal. ~~It was a big one.~~

For <u>coherence</u> (Tab 10), place pronouns as close as possible to their antecedents—distance increases the likelihood of ambiguity.

- *, praised for its architectural design, is* .
  The office building next to City Hall ~~is praised for its architectural design.~~

A general (or broad) reference or one that has no real antecedent is a problem that often occurs when the word *this* is used by itself.

- *experience*
  He deals with personnel problems in his work. This helps him in his community service projects.

Another common problem is a hidden reference, which has only an implied antecedent.

- A high-lipid, low-carbohydrate diet is "ketogenic" because it
  the   *of ketone bodies*
  favors ~~their~~ formation.

Do not repeat an antecedent in parentheses following the pronoun. If you feel you must identify the pronoun's antecedent in that way, rewrite the sentence.

AWKWARD	The senior partner first met Bob Evans when he (Evans) was a trainee.
IMPROVED	Bob Evans was a trainee when the senior partner first met him. [or "When the senior partner first met him, Bob Evans was a trainee."]

For advice on avoiding pronoun-reference problems with gender, see <u>biased language</u> (Tab 10).

pronouns

A pronoun is a word that is used as a substitute for a <u>noun</u> (the noun for which a pronoun substitutes is called the *antecedent*). Using pronouns in place of nouns relieves the monotony of repeating the same noun over and over. See also <u>pronoun reference</u>.

Personal pronouns refer to the person or people speaking (*I, me, my, mine; we, us, our, ours*); the person or people spoken to (*you, your, yours*); or the person, people, or thing(s) spoken of (*he, him, his; she, her, hers; it, its; they, them, their, theirs*). See also <u>point of view</u> (Tab 1) and <u>person</u>.

- If *their* figures are correct, *ours* must be in error.

Demonstrative pronouns (*this, these, that, those*) indicate or point out the thing being referred to.

- *This* is my desk. *These* are my coworkers. *That* will be a difficult job. *Those* are incorrect figures.

Relative pronouns (*who, whom, which, that*) perform a dual function: (1) They take the place of nouns and (2) they connect and establish the relationship between a dependent <u>clause</u> and its main clause.

- The department manager decided *who* would be hired.

Interrogative pronouns (*who, whom, what, which*) are used to ask questions.

- *What* is the trouble?

Indefinite pronouns specify a class or group of persons or things rather than a particular person or thing (*all, another, any, anyone, anything, both, each, either, everybody, few, many, most, much, neither, nobody, none, several, some, such*).

- Not *everyone* liked the new procedures; *some* even refused to follow them.

A *reflexive pronoun*, which always ends with the suffix *-self* or *-selves*, indicates that the subject of the sentence acts upon itself. See also <u>sentence construction</u>.

- The electrician accidentally shocked *herself*.

The reflexive pronouns are *myself, yourself, himself, herself, itself, oneself, ourselves, yourselves,* and *themselves*. *Myself* is not a substitute for *I* or *me* as a personal pronoun.

- Victor and ~~myself~~ *I* completed the report on time.

- The assignment was given to Ingrid and ~~myself~~ *me*.

Intensive pronouns are identical in form to the reflexive pronouns, but they perform a different function: Intensive pronouns emphasize their antecedents.

- I *myself* asked the same question.

Reciprocal pronouns (*one another, each other*) indicate the relationship of one item to another. *Each other* is commonly used when referring to two persons or things and *one another* when referring to more than two.

- Lashell and Kara work well with *each other*.
- The crew members work well with *one another*.

Case

Pronouns have forms to show the subjective, objective, and possessive cases.

SINGULAR	SUBJECTIVE	OBJECTIVE	POSSESSIVE
First person	I	me	my, mine
Second person	you	you	your, yours
Third person	he, she, it	him, her, it	his, her, hers, its

PLURAL	SUBJECTIVE	OBJECTIVE	POSSESSIVE
First person	we	us	our, ours
Second person	you	you	your, yours
Third person	they	them	their, theirs

 TIP FOR USING POSSESSIVE PRONOUNS

In many languages, possessive pronouns agree in number and gender with the nouns they modify. In English, however, possessive pronouns agree in number and gender with their antecedents. Check your writing carefully for agreement between a possessive pronoun and the word, phrase, or clause to which it refers.

- The *woman* brought *her* brother a cup of soup.

- *Robert* sent *his* mother flowers on Mother's Day.

A pronoun that functions as the subject of a clause or sentence is in the subjective case (*I, we, he, she, it, you, they, who*). The subjective case is also used when the pronoun follows a linking <u>verb</u>.

- *She* is my boss.

- My boss is *she*.

A pronoun that functions as the object of a verb or <u>preposition</u> is in the objective case (*me, us, him, her, it, you, them, whom*).

- Ms. Davis hired Tom and *me*.
  [object of verb]

- Between *you* and *me*, she's wrong.
  [object of preposition]

A pronoun that expresses ownership is in the <u>possessive case</u> (*my, mine, our, ours, his, her, hers, its, your, yours, their, theirs, whose*).

- He took *his* notes with him on the business trip.

- We took *our* notes with us on the business trip.

11

Grammar

A pronoun <u>appositive</u> takes the case of its antecedent.

- Two systems analysts, Joe and *I*, were selected to represent the company.
  [*Joe and I* is in apposition to the subject, *two systems analysts*, and must therefore be in the subjective case.]

- The manager selected two representatives—Joe and *me*.
  [*Joe and me* is in apposition to *two representatives*, which is the object of the verb, *selected*, and therefore must be in the objective case.]

If you have difficulty determining the case of a compound pronoun, try using the pronoun singly.

- In his letter, Eldon mentioned *him* and *me*.
  In his letter, Eldon mentioned *him*.
  In his letter, Eldon mentioned *me*.

- *They* and *we* must discuss the terms of the merger.
  They must discuss the terms of the merger.
  We must discuss the terms of the merger.

When a pronoun modifies a noun, try it without the noun to determine its case.

- [*We/Us*] pilots fly our own planes.
  We fly our own planes.
  [You would not write, "*Us* fly our own planes."]

- He addressed his remarks directly to [*we/us*] technicians.
  He addressed his remarks directly to *us*.
  [You would not write, "He addressed his remarks directly to *we*."]

Gender

A pronoun must agree in gender with its antecedent. A problem sometimes occurs because the masculine pronoun has traditionally been used to refer to both sexes. To avoid the sexual bias implied in such usage, use *he or she* or the plural form of the pronoun, *they*.

- *All*
  ~~Each~~ may stay or go as ~~he chooses.~~ *they choose.*

As in this example, when the singular pronoun (*he*) changes to the plural (*they*), the singular indefinite pronoun (*each*) must also change to its plural form (*all*). See also <u>biased language</u> (Tab 10).

Number

Number is a frequent problem with only a few indefinite pronouns (*each, either, neither,* and those ending with *-body* or *-one,* such as

anybody, anyone, everybody, everyone, nobody, no one, somebody, someone)
that are normally singular and so require singular verbs and are referred
to by singular pronouns.

- As *each member arrives* for the meeting, please hand *him or her* a
  copy of the confidential report. *Everyone* must return the copy
  before *he or she* leaves. *Everybody* on the committee *understands*
  that *neither* of our major competitors *is* aware of the new process
  we have developed.

Person

Third-person personal pronouns usually have antecedents.

- Gina presented the report to the members of the board of directors. *She* [Gina] first summarized *it* [the report] for *them* [the
  directors] and then asked for questions.

First- and second-person personal pronouns do not normally require
antecedents.

- *I* like my job.

- *You* were there at the time.

- *We* all worked hard on the project.

restrictive and nonrestrictive elements

Modifying <u>phrases</u> and <u>clauses</u> may be either restrictive or nonrestrictive. A *nonrestrictive phrase or clause* provides additional information
about what it modifies, but it does not restrict the meaning of what it
modifies. A nonrestrictive phrase or clause can be removed without
changing the essential meaning of the sentence. It is a parenthetical element that is set off by <u>commas</u> (Tab 12) to show its loose relationship
with the rest of the sentence.

NONRESTRICTIVE   The annual report, *which was distributed
                  yesterday*, shows that sales increased 20 percent
                  last year.

A *restrictive phrase or clause* limits, or restricts, the meaning of what it
modifies. If it were removed, the essential meaning of the sentence
would change. Because a restrictive phrase or clause is essential to the
meaning of the sentence, it is never set off by commas.

RESTRICTIVE   All employees *wishing to donate blood* may take
                  Thursday afternoon off.

11

Grammar

Writers need to distinguish between nonrestrictive and restrictive elements. The same sentence can take on two entirely different meanings, depending on whether a modifying element is set off by commas (because it is nonrestrictive) or is not (because it is restrictive). A slip by the writer can not only mislead readers but also embarrass the writer.

MISLEADING   He gave a poor performance evaluation to the staff members who protested to the Human Resources Department.
[This suggests that he gave the poor evaluation because the staff members had protested.]

ACCURATE   He gave a poor performance evaluation to the staff members, who protested to the Human Resources Department.
[This suggests that the staff members protested because of the poor evaluation.]

Use *which* to introduce nonrestrictive clauses and *that* to introduce restrictive clauses.

NONRESTRICTIVE   After John left the restaurant, *which* is one of the finest in New York, he came directly to my office.

RESTRICTIVE   Companies *that* diversify usually succeed.

11 sentence construction

DIRECTORY

A sentence is the most fundamental and versatile tool available to writers. Sentences generally flow from a subject to a <u>verb</u> to any <u>objects</u>, <u>complements</u>, or <u>modifiers</u>, but they can be ordered in a variety of ways to achieve <u>emphasis</u> (Tab 10). When shifting word order for emphasis, however, be aware that word order can make a great difference in the meaning of a sentence.

- He was *only* the accountant.
- He was the *only* accountant.

The most basic components of sentences are subjects and predicates.

Subjects

The *subject* of a sentence is a <u>noun</u> or <u>pronoun</u> (and its modifiers) about which the predicate of the sentence makes a statement. Although a subject may appear anywhere in a sentence, it most often appears at the beginning. ("*To increase sales* is our goal.") Grammatically, a subject must agree with its verb in number.

- *These departments have* much in common.
- *This department has* several functions.

The subject is the actor in sentences using the active <u>voice</u>.

- *The Webmaster reported* an increase in site visits for May.

A *compound subject* has two or more substantives (nouns or noun equivalents) as the subject of one verb.

- *The president* and *the treasurer* agreed to begin the audit.

 TIP FOR UNDERSTANDING THE SUBJECT OF A SENTENCE

In English, every sentence, except commands, must have an explicit subject.

- *Paul* worked fast. ~~Established~~ the parameters for the project.
  He established

In commands, the subject *you* is understood and is used only for emphasis.

- (*You*) Meet me at the airport at 6:30 tomorrow morning.
- (*You*) Do your homework, young man.
  [parent to child]

If you move the subject from its normal position (subject-verb-object), English often requires you to replace the subject with an expletive (*there*, *it*). In this construction, the verb agrees with the subject that follows it.

- *There are* two files on the desk.
  [The subject is *files*.]
- *It is* presumptuous for me to speak for Jim.
  [The subject is *to speak for Jim*.]

Time, distance, weather, temperature, and environmental expressions use *it* as their subject.

- *It* is ten o'clock.
- *It* is ten miles down the road.
- *It* seldom snows in Florida.
- *It* is very hot in Jorge's office.

11

Grammar

Predicates

The *predicate* is the part of a sentence that makes an assertion about the subject and completes the thought of the sentence.

- Bill *has piloted the corporate jet.*

The *simple predicate* is the verb and any helping verbs (*has piloted*). The *complete predicate* is the verb and any modifiers, objects, or complements (*has piloted the corporate jet*). A *compound predicate* consists of two or more verbs with the same subject.

- The company *tried* but *did not succeed* in that field.

Such constructions help achieve <u>conciseness</u> (Tab 10) in writing. A *predicate nominative* is a noun construction that follows a linking verb and renames the subject.

- She is my *attorney.*
  [noun]

- His excuse was *that he had been sick.*
  [noun clause]

Sentence Types

Sentences may be classified according to *structure* (simple, compound, complex, compound-complex); *intention* (declarative, interrogative, imperative, exclamatory); and *stylistic use* (loose, periodic, minor).

Structure.   A *simple sentence* consists of one independent clause. At its most basic, a simple sentence contains only a subject and a predicate.

- Profits [subject] rose [predicate].

A *compound sentence* consists of two or more independent clauses connected by a comma and a coordinating <u>conjunction</u>, by a <u>semicolon</u> (Tab 12), or by a semicolon and a conjunctive <u>adverb</u>.

- Drilling is the only way to collect samples of the layers of sediment below the ocean floor, *but* it is not the only way to gather information about these strata.
  [comma and coordinating conjunction]

- The chemical composition of seawater bears little resemblance to that of river water; the various elements are present in entirely different proportions.
  [semicolon]

- It was 500 miles to the site; *therefore,* we made arrangements to fly.
  [semicolon and conjunctive adverb]

A *complex sentence* contains one independent clause and at least one dependent clause that expresses a subordinate idea.

- The generator will shut off automatically [independent clause] if the temperature rises above a specified point [dependent clause].

A *compound-complex sentence* consists of two or more independent clauses plus at least one dependent clause.

- Productivity is central to controlling inflation [independent clause]; when productivity rises [dependent clause], employers can raise wages without raising prices [independent clause].

Intention.   A *declarative sentence* conveys information or makes a factual statement. ("The motor powers the conveyor belt.") An *interrogative sentence* asks a direct question. ("Does the conveyor belt run constantly?") An *imperative sentence* issues a command. ("Submit your résumé online.") An *exclamatory sentence* is an emphatic expression of feeling, fact, or opinion. It is a declarative sentence that is stated with great feeling. ("The files were deleted!")

Stylistic Use.   A *loose sentence* makes its major point at the beginning and then adds subordinate phrases and clauses that develop or modify that major point. A loose sentence could end at one or more points before it actually does end, as the periods in brackets illustrate in the following sentence:

- It went up[.], a great ball of fire about a mile in diameter[.], an elemental force freed from its bonds[.] after being chained for billions of years.

A *periodic sentence* delays its main ideas until the end by presenting subordinate ideas or modifiers first.

- During the last century, the attitude of the American citizen toward automation underwent a profound change.

A *minor sentence* is an incomplete sentence that makes sense in its context because the missing element is clearly implied by the preceding sentence.

- In view of these facts, is the service contract really useful? *Or economical?*

Constructing Effective Sentences

The subject-verb-object pattern is effective because it is most familiar to readers. In "The company increased profits," we know the subject (*company*) and the object (*profits*) by their positions relative to the verb (*increased*).

An *inverted sentence* places the elements in an unexpected order, thus emphasizing the point by attracting the readers' attention in declarative sentences.

- A better job I never had.
  [direct object-subject-verb]

- More optimistic I have never been.
  [subjective complement-subject-linking verb]

- A poor image we presented.
  [complement-subject-verb]

Use uncomplicated sentences to state complex ideas. If readers have to cope with a complicated sentence in addition to a complex idea, they are likely to become confused. Just as simpler sentences make complex ideas more digestible, a complex sentence construction makes a series of simple ideas more smooth and less choppy.

Avoid loading sentences with a number of thoughts carelessly tacked together. Such sentences are monotonous and hard to read because all the ideas seem to be of equal importance. Rather, distinguish the relative importance of sentence elements with <u>subordination</u> (Tab 10). See also <u>garbled sentences</u> (Tab 10).

LOADED   We started the program three years ago, only three members were on the staff, and each member was responsible for a separate state, but it was not an efficient operation.

IMPROVED   When we started the program three years ago, only three members were on the staff, each responsible for a separate state; however, that arrangement was not efficient.

Express coordinate or equivalent ideas in similar form. The structure of the sentence helps readers grasp the similarity of its components, as illustrated in <u>parallel structure</u> (Tab 10).

 TIP FOR UNDERSTANDING THE REQUIREMENTS OF A SENTENCE

- A sentence must start with a capital letter.
- A sentence must end with a period, a question mark, or an exclamation point.
- A sentence must have a subject.
- A sentence must have a verb.
- A sentence must conform to subject-verb-object word order (or inverted word order for questions or emphasis).
- A sentence must express an idea that can stand on its own (called the *main*, or *independent*, *clause*).

sentence faults

A number of problems can create sentence faults, including faulty <u>sub-ordination</u> (Tab 10), <u>clauses</u> with no subjects, rambling sentences, omitted <u>verbs</u>, and illogical assertions.

Faulty subordination occurs when a grammatically subordinate element contains the main idea of the sentence or when a subordinate element is so long or detailed that it obscures the main idea. Both of the following sentences are logical, depending on what the writer intends as the main idea and as the subordinate element.

- Although the new filing system saves money, many of the staff are unhappy with it.
  [If the main point is that *many of the staff are unhappy*, this sentence is correct.]
- The new filing system saves money, although many of the staff are unhappy with it.
  [If the main point is that *the new filing system saves money*, this sentence is correct.]

In the following example, the subordinate element overwhelms the main point.

FAULTY   Because the noise level in the assembly area on a typical shift is as loud as a smoke detector's alarm ten feet away, employees often develop hearing problems.

IMPROVED   Employees in the assembly area often develop hearing problems because the noise level on a typical shift is as loud as a smoke detector's alarm ten feet away.

Missing subjects occur when writers inappropriately assume a subject that they do not state in the clause. See also <u>sentence fragments</u>.

INCOMPLETE   Your application program can request to end the session after the next command.
             [Your application program can request *who* or *what* to end the session?]

COMPLETE   Your application program can request *the host program* to end the session after the next command.

Rambling sentences contain more information than the reader can comfortably absorb. The obvious remedy for a rambling sentence is to divide it into two or more sentences. When you do that, put the

11

Grammar

main message of the rambling sentence into the first of the revised sentences.

RAMBLING   The payment to which a subcontractor is entitled should be made promptly in order that in the event of a subsequent contractual dispute we, as general contractors, may not be held in default of our contract by virtue of nonpayment.

DIRECT   Pay subcontractors promptly. Then if a contractual dispute occurs, we cannot be held in default of our contract because of nonpayment.

Missing verbs produce some sentence faults.

- I never have *written* and probably never will write the annual report.

Faulty logic results when a predicate makes an illogical assertion about its subject. "Mr. Wilson's *job* is a sales representative" is not logical, but "*Mr. Wilson* is a sales representative" is logical. "Jim's *height* is six feet tall" is not logical, but "*Jim* is six feet tall" is logical. See also <u>logic errors</u> (Tab 10).

sentence fragments

A sentence fragment is an incomplete grammatical unit that is punctuated as a sentence.

FRAGMENT   And quit his job.
SENTENCE   He quit his job.

A sentence fragment lacks either a subject or a <u>verb</u> or is a subordinate <u>clause</u> or <u>phrase</u>. Sentence fragments are often introduced by relative <u>pronouns</u> (*who, whom, which, that*) or subordinating <u>conjunctions</u> (such as *although, because, if, when, while*).

- The new manager instituted several new policies*, although* ~~Although~~

  she didn't clear them with Human Resources.

A sentence must contain a finite verb; verbals (nonfinite) do not function as verbs. The following sentence fragments use verbals (*providing, to work*) that cannot function as finite verbs.

FRAGMENT   *Providing* all employees with disability insurance.
SENTENCE   The company *provides* all employees with disability insurance.

FRAGMENT   *To work* a 40-hour week.

SENTENCE   Most of our employees *must work* a 40-hour week.

Explanatory phrases beginning with *such as*, *for example*, and similar terms often lead writers to create sentence fragments.

- The staff wants additional benefits. ~~For example,~~ *, such as* the use of company cars.

A hopelessly snarled fragment simply must be rewritten. To rewrite such a fragment, pull the main points out of the fragment, list them in the proper sequence, and then rewrite the sentence as illustrated in garbled sentences (Tab 10). See also sentence construction and sentence faults.

spelling (*see* Tab 12)

tense

DIRECTORY

Past Tense 346	Future Tense 347
Past-Perfect Tense 346	Future-Perfect Tense 347
Present Tense 346	Shift in Tense 347
Present-Perfect Tense 347	

Tense is the grammatical term for verb forms that indicate time distinctions. The six tenses in English are past, past perfect, present, present perfect, future, and future perfect. Each tense also has a corresponding progressive form.

TENSE	BASIC FORM	PROGRESSIVE FORM
Past	I began	I was beginning
Past perfect	I had begun	I had been beginning
Present	I begin	I am beginning
Present perfect	I have begun	I have been beginning
Future	I will begin	I will be beginning
Future perfect	I will have begun	I will have been beginning

11

Grammar

Perfect tenses allow you to express a prior action or condition that continues in a present, past, or future time.

PAST PERFECT	I *had begun* to read the manual when the lights went out.
PRESENT PERFECT	I *have begun* to write the annual report and will continue for the rest of the month.
FUTURE PERFECT	I *will have begun* this project by the time funds are allocated.

Progressive tenses allow you to describe some ongoing action or condition in the present, past, or future.

PAST PROGRESSIVE	I *was beginning* to think we would not finish by the deadline.
PRESENT PROGRESSIVE	I *am beginning* to be concerned that we will not meet the deadline.
FUTURE PROGRESSIVE	I *will be requesting* a leave of absence when this project is finished.

Past Tense

The simple past tense indicates that an action took place in its entirety in the past. The past tense is usually formed by adding -*d* or -*ed* to the root form of the verb. ("We *closed* the office early yesterday.")

Past-Perfect Tense

The past-perfect tense (also called *pluperfect*) indicates that one past event preceded another. It is formed by combining the helping verb *had* with the past-participle form of the main verb. ("He *had finished* by the time I arrived.")

Present Tense

The simple present tense represents action occurring in the present, without any indication of time duration. ("I *ride* the train.")

A general truth is always expressed in the present tense. ("Time *heals* all wounds.") The present tense can be used to present actions or conditions that have no time restrictions. ("Water *boils* at 212 degrees Fahrenheit.") Similarly, the present tense can be used to indicate habitual action. ("I *pass* the coffee shop every day.") The present tense is also used for the "historical present," as in newspaper headlines ("Dow Jones *Reaches* a High for the Year") or as in references to an author's opinion or a work's contents — even though it was written in the past and the author is no longer living.

- In *Post-Capitalist Society*, Peter Drucker argues that the educated person will need "to live and work simultaneously in two cultures — that of the 'intellectual,' who focuses on words and ideas, and that of the 'manager,' who focuses on people and work" (215).

Present-Perfect Tense

The present-perfect tense describes something from the recent past that has a bearing on the present — a period of time before the present but after the simple past. The present-perfect tense is formed by combining a form of the helping verb *have* with the past-participle form of the main verb. ("We *have finished* the draft and can now revise it.")

Future Tense

The simple future tense indicates a time that will occur after the present. It uses the helping verb *will* (or *shall*) plus the main verb. ("I *will finish* the job tomorrow.") Do not use the future tense needlessly; doing so merely adds complexity.

- This system ~~will be~~ *is* explained on page 3.
- When you press this button, the feeder ~~will move~~ *moves* the paper into position.

Future-Perfect Tense

The future-perfect tense indicates action that will have been completed at the time of or before another future action. It combines *will have* and the past participle of the main verb. ("She *will have driven* 1,400 miles by the time she returns.")

Shift in Tense

Be consistent in your use of tense. The only legitimate shift in tense records a real change in time. Illogical shifts in tense will only confuse your readers.

- Before he visited the facility, the manager ~~meets~~ *met* with the staff.

TIP FOR USING THE PROGRESSIVE FORM

The progressive form of the verb is composed of two features: a form of the helping verb *be* and the *-ing* form of the base verb.

PRESENT PROGRESSIVE	I *am updating* the Web site.
PAST PROGRESSIVE	I *was updating* the Web site last week.
FUTURE PROGRESSIVE	I *will be updating* the Web site regularly.

The present progressive is used in three ways:

1. To refer to an action that is in progress at the moment of speaking or writing:

   • The technician *is repairing* the copier.

2. To highlight that a state or an action is not permanent:

   • The office temp *is helping* us for a few weeks.

3. To express future plans:

   • The summer intern *is leaving* to return to school this Friday.

The past progressive is used to refer to a continuing action or condition in the past, usually with specified limits.

• I *was failing* calculus until I got a tutor.

The future progressive is used to refer to a continuous action or condition in the future.

• We *will be monitoring* his condition all night.

Verbs that express mental activity (*believe, know, see,* and so on) are generally not used in the progressive.

    believe
• I ~~am believing~~ the defendant's testimony.
    ^

---

verbs

A verb is a word or group of words that describes an action ("The copier *jammed* at the beginning of the job"), states how something or someone is affected by an action ("He *was disappointed* that the proposal was rejected"), or affirms a state of existence ("She *is* a district manager now").

Types of Verbs

Verbs are either transitive or intransitive. A *transitive verb* requires a direct <u>object</u> to complete its meaning.

- They *laid* the foundation on October 24.
  [*Foundation* is the direct object of the transitive verb *laid*.]

- Rosalie Anderson *wrote* the treasurer a letter.
  [*Letter* is the direct object of the transitive verb *wrote*.]

An *intransitive verb* does not require an object to complete its meaning. It makes a full assertion about the subject without assistance (although it may have <u>modifiers</u>).

- The engine *ran*.

- The engine *ran* smoothly and quietly.

A *linking verb* is an intransitive verb that links a <u>complement</u> to the subject.

- The carpet *is* stained.
  [*Is* is a linking verb; *stained* is a subjective complement.]

Some intransitive verbs, such as *be*, *become*, *seem*, and *appear*, are almost always linking verbs. A number of others, such as *look*, *sound*, *taste*, *smell*, and *feel*, can function as either linking verbs or simple intransitive verbs. If you are unsure about whether one of those verbs is a linking verb, try substituting *seem*; if the sentence still makes sense, the verb is probably a linking verb.

- Their antennae *feel* delicate.
  [*Seem* can be substituted for *feel*—thus *feel* is a linking verb.]

- Their antennae *feel* delicately for their prey.
  [*Seem* cannot be substituted for *feel*; in this case, *feel* is a simple intransitive verb.]

Forms of Verbs

Verbs are also described as being either finite or nonfinite.

Finite Verbs.   A finite verb is the main verb of a <u>clause</u> or sentence. It makes an assertion about its subject and often serves as the only verb in its clause or sentence. ("The telephone *rang*, and the receptionist *answered* it.") See also <u>sentence construction</u>.

11

Grammar

A helping verb (sometimes called an *auxiliary verb*) is used in a verb phrase to help indicate mood, tense, and voice. ("The phone *had* rung.") Phrases that function as helping verbs are often made up of combinations with the sign of the infinitive, *to* (for example, *am going to, is about to, has to,* and *ought to*). The helping verb always precedes the main verb, although other words may intervene. ("Machines *will* never completely *replace* people.")

Nonfinite Verbs.   Nonfinite verbs are verbals—verb forms that function as nouns, adjectives, or adverbs.

A *gerund* is a noun that is derived from the *-ing* form of a verb. ("*Seeing* is *believing*.") An *infinitive*, which uses the root form of a verb (usually preceded by *to*), can function as a noun, an adverb, or an adjective.

- He hates *to complain.*
  [noun, direct object of *hates*]

- The valve closes *to stop* the flow.
  [adverb, modifies *closes*]

- This is the proposal *to consider.*
  [adjective, modifies *proposal*]

A *participle* is a verb form that can function as an adjective.

- The *rejected* proposal may be resubmitted when the concerns are addressed.
  [*Rejected* is a verb form that is used as an adjective modifying *proposal.*]

Properties of Verbs

Verbs must (1) agree in person with personal pronouns functioning as subjects, (2) agree in tense and number with their subjects, and (3) be in the appropriate voice.

Person is the term for the form of a personal pronoun that indicates whether the pronoun refers to the speaker, the person spoken to, or the person (or thing) spoken about. Verbs change their forms to agree in person with their subjects.

- I *see* [first person] a yellow tint, but she *sees* [third person] a yellow-green hue.

Tense refers to verb forms that indicate time distinctions. The six tenses are past, past perfect, present, present perfect, future, and future perfect.

Number refers to the two forms of a verb that indicate whether the subject of a verb is singular ("The copier *was* repaired" [singular]) or plural ("The copiers *were* repaired" [plural]).

Most verbs show the singular of the present tense by adding *-s* or *-es* (he *stands*, she *works*, it *goes*), and they show the plural without *-s* or *-es* (they *stand*, we *work*, they *go*). The verb *to be*, however, normally changes form to indicate the singular ("I *am* ready" [singular]) or plural ("We *are* ready" [plural]).

Voice refers to the two forms of a verb that indicate whether the subject of the verb acts or receives the action. The verb is in the *active voice* if the subject of the verb acts. ("The bacteria *grow*.") The verb is in the *passive voice* if the verb receives the action. ("The bacteria *are grown* in a petri dish.")

 WEB LINK CONJUGATION OF VERBS

The conjugation of a verb arranges all forms of the verb so that the differences caused by the changing of the tense, number, person, and voice are readily apparent. For a chart showing the full conjugation of the verb *drive*, see *bedfordstmartins.com/alred*, and select *Links Library*.

 TIP FOR AVOIDING SHIFTS IN VOICE, MOOD, OR TENSE

To achieve clarity in your writing, you must maintain consistency and avoid shifts. A shift is an abrupt change in voice, mood, or tense. Pay special attention when you edit your writing to check for the following types of shifts.

VOICE

- The captain permits his crew to go ashore, but ~~they are not~~ *he does not permit* *them* ~~permitted~~ to go downtown.

  [The entire sentence is now in the active voice.]

MOOD

- Reboot your computer/ and ~~you should~~ empty the cache.
  [The entire sentence is now in the imperative mood.]

TENSE

- I was working quickly, and suddenly a box ~~falls~~ *fell* off the conveyor belt and ~~breaks~~ *broke* my foot.

  [The entire sentence is now in the past tense.]

voice

In grammar, *voice* indicates the relation of the subject to the action of the <u>verb</u>. When the verb is in the *active voice*, the subject acts; when it is in the *passive voice*, the subject is acted upon.

> **ACTIVE**   David Cohen *wrote* the newsletter article.
> [The subject, *David Cohen*, performs the action; the verb, *wrote*, describes the action.]
>
> **PASSIVE**   The newsletter article *was written* by David Cohen.
> [The subject, *the newsletter article*, is acted upon; the verb, *was written*, describes the action.]

The two sentences say the same thing, but each has a different emphasis: The first emphasizes *David Cohen*; the second emphasizes *the newsletter article*. In business writing, it is often important to emphasize who or what performs an action. Further, the passive-voice version is indirect because it places the performer of the action behind the verb instead of in front of it. Because the active voice is generally more direct, more concise, and easier for readers to understand, use the active voice unless the passive voice is more appropriate, as described on pages 353–54. Whether you use the active voice or the passive voice, be careful not to shift voices within a sentence.

- David Cohen corrected the inaccuracy as soon as ~~it was identified~~
  ~~by~~ the editor. *identified it* ^

Using the Active Voice

Improving Clarity.   The active voice improves clarity and avoids confusion, especially in instructions and policies and procedures.

> **PASSIVE**   Sections B and C *should be checked* for errors.
> [Are they already checked?]
>
> **ACTIVE**   *Check* sections B and C for errors.
> [The performer of the action, *you*, is understood: (*You*) *Check* the sections.]

Active voice can also help avoid <u>dangling modifiers</u>.

> **PASSIVE**   Hurrying to complete the work, the cables *were connected* improperly.
> [*Who* was hurrying? The implication is the cables were hurrying!]

ACTIVE   Hurrying to complete the work, the technician *connected* the cables improperly.
             [Here, *hurrying to complete the work* properly modifies the performer of the action: *the technician.*]

Highlighting Subjects.   One difficulty with passive sentences is that they can bury the performer of the action in prepositional <u>phrases</u> and <u>expletives</u> (Tab 10).

PASSIVE   It *was reported by* the maintenance staff that the new model is defective.

ACTIVE   The maintenance staff *reported* that the new model is defective.

Sometimes writers using the passive voice fail to name the performer—information that might be missed and important.

PASSIVE   The problem *was discovered* yesterday.

ACTIVE   The attending physician *discovered* the problem yesterday.

Achieving Conciseness.   The active voice helps achieve <u>conciseness</u> (Tab 10) because it eliminates the need for an additional helping verb as well as an extra <u>preposition</u> to identify the performer of the action.

PASSIVE   Arbitrary changes in policy *are resented by* employees.

ACTIVE   Employees *resent* arbitrary changes in policy.

The active-voice version takes one verb (*resent*); the passive-voice version takes two verbs (*are resented*) and an extra preposition (*by*).

Using the Passive Voice

The passive voice is sometimes effective or even necessary. Indeed, for reasons of tact and diplomacy, you might need to use the passive voice to avoid an accusation.

ACTIVE   Your staff *did not meet* the sales quota last month.

PASSIVE   The sales quota *was not met* last month.

⬧ ETHICS NOTE   Be careful not to use the passive voice to evade responsibility or to obscure an issue or information that readers should know.

- Several mistakes *were made.*
  [*Who* made the mistakes?]

- It *has been decided.*
  [*Who* has decided?]

See also <u>ethics in writing</u> (Tab 1). ✦

11

Grammar

When the performer of the action is either unknown or unimportant, use the passive voice. ("The copper deposit *was discovered* in 1929.") When the performer of the action is less important than the receiver of that action, the passive voice is sometimes more appropriate. ("Ann Bryant *was presented* with an award by the president.")

When you are explaining an operation in which the reader is not actively involved or when you are explaining a process or a procedure, the passive voice may be more appropriate. In the following example, anyone—it really does not matter who—could be the performer of the action.

- Area strip mining *is used* in regions of flat to gently rolling terrain, like that found in the Midwest. Depending on applicable reclamation laws, the topsoil *may be removed* from the area *to be mined*, *stored*, and later *reapplied* as surface material during reclamation of the mined land. After the removal of the topsoil, a trench *is cut* through the overburden to expose the upper surface of the coal to be mined. The overburden from the first cut *is placed* on the unmined land adjacent to the cut. After the first cut *has been completed*, the coal *is removed*.

Do not, however, simply assume that any such explanation should be in the passive voice; in fact, as in the following example, the active voice is often more effective.

- In the operation of an internal combustion engine, an explosion in the combustion chamber *forces* the pistons down in the cylinders. The movement of the pistons in the cylinders *turns* the crankshaft.

Ask yourself, "Would it be of any advantage to the reader to know the performer of the action?" If the answer is yes, use the active voice, as in the previous example.

11

Grammar

ESL TIP FOR CHOOSING VOICE

Different languages place different values on active-voice and passive-voice constructions. In some languages, the passive voice is used frequently; in others, hardly at all. As a nonnative speaker of English, you may have a tendency to follow the pattern of your native language. But remember, even though business writing may sometimes require the passive voice, active verbs are highly valued in English.

12

Punctuation
and Mechanics

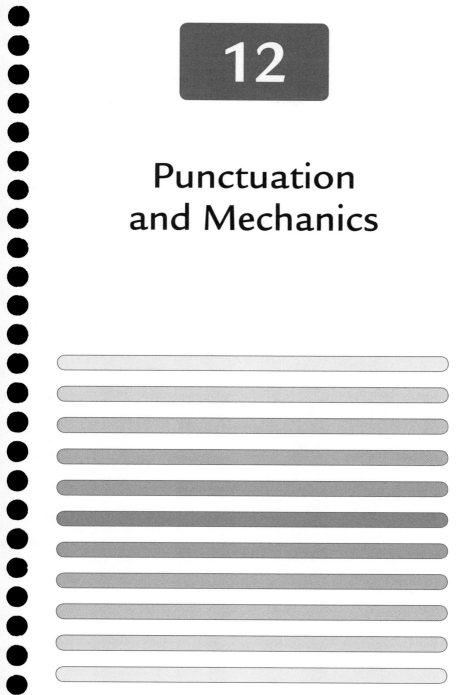

Preview

Understanding punctuation and mechanics enables you as a writer to communicate clearly and precisely. Punctuation is a system of symbols that helps readers understand the structural relationship within a sentence. The use of punctuation is determined by grammatical convention and a writer's intention.

Marks of punctuation may link, separate, enclose, indicate omissions, terminate, and classify. This section provides detailed information on each of the 13 marks of punctuation as well as entries on the mechanics of writing, including the use of <u>abbreviations</u>, <u>capitalization</u>, <u>contractions</u>, <u>dates</u>, <u>ellipses</u>, <u>italics</u>, and <u>numbers</u>.

12

Punctuation and Mechanics

abbreviations

Abbreviations are shortened versions of words or combinations of the first letters of words (Corp./Corporation, URL/Uniform Resource Locator). Abbreviations, if used appropriately, can be convenient for both the reader and the writer. Like symbols, they can be important space savers in business writing.

Abbreviations that are formed by combining the initial letter of each word in a multiword term are called *initialisms*. Initialisms are pronounced as separate letters (SEC/Securities and Exchange Commission). Abbreviations that combine the first letter or letters of several words—and can be pronounced as a word—are called *acronyms* (PIN/personal identification number, LAN/local area network).

Using Abbreviations

In business, industry, and government, specialists and those working together on particular projects often use abbreviations. The most important consideration in the use of abbreviations is whether they will be understood by your <u>audience</u> (Tab 1). The same abbreviation, for example, can have two different meanings (NEA stands for both the National Education Association and the National Endowment for the Arts). Like <u>jargon</u> (Tab 10), shortened forms are easily understood within a group of specialists; outside the group, however, shortened forms might be incomprehensible. In fact, abbreviations can be easily overused, either as an <u>affectation</u> (Tab 10) or in a misguided attempt to make writing concise, even with <u>instant messaging</u> (Tab 2) where abbreviations are often used. Remember that memos, e-mail, or reports addressed to specific people may be read by other people—you must consider those secondary audiences as well. A good rule to follow is "when in doubt, spell it out."

12

Punctuation and Mechanics

Writer's Checklist: Using Abbreviations

☑ Except for commonly used abbreviations (U.S., a.m.), spell out a term to be abbreviated the first time it is used, followed by the abbreviation in parentheses. Thereafter, the abbreviation may be used alone.

☑ In long documents, repeat the full term in parentheses after the abbreviation at regular intervals to remind readers of the abbreviation's meaning, as in "Remember to submit the CAR (Capital Appropriations Request) by . . ."

☑ Do not add an additional period at the end of a sentence that ends with an abbreviation. ("The official name of the company is Data-Base, Inc.")

☑ For abbreviations specific to your profession or discipline, use a style guide recommended by your professional organization or company. (A list of style guides appears online at *bedfordstmartins .com/alred*.)

☑ Write acronyms in capital letters without periods. The only exceptions are acronyms that have become accepted as common nouns, which are written in lowercase letters, such as *scuba* (*s*elf-*c*ontained *u*nderwater *b*reathing *a*pparatus).

☑ Generally, use periods for lowercase initialisms (a.k.a., d.b.a., p.m.) but not for uppercase ones (GDP, IRA, UFO). Exceptions include geographic names (U.S., U.K., E.U.) and the traditional expression of academic degrees (B.A., M.B.A., Ph.D.).

☑ Form the plural of an acronym or initialism by adding a lowercase *s*. Do not use an **apostrophe** (CARs, DVDs).

☑ Do not follow an abbreviation with a word that repeats the final term in the abbreviation (ATM location *not* ATM machine location).

☑ Do not make up your own abbreviations; they will confuse readers.

Forming Abbreviations

Names of Organizations.   A company may include in its name a term such as *Brothers, Incorporated, Corporation, Company,* or *Limited Liability Company.* If the term is abbreviated in the official company name that appears on letterhead stationery or on its Web site, use the abbreviated form: *Bros., Inc., Corp., Co.,* or *LLC.* If the term is not abbreviated in the official name, spell it out in writing, except with addresses, footnotes, bibliographies, and lists where abbreviations may be used. Likewise, use an ampersand (&) only if it appears in the official company name. For names of divisions within organizations, terms such as *Department* and *Division* should be abbreviated only when space is limited (*Dept.* and *Div.*).

Measurements. Except for abbreviations that may be confused with words (*in.* for *inch* and *gal.* for *gallon*), abbreviations of measurement do not require periods (*yd* for *yard* and *qt* for *quart*). Abbreviations of units of measure are identical in the singular and plural: 1 *cm* and 15 *cm* (*not* 15 *cms*). Some abbreviations can be used in combination with other symbols (°F for *degrees Fahrenheit* and *ft²* for *square feet*).

The following list includes abbreviations for the basic units of the International System of Units (SI), the metric system. This system not only is used in science but also is used in international commerce and trade.

MEASUREMENT	UNIT	ABBREVIATION
length	meter	m
mass	kilogram	kg
time	second	s
electric current	ampere	A
thermodynamic temperature	kelvin	K
amount of substance	mole	mol
luminous intensity	candela	cd

For additional definitions and background, see the National Institute of Standards and Technology Web site at *http://physics.nist.gov/cuu/Units/units.html*. For information on abbreviating dates and time, see numbers.

Personal Names and Titles. Personal names generally should not be abbreviated: Thomas (*not* Thos.) and William (*not* Wm.). An academic, civil, religious, or military title should be spelled out and in lowercase when it does not precede a name. ("The *captain* wanted to check the orders.") When they precede names, some titles are customarily abbreviated (Dr. Smith, Mr. Mills, Ms. Katz).

An abbreviation of a title may follow the name; however, be certain that it does not duplicate a title that appears before the name (Angeline Martinez, Ph.D. *or* Dr. Angeline Martinez). When addressing correspondence (Tab 7) and including names in other documents, you normally should spell out titles (The Honorable Mary J. Holt; Professor Charles Matlin). Traditionally, periods are used with academic degrees, although they are sometimes omitted (M.A./MA, M.B.A./MBA, Ph.D./PhD).

Common Scholarly Abbreviations. The following is a partial list of abbreviations commonly used in reference books and for documenting sources in research papers and reports. Other than in formal scholarly work, generally avoid such abbreviations.

12 Punctuation and Mechanics

anon.	anonymous
bibliog.	bibliography, bibliographer, bibliographic
ca., c.	*circa*, "about" (used with approximate dates: ca. 1756)
cf.	*confer*, "compare"
chap.	chapter
diss.	dissertation
ed., eds.	edited by, editor(s), edition(s)
e.g.	*exempli gratia*, "for example"
esp.	especially
et al.	*et alii*, "and others"
etc.	*et cetera*, "and so forth"
ff.	and the following page(s) or line(s)
GPO	Government Printing Office, Washington, D.C.
i.e.	*id est*, "that is"
MS, MSS	manuscript, manuscripts
n., nn.	note, notes (used immediately after page number: 56n., 56n.3, 56nn.3–5)
N.B., n.b.	*nota bene*, "take notice, mark well"
n.d.	no date (of publication)
n.p.	no place (of publication); no publisher; no page
p., pp.	page, pages
proc.	proceedings
pub.	published by, publisher, publication
rev.	revised by, revised, revision; review, reviewed by (Spell out "review" where "rev." might be ambiguous.)
rpt.	reprinted by, reprint
sec., secs.	section, sections
sic	so, thus; inserted in brackets ([*sic*]) after a misspelled or wrongly used word in quotations
supp., suppl.	supplement
trans.	translated by, translator, translation
UP	University Press (used in MLA style, as in "Oxford UP")
viz.	*videlicet*, "namely"
vol., vols.	volume, volumes
vs., v.	*versus*, "against" (*v.* preferred in titles of legal cases)

WEB LINK USING ABBREVIATIONS

For links to Web sites specifying standard abbreviations and acronyms, including U.S. Postal Service abbreviations, see *bedfordstmartins.com/alred*, and select *Links Library*.

apostrophes

An apostrophe (') is used to show possession or to indicate the omission of letters. Sometimes it is also used to avoid confusion with certain plurals of words, letters, and abbreviations.

Showing Possession

An apostrophe is used with an *s* to form the possessive case of some nouns (the *report's* title). For further advice on using apostrophes to show possession, see possessive case (Tab 11).

Indicating Omission

An apostrophe is used to mark the omission of letters or numbers in a contraction or a date (*can't, I'm, I'll*; the class of *'11*).

Forming Plurals

An apostrophe can be used in forming the plurals of letters, words, or lowercase abbreviations if confusion might result from using *s* alone.

- The search program does not find *a*'s and *i*'s.
- Do not replace all *of which*'s in the document.
- *I*'s need to be distinguished from the number 1.
- Check for any c.o.d.'s.

In general, however, add only *s* in roman (or regular) type when referring to words as words or capital letters. See also italics.

- Five *and*s appear in the first sentence.
- The applicants received *A*s and *B*s in their courses.

Do not use an apostrophe for plurals of abbreviations with all capital letters (PDFs) or a final capital letter (ten Ph.D.s) or for plurals of numbers (7s, the late 1990s).

brackets

The primary use of brackets ([ ]) is to enclose a word or words inserted by the writer or editor into a quotation.

- The text stated, "Hypertext systems can be categorized as either modest [not modifiable] or robust [modifiable]."

Brackets are used to set off a parenthetical item within parentheses.

- We must credit Emanuel Foose (and his brother Emilio [1912–1982]) for founding the institute.

Brackets are also used to insert the Latin word *sic*, which is a scholarly abbreviation that indicates a writer has quoted material exactly as it appears in the original, even though it contains a misspelled or wrongly used word.

- The contract states, "Tinted windows will be installed to protect against son [*sic*] damage."

See also quotations (Tab 3).

capitalization

DIRECTORY

The use of capital, or uppercase, letters is determined by custom. Capital letters are used to call attention to certain words, such as proper nouns and the first word of a sentence. Use capital letters carefully because they can affect a word's meaning (march/March, china/China) and because a spell checker would fail to identify such an error.

Proper Nouns

Capitalize proper nouns that name specific persons, places, or things (Pat Wilde, Peru, Business Writing 205, Microsoft). When in doubt, check a current dictionary.

Common Nouns

Common nouns name general classes or categories of people, places, things, concepts, or qualities rather than specific ones and are not capitalized (business writing class, company, person, country).

First Words

The first letter of the first word in a sentence is always capitalized. ("Of the plans submitted, ours is best.") The first word after a colon is capitalized when the colon introduces two or more sentences (independent clauses) or if the colon precedes a statement requiring special emphasis.

- The meeting will address only one issue: What is the firm's role in environmental protection?

If a subordinate element follows the colon or if the thought is closely related, use a lowercase letter following the colon.

- We kept working for one reason: the approaching deadline.

The first word of a complete sentence in <u>quotation marks</u> is capitalized.

- Peter Drucker said, "The most important thing in communication is to hear what isn't being said."

The first word in the salutation (Dear Mr. Smith:) and complimentary close (Sincerely yours,) are capitalized, as are the names of the recipients. See also <u>letters</u> (Tab 7).

Specific Groups

Capitalize the names of ethnic groups, religions, and nationalities (Native American, Christianity, Mongolian). Do not capitalize the names of social and economic groups (middle class, unemployed).

Specific Places

Capitalize the names of all political divisions (Ward Six, Chicago, Cook County, Illinois) and geographical divisions (Europe, Asia, North America, the Middle East). Do not capitalize geographic features unless they are part of a proper name.

- The mountains in some areas, such as the *Great Smoky Mountains*, make radio transmission difficult.

The words *north, south, east,* and *west* are capitalized when they refer to sections of the country but not when they refer to directions.

- I may relocate further *west*, but my family will remain in the *South*.

Specific Institutions, Events, and Concepts

Capitalize the names of institutions, organizations, and associations (U.S. Department of Health and Human Services). An organization usually capitalizes the names of its internal divisions and departments (Aeronautics Division, Human Resources Department). Types of

12

Punctuation and Mechanics

organizations are not capitalized unless they are part of an official name (a business communication association; Association for Business Communication). Capitalize historical events (the Great Depression of the 1930s). Capitalize words that designate holidays, specific periods of time, months, or days of the week (Labor Day, the Renaissance, January, Monday). Do not capitalize seasons of the year (spring, summer, autumn, winter).

Titles of Works

Capitalize the initial letters of the first, last, and major words in the title of a book, an article, a play, or a film. Do not capitalize <u>articles</u> (Tab 11), coordinating <u>conjunctions</u> (Tab 11), or <u>prepositions</u> (Tab 11) unless they begin or end the title (*The Lives of a Cell*). Capitalize prepositions within titles when they contain five or more letters (*Between, Within, Until, After*), unless you are following a style that recommends otherwise. The same rules apply to the subject lines of e-mails or memos.

Professional and Personal Titles

Titles preceding proper names are capitalized (Ms. Berger, Senator Lieberman). Appositives following proper names normally are not capitalized (Joseph Lieberman, *senator* from Connecticut). However, the word *President* is often capitalized when it refers to the chief executive of a national government. See <u>appositives</u> (Tab 11).

Job titles used with personal names are capitalized (Ho-shik Kim, *Division Manager*). Job titles used without personal names are not capitalized. ("The *division manager* will meet us tomorrow.") Use capital letters to designate family relationships only when they occur before a name (my uncle, Uncle Fred).

Abbreviations and Letters

Capitalize <u>abbreviations</u> if the words they stand for would be capitalized, such as M.B.A. (Master of Business Administration). Capitalize letters that serve as names or indicate shapes (vitamin B, T-square, U-turn, I-beam).

Miscellaneous Capitalizations

The first word of a complete sentence enclosed in <u>dashes</u>, <u>brackets</u>, or <u>parentheses</u> is not capitalized when it appears as part of another sentence.

- We must improve our safety record this year (accidents last year were up 10 percent).

colons

The colon (:) is a mark of introduction that alerts readers to the close connection between the preceding statement and what follows.

Colons in Sentences

A colon links independent clauses to words, phrases, clauses, or lists that identify, rename, explain, emphasize, amplify, or illustrate the sentence that precedes the colon.

- Two topics will be discussed: *the new accounting system and the new bookkeeping procedures.*
  [phrases that identify]

- Only one thing will satisfy Mr. Sturgess: *our finished report.*
  [appositive (renaming) phrase for emphasis]

- Any organization is confronted with two separate, though related, information problems: *It must maintain an effective internal communication system and an effective external communication system.*
  [clause to amplify and explain]

- Heart patients should make key lifestyle changes: *stop smoking, exercise regularly, eat a low-fat diet, and reduce stress.*
  [list to identify and illustrate]

Colons with Salutations, Titles, Citations, and Numbers

A colon follows the salutation in business <u>letters</u> (Tab 7), even when the salutation refers to a person by first name.

- Dear Professor Jeffers: *or* Dear Georgia:

Colons separate titles from subtitles and separate references to sections of works in citations. See also <u>documenting sources</u> (Tab 3).

- "'We Regret to Inform You': Toward a New Theory of Negative Messages"

- Genesis 10:16
  [chapter 10, verse 16]

Colons separate numbers in time references and indicate numerical ratios.

- 9:30 a.m.
  [9 hours and 30 minutes]

- The cement is mixed with water and sand at 5:3:1.
  [The colon is read as the word *to*.]

Punctuation and Capitalization with Colons

A colon always goes outside <u>quotation marks</u>.

- This was the real meaning of the manager's "suggestion": Cooperation within our department must improve.

As this example shows, the first word after a colon may be capitalized if the statement following the colon is a complete sentence and functions as a formal statement or question. If the element following the colon is subordinate, however, use a lowercase letter to begin that element. See also <u>capitalization</u>.

- We have only one way to stay within our present budget: to reduce expenditures for research and development.

Unnecessary Colons

Do not place a colon between a <u>verb</u> (Tab 11) and its objects.

- Three fluids that clean pipettes are ⫻ water, alcohol, and acetone.

Likewise, do not use a colon between a <u>preposition</u> (Tab 11) and its object.

- I may be transferred to ⫻ Tucson, Boston, or Miami.

Do not insert a colon after *including, such as,* or *for example* to introduce a simple list.

- Office computers should not be used for activities such as ⫻ personal e-mail, Web surfing, Internet shopping, and playing computer games.

One common exception is made when a verb or preposition is followed by a stacked <u>list</u> (Tab 6); however, it may be possible to introduce the list with a complete sentence instead.

The following corporations
- ~~Corporations that~~ manufacture computers ~~include~~ :

| Apple | Compaq | Dell |
| Gateway | IBM | Sony |

comma splice

A comma splice is a grammatical error in which two independent <u>clauses</u> (Tab 11) are joined by only a <u>comma</u>.

INCORRECT   It was 500 miles to the facility, we arranged to fly.

A comma splice can be corrected in several ways.

1. Substitute a <u>semicolon</u>, a semicolon and a conjunctive <u>adverb</u> (Tab 11), or a comma and a coordinating <u>conjunction</u> (Tab 11).

   - It was 500 miles to the facility; we arranged to fly.
   - It was 500 miles to the facility; *therefore*, we arranged to fly.
   - It was 500 miles to the facility, *so* we arranged to fly.

2. Create two sentences.

   - It was 500 miles to the facility. *We* arranged to fly.

3. Subordinate one clause to the other. (See <u>subordination</u>, Tab 10.)

   - *Because it was 500 miles to the facility*, we arranged to fly.

See also <u>sentence construction</u> (Tab 11) and <u>sentence faults</u> (Tab 11).

commas

Like all punctuation, the comma (,) helps readers understand the writer's meaning and prevents ambiguity. Notice how the comma helps make the meaning clear in the second example.

AMBIGUOUS   To be successful managers with MBAs must continue to learn.

CLEAR   To be successful, managers with MBAs must continue to learn.
[The comma makes clear where the main part of the sentence begins.]

Do not follow the old myth that you should insert a comma wherever you would pause if you were speaking. Although you would pause

12

Punctuation and Mechanics

wherever you encounter a comma, you should not insert a comma wherever you might pause. Effective use of commas depends on an understanding of <u>sentence construction</u> (Tab 11).

Linking Independent Clauses

Use a comma before a coordinating conjunction (*and*, *but*, *or*, *nor*, and sometimes *so*, *yet*, and *for*) that links independent <u>clauses</u> (Tab 11).

- The new microwave disinfection system was delivered, *but* the installation will require an additional week.

However, if two independent clauses are short and closely related—and there is no danger of confusing the reader—the comma may be omitted. Both of the following examples are correct.

- The cable snapped and the power failed.
- The cable snapped, and the power failed.

Enclosing Elements

Commas are used to enclose nonessential information in nonrestrictive clauses, phrases, and parenthetical elements. See also <u>restrictive and nonrestrictive elements</u> (Tab 11).

- Our new factory, *which began operations last month*, should add 25 percent to total output.
  [nonrestrictive clause]

- The accountant, *working quickly and efficiently*, finished early.
  [nonrestrictive phrase]

- We can, *of course*, expect their lawyer to call us.
  [parenthetical element]

Yes and *no* are set off by commas in such uses as the following:

- I agree with you, *yes*.
- *No*, I do not think we can finish by the deadline.

A direct address should be enclosed in commas.

- You will note, *Jeff*, that the budget figure matches our estimate.

An appositive phrase (which re-identifies another expression in the sentence) is enclosed in commas.

- Our company, *NT Insurance Group*, won several awards last year.

Interrupting parenthetical and transitional words or phrases are usually set off with commas. See also <u>transition</u> (Tab 10).

- The report, *therefore*, needs to be revised.

Commas are omitted when the word or phrase does not interrupt the continuity of thought.

- I *therefore* suggest that we begin construction.

For other means of punctuating parenthetical elements, see <u>dashes</u> and <u>parentheses</u>.

Introducing Elements

Clauses and Phrases.   In general, place a comma after an introductory clause or phrase, especially if it is long, to identify where the introductory element ends and the main part of the sentence begins.

- *Because we have not yet reached our hiring goals for the Sales Division,* we recommend the development of an aggressive recruiting program.

A long modifying phrase that precedes the main clause should always be followed by a comma.

- *During the first series of field-performance tests at our Colorado proving ground,* the new engine failed to meet our expectations.

When an introductory phrase is short and closely related to the main clause, the comma may be omitted.

- *In two seconds* a 5°C temperature rise occurs in the test tube.

A comma should always follow an absolute phrase, which modifies the whole sentence.

- *The presentation completed,* we returned to our offices.

Words and Quotations.   Certain types of introductory words are followed by a comma. One example is a transitional word or phrase (*however, in addition*) that connects the preceding clause or sentence with the thought that follows.

- *Furthermore,* we should include college job fairs in our recruiting plans, provided our budget is approved.
- *For example,* this change will make us more competitive in the global marketplace.

When an <u>adverb</u> (Tab 11) closely modifies the <u>verb</u> (Tab 11) or the entire sentence, it should not be followed by a comma.

12

Punctuation and Mechanics

- *Perhaps* we can still solve the turnover problem. *Certainly* we should try.
  [*Perhaps* and *certainly* closely modify each statement.]

A proper noun used in an introductory direct address is followed by a comma, as is an interjection (such as *oh, well, why, indeed, yes,* and *no*).

- *Nancy,* enclosed is the article you asked me to review.
  [direct address]

- *Indeed,* I will ensure that your request is forwarded.
  [interjection]

Use a comma to separate a direct quotation from its introduction.

- Morton and Lucia White *said,* "People live in cities but dream of the countryside."

Do not use a comma when giving an indirect quotation.

- Morton and Lucia White *said that* people dream of the country-side, even though they live in cities.

Separating Items in a Series

Although the comma before the last item in a series is sometimes omitted, it is generally clearer to include it.

- Random House, Bantam, Doubleday, and Dell were individual publishing companies.
  [Without the final comma, "Doubleday and Dell" might refer to one company or two.]

Phrases and clauses in coordinate series are also punctuated with commas.

- Plants absorb noxious gases, act as receptors of dirt particles, and cleanse the air of other impurities.

When phrases or clauses in a series contain commas, use <u>semicolons</u> rather than commas to separate the items.

- Among those present were John Howard, President of the Howard Paper Company; Thomas Martin, CEO of AIR Recycling, Inc.; and Larry Stanley, President of Northland Papers.

When <u>adjectives</u> (Tab 11) modifying the same noun can be reversed and make sense, or when they can be separated by *and* or *or*, they should be separated by commas.

- The aircraft featured a *modern, sleek, swept-wing* design.

When an adjective modifies a phrase, no comma is required.

- She was investigating the *damaged inventory-control system.*
  [The adjective *damaged* modifies the phrase *inventory-control system.*]

Never separate a final adjective from its noun.

- He is a conscientious, honest, reliable,/ worker.

Clarifying and Contrasting

Use a comma to separate two contrasting thoughts or ideas.

- The project was finished on time, but not within the budget.

Use a comma after an independent clause that is only loosely related to the dependent clause that follows it or that could be misread without the comma.

- I should be able to finish the plan by July, even though I lost time because of illness.

Showing Omissions

A comma sometimes replaces a verb in certain elliptical constructions.

- Some were punctual; *others, late.*
  [The comma replaces *were.*]

It is better, however, to avoid such constructions in business writing.

Using with Numbers and Names

Commas are conventionally used to separate distinct items. Use commas between the elements of an address written on the same line (but not between the state and the zip code).

- Kristen James, 4119 Mill Road, Dayton, Ohio 45401

A full date that is written in month-day-year format uses a comma preceding and following the year.

- November 30, 2025, is the payoff date.

Do not use commas for dates in the day-month-year format, which is used in many parts of the world and by the U.S. military. See also international correspondence (Tab 7).

- Note that 30 November 2025 is the payoff date.

No commas are used when showing only the month and year or month and day in a <u>date</u>.

- The target date of May 2015 is optimistic, so I would like to meet on March 4 to discuss our options.

Use commas to separate the elements of Arabic numbers.

- 1,528,200 feet

However, because many countries use the comma as the decimal marker, use spaces or periods rather than commas in international documents.

- 1.528.200 meters *or* 1 528 200 meters

A comma may be substituted for the colon in the salutation of a personal letter or e-mail. Do not, however, use a comma in the salutation of a business letter or e-mail, even if you use the person's first name.

- Dear Marie,
  [personal letter or e-mail]

- Dear Marie:
  [business letter or e-mail]

Use commas to separate the elements of geographical names.

- Toronto, Ontario, Canada

Use a comma to separate names that are reversed (Smith, Alvin) and names with professional <u>abbreviations</u>.

- Jim Rogers Jr., M.D., chaired the conference.
  [*Jr.* or *Sr.* does not require a comma.]

Using with Other Punctuation

Conjunctive adverbs (*however, nevertheless, consequently, for example, on the other hand*) that join independent clauses are preceded by a <u>semicolon</u> and followed by a comma. Such adverbs function both as <u>modifiers</u> (Tab 11) and as connectives.

- The idea is good; *however*, our budget is not sufficient.

As shown earlier in this entry, use semicolons rather than commas to separate items in a series when the items themselves contain commas.

When a comma should follow a phrase or clause that ends with words in parentheses, the comma always appears outside the closing parenthesis.

- Although we left late (at 7:30 p.m.), we arrived in time for the keynote address.

Commas always go inside <u>quotation marks</u>.

- The status display indicates "*ready*," but the unit requires an additional warm-up period.

Except with abbreviations, a comma should not be used with a dash, an <u>exclamation mark</u>, a <u>period</u>, or a <u>question mark</u>.

- "Have you finished the project?⁄" she asked.

Avoiding Unnecessary Commas

A number of common writing errors involve placing commas where they do not belong. As stated earlier, such errors often occur because writers assume that a pause in a sentence should be indicated by a comma.

Do not place a comma between a subject and verb or between a verb and its <u>object</u> (Tab 11).

- The location of our booth at this year's conference⁄ made attracting visitors difficult.

- She has often said⁄ that one company's failure is another's opportunity.

Do not use a comma between the elements of a compound subject or compound predicate consisting of only two elements.

- The director of the design department⁄ and the supervisor of the quality-control section were opposed to the new schedules.

- The design director listed five major objections⁄ and asked that the new schedule be reconsidered.

Do not include a comma after a coordinating conjunction such as *and* or *but*.

- The chairperson formally adjourned the meeting, but⁄ the members of the committee continued to argue.

Do not place a comma before the first item or after the last item of a series.

- The new products we are considering include⁄ calculators, scanners, and cameras.

- It was a fast, simple, inexpensive⁄ process.

12

Punctuation and
Mechanics

Do not use a comma to separate a prepositional phrase from the rest of the sentence unnecessarily.

- We discussed the final report⁄ on the new project.

contractions

A contraction is a shortened spelling of a word or phrase with an **apostrophe** substituting for the missing letter or letters (*cannot/can't*; *have not/haven't*; *will not/won't*; *it is/it's*). Contractions are often used in speech and informal writing; they are generally not appropriate in reports, proposals, and formal correspondence. See also **business writing style** (Tab 10).

dashes

The dash (—) can perform all the punctuation duties of linking, separating, and enclosing. The dash, sometimes indicated by two consecutive **hyphens,** can also indicate the omission of letters. ("Mr. A— admitted his error.")

Use the dash cautiously to indicate more **emphasis** (Tab 10), informality, or abruptness than the other punctuation marks would show. A dash can emphasize a sharp turn in thought.

- The project will end May 15—unless we receive additional funding.

A dash can indicate an emphatic pause.

- The project will begin—after we are under contract.

Sometimes, to emphasize contrast, a dash is used with *but*.

- We completed the survey quickly—*but* the results were not accurate.

A dash can be used before a final summarizing statement or before repetition that has the effect of an afterthought.

- It was hot near the heat-treating ovens—steaming hot.

Such a statement may also complete the meaning of the clause preceding the dash.

- We try to write as we speak—or so we believe.

Dashes set off parenthetical elements more sharply and emphatically than <u>commas</u>. Unlike dashes, <u>parentheses</u> tend to deemphasize what they enclose. Compare the following sentences:

- Only one person—the president—can authorize such activity.
- Only one person, the president, can authorize such activity.
- Only one person (the president) can authorize such activity.

Dashes can be used to set off parenthetical elements that contain commas.

- Three of the applicants—John Evans, Rosalita Fontiana, and Kyong-Shik Choi—seem well qualified for the job.

The first word after a dash is capitalized only if it is a proper <u>noun</u> (Tab 11).

dates

In the United States, full dates are generally written in the month-day-year format, with a comma preceding and following the year.

- November 30, 2025, is the payoff date.

Do not use <u>commas</u> in the day-month-year format, which is used in many parts of the world and by the U.S. military.

- Note that 30 November 2025 is the payoff date.

No commas are used when showing only the month-year or month-day in a date.

- The target date of May 2015 is optimistic, so I would like to meet on March 4 to discuss our options.

When writing days of the month without the year, use the cardinal number ("March 4") rather than the ordinal number ("March 4th"). Of course, in speech or <u>presentations</u> (Tab 9), use the ordinal number ("March fourth").

Avoid the strictly numerical form for dates (11/6/15) because the date is not always immediately clear, especially in <u>international correspondence</u> (Tab 7). In many countries, 11/6/15 means June 11, 2015, rather than November 6, 2015. Writing out the name of the month makes the entire date immediately clear to all readers.

Centuries often cause confusion with <u>numbers</u> because their spelled-out forms, which are not capitalized, do not correspond with their numeral designations. The twentieth century, for example, is the 1900s: 1900–1999.

When the century is written as a noun, do not use a <u>hyphen</u>.

- During the twentieth century, technology transformed business practices.

When the centuries are written as adjectives, however, use hyphens.

- Twenty-first-century technology relies on dependable power sources.

ellipses

An ellipsis is the omission of words from quoted material; it is indicated by three spaced <u>periods</u> called *ellipsis points* (. . .). When you use ellipsis points, omit original punctuation marks, unless they are necessary for clarity or the omitted material comes at the end of a quoted sentence.

ORIGINAL TEXT	"Promotional material sometimes carries a fee, particularly in high-volume distribution to schools, although prices for these publications are much lower than the development costs when all factors are considered."
WITH OMISSION AND ELLIPSIS POINTS	"Promotional material sometimes carries a fee . . . although prices for these publications are much lower than the development costs. . . ."

Notice in the preceding example that the final period is retained and what remains of the quotation is grammatically complete. When the omitted part of the quotation is preceded by a period, retain the period and add the three ellipsis points after it, as in the following example:

ORIGINAL TEXT	"Of the 172 major ethics cases reported, 57 percent were found to involve un-substantiated concerns. Misinformation was the cause of unfounded concerns of misconduct in 72 cases. Forty-four cases, or 26 percent of the total cases reported, involved incidents partly substantiated by ethics officers as serious misconduct."
WITH OMISSION AND ELLIPSIS POINTS	"Of the 172 major ethics cases reported, 57 percent were found to involve unsub-stantiated concerns. . . . Forty-four cases, or 26 percent of the total cases reported, involved incidents partly substantiated by ethics officers as serious misconduct."

Do not use ellipsis points when the beginning of a quoted sentence is omitted. Notice in the following example that the comma is dropped to prevent a grammatical error.

- The ethics report states that "26 percent of the total cases reported involved incidents partly substantiated by ethics officers as serious misconduct."

See also <u>quotations</u> (Tab 3).

exclamation marks

The exclamation mark (!) indicates strong feeling, urgency, elation, or surprise ("Hurry!" "Great!" "Wow!"). However, it cannot make an argument more convincing, lend force to a weak statement, or call attention to an intended irony.

An exclamation mark can be used after a whole sentence or an element of a sentence.

- This meeting—please note it well!—concerns our budget deficit.

When used with <u>quotation marks</u>, the exclamation mark goes outside, unless what is quoted is an exclamation.

- The paramedic shouted, "Don't touch the victim!" The bystander then, according to a witness, "jumped like a kangaroo"!

In instructions, the exclamation mark is often used in cautions and warnings ("Danger!" "Stop!"). See also <u>emphasis</u> (Tab 10).

hyphens

The hyphen (-) is used primarily for linking and separating words and parts of words. The hyphen often improves the clarity of writing. The hyphen is sometimes confused with the <u>dash,</u> which is longer and has many other functions.

Hyphens with Compound Words

Some compound words are formed with hyphens (able-bodied, over-the-counter). Hyphens are also used with multiword <u>numbers</u> from twenty-one through ninety-nine and fractions when they are written out (three-quarters). Most current dictionaries indicate whether compound words are hyphenated, written as one word, or written as separate words.

Hyphens with Modifiers

Two- and three-word <u>modifiers</u> (Tab 11) that express a single thought are hyphenated when they precede a <u>noun</u> (Tab 11).

- It was a *well-written* report.

However, a modifying phrase is not hyphenated when it follows the noun it modifies.

- The report was *well written*.

If each of the words can modify the noun without the aid of the other modifying word or words, do not use a hyphen (a *new laser* printer). If the first word is an <u>adverb</u> (Tab 11) ending in *-ly*, do not use a hyphen (a *privately held* company). A hyphen is always used as part of a letter or number modifier (A-frame house, 17-inch screen).

In a series of unit modifiers that all have the same term following the hyphen, the term following the hyphen need not be repeated throughout the series; for greater smoothness and brevity, use the term only at the end of the series.

- The third-, fourth-, and fifth-floor rooms were recently painted.

Hyphens with Prefixes and Suffixes

A hyphen is used with a prefix when the root word is a proper noun (pre-Columbian, anti-American, post-Newtonian). A hyphen may be used when the prefix ends and the root word begins with the same vowel (re-enter, anti-inflammatory). A hyphen is used when *ex-* means "former" (ex-president, ex-spouse). A hyphen may be used to emphasize a prefix. ("He is *anti-change*.") The suffix *-elect* is hyphenated (president-elect).

Hyphens and Clarity

The presence or absence of a hyphen can alter the meaning of a sentence.

AMBIGUOUS   We need a biological waste management system.

That sentence could mean one of two things: (1) We need a system to manage "biological waste," or (2) We need a "biological" system to manage waste.

CLEAR   We need a *biological-waste* management system. [1]
CLEAR   We need a biological *waste-management* system. [2]

To avoid confusion, some words and modifiers should always be hyphenated. *Re-cover* does not mean the same thing as *recover*, for example; the same is true of *re-sign* and *resign* and *un-ionized* and *unionized*.

Other Uses of the Hyphen

Hyphens are used between letters showing how a word is spelled.

* In his e-mail, he misspelled *believed* as b-e-l-e-i-v-e-d.

A hyphen can stand for *to* or *through* between letters and numbers (pages 44-46, the Detroit-Toledo Expressway, A-L and M-Z).

Writer's Checklist: Using Hyphens to Divide Words

- ☑ Do not divide one-syllable words.
- ☑ Divide words at syllable breaks, which you can determine with a dictionary.
- ☑ Do not divide a word if only one letter would remain at the end of a line or if fewer than three letters would start a new line.
- ☑ Do not divide a word at the end of a page; carry it over to the next page.
- ☑ If a word already has a hyphen in its spelling, divide the word at the existing hyphen.
- ☑ Do not use a hyphen to break a URL or an e-mail address at the end of a line because it may confuse readers who could assume that the hyphen is part of the address.

italics

Italics is a style of type used to denote <u>emphasis</u> (Tab 10) and to distinguish foreign expressions, book titles, and certain other elements. *This sentence is printed in italics.* Italic type is often signaled by underlining in manuscripts submitted for publication or where italic font is not available (see also <u>e-mail</u>, Tab 2). You may need to italicize words that require special emphasis in a sentence. ("Contrary to projections, sales have *not* improved.") Do not overuse italics for emphasis, however. ("*This* will hurt *you* more than *me*.")

Foreign Words and Phrases

Foreign words and phrases are italicized (*bonjour, guten tag*, the sign said "*Se habla español*"). Foreign words that have been fully assimilated into English need not be italicized (cliché, etiquette, vis-à-vis, de facto,

12

Punctuation and Mechanics

résumé). When in doubt about whether to italicize a word, consult a current dictionary.

Titles

Italicize the titles of separately published documents, such as books, periodicals, newspapers, pamphlets, brochures, legal cases, movies, and television programs.

- The book *Turning Workplace Conflicts into Collaboration* was reviewed in the *New York Times*.

<u>Abbreviations</u> of such titles are italicized if their spelled-out forms would be italicized.

- The *NYT* is one of the nation's oldest newspapers.

Italicize the titles of compact discs, videotapes, plays, long poems, paintings, sculptures, and long musical works.

CD-ROM	*Computer Security Tutorial on CD-ROM*
PLAY	Arthur Miller's *Death of a Salesman*
LONG POEM	T. S. Eliot's *The Wasteland*
MUSICAL WORK	Gershwin's *Porgy and Bess*

Use <u>quotation marks</u> for parts of publications, such as chapters of books and articles or sections within periodicals.

Proper Names

The names of ships, trains, and aircraft (but not the companies or governments that own them) are italicized (U.S. aircraft carrier *Independence*, U.S. space shuttle *Endeavour*). Craft that are known by model or serial designations are not italicized (DC-7, Boeing 747).

Words, Letters, and Figures

Words, letters, and figures discussed as such are italicized.

- The word *inflammable* is often misinterpreted.
- The *S* and *6* keys on my keyboard do not function.

Subheads

Subheads in a report are sometimes italicized.

- *Training Managers.* We are leading the way in developing first-line managers who not only are professionally competent but . . .

See also <u>headings</u> (Tab 6) and <u>layout and design</u> (Tab 6).

numbers

The standards for using numbers vary; however, unless you are following an organizational or a professional style manual, observe the following guidelines.

Numerals or Words

Write numbers from zero through ten as words, and write numbers above ten as numerals.

- I rehearsed my presentation *three* times.
- The association added *150* new members.

Spell out numbers that begin a sentence, however, even if they would otherwise be written as numerals.

- *One hundred and fifty* new members joined the association.

If spelling out such a number seems awkward, rewrite the sentence so that the number does not appear at the beginning. ("We added *150* new members.")
Spell out approximate and round numbers.

- We've had *over a thousand* requests this month.

In most writing, spell out small ordinal numbers when they express degree or sequence (first, second; *but* 27th, 42nd), when they are single words (our nineteenth year), or when they modify the word *century* (the twenty-first century). However, avoid ordinal numbers in <u>dates</u> (use March 30 or 30 March, not March 30th).

Plurals

Indicate the plural of numerals by adding -*s* (7s, the late 1990s). Form the plural of a written number (like any noun) by adding -*s* or -*es* or by dropping the *y* and adding -*ies* (elevens, sixes, twenties). See also <u>apostrophes</u>.

12

Punctuation and Mechanics

Measurements

Express units of measurement as numerals (3 miles, 45 cubic feet, 9 meters). When numbers run together in the same phrase, write one as a numeral and the other as a word.

- The order was for ~~12~~ *twelve* 6-foot tables.

Generally give percentages as numerals and write out the word *percent*. ("Approximately *85 percent* of the land has been sold.") However, in a table, use a numeral followed by the percent symbol (85%).

Fractions

Express fractions as numerals when they are written with whole numbers ($27^1/_2$ inches, $4^1/_4$ miles). Spell out fractions when they are expressed without a whole number (one-fourth, seven-eighths). Always write decimal numbers as numerals (5.21 meters).

Money

In general, use numerals to express exact or approximate amounts of money.

- We need to charge *$28.95* per unit.
- The new system costs *$60,000*.

Use words to express indefinite amounts of money.

- The printing system may cost *several thousand dollars*.

Use numerals and words for rounded amounts of money over one million dollars.

- The contract is worth *$6.8 million*.

Use numerals for more complex or exact amounts.

- The corporation paid *$2,452,500* in taxes last year.

For amounts under a dollar, ordinarily use numerals and the word *cents* ("The pens cost *75 cents* each"), unless other numerals that require dollar signs appear in the same sentence.

- The business-card holders cost *$10.49* each, the pens cost *$.75* each, and the pencil cup holders cost *$6.49* each.

ESL TIP FOR PUNCTUATING NUMBERS

Some rules for punctuating numbers in English are summarized as follows:

Use a comma to separate numbers with four or more digits into groups of three, starting from the right (*5,289,112,001* atoms).

Do not use a comma in years, house numbers, zip codes, and page numbers, even with four or more digits.

- June *2009*
- *92401* East Alameda Drive
- The zip code is *91601*.
- Page *1204*

Use a period to represent the decimal point (*4.2* percent, *$3,742,097.43*). See also <u>global communication</u> (Tab 1) and <u>global graphics</u> (Tab 6).

Time

Divide hours and minutes with <u>colons</u> when *a.m.* or *p.m.* follows (*7:30* a.m., *11:30* p.m.). Do not use colons with the 24-hour system (0730, 2330). Spelled-out time is not followed by *a.m.* or *p.m.* (seven o'clock in the evening).

Dates

In the United States dates are usually written in a month-day-year sequence (August 11, 2009). Never use the strictly numerical form for dates (8/11/09) because the date is not immediately clear, especially in <u>international correspondence</u> (Tab 7).

Addresses

Spell out numbered streets from one to ten unless space is at a premium (East Tenth Street). Write building numbers as numerals. The only exception is the building number *one* (One East Monument Street). Write highway numbers as numerals (U.S. 40, Ohio 271, I-94).

Documents

Page numbers are written as numerals in manuscripts (page 37). Chapter and volume numbers may appear as numerals or words

12

Punctuation and
Mechanics

(Chapter 2 or Chapter Two, Volume 1 or Volume One), but be consistent. Express figure and table numbers as numerals (Figure 4, Table 3).

Do not follow a word representing a number with a numeral in parentheses that represents the same number. Doing so is redundant.

- Send five ~~(5)~~ copies of the report.

parentheses

Parentheses are used to enclose explanatory or digressive words, phrases, or sentences. Material in parentheses often clarifies or defines the preceding text without altering its meaning.

- She severely bruised her tibia (or shinbone) in the accident.

Parenthetical information may not be essential to a sentence (in fact, parentheses deemphasize the enclosed material), but it may be helpful to some readers.

Parenthetical material does not affect the punctuation of a sentence, and any punctuation (such as a <u>comma</u> or <u>period</u>) should appear following the closing parenthesis.

- She could not fully extend her knee because of a torn meniscus (or cartilage), and she suffered pain from a severely bruised tibia (or shinbone).

When a complete sentence within parentheses stands independently, the ending punctuation is placed inside the final parenthesis.

- The project director listed the problems her staff faced. (This was the third time she had complained to the board.)

For some constructions, however, you should consider using <u>subordination</u> (Tab 10) rather than parentheses.

- The early tests showed little damage *, which pleased the attending physician,* ~~(the attending physician was pleased),~~ but later scans revealed abdominal trauma.

Parentheses also are used to enclose numerals or letters that indicate sequence.

- The following sections deal with (1) preparation, (2) research, (3) organization, (4) writing, and (5) revision.

Do not follow spelled-out <u>numbers</u> with numerals in parentheses representing the same numbers.

- Send five ~~(5)~~ copies of the report.

Use brackets to set off a parenthetical item that is already within parentheses.

- We should be sure to give Emanuel Foose (and his brother Emilio [1912–1982]) credit for his part in founding the institute.

See also documenting sources (Tab 3) and quotations (Tab 3).

periods

A period usually indicates the end of a declarative or an imperative sentence. Periods also link when used as leaders (as in rows of periods in tables of contents) and indicate omissions when used as ellipses. Periods are also used to end questions that are actually polite requests or instructions to which an affirmative response is assumed. ("Will you call me as soon as he arrives.") See also sentence construction (Tab 11).

Periods in Quotations

Use a comma, not a period, after a declarative sentence that is quoted in the context of another sentence.

- "There is every chance of success," she stated.

A period is placed inside quotation marks.

- He stated clearly, "My vote is yes."

See also quotations (Tab 3).

Periods with Parentheses

Place a period outside the final parenthesis when a parenthetical element ends a sentence.

- The institute was founded by Harry Denman (1902–1972).

Place a period inside the final parenthesis when a complete sentence stands independently within parentheses.

- The project director listed the problems her staff faced. (This was the third time she had complained to the board.)

Other Uses of Periods

Use periods after initials in names (Wilma T. Grant, J. P. Morgan). Use periods as decimal points with numbers (27.3 degrees Celsius, $540.26, 6.9 percent). Use periods to indicate certain abbreviations (Ms., Dr., Inc.).

When a sentence ends with an abbreviation that ends with a period, do not add another period. ("Please meet me at 3:30 p.m.") Use periods following the numerals in a numbered list and following lists with complete sentences.

- 1. Enter your name and PIN.

  2. Enter your address with zip code.

  3. Enter your home telephone number.

Period Faults

The incorrect use of a period is sometimes referred to as a *period fault*. When a period is inserted prematurely, the result is a <u>sentence fragment</u> (Tab 11).

FRAGMENT   After a long day at the office during which we finished the quarterly report. We left hurriedly for home.

SENTENCE   After a long day at the office, during which we finished the quarterly report, we left hurriedly for home.

When two independent clauses are joined without any punctuation, the result is a *fused*, or *run-on*, *sentence*. Adding a period between the clauses is one way to correct a run-on sentence.

RUN-ON   Bill was late for ten days in a row Ms. Sturgess had to dismiss him.

CORRECT   Bill was late for ten days in a row. Ms. Sturgess had to dismiss him.

Other options are to add a comma and a coordinating conjunction (*and, but, for, or, nor, so, yet*) between the clauses, to add a <u>semicolon</u>, or to add a semicolon with a conjunctive <u>adverb</u> (Tab 11), such as *therefore* or *however*.

12 question marks

The question mark (?) most often ends a sentence that is a direct question or request.

- Where did you put the tax report?
  [direct question]

- Will you e-mail me if your shipment does not arrive by June 10?
  [request]

Use a question mark to end a statement that has an interrogative meaning—a statement that is declarative in form but asks a question.

- The tax report is finished?
  [question in declarative form]

Question marks may follow a series of separate items within an interrogative sentence.

- Do you remember the date of the contract? its terms? whether you signed it?

Use a question mark to end an interrogative clause within a declarative sentence.

- It was not until July (or was it August?) that we submitted the report.

Retain the question mark in a title that is being cited, even though the sentence in which it appears has not ended.

- *Can Investments Be Protected?* is the title of her book.

Never use a question mark to end a sentence that is an indirect question.

- He asked me where I put the tax report?
  ^

When a question is a polite request or an instruction to which an affirmative response is assumed, a question mark is not necessary.

- Will you call me as soon as he arrives.
  [polite request]

When used with <u>quotations</u> (Tab 3), the placement of the question mark is important. When the writer is asking a question, the question mark belongs outside the <u>quotation marks</u>.

- Did she actually say, "I don't think the project should continue"?

If the quotation itself is a question, the question mark goes inside the quotation marks.

- She asked, "Do we have enough funding?"

If both cases apply—the writer is asking a question and the quotation itself is a question—use a single question mark inside the quotation marks.

- Did she ask, "Do we have enough funding?"

quotation marks

Quotation marks (" ") are used to enclose a direct quotation of spoken or written words. Quotation marks have other special uses, but they should not be used for <u>emphasis</u> (Tab 10).

Direct Quotations

Enclose in quotation marks anything that is quoted word for word (a direct quotation) from speech or written material.

- She said clearly, "I want the progress report by three o'clock."

Do not enclose indirect quotations—usually introduced by the word *that*—in quotation marks. Indirect quotations are paraphrases of a writer's or speaker's words or ideas.

- She said that she wanted the progress report by three o'clock.

See also paraphrasing (Tab 3).

◼ ETHICS NOTE When you use quotation marks to indicate that you are quoting, do not make any changes or omissions in the quoted material unless you clearly indicate what you have done. For further information on incorporating quoted material and inserting comments, see plagiarism (Tab 3) and quotations (Tab 3). ✦

Use single quotation marks (' ') to enclose a quotation that appears within a quotation.

- John said, "Jane told me that she was going to 'stay with the project if it takes all year.'"

Words and Phrases

Use quotation marks to set off special words or terms only to point out that the term is used in context for a unique or special purpose (that is, in the sense of the term *so-called*).

- A remarkable chain of events caused the sinking of the "unsinkable" *Titanic* on its maiden voyage.

Slang, colloquial expressions, and attempts at humor, although infrequent in workplace writing, should seldom be set off by quotation marks.

- Our first six months amounted to a *shakedown cruise.* ~~"shakedown cruise."~~

Titles of Works

Use quotation marks to enclose titles of reports, short stories, articles, essays, single episodes of radio and television programs, and short musical works (including songs). However, do not use quotation marks for titles of books and periodicals, which should appear in italics.

- His report, "Effects of Government Regulations on Motorcycle Safety," cited the article "No-Fault Insurance and Motorcycles," published in *American Motorcyclist* magazine.

Use quotation marks for parts of publications, such as chapters of books and articles or sections within periodicals.

- "Bad Writing," an article by Barbara Wallraff, appeared in the "On Language" column of the *New York Times*.

Some titles, by convention, are not set off by quotation marks, underlining, or italics, although they are capitalized.

- Professional Writing [college course title], the Bible, the Constitution, Lincoln's Gettysburg Address, the Lands' End Catalog

Punctuation

Commas and periods always go inside closing quotation marks.

- "Reading *Computer World* gives me the insider's view," he says, adding, "It's like a conversation with the top experts."

Semicolons and colons always go outside closing quotation marks.

- He said, "I will pay the full amount"; this statement surprised us.

All other punctuation follows the logic of the context: If the punctuation is part of the material quoted, it goes inside the quotation marks; if the punctuation is not part of the material quoted, it goes outside the quotation marks.

semicolons

The semicolon (;) links independent clauses (Tab 11) or other sentence elements of equal weight and grammatical rank when they are not joined by a comma and a conjunction (Tab 11). The semicolon indicates a greater pause between clauses than does a comma but not as great a pause as a period.

Independent clauses joined by a semicolon should balance or contrast with each other, and the relationship between the two statements should be so clear that further explanation is not necessary.

- The new Web site was a success; every division reported increased online sales.

Do not use a semicolon between a dependent clause and its main clause.

- No one applied for the position; even though it was heavily advertised.

With Strong Connectives

In complicated sentences, a semicolon may be used before transitional words or phrases (*that is, for example, namely*) that introduce examples or further explanation. See also transition (Tab 10).

- The press understands Commissioner Curran's position on the issue; *that is*, local funds should not be used for the highway project.

A semicolon should also be used before conjunctive adverbs (*therefore, moreover, consequently, furthermore, indeed, in fact, however*) that connect independent clauses.

- The test results are not complete; *therefore*, I cannot make a recommendation.
  [The semicolon shows that *therefore* belongs to the second clause.]

For Clarity in Long Sentences

Use a semicolon between two independent clauses connected by a coordinating conjunction (*and, but, for, or, nor, so, yet*) if the clauses are long and contain other punctuation.

- In most cases, these individuals are executives, bankers, or lawyers; *but* they do not, as the press seems to believe, simply push the button of their economic power to affect local politics.

A semicolon may also be used if any items in a series contain commas.

- Among those present were John Howard, president of the Omega Paper Company; Carol Delgado, president of Environex Corporation; and Larry Stanley, president of Stanley Papers.

Use parentheses or dashes, not semicolons, to enclose a parenthetical element that contains commas.

- All affected job classifications (receptionist, secretary, transcriptionist, and clerk) will be upgraded this month.

Use a colon, not a semicolon, as a mark of anticipation or enumeration.

- Three decontamination methods are under consideration: a zeolite-resin system, an evaporation system, and a filtration system.

The semicolon always appears outside closing quotation marks.

- The attorney said, "You must be accurate"; her client replied, "I will."

slashes

The slash (/)—also called *slant line*, *diagonal*, *virgule*, *bar*, and *solidus*—both separates and shows omission. The slash can indicate alternatives or combinations.

- David's telephone numbers are (800) 549-2278/2235.
- Check the on/off switch before you leave.

The slash often indicates omitted words and letters.

- miles/hour (miles per hour); w/o (without)

In fractions and mathematical expressions, the slash separates the numerator from the denominator (3/4 for three-fourths; x/y for x over y).

Although the slash is used informally with <u>dates</u> (5/9/09), avoid this form in business writing, especially in <u>international correspondence</u> (Tab 7).

The forward slash often separates items in URL (uniform resource locator) addresses for sites on the Internet (*bedfordstmartins.com/alred*). The backward slash is used to separate parts of file names (*c:\myfiles\ reports\annual09.doc*).

spelling

Because spelling errors in your documents can confuse readers and damage your credibility, careful <u>proofreading</u> (Tab 1) is essential. The use of a spell checker is crucial; however, it will not catch all mistakes, especially those in personal and company names. It cannot detect a spelling error if the error results in a valid word; for example, if you mean *to* but inadvertently type *too*, the spell checker will not detect the error. Likewise, spell checkers will not detect errors in the names of people, places, and organizations. If you are unsure about the spelling of a word, do not rely on guesswork or a spell checker—consult a standard dictionary or style guide.

12

Punctuation and
Mechanics

Appendix: Usage

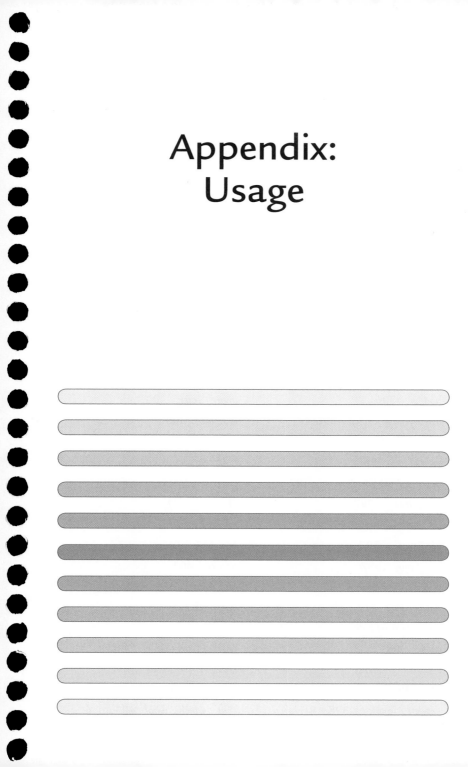

Preview

Usage describes the choices we make among the various words and constructions available in our language. The line between standard and nonstandard English, or between formal and informal English, is determined by these choices. Your choices in any writing situation should be guided by appropriateness: Is the word or expression appropriate to your audience and subject? When it is, you are practicing good usage. A good dictionary is also an invaluable aid in helping you select the right word. (See Tab 10, "Style and Clarity.")

 WEB LINK ONLINE DICTIONARIES

Dictionary.com provides a multisource search that displays definitions and thesaurus entries from a number of major dictionaries and references. For this resource and others, see *bedfordstmartins.com/alred*, and select *Links Library*.

---

a lot   *A lot* is often incorrectly written as one word (*alot*). The phrase *a lot* is informal and often too vague for business writing. Use *many* or *numerous* for estimates or give a specific number or amount.

• We received a̶ ̶l̶o̶t̶ ̶o̶f̶ e-mails supporting the new policy.
    152

above   Avoid using *above* to refer to a preceding passage or visual because its reference is often vague. The same is true of *aforesaid* and *aforementioned*. To refer to something previously mentioned, repeat the noun or pronoun, or construct your paragraph so that your reference is obvious.

• Please complete and submit t̶h̶e̶ ̶a̶b̶o̶v̶e̶ by March 1.
    your travel voucher

accept / except   *Accept* is a verb meaning "consent to," "agree to take," or "admit willingly." ("I *accept* the responsibility.") *Except* is normally used as a preposition meaning "other than" or "excluding." ("We agreed on everything *except* the schedule.")

affect / effect   *Affect* is a verb that means "influence." ("The decision could *affect* the company's stock value.") *Effect* can function as a noun that means "result" ("The decision had a positive *effect*") or as a verb that means "bring about" or "cause." However, avoid *effect* as a verb when you can replace it with a less formal word, such as *make* or *produce*.

• The new manager will e̶f̶f̶e̶c̶t̶ several changes to improve morale.
    make

Appendix: Usage

also   *Also* is an adverb that means "additionally." ("Two 5,000-gallon tanks are on-site, and several 2,500-gallon tanks are *also* available.") *Also* should not be used as a connective in the sense of "and."

- He brought the reports, the memos, ~~also~~ the section supervisor's recommendations.
  (insert: and)

Avoid opening sentences with *also*. It is a weak transitional word that suggests an afterthought rather than planned writing.

- ~~Also~~ he brought a cost analysis to support his proposal.
  (insert: In addition,)

- ~~Also, he~~ brought cost analysis data to support his proposal.
  (insert: He also)

amount / number   *Amount* is used with things that are thought of in bulk and that cannot be counted (mass nouns), as in "the *amount* of electricity." *Number* is used with things that can be counted as individual items (count nouns), as in "the *number* of employees."

and/or   *And/or* means that either both circumstances are possible or only one of two circumstances is possible. This term is awkward and confusing because it makes the reader stop to puzzle over your distinction.

AWKWARD	Use A *and/or* B.
IMPROVED	Use A or B or both.

as / because / since   *As*, *because*, and *since* are commonly used to mean "because." To express cause, *because* is the strongest and most specific connective in unequivocally stating a causal relationship. ("*Because* she did not have an MBA, she was not offered the job.")

Since is a weak substitute for *because* as a connective to express cause. However, *since* is an appropriate connective when the emphasis is on circumstance, condition, or time rather than on cause and effect. ("*Since* it went public, the company has earned a profit every year.")

As is the least definite connective to indicate cause; its use for that purpose is best avoided.

as such   The phrase *as such* is seldom useful and should be omitted.

- Patients~~, as such,~~ should be partners in their treatment decisions.

as well as   Do not use *as well as* with *both*. The two expressions have similar meanings; use one or the other and adjust the verb as needed.

- Both General Motors ~~as well as~~ Ford ~~is~~ marketing hybrid vehicles.
  (insert: and ... are)

- ~~Both~~ General Motors as well as Ford is marketing hybrid vehicles.

average / median / mean   The *average* (or arithmetic *mean*) is determined by adding two or more quantities and dividing the sum by the number of items totaled. For example, if one report is 10 pages, another is 30 pages, and a third is 20 pages, their *average* length is 20 pages. It is incorrect to say that "each report averages 20 pages" because each report is a specific length.

> *The three reports average*
* ~~Each report averages~~ 20 pages.
  ^

The *median* is the middle number in a sequence of numbers. For example, the *median* of the series 1, 3, 4, 7, 8 is 4.

bad / badly   *Bad* is the adjective form that follows such linking verbs as *feel* and *look*. ("We don't want to look *bad* at the meeting.") *Badly* is an adverb. ("The shipment was *badly* damaged.") To say "I feel *badly*" would mean, literally, that your sense of touch is impaired.

between / among   *Between* is normally used to relate two items or persons. ("Preferred stock offers a middle ground *between* bonds and common stock.") *Among* is used to relate more than two. ("The subcontracting was distributed *among* three firms.")

bi- / semi-   When used with periods of time, *bi-* means "two" or "every two," as in *bimonthly*, which means "once in two months." When used with periods of time, *semi-* means "half of" or "occurring twice within a period of time." *Semimonthly* means "twice a month." Both *bi-* and *semi-* normally are joined with the following element without a space or hyphen.

can / may   In writing, *can* refers to capability. ("I *can* have the project finished today.") *May* refers to possibility ("I *may* be in Boston on Monday.") or permission ("*May* I leave early?").

criteria / criterion   *Criterion* is a singular noun meaning "an established standard for judging or testing." *Criteria* and *criterions* are both acceptable plural forms of *criterion*, but *criteria* is generally preferred.

data   In formal and scholarly writing, *data* is generally used as a plural, with *datum* as the singular form. In much informal writing, however, *data* is considered a collective singular noun. Base your usage on whether your readers should consider the data as a single collection or as a group of individual facts. Whichever you use, be sure that your pronouns and verbs agree in number with the selected usage.

different from / different than   In formal writing, the preposition *from* is used with *different*. ("The product I received is *different from* the one I ordered.") *Different than* is used when it is followed by a clause. ("The actual cost was *different than* we estimated in our proposal.")

each   When *each* is used as a subject, it takes a singular verb or pronoun. ("*Each* of the reports *is* to be submitted ten weeks after *it* is assigned.") When *each* refers to a plural subject, it takes a plural verb or pronoun. ("The reports *each have* company logos on *their* title pages.")

e.g. / i.e.   The abbreviation *e.g.* stands for the Latin *exempli gratia*, meaning "for example"; *i.e.* stands for the Latin *id est*, meaning "that is." Because the English expressions (*for example* and *that is*) are clear to all readers, avoid the Latin *e.g.* and *i.e.* abbreviations except to save space in notes and visuals. If you must use *i.e.* or *e.g.*, do not italicize either and punctuate them as follows. If *i.e.* or *e.g.* connects two independent clauses, a semicolon should precede the abbreviation and a comma should follow it.

- The conference reflected international viewpoints; e.g., speakers included Germans, Italians, Japanese, Chinese, and Americans.

If *i.e.* or *e.g.* connects a noun and an appositive, a comma should precede it and follow it.

- The conference included speakers from five countries, i.e., Germany, Italy, Japan, China, and the United States.

etc.   *Etc.* is an abbreviation for the Latin *et cetera*, meaning "and others" or "and so on." Therefore, do not use the redundant phrase *and etc.* Likewise, do not use *etc.* at the end of a series introduced by the phrases *such as* and *for example*—those phrases already indicate unnamed items of the same category. Use *etc.* with a logical progression (1, 2, 3, etc.) and when at least two items are named. Do not italicize *etc.*

- The sorting machine processes coins (~~for example~~ pennies, nickels, ~~and~~ etc.) and then packages them for redistribution.

Otherwise, avoid *etc.* because the reader may not be able to infer what other items a list might include.

VAGUE	He will bring note pads, paper clips, etc., to the trade show.
CLEAR	He will bring note pads, paper clips, and other office supplies to the trade show.

explicit / implicit   An *explicit* statement is one expressed directly, with precision and clarity.

- He gave us *explicit* directions to the Wausau facility.

An *implicit* meaning is one that is not directly expressed.

- Although the CEO did not mention the lawsuit directly, the company's commitment to ethical practices was *implicit* in her speech.

fact   Expressions containing the word *fact* ("due to the *fact* that," "except for the *fact* that," "as a matter of *fact*," or "because of the *fact* that") are often wordy substitutes for more accurate terms.

Because
- ~~Due to the fact that~~ the sales force has a high turnover rate, sales
  ^
  have declined.

Do not use the word *fact* to refer to matters of judgment or opinion.

In my opinion,
- ~~It is a fact that~~ sales are poor in the Midwest because of insuffi-
  ^
  cient market research.

The word *fact* is, of course, valid when facts are what is meant.

- Our tests uncovered numerous *facts* to support your conclusion.

few / a few   In certain contexts, *few* carries more negative overtones than does the phrase *a few*.

NEGATIVE   The report offers *few* helpful ideas.
POSITIVE   The report offers *a few* helpful ideas.

fewer / less   *Fewer* refers to items that can be counted (count nouns). ("*Fewer* employees retired than we expected.") *Less* refers to mass quantities or amounts (mass nouns). ("We had much *less* rain this year than forecasts predicted.")

first / firstly   *First* and *firstly* are both adverbs. Avoid *firstly* in favor of *first*, which sounds less stiff than *firstly*. The same is true of other ordinal numbers, such as *second*, *third*, and so on.

former / latter   *Former* and *latter* should be used to refer to only two items in a sentence or paragraph.

- The president and his aide emerged from the conference, the *former* looking nervous and the *latter* looking glum.

Because these terms make the reader look to previous material to identify the reference, they complicate reading and are best avoided.

good / well   *Good* is an adjective and *well* is an adverb.

ADJECTIVE   Janet presented a *good* plan.
ADVERB   Janet presented the plan *well*.

Well also can be used as an adjective to describe health (a *well* child, *wellness* programs).

he / she   The use of either *he* or *she* to refer to both sexes excludes half of the population. To avoid this problem, you could use the phrases *he or she* and *his or her*. ("Whoever is appointed will find *his or her* task difficult.") However, *he or she* and *his or her* are clumsy when used repeatedly, as are *he/she* and similar constructions. One solution is to reword the sentence to use a plural pronoun; if you do, change the nouns or other pronouns to match the plural form.

-   *Administrators*   *their jobs*
  ~~The administrator~~ cannot do ~~his or her job~~ until
                   ^   ^

    they understand
  ~~he or she understands~~ the organization's culture.
    ^

In other cases, you may be able to avoid using a pronoun altogether.

-                          *an*
  Everyone must submit ~~his or her~~ expense report by Monday.
                       ^

Of course, a pronoun cannot always be omitted without changing the meaning of a sentence.

    Another solution is to omit troublesome pronouns by using the imperative mood.

-   *Submit all*   *s*
  ~~Everyone must submit his or her~~ expense report by
   ^   ^

  Monday.

imply / infer   If you *imply* something, you hint at or suggest it. ("Her e-mail *implied* that the project would be delayed.") If you *infer* something, you reach a conclusion based on evidence or interpretation. ("The manager *inferred* from the e-mail that the project would be delayed.")

in / into   *In* means "inside of"; *into* implies movement from the outside to the inside. ("We were *in* a meeting when the intern brought copies of the contract *into* the conference room.")

its / it's   *Its* is a possessive pronoun and does not use an apostrophe. *It's* is a contraction of *it is*.

- *It's* important that the sales department meet *its* quota.

kind of / sort of   The phrases *kind of* and *sort of* should be used only to refer to a class or type of things. ("We require a special *kind of* training to ensure employee safety.") Do not use *kind of* or *sort of* to mean "rather," "somewhat," or "somehow."

lay / lie   *Lay* is a transitive verb—a verb that requires a direct object to complete its meaning—that means "place" or "put."

- We will *lay* the foundation one section at a time.

The past-tense form of *lay* is *laid*.

- We *laid* the first section of the foundation last month.

The perfect-tense form of *lay* is also *laid*.

- Since June, we *have laid* all but two sections of the foundation.

Lay is frequently confused with *lie*, which is an intransitive verb—a verb that does not require an object to complete its meaning—that means "recline" or "remain."

- A person in shock should *lie* down with legs slightly elevated.

The past-tense form of *lie* is *lay* (not *lied*). This form causes the confusion between *lie* and *lay*.

- The injured employee *lay* still for approximately five minutes.

The perfect-tense form of *lie* is *lain*.

- The injured employee *had lain* still for five minutes before the EMTs arrived.

like / as   To avoid confusion between *like* and *as*, remember that *like* is a preposition and *as* (or *as if*) is a conjunction. Use *like* with a noun or pronoun that is not followed by a verb.

- The new supervisor behaves *like* a novice.

Use *as* before clauses, which contain verbs.

- He responded *as* we expected he would.
- The presentation seemed *as if* it would never end.

Like and *as* are used in comparisons: *Like* is used in constructions that omit the verb, and *as* is used when the verb is retained.

- He adapted to the new system *like* a duck to water.
- He adapted to the new system *as* a duck adapts to water.

media / medium   *Media* is the plural of *medium* and should always be used with a plural verb.

- Many communication *media are* available today.
- The Internet *is* a multifaceted *medium*.

Ms. / Miss / Mrs.   *Ms.* is used in business and public life to address or refer to a woman, especially if her marital status is either unknown or irrelevant to the context. Traditionally, *Miss* is used to refer to an unmarried woman, and *Mrs.* is used to refer to a married woman. Some women may indicate a preference for *Ms.*, *Miss*, or *Mrs.*, which you should honor. If a woman has an academic or a professional title, use the appropriate form of address (*Doctor, Professor, Captain*) instead of *Ms.*, *Miss*, or *Mrs.*

nature   *Nature*, when used to mean "kind" or "sort," is vague. Avoid this usage in your writing. Say exactly what you mean.

- The ~~nature of~~ *exclusionary clause in* the contract caused the problem.

on / onto / upon   *On* is normally used as a preposition meaning "attached to" or "located at." ("Install the shelf *on* the north wall.") *On* also stresses a position of rest. ("The victim lay *on* the stretcher.") *Onto* implies movement to a position on or movement up and on. ("The commuters surged *onto* the platform.") *Upon* emphasizes movement or a condition. ("The report is due *upon* completion of the project.")

only   The word *only* should be placed immediately before the word or phrase it modifies.

- We ~~only~~ lack *only* financial backing.

Be careful with the placement of *only* because it can change the meaning of a sentence.

- *Only* he said that he was tired.
  [He alone said that he was tired.]

- He *only* said that he was tired.
  [He actually was not tired, although he said he was.]

- He said *only* that he was tired.
  [He said nothing except that he was tired.]

- He said that he was *only* tired.
  [He said that he was nothing except tired.]

per   When *per* is used to mean "for each," "by means of," "through," or "on account of," it is appropriate (*per* annum, *per* capita, *per* diem, *per* head). When used to mean "according to" (*per* your request, *per* your order), the expression is jargon and should be avoided.

- As ~~per our discussion,~~ *we discussed,* I will send revised instructions.

percent / percentage   *Percent* is normally used instead of the symbol % ("only 15 *percent*"), except in tables, where space is at a premium. *Percentage*, which is never used with numbers, indicates a general size ("only a small *percentage*").

reason is [because]   Replace the redundant phrase *the reason is because* with *the reason is that* or simply *because*.

regardless   Always use *regardless* instead of the nonstandard *irregardless*, which expresses a double negative. The prefix *ir-* renders the base word negative, but *regardless* is already negative, meaning "unmindful."

that / which / who   The word *that* is often overused and can foster wordiness.

- I ~~think that when~~ this project is finished, ~~that~~ you should publish

  the results.

However, include *that* in a sentence if it avoids ambiguity or improves the pace.

- Some designers fail to appreciate the workers who operate *that*

  equipment constitute an important safety system.

Use *which*, not *that*, with nonrestrictive clauses (clauses that do not change the meaning of the basic sentence).

NONRESTRICTIVE	After John left the law firm, *which* is the largest in the region, he started a private practice.
RESTRICTIVE	Companies *that* diversify usually succeed.

That and *which* should refer to animals and things; *who* should refer to people.

- Dr. Cynthia Winter, *who* recently joined the clinic, treated a dog *that* was severely burned.

there / their / they're   *There* is an expletive (a word that fills the position of another word, phrase, or clause) or an adverb.

EXPLETIVE	*There* were more than 1,500 people at the conference.
ADVERB	More than 1,500 people were *there*.

Their is the possessive case form of *they*. ("Managers check *their* e-mail regularly.") *They're* is a contraction of *they are*. ("Clients tell us *they're* pleased with our services.")

to / too / two   *To*, *too*, and *two* are frequently confused because they sound alike. *To* is used as a preposition or to mark an infinitive.

- Send the report *to* the district manager.
  [preposition]

- I do not wish *to* attend.
  [mark of the infinitive]

Too is an adverb meaning "excessively" or "also."

- The price was *too* high.
  [excessively]

- I, *too*, thought it was high.
  [also]

Two is a number (*two* buildings, *two* concepts).

utilize   Do not use *utilize* as a long variant of *use*, which is the general word for "employ for some purpose." *Use* will almost always be clearer and less pretentious.

via   *Via* is Latin for "by way of." The term should be used only in routing instructions.

- The package was shipped *via* FedEx.

- Her project was funded ~~via~~ the recent legislation.
  as a result of ^

when / where / that   *When and if* (or *if and when*) is a colloquial expression that should not be used in writing.

- When ~~and if~~ funding is approved, you will get the position.

- ~~When and if~~ funding is approved, you will get the position.
  If ^

In phrases using the *where . . . at* construction, *at* is unnecessary and should be omitted.

- Where is his office ~~at~~?

Do not substitute *where* for *that* to anticipate an idea or fact to follow.

- I read in the newsletter ~~where~~ sales increased last quarter.
  that ^

whether   *Whether* communicates the notion of a choice. The use of *whether or not* to indicate a choice between alternatives is redundant.

* The client asked whether ~~or not~~ the proposal was finished.

The phrase *as to whether* is clumsy and redundant. Either use *whether* alone or omit it altogether.

* ~~As to whether we will~~ commit to a long-term ~~contract, we have~~

  ~~decided to do so.~~

  We have decided to   *contract.*

while   *While*, meaning "during an interval of time," is sometimes substituted for connectives like *and*, *but*, *although*, and *whereas*. Used as a connective in that way, *while* often causes ambiguity.

* Ian Evans is sales manager, ~~while~~ Joan Thomas is a vice president

  and

  for research.

Do not use *while* to mean *although* or *whereas*.

* ~~While~~ Ryan Sims is retired, he serves as our financial consultant.

  Although

Restrict *while* to its meaning of "during the time that."

* I'll have to catch up on my reading *while* I am on vacation.

who / whom   *Who* is a subjective case pronoun, and *whom* is the objective case form of *who*. When in doubt about which form to use, substitute a personal pronoun to see which one fits. If *he*, *she*, or *they* fits, use *who*.

* *Who* is the training coordinator?
  [You would say, "*She* is the training coordinator."]

If *him*, *her*, or *them* fits, use *whom*.

* It depends on *whom*?
  [You would say, "It depends on *them*."]

who's / whose / of which   *Who's* is the contraction of *who is*. ("*Who's* scheduled today?") *Whose* is the possessive case of *who*. ("Consider *whose* budget should be cut.")
      Normally, *whose* is used with persons, and *of which* is used with inanimate objects.

* The employee *whose* car had been towed away was angry.

* The report recommended over 100 changes, more than half *of which* the client approved.

If *of which* causes a sentence to sound awkward, *whose* may be used with inanimate objects. (Compare: "The business the profits *of which* steadily declined" versus "The business *whose* profits steadily declined.")

your / you're   *Your* is a possessive pronoun ("*your* wallet"); *you're* is the contraction of *you are* ("*You're* late for the meeting"). If you tend to confuse *your* with *you're,* use the search function to review for both terms during <u>proofreading</u> (Tab 1).

Acknowledgments (continued)

Figure 3–4: "MLA Sample List of Works Cited." Reprinted with the permission of Susan Litzinger, a student at Pennsylvania State University, Altoona.

Figure 5–2: "Formal Report." Reprinted with the permission of Susan Litzinger, a student at Pennsylvania State University, Altoona.

Figure 6–1: "Conventional Line Drawing for a Retail Catalog." Reprinted with the permission of the DeSantis Collection.

Figure 6–7: "International Organization for Standardization Symbols." The material taken from "Graphic Symbols to Address Consumer Needs" by John Perry, in ISO Bulletin, March 2003, is reproduced with the permission of the International Organization for Standardization, ISO. This standard can be obtained from any ISO member and from the Web site of the ISO Central Secretariat at the following address: www.iso.org. Copyright © 2003 by ISO. Reprinted with permission.

Figure 7–2: (heavily adapted) "Adjustment Letter." Reprinted with the permission of American Airlines, AMR Corporation, Inc. All rights reserved.

Figure 8–8: "Résumé." Prepared by Kim Isaacs, Advanced Career Systems, Inc. Reprinted with permission.

Figure 8–12: "Advanced Résumé." Prepared by Kim Isaacs, Advanced Career Systems, Inc. Reprinted with permission.

Index

Proofreaders' Marks

The marks illustrated on this page are commonly used by editors and proofreaders. These marks are also useful when revising your own writing and when collaborating with others.

MARK/SYMBOL	MEANING	EXAMPLE	CORRECTED TYPE
	Delete	the ~~manager's~~ report	the report
	Insert	the report (manager's)	the manager's report
(stet)	Let stand	the manager's report	the manager's report
(cap)	Capitalize	the monday meeting	the Monday meeting
(lc)	Lowercase	the Monday Meeting	the Monday meeting
(tr)	Transpose	the cover lettre	the cover letter
	Close space	a loud speaker	a loudspeaker
#	Insert space	a loudspeaker	a loud speaker
¶	Paragraph	...report. The meeting...	...report. The meeting...
	Run in with previous line or paragraph	...report. The meeting...	...report. The meeting...
(ital)	Italicize	the New York Times	the *New York Times*
(bf)	Boldface	Use boldface sparingly.	Use **boldface** sparingly.
⊙	Insert period	I wrote the e-mail	I wrote the e-mail.
	Insert comma	However we cannot...	However, we cannot...
=	Insert hyphen	clear cut decision	clear-cut decision
	Insert em dash	Our goal productivity	Our goal—productivity
∧ or :|	Insert colon	We need the following	We need the following:
∧ or ;|	Insert semicolon	we finished we achieved	we finished; we achieved
	Insert quotation marks	He said, I agree.	He said, "I agree."
	Insert apostrophe	the managers report	the manager's report

How to Use This Book

The Business Writer's Companion offers a concise yet thorough guide to business writing and communication in an easy-to-use format.

- **Twelve tabbed sections** organize the book's entries in thematic groups. A **brief table of contents** on the inside front cover provides a convenient listing of all twelve tabs.
- **Alphabetically arranged entries** within each tabbed section make it easy to find the specific topic you are looking for. At the beginning of each tab, a brief **Preview** discusses the entries in that section and lists them with page numbers.
- **Underlined cross-references** in each entry link to related entries, both within the same section and in other sections. **Tab numbers** appear in parentheses after cross-references to entries in other tabbed sections.
- A **complete list of model documents** at the front of the book helps you easily find the examples of business writing throughout the book.
- A **complete table of contents** at the front of the book lists all the entries, figures, Writer's Checklists, and other features.
- A **user-friendly index** provides a comprehensive listing of terms and topics covered in the book, including topics that are not featured as main entries.
- **Web Links** and **Digital Tips** throughout the book point to expanded information, additional sample documents, and related resources that can be found on the book's companion Web site at **<bedfordstmartins.com/alred>**.

A concise but comprehensive reference for writing in class and on the job.

An easy-access guide to the most common types of business writing and communication, *The Business Writer's Companion* places writing in a real-world context with hundreds of business writing topics and more than sixty sample documents. Always anticipating the needs of today's business writers, the sixth edition includes updated information on the technologies that are integral to workplace writing and offers tips about professionalism.

You get more help online for free at bedfordstmartins.com/alred.

Visit the companion Web site for *The Business Writer's Companion* to find more examples, guidelines, and checklists to support your writing—all for free.

ISBN-13: 978-0-312-63132-1
ISBN-10: 0-312-63132-4

BEDFORD/ST. MARTIN'S
bedfordstmartins.com

90000

9 780312 631321